LANGUAGE THEORIES AND EDUCATIONAL PRACTICE

David Piper

Mellen Research University Press
San Francisco

Library of Congress Cataloging-in-Publication Data

Piper, David, 1947-
   Language theories and educational practice / David Piper.
      p.   cm.
   Includes bibliographical references and index.
   ISBN 0-7734-9864-8
   1. Applied linguistics. 2. Language and education. I. Title.
P129.P56   1992
418--dc20   92-28795
                                                            CIP

Copyright   ©1992 David Piper.

Editorial Inquiries:

Mellen Research University Press
534 Pacific Avenue
San Francisco
CA 94133

Order Fulfillment:

The Edwin Mellen Press
P.O. Box 450
Lewiston, NY 14092
USA

Printed in the United States of America

This book is dedicated to the memory of my parents, whose fascination with language inspired my own.

TABLE OF CONTENTS

Preface	*iii*
Acknowledgements	*v*
Chapter One: Models of Language	*1*
Chapter Two: Fundamental Ideas about Language I: Language as Object	*17*
Chapter Three: Fundamental Ideas about Language II: Language and Subjective Experience	*45*
Chapter Four: Language and Biology	*69*
Chapter Five: Grammars	*116*
Chapter Six: Language and Cognitive Psychology: The Processing of Linguistic Structures	*170*
Chapter Seven: Language in Culture and Society	*213*
Chapter Eight: Language and Philosophy	*271*
Chapter Nine: Semiotics: The Interpretation of Signs	*324*

Chapter Ten: Theory and Practice: The Epistemic Spectrum of Language	*370*
Appendix A	*425*
Appendix B	*426*
References	*427*
Index of Names	*443*
Index of Subjects	*447*

PREFACE

Although there are many introductory textbooks in linguistics, in sociolinguistics, in psycholinguistics and other specialist areas, there are few that cover a variety of perspectives on language. Over a decade of involvement with introductory linguistics courses for teachers has convinced me of the need for such a broader approach to language, an approach that allows students to view language from different perspectives, and to see these perspectives in relation to each other.

The book is principally addressed to graduate students in language education, but may also be of interest to others, including administrators and majors in other curriculum areas having an interest in the involvement of language in their specialized subjects. While an introductory course in linguistics will certainly make several passages easier to read, the book has been written in such a way that it can be followed without such a background. The focus throughout is on *concepts*, rather than technical details, expect, as in the introduction to Transformational-generative grammar in Chapter Five, where such details are required for illustration of the nature of a theory.

There are three parts to the book. The first three chapters introduce several central and recurring ideas in language studies organized into "subjective" vs. "objective" orientations. Chapters Four through Nine look at theories of language developed within the traditional disciplines. The final chapter returns to the dichotomy between "subjective" and "objective" orientations to language and places the division in the wider context of current theorizing about the nature of knowledge. The conclusion is that a framework for educational practice should be pragmatically-based in a way that allows practitioners to draw on the wide *range* of language theorizing. Such a framework will avoid dogmatic faith in or adherence to any one definition of language.

In writing this book, I have become even more aware than I was before of the dangers of attempting to describe the phenomenon of language in its own terms. Any attempted escape from the language of normal discourse to a "higher" or "meta-" language, however, as several discussions in the text make clear, is doomed to failure. In this limited sense, we may appear to be "trapped" or "imprisoned" by our language. But, of course, it is also our liberation and, ultimately, we have to find ways of using it that are compatible with its own explanation. This, perhaps, is the most important academic motivation of all for writing this book--not only to take a trip around the boundaries of what we think we know about language, but also to explore the role of language in this knowledge. As those working in Artificial Intelligence, or anyone trying to program a machine to act like a human being, have had especially good reason to recognize, trying to explain language is a humbling experience. Given its centrality in our lives, our cultures, our thinking and being, this is no doubt as it should be. My main hope for this text is that it will, more than the standard texts in linguistics, encourage others to join the search for a more resilient and durable basis for practice in all aspects of language education than has been evident in the fads and "paradigms" of the past few decades. Such a challenge can only be met, I believe, from further concentration on fundamentals.

ACKNOWLEDGEMENTS

I am especially grateful to three people who have helped in the development of the manuscript. The first is my wife, Terry, who, apart from having given me invaluable advice about matters ranging from the presentation of ideas to formatting, has also done far more than her fair share of the housework during the course of writing. Second, I have received a great deal of help from two graduate assistants, Sheila MacDonald and Jiang Yan, both of whom, although they were originally cast in an editing role, have made contributions to the content. In addition to her sterling editorial work, Sheila has been responsible for eradicating many of the politically incorrect expressions which all too easily arise when a male writes about language--especially about language, society, and gender. She has also been a constant force working towards clarity of expression. In addition to the arduous task of final copy editing, Yan, a student from Shanghai, provided the details on Chinese characters, together with interesting discussions about language and culture. Any remaining errors or inadequacies of expression are, of course, my own. Finally, I would also like to thank Saint Mary's University, for providing graduate assistantship financing and a grant-in-aid of publication.

David Piper, Associate Professor
Faculty of Education
Saint Mary's University
Halifax, Nova Scotia, Canada

CHAPTER ONE

Models of Language

What contribution can the study of language make to our understanding of human nature? In one or another manifestation, this question threads its way through modern Western thought....And in the nineteenth and twentieth centuries, as linguistics, philosophy, and psychology have uneasily tried to go their separate ways, the classical problems of language and mind have inevitably reappeared and have served to link these diverging fields and to give direction and significance to their efforts. There have been signs in the past decade that the rather artificial separation of disciplines may be coming to an end.
(N. Chomsky, 1972, *Language and Mind*)

The Study of Language in Education

There are many reasons for language educators and others responsible for language education to pay close attention to recent and contemporary developments in language theory. One such reason is that with the formation of increasingly multi-ethnic societies there is a corresponding need for awareness about the linguistic and cultural influences on second language learning. Another lies in the need for greater understanding about the relations between first language development, social identity and school performance. A third reason lies in the need to develop educational programmes for children or adults who for one cause or another have communication disorders, or who do not become fully literate--conditions which increasingly alienate them in a world of sophisticated information-processing.

Apart from conspicuous areas of educational concern such as these, however, there is perhaps a less obvious motivation for those working in the field of education to learn more about language. Recent insights into the nature of language make it clear that the exploration of language is inseparable from that of foundational aspects of the educational enterprise as a whole. Many of the recent findings about language are so far-reaching that they influence our thinking about the very nature of the civilizations and cultures in which education takes place. Language theories have also become significant in debates about such matters as the nature and range of curricula in schools and the analysis of the ideological bases of schooling. It follows, then, that learning about language theories may lead to valuable insights into the nature of education and society in general.

Courses on Language for Teachers

Among other documents, the influential Bullock Report published in Great Britain (1975) strongly promoted the idea that *all* school teachers should to some extent regard themselves as language teachers, so pervasive are the connections between language and all types of knowledge across the curriculum. This conviction has also been expressed in one form or another in both the United States and Canada over the past decade. One way the conviction has been expressed in North America has been through the development in teacher education programs of courses in reading across the content areas, and many British and North American educators are now also introduced in their programs to the linguistic challenges they will face in the classroom relating to the academic growth of children from non English-speaking minority groups. As previously suggested, though, it is not just classroom teachers who now face the new challenges of ensuring growth in language and literacy across the curriculum: It is also those working in the areas of assessment, remediation, counselling, curriculum development and administration. So strong are the ties between language, cognition, society, and learning, that all of these professionals at one time or another must make decisions which potentially involve foundational ideas about the nature and purpose of language. It is now widely acknowledged that greater understanding about language should be a priority for all students and professionals concerned with education or with human development more generally.

A great deal of thinking has already been devoted to the question of what should be specifically included in courses on language designed for educators. One response to the need for more university courses on language has been the response of those who propose a new academic classification, "educational linguistics." Stubbs (1985) has provided an articulate rationale for grounding courses on language for practitioners in descriptive linguistics, and his proposals call for teachers to become proficient at analyzing language in terms of traditional linguistic categories. Both McArthur (1983) and Hawkins (1984) have also proposed programmes for educators which concentrate on linguistic analysis, although it should be added that their orientations, like that of Stubbs, also embrace a concern with many social aspects of language use. While these authors have emphasized the need for greater understanding of language within education, however, their approaches have largely remained focused on the kinds of analysis developed solely within the field of linguistics.

The Need for a Multifaceted and Interdisciplinary Approach

Enough has already been said to suggest that the tentacles of language theory stretch in many directions. Indeed, it is likely that there are many more points of contact between language theories and education yet remaining to be discovered. Not surprisingly, the realization that linguistic issues are pervasive in education means also that language is nothing if not complex: Language is all of being "logical," "social," and "cognitive" and "affective" in nature. For this reason, it is becoming increasingly clear that the discipline of "linguistics" (or "linguistic science" as it is sometimes called) may provide too narrow a focus for any complete explanation of language. Alternatively, linguistics must be conceived more broadly than has traditionally been the case if it is to continue to make a rich contribution to our understanding of *communication*. The approach taken here (in line with Chomsky's comments quoted at the beginning of this chapter) is an interdisciplinary one which works towards the ultimate *integration* of ideas pursued in linguistics with those pursued by other kinds of theorists.

The attempt to move beyond the traditional bounds of linguistics involves avoiding some of the constraints of particular modes of analysis developed by theoretical linguists. As a discipline, linguistics is essentially reductionist or "atomistic," involving the dissection of language into its component parts together with description of the abstract systems of rules which govern the relationships between these atomistic parts. Although both sociolinguists and psycholinguists have considerably broadened the scope of linguistic theorizing, an essential characteristic of much of their work lies in the direct relating of social or psychological variables to the structures identified in the descriptive grammars of formal linguists. Great progress has been made through these approaches but a fundamental problem yet remains in typical sociolinguistic or psycholinguistic explanations, just as it does in the explanations of language put forward by grammarians. This is the *epistemological* problem of an inabilitiy to establish clearly that linguistic structures bear any direct relation to categories of knowledge used by individuals. It must be stressed that for educators interested in language processing this is a particularly intransigent problem, since most aspects of educating seem to depend not upon understanding the knowledge and thoughts of individuals in abstract terms but, rather, upon understanding the *everyday* categories of knowledge they use to make decisions and on the basis of which they learn. It should come as no surprise, then, that the many descriptions of language processing that have linguistic structures at their foundation may be unsuited to the kinds of tasks faced by educators or to the kinds of insights they need. One of the advantages of a multi-disciplinary approach to language in education, then, is that it ensures some sensitivity to the question of what different kinds of personal knowledge are relevant to language learning and use.

Diverse Aspects of Language

What are some of these facets or aspects of language that cannot be captured by reducing it into its component structural parts? The idea that there are more opaque aspects of language that do not readily yield to formal description seems to have been recognized by earlier language theorists, such as the eighteenth century scholar, von Humboldt, but seems to have become less predominant in the work of many recent formal linguistics. Robins, in an analysis of von Humboldt's contribution to the history of the study of language makes the point that

> ...no matter how much one analyses and describes a language, something of its essential nature remains unsaid... (Robins, 1967, p. 175)

This captures a crucial point about the structural description of language, and it is this: No matter how exhaustive and rigorous our inquiries may be, it seems that we can never completely explain language in terms of "scientific" predictions about what is said or written--it is simply part of the nature of language to be multi-faceted and in many ways *un*predictable, and it will never fully reveal its secrets solely through the scrutiny of formal linguists. The central message here is that *language is always more the sum of its parts*.

Wachterhauser, a contemporary scholar in the field of *hermeneutics*, suggests one direction where further searching for less atomistic and more holistic aspects of language might lead us. He argues that:

> A principal vehicle by which the past is transported into the present and carried over into the future is language. Our involvement in language is responsible for the fact that all understanding occurs in a historical context where our historically formed present informs our interpretation of any topic or subject. It is the 'institution' of language that ensures that all understanding is historically mediated. (1986, p.9)

If we accept the idea that language is inherited as the central medium through which any individual views the world, then it is but a small step to the realization that its essential nature is to be part of the substance of consciousness itself. This challenging idea strongly implies that everything we do with language, including the formulation of linguistic theories, is governed by personal, subconscious, and historical forces of which we are not always aware. On this view, then, the examination of language should be treated as inseparable from that of subjective consciousness (both individual and social) and of the foundations of personal experience and expression. From this perspective, objective analysis, just like any other activities that involve categorizing aspects of the world around us, will be understood as being strongly influenced by subjectively-driven reactions and intentions. As we shall see, this view is as compelling for phenomenologists and semioticians as the development of formal "objective" analyses of language is for linguists.

Despite the fact that the "objective" and "subjective" perspectives on language are crucially different (the former strives to turn language into an object susceptible to formal empirical reasoning, while the latter is predicated on the perceived inseparability of linguistic phenomena from those of conscious and subconscious knowledge), an interdisciplinary approach will naturally view them as the two extreme points of a spectrum across which language theories can be located. These "subjective" and "objective" orientations, then, will be treated here as methodological emphases rather than as absolute or mutually-exclusive positions.

Coming to Terms with Multiple Perspectives

A good skeptical question at this point might be: "Well, if there are so many compelling but different views about language, how can we hope to draw clear and well-justified relations between language theory and educational practice?" For the present, let us simply observe that there are several logical alternatives open to us in forging links between theory and practice. A first possibility is that practitioners might simply choose the one approach to language they prefer or find particularly accessible (for example, the "functional" approach or the "grammatical" approach) and then simply apply it uniformly across their practice. Such a position might appropriately be called "practitioner-based eclecticism," and it is an approach to the problem which at least has the advantage of consistency. This particular brand of eclecticism, however, is vulnerable to the criticism that it fails to meet the *multiple* challenges and *differing* demands of a variety of educational situations.

A second possibility lies in a more complex form of eclecticism, one which involves adopting different language models for different particular educational purposes. In this way, a practitioner might, for example, choose a "functional" approach for an elementary arts class but a "syntactic" approach for the purposes of assessing the progress of some adolescent English-as-a-second-language (ESL) students in whose education she or he might be involved. This second kind of eclecticism might be called "student-based" eclecticism. Here, choices of different approaches will be founded on a genuine attempt to match particular theories to particular practices on grounds that they are well-suited to each other. It is only a practitioner taking the latter of these alternatives, of course, who is likely to wish to delve deeper into the matters covered here!

A further more ambitious approach than either of those so far mentioned is to attempt to ground practice on some form of integration of language theories as the basis for applied thinking and action. Most theories will find a place on the spectrum between the opposed subjective-objective extremes and it is a contention here that *both* orientations are of equal value and, indeed, that they must both be somehow integrated in any over-arching description of language that is to provide a substantial base for educational practice.

Domains of Educational Discussion

Some justification for an interdisciplinary understanding of language in education has now been presented. Finally in this chapter, it is useful to identify some of the particular issues in education where such understanding will be of greatest value.

Language and Cognitive Development

Over the last three decades much attention has been devoted to the question of how children acquire language and of how language learning relates to cognition. One important development that has taken place in the field of language acquisition has been the increasing recognition that language learners combine *many* sources of information during learning.

The central spurs to communicative development appear to lie in children's need to gain some functional control over their environments and it is now clear that children do *not* learn language merely by paying attention to the linguistic "input" of those around them. Children, moreover, communicate in quite sophisticated ways *before* they have learned their mother-tongues. Many researchers argue that in the early stages of life young children have numerous organized sensory experiences that are not mediated by language. Although they may communicate a great deal, then, it appears that very young children have not yet learned to *label* their experiences; they do not use recognizable signs or symbols in a systematic way.

At some point, however, both the presence of language as a sensory phenomenon in itself (that is, through the sounds of the utterances of parents or others) and the pragmatic need to deal functionally with the environment spark children's drive to bring the representations of sensory experience (in the form of raw images, raw clusters of feelings, tastes, smells or sounds) together with the symbolic representations they hear. A more formal way of stating this process is to say that children "map" the verbal forms which they regularly hear onto these prior experiences (Macnamara, 1972; Nelson, 1974). In addition to this process of cognitive-linguistic mapping, it is likely that in the initial stages of learning children also produce imitations of various kinds on the basis of what they hear from those around them-- although it is quite clear that imitation per se is unable to explain children's abstractions and generalizations of the rules of the language they hear to new productive forms of their own, forms such as *writed* for *wrote* or *seed* for *saw*, which show overgeneralization of the rules for the formation of past tenses of *regular* to *irregular* English verbs. It seems likely that children at some time or another use almost every strategy they can in order to join the union of those who speak.

Language, thought, and their interaction

The claim that language and cognitive development are intimately related bears close relation to the claim that language and thought are themselves inseparable. While arguments continue concerning the details of the mutual dependency between language and thought, however, the central point upon which most current theorists and researchers agree is that the development of cognition and language is a process of *mutual interaction*. Categories of thought and categories of language, that is to say, are shaped by each other. Bever emphasized this idea as early as 1970 when he wrote, albeit within an essentially formal-linguistic orientation, that:

> Language has various manifestations, each of which draws on and contributes to structural constraints on the language created by every other subsystem. During the first decade of his life a child simultaneously learns all these systems--primarily how to talk in sentences, how to understand sentences, and how to predict new sentences in his language. These and other cognitive skills can *mutually influence each other as the child acquires them and as they are integrated in adult language behavior*. (p. 280; italics added)

Several interactionist models of language acquisition have been developed over the past decade, a good current example of which is the "competition model" of Bates and MacWhinney (1987).

Related questions for educators

The notion that cognitive and linguistic development coexist interactively leads to many questions of particular interest to educators. A partial list might be as follows:

> Given what we know about the relations between linguistic and cognitive development, how can academic work be sequenced to maximize the chances of learning?
> Do linguistically-based assessments of children actually measure their cognitive abilities? This is a particularly relevant question for those concerned with assessing students from other first-language backgrounds or with various kinds of impairments.
> How can the experiences of exceptional students such as those called "learning-disabled" be enriched in order to stimulate cognitive-linguistic interaction?
> Are children from other first-language groups in some way "locked" into the particular cognitive-linguistic categories they have developed prior to second language learning?

Language and Social Development

Another major influence on the study of language development has arisen out of the recognition that close relations exist between social forces, language learning, and use. Whereas twenty or thirty years ago it was possible to promote explanations of language development cast more or less exclusively in terms of structural or grammatical categories, it is now recognized that the processes of language learning involve many social variables that are not so readily captured by purely grammatical descriptions. Theorists such as Trudgill (e.g. Trudgill, 1983) have long stressed that part of the goal of full acquisition is the ability of speakers to recognize the need to switch *registers* in order to fit in with the demands of different situations and different levels of social status represented by other communicators. It is recognized that both children, and indeed, all language learners have to know much more than the grammatical systems of languages they are acquiring: Learning about language registers also involves knowing about the *codes* which underlie language use in particular social situations, codes which are expressed through intonation, accent and gesture, as well as through syntax. Sociolinguists have also recognized the significance of dialects in reinforcing the social identities of the members of groups who share them.

Communicative competence

Researchers have further observed that the relationship between society and language is an even deeper one than is reflected in overt measurable phenomena such as registers and dialects. Of particular significance has been the investigation of *communicative competence* initiated by the sociologist, Del Hymes (1971), as part of a critique of the limited conception of "linguistic" or "grammatical" competence espoused by Chomsky and his successors. Achieving full communicative competence necessarily involves knowing more than just how to follow grammatical rules; it also involves sensitivity to wider aspects of social interaction such as how to take turns during conversations, how to interrupt in order to clarify meaning, or even when *not* to speak. According to communicative competence theory, in addition to grammatical competence, fluent speakers of any language have *sociolinguistic* competence, which permits them to judge, for example, the intentions of other speakers or the appropriateness of language in varied settings. They also have *discourse* competence, which enables the processing not just of sentences, but of entire organized texts, and they have *strategic* competence, enabling them, for example, to get things clarified if they are not clear at first speaking or hearing (see e.g. Savignon, 1983). It has also been recognized that language is partly *functional*, a tool for "doing things." This is an idea given special emphasis in the work of Halliday (e.g. Halliday, 1976) and in the work of the "speech act" philosophers (see Chapter Eight, below).

Language and identity

Over the past decade, Halliday and other language theorists have written of yet another significant aspect of the relationship between language and society, namely, the particular part that language plays in the development of cultural and personal identity. Saville-Troike (1982) makes this connection clear:

> At a societal level, language serves many functions. Chief among these...is that language creates/reinforces boundaries, unifying its speakers as members of a single speech community, and excluding outsiders from intra-group communication ....Linguistic features are often employed by people, consciously or unconsciously, to identify themselves and others, and thus serve to mark and maintain various social categories and divisions. (p. 15)

Halliday (1978), and Gumperz and Cook-Gumperz (1982), go even further in their analysis of the strong bonds between language and social identity by arguing that social structures and institutions themselves are strongly influenced by language and by the attitudes expressed through language. These influences often relate to more subtle and subliminal aspects of language that are difficult to capture in formal description. It is the central challenge of various kinds of *discourse analysis*, however, to show how language affects both individuals' experiences of their own identity and also the shapes of their social and their working lives. Interest in the social aspects of language, then, forces us well beyond the boundaries of descriptive linguistics.

Related questions for educators

Some of the most trenchant current questions in education relating to language and social development are as follows:

What effect does the relationship between sociolinguistic variation and individual identity have on academic achievement?

Do teachers typically identify, through their language, with cultural and social groups that are alien to many of their students and, if so, what are the related educational implications?

How are cultural and sub-cultural groupings of students in schools reflected in the forms of their language use?

Which students face home-school language switching of various kinds, and what impact does this have on their educational experiences?

Once again, these are some of the questions which are easier to resolve with greater understanding about language from multiple perspectives.

Abnormal Language Growth

Even a cursory glance at an up-to-date special education textbook will show that the topics of communication and language are especially relevant to the field of *exceptionality* and that these topics are no longer principally tied to the discussion of "speech impairments." Full communicative competence is now the primary educational goal across a range of physically and mentally challenging conditions. In the case of the mentally challenged, for instance, one major current objective is to enable clients to live as normal a life as possible within the larger social community around them--an objective towards which language education plays a central role. Another example from the field of special education is *autism* with its central characteristic of severe communicative delay. For a long time, the primary goal with autistic patients has been to unlock and develop any potential they may have for communicating through natural language.

In the case of sensory (auditory or visual) impairments, language education is equally important. In cases of hearing impairment, a primary educational objective, once again, is to maximize the individual's potential for full communicative competence, and there has been a shift away from restrictive sign systems, which tend to limit the range of potential communication with others, towards *total-communication* approaches that make optimal use of any and all teaching approaches which have the potential to develop full communication between the hearing impaired and all sorts of other language users. In the case of visual impairments, there have been significant discoveries about the particular problems individuals face in developing concepts without the power of sight, and without the advantage of visually-based associations to reinforce language development (Winzer et al., 1987). There is reason to believe, however, that when optimal provisions are made even children who are fully blind can develop advanced levels of communicative competence (Landau & Gleitman, 1985).

In cases of physical impairments such as cerebral palsy or multiple sclerosis, language development is also a key educational objective. Theories of language development now also enter discussion of learning disabilities, and are central to understanding impediments to literacy falling within the class of conditions known as *dyslexia*.

Language and brain damage

There is also a burgeoning literature on the damaging effects on communicative competence and performance imposed by brain traumas of various kinds and on those leading to types of *aphasia*. Studies of aphasia are especially significant and fascinating because they provide data that cast light on normal language processing. Following the work of two pioneers in the neurology of language, Broca and Wernicke, both of whom identified relations between particular locations of brain lesions and particular kinds of language breakdown, many researchers have pursued the objectives of isolating damaged parts of the brain and describing the relations between these areas and various forms of abnormal language behavior. This orientation raises further interesting general questions about the relationships between physiology and language (see Chapter Four).

Related questions for educators

Some of the key current questions about language and all these various forms of impairments, then, are as follows:

> To what extent do language deficits represent cognitive deficits, and what are the educational implications of the relationship?
> To what extent are language deficits tied to social aspects of language? In particular, how may educational procedures tend to restrict or to liberate communicative competence?
> What, if any, are the direct relations between communicative impairment and physiological structure, and which of the various available models of linguistic organization in the brain provides the richest description for educational practice?
> What can abnormal language processing tell us about normal cognitive, social, and linguistic development and behavior?

Summary

The intention in this chapter has been to establish that language and communication are central issues across the range of educational practice, and that further understanding about language is therefore of great value to students and professionals in the field of education. The study of language for educators, however, if it is to provide a base that is sufficiently rich for educational practice, must be both broad and multi-disciplinary: Theorizing about language has been a preoccupation not only of linguists but also of philosophers, psychologists, anthropologists, sociologists, and others, and all of these perspectives are of importance for educators.

Despite the complexity of language studies, however, several ideas or themes in language theory can be identified which emerge time and again in discussions about education and which are distributed across a spectrum which can be identified in terms of the polarized tendencies to emphasize the "objective" or "subjective" aspects of language. In the next two chapters, an overview of these two perspectives will be presented, while in Chapters Four through Nine, a more detailed examination of language theories will be presented from the perspectives of the central disciplines involved in the study of language. In these more detailed overviews, the foundational ideas presented in Chapters Two and Three will constantly emerge in one form or another, and it will be the main objective to see how they have been incorporated and extended in the work of theorists working within their separate disciplines. Following these overviews, we will return to consider the possibility of relating language theories to practice within a multi-disciplinary framework.

CHAPTER TWO

Fundamental Ideas about Language I: Language as Object

By the scientific study of language is meant its investigation by means of controlled and verifiable observations and with reference to some general theory of language-structure. The chief difficulty facing the person who comes new to the study of linguistics is that of being prepared to look at language objectively....There are all sorts of social and nationalistic prejudices associated with language, and many popular misconceptions fostered by the distorted version of traditional grammar that is frequently taught in the schools. To free one's mind of these prejudices and misconceptions is indeed difficult; but it is both a necessary and rewarding first step. (John Lyons, *Introduction to Theoretical Linguistics*, 1968)

What *is* the general character of those rules which must in some sense have been mastered by anyone who speaks and understands a given language?....It seems to me that there is only one type of answer that has ever been seriously advanced or developed, or needs to be seriously considered....This is an answer which rests on the notion of truth-conditions. (P. F. Strawson, *Logico-Linguistic Papers*, 1971)

Introduction

The above two quotations have in common that they represent, albeit in contrasting ways, an essentially objective orientation to the description of language. The first, by a linguist, emphasizes the rigor of the scientific method while the second, by a philosopher, emphasizes the rigor of logic as the basis for meaning in language. What further characterizes these approaches to language is that they each reflect a belief in the potency of various kinds of *rules* at the core of language. Here, language is primarily conceived in terms of its objectively-definable *systematicity*.

The eight dominant ideas about language reviewed in this and the next chapter surface repeatedly in one form or another in discussions about language and education. Collectively, they define the central territory in which language theorizing takes place. In this chapter, four ideas will be presented which represent the objective end of the analytic spectrum, while the next chapter will be reserved for four more subjectively-oriented ideas about language.

Within the objective approach, language can (and almost always is) examined independently from the everyday performance of actual speakers, and the focus is almost exclusively upon developing abstract descriptions of grammatical competence. The four objectively-oriented views are as follows. First, there is the idea that language is *dynamic* in a way which can be captured by a formalized system of rules. Second, there is the idea that language is *structured*, and that meaning and communication crucially depend upon the relations between its structural elements. The third idea is that *innate mechanisms* underlie human language processing, mechanisms that can be discovered by detailed scientific attention to the common or "universal" features held to underlie all languages. The fourth idea is that articulated by Strawson in the quotation above, namely, that language relies for its meaning on *truth-values* as they are expressed within the formal rule-systems described by logicians.

Before moving on to explore each of these ideas in more detail, it should be noted that the familiar *behaviorist* idea that "language is a set of habits"--even though it bears a close relation to structuralism, has been deliberately omitted from discussion here. The reason for this is simple: While this notion was indeed once highly influential, particularly following the publication of Bloomfield's *Language* in 1933 up until the famous rebuttal by Chomsky (1959) of Skinner's *Verbal Behavior* (1957), it no longer receives wide support or discussion. Although some behaviorist techniques are still used in the education of children or adults with severe emotional and communicative disorders, such as those to be found in cases of autism, the central assumption that today underlies the field of language studies is that communication involves constant and active *cognitive* processing and not merely habit-driven responses. Unlike the behaviorists, who disparaged anything in the description of language other than observable behavior in response to environmental stimuli, it is now an orthodox assumption that communication involves mental states, or *mind*. All the seminal ideas to be introduced here and in the following chapter remain influential, and each is consistent with this fundamental and widely-held belief in the existence of mental processing in the mediation of behavior.

Four Objectively-oriented Ideas about Language

1. Language is a Dynamic Rule-governed System.

It was the early nineteenth century Prussian scholar, Wilhelm von Humboldt, who first articulated many of the thoughts developed by linguists in our own century. Unlike most of his contemporaries, who focused on historical and comparative aspects of different languages, Humboldt, who was a politician and statesman as well as a scholar, focused his attention on the *nature* of language as it is used in speech communities. One of his influential ideas about language is captured in his observation that "[s]peech, in its true essence, is constantly and at any moment ephemeral,...itself not a product (*ergon*) but an activity (*energeia*)" (translated in Hörmann, 1971, p. 2). Energeia referred to the creative linguistic ability characteristic of all language users, and Humboldt stressed that language was both dynamic and open-ended in that an infinite variety of expression could be wrought out of the finite means provided in the sound systems of natural languages. In explaining this infinite flexibility of language, Humboldt also drew a distinction between the *inner* form of language--that is, the patterns and structures of grammars and meanings shared by individuals within discrete language groups--and the *outer* form of language, the raw transmitted sounds themselves.

Chomsky's revival and extension of von Humboldt

In the twentieth century, it has been the linguist, Chomsky (e.g. Chomsky 1957; 1965), who has most enthusiastically developed Humboldt's idea about the creative essence of language, an idea that he incorporated into his development of the transformational-generative theory of language. At the beginning of *Aspects of the theory of syntax* (1965), Chomsky acknowledged his indebtedness to Humboldt for the idea that the underlying form of language was best conceived as a system of dynamic processes. Adapting Humboldt's division between outer and inner language, Chomsky defined linguistic *competence* as "the speaker-hearer's knowledge" of the dynamic inner properties of the language he spoke. Competence was to be kept conceptually distinct from *performance*, which he defined as "the actual use of language in concrete situations" (p. 4).

It will help to understand Chomsky's interpretation of Humboldt's "energeia" more fully if we look closely at several other claims Chomsky makes at the beginning of *Aspects*. First, he states that "one of the qualities that all languages have in common is their 'creative' aspect," a property of language allowing the expression of an infinite variety of thoughts (p. 6). Second, the locus of dynamic creativity resides ultimately in a *universal* system of rules which he claims to underlie all languages and the particular grammars that are acquired by children. He believes, moreover, that this universal system is innate (see Idea Four, below).

Third, Chomsky has argued that the primary goal of linguistic theory is to account for the inner systems of dynamic creative rules unconsciously known by language-users; that is, to account for their competence and not for the less ideal characteristics of their everyday performance. Chomsky also recognizes in *Aspects* the potential of *generative* rules as they have already been developed in mathematics for providing the central mechanism by which such a dynamic description of language could be developed. He expresses this recognition as follows:

> ...by a generative grammar I mean simply a system of rules that in some explicit and well-defined way assigns structural descriptions to sentences. (p. 8)

> Obviously, every speaker of a language has mastered and internalized a generative grammar that expresses his knowledge of his language....a generative grammar attempts to specify what the speaker actually knows, not what he may report about his knowledge. (p. 8)

Generative grammar as a theory of language

The next step in Chomsky's progress towards developing a grammatical theory of language to reflect its infinite creative potential is to demonstrate *how* generative rules can be incorporated into a grammatical system. To achieve this, Chomsky turns to the observation that all speakers as a part of their competence (or of their "native-speaker intuition") are aware of similarities between certain kinds of sentences. Speakers of English, for example, know that the simple sentence *Frost conducts interviews* is related to the sentences *Frost doesn't conduct interviews, Doesn't Frost conduct interviews? Frost conducts interviews, doesn't he? Interviews are conducted by Frost*, and so on. Native speakers of English, in other words, recognize to some extent that these sentences are transformed versions of each other. According to Chomsky, speakers of English also recognize that the most basic of these sentences is the first one--the active, affirmative, declarative sentence *Frost conducts interviews*.

While many of these points had been recognized prior to Chomsky's work (in particular, by one of his teachers, Zelig Harris) it was Chomsky's revolutionary step to put all of this together and to show that this knowledge about language could be captured by postulating two levels of structure. The first of these levels is *deep structure*, in which *kernel* sentences such as *Frost conducts interviews* are formed, and the second is *surface structure*, where all the other transformed sentences related to it may be expressed. The dynamic mechanism, which relates these two levels--which takes deep structure forms as input and which produces the various surface-structural possibilities--is a set of *transformational-generative rules*.

According to Chomsky, the operation of these rules, if they are properly constructed, yields only *grammatical* surface structure. In this way, the specification of the rules constitutes an essential part of the theoretical description, or grammar, of English. Each of the sentences in the related set described above can be *derived* from the kernel sentence by passing it through various generative transformational operations which both yield the alternative surface forms and guarantee that they are grammatical.

Transformational rules and sentence families

The next crucial step in Chomsky's thinking was to extend the capacity of transformational rules to capture one further characteristic of natural languages. Specifically, these rules would have to generate complex sentences such as *Carter, who lives in Georgia, grows oversized peanuts*. Complex sentences like this can be viewed, of course, to be the result of combining simple sentences. In this case, the complex sentence is constructed out of the simple sentences *Carter grows peanuts, Carter lives in Georgia,* and *The peanuts are oversized*. The extra characteristic that Chomsky had to incorporate into the grammar in order to account for the production of complex sentences was that the rules had to be *cyclical* in nature. The sequence of operations begins with the sentences to be embedded in the main sentence, *Carter grows peanuts* (i.e. the sentences *Carter lives in Georgia* and *The peanuts are oversized*), and then returns to the beginning again to deal with the business of organizing the embedded sentences and the main sentence as an entire syntactic unit (deleting on the way elements appearing only in deep structure--"the peanuts are..." --and replacing "Carter" with *who* at the beginning of the relative clause). The property of the rules which allowed them to recycle in this way is known as *recursion*, and this mechanism (which, theoretically at least, can operate an infinite number of times to generate hugely complex (but probably uninterpretable) sentences, guarantees that the transformational-generative rules in a Chomskyan grammar do indeed reflect one aspect of the infinite creativity embodied in language. Chomsky, then, apparently succeeded in formalizing with precision the creative aspect of language about which von Humboldt had written more than a century earlier.

What does Chomskyan theory "explain"?

As has been suggested, Chomsky's synthesis of these ideas in building a theory of linguistic competence can justifiably be called "revolutionary." His original theory is still being developed by many linguists, and it will be a central task in Chapter Five to trace the theory through to its current status. At this point, however, it is important to recognize that, despite the infinite levels of descriptive sophistication to which transformational grammarians can aspire, a very significant question yet remains for those concerned with practice: If transformational grammar does, indeed, constitute a viable "theory" of language, what is it about language that the theory actually explains? As Chomsky has been careful to point out, although the system of rules in some way accurately describes speakers' knowledge, it does *not* do so in a way which accounts for the actual processes of language use. There is no correspondence, in other words, between the actual formulations of the dynamic rules by linguists, on the one hand, and the details of the actual mental operations of language-users, on the other. One very straightforward demonstration of this, indeed, is that the linguistic rules can actually be constructed in many equivalent but different ways--there simply is no way of specifying an unambiguous relation between the transformational-generative descriptions of linguists and what goes on in our heads. Another indication of the discrepancy between linguistic description and psychological processing here is that if there were a correspondence between the two, then the time taken to process a sentence should reflect the number of transformations applying to it. As we shall see later, researchers have found that this is simply not true.

If language-users do not process language by way of generative transformational rules, then, Chomskyan rules can only be held to "explain" something else other than such processing. For practitioners, this is a significant and critical point to recognize, since it means that in this case the relations between theory and practice must be, at best, only indirect.

2. Language is Structured

The posthumous publication in 1916 of the lecture notes of Ferdinand de Saussure, comprising his famous *Course in General Linguistics*, has often been cited as the inception of modern linguistics. Despite the perspicacity and novelty of Saussure's thinking about many fundamental problems and challenges in the description of language, nevertheless, it is clear that Saussure, like Chomsky, was indebted to the earlier innovations of Humboldt. It was Saussure who provided some important intermediary steps in the development from Humboldt's distinction between inner and outer language forms to Chomsky's distinction between competence and performance. And it was Saussure who laid the foundations for the *structuralist* analysis of language.

Saussure's dichotomies

Saussure's most influential ideas were expressed in the form of five dichotomies relating to the analysis and description of language, each of which contributes to further elaboration of Humboldt's distinction between inner and outer language.

A: langue vs. parole:

The first of these dichotomies is Saussure's distinction between *langue* and *parole*. This is the distinction, respectively, between the abstract system of language known by speakers within a given language community and the actual manifestations of speech utterances respectively. This distinction provided a direct foundation for Chomsky's later development of the distinction between competence and performance. The force of Saussure's original dichotomy was directed towards organizing linguistics into a "science," and a particularly clear statement in the *Course* about langue and parole is as follows:

> In separating language [langue] from speaking [parole] we are at the same time separating: (1) what is social from what is individual; and (2) what is essential from what is accessory and more or less accidental. Language... never requires premeditation, and reflection enters in only for the purpose of classification... Speaking, on the contrary, is an individual act. It is willful and intellectual. (1974, p.14)

Saussure's intent in separating speech from the underlying system of language was to establish that the many meanings produced in actual speech can only exist in the context of an underlying and unified system of shared reference points. The significance of this idea is brought out in a further argument Saussure put forward to counter the idea that language *change* might be fundamentally wrought out of modifications in speech. As an example of such modification, the fairly recent North American neologism *winterize*, the result of combining *winter* and the verb-forming morpheme *-ize*, represents a new language category essentially developed through *parole*. Saussure argued, first, that all such new forms in the language were straightforward analogies which could not be formed without the stable units of *langue* (the noun *winter*, and the morpheme *-ize* as it already occurs in words predating *winterize* such as *finalize*, *modernize*, *stabilize*, and so on). Secondly, he argued that neologisms such as *winterize*, rather than breaking language down in some way, tend to reinforce existing categories. Combining morphemes into novel words, then, ensures their continuing productive use in languages.

B: substance vs. form:

If language units (such as *winterize*) are developed by way of analogy to other similar forms, it means that all these units must exist in langue in the form of *organized structural relationships* to each other. *Winterize*, to stretch the example further, can be used precisely (and only) because language-users recognize a relationship between this word and others (e.g. finalize). It will also be true, then, that all other words (or their individual meaning-bearing sub-parts, *morphemes*) gain their meaning in parole only from their underlying structural relations to each other. To take another example, the color *blue* will be understood because it fits into an underlying pattern of related words such as *white, brown, teal*, and so on: It exists in a structural network with other terms in *langue*, and it is always understood during the contingencies of parole on the basis of its participation in these underlying structural relationships. According to Saussure, then, the occurrence in the real world of an expression such as *The Denver plane is late*, while it may differ in interpretation from one occasion to another, yet still retains the same *form*. Although the interpretation of substance may differ from situation to situation, its reference can only vary in this way due to the stable underlying system of language forms against which background of shared knowledge it is uttered. It is this latter concept which forms the basis of linguistic structuralism, a mode of analysis which has played a crucial role in the history of thinking about language from Saussure to the present.

C: signifier vs. signified:

To make this latter point clear, Saussure further distinguished two aspects of language *signs* from each other; the *signifier*, which was the name he gave to actual real-world phonological sequences spoken and heard, and the *signified*, which referred to the abstract "sound image" in the formal system shared by the particular language community. Saussure emphasized that the relationship between the signifier and signified aspects of signs, moreover, was an arbitrary one--there is no absolute or intrinsic reason why the particular sounds which make up the utterance "Denver plane," for example, should be the ones chosen for signification of the meaning. This point is made clear by indicating how different languages make use of different signifiers--plane is *avion* in French, but *aeroplano* in Italian, and so on. The goal of linguistics, according to Saussure, was to show how all these arbitrary and variant signs fit together in the structured labyrinth of *langue*.

The next step in Saussure's analysis also follows logically, and it is a crucial one for the development of structuralist thinking as a whole. If linguistic units are to be defined in terms of their formal relations to each other within the internal system of language, then their definition depends essentially upon describing their *differences* or *contrasts* with one another. Saussure expressed this idea by saying that the "most precise characteristic of [language signs] is in being what the others are not" (*Course*, p. 118). Yet another way of putting this is to say that linguistic units have *values*, and that these values are established in relation to other values. A good analogy here might be that of banknotes, since they have exchange value only for certain merchandise or in relation to other monetary systems, their value being thus established by way of these relationships. This network of relations can also be conceived, as Saussure argued, in terms of the *oppositions* of "signifieds" to each other within the underlying system of langue. Different languages, of course, will have quite different underlying systems of oppositions, and Saussure illustrated this with reference to the uses of *mouton* in French and of *mutton* and *sheep* in English (*Course* pp. 115-116). Although these two words may appear on the surface to be equivalent translations of each other, it is clear that a French and an English speaker do not have exactly the same concept in mind since the terms *sheep* and *mouton* have different underlying values within their respective language systems. This results from the fact that part of the meaning of *sheep* in English is determined by its known contrast with, its known opposition to, *mutton*, whereas there is no corresponding contrast between *mouton* and some other term in French (and therefore no pejoratives such as "mutton dressed up to look like lamb"-- perhaps reflecting the higher status of haute couture and French cuisine). As we shall see, however, the major line of development from Saussure's ideas about structural opposition is through analysis of oppositions between individual sounds in the phonological systems of different languages.

In summary, it was Saussure's influential perception that descriptions of language must demonstrate the relations between linguistic units in the underlying structure of forms shared by communities of language-users (*langue*), and that such demonstrations will involve analyzing the distinctions maintaining them in opposition to each other. The last two dichotomies set forth in the *Course* each give further elaboration of how the underlying differences between forms could and should be analyzed.

D: syntagmatic vs. paradigmatic:

The fourth dichotomy is between *syntagmatic* and *paradigmatic* relations among linguistic units. This represents a distinction between the kinds of 'horizontal' relations between units in language sequences or chains (*the* [article] followed by *rain* [noun] followed by *in* [preposition] followed by *Spain* [noun] and so on) and the 'vertical' relations existing between items such that the sequential 'slot' taken by rain could also be taken by any number of members of a huge set of possible entries (*bullfights*, *opera-houses*, and so on).

E: diachronic vs. synchronic:

The fifth distinction, between *synchronic* (current) and *diachronic* (historical) aspects of language analysis reflected Saussure's perception that the most central task of linguists was to describe language systems as they are structured at particular points in time rather than to describe the historical changes by way of which languages came to their current states of development (and of which speakers are largely unaware). Saussure emphasized that analyzing language historically, or longitudinally, was not the same as analyzing it cross-sectionally as a current system and that it was the latter kind of analysis which was most vital, since it had more to do with how people actually communicate with each other.

The development of Saussurean principles

It was a group of theorists meeting regularly during the nineteen twenties and thirties in Prague (and sometimes known as the "Prague School" of linguists) who developed Saussurean concepts into fully-fledged structuralism. Although these linguists were interested in all aspects of language systems, their most complete and influential work was on the structure of sound systems, on phonology. The basis for the development of the concept of the phoneme was Saussure's distinction between langue and parole. Actual speech sounds produced and heard in the real world, they argued, belonged to parole, whereas phonemes were abstract entities belonging to langue. The second idea developed from Saussure was that of structural opposition, the idea (introduced above) that language units gain meaning only through their relations between each other and not through any absolute properties they might have in isolation from each other.

The key figure in the development of structural phonology was Trubetzkoy, who elaborated and classified various kinds of oppositions found between phonemes in natural languages. His work became somewhat technical and complicated, but for present purposes the following simplified account of his thinking will suffice.

Before Trubetzkoy's contributions, it had long been realized that English sounds (or *phones*) such as [p], [t] and [d] differed in terms of how they were produced in the articulatory system. The sound [p], for example, is produced by closing the lips tightly, building up some air pressure behind them and then suddenly releasing all of this pressure when the lips are opened. The sound [t] is made by the same kind of "plosive" process, except that the point of closure of the air passage is not at the lips but is made, rather, by placing the tip of the tongue tightly up against the palatal ridge located behind the top teeth (commonly known as the alveolar ridge). The sound [d] is produced in exactly the same way as the sound [t], except that the vocal cords are set in motion making [d] a voiced sound and [t] an unvoiced sound. It is possible to continue this traditional descriptive process until all the sounds of English are uniquely identified and, indeed, this continues to be a very useful mode of analysis--especially for those working with second language learners or with subjects having speech impairments of various kinds--since the description focuses naturally upon aspects of the articulation in need of improvement or remediation.

This kind of analysis, however, was essentially *phonetic* in orientation, focusing on the transcription and analysis of actual sounds as they might be received, for instance, by some kind of mechanical recording device. The structuralist focus initiated by Trubetzkoy was at the more abstract phonological level (the level of the organization of sounds in human minds) and it centered on the attempt to find the sets of distinctive features between sounds. The Prague School linguists held that it was these features which kept phonemes apart in the minds of language-users and which allowed them to do their job of making meaningful distinctions in communication. The significance of pursuing this more abstract level of definition will become clearer, perhaps, following a short portrayal of the place and nature of individual sounds in meaningful communication.

Phones vs. phonemes:

Although it is in general true that the sound [t] is produced in the way described above, there is still a wide variety of ways in which the sound [t] can be pronounced. Indeed, it is acoustically different for every speaker who produces the sound and it is acoustically different for every verbal context in which it is uttered. To take an example, the sound [t] is not the same at the beginning of the word *tent* as it is at the end of the word--and it is not the same in Mary's, Spike's, Major's, or Bush's pronunciation of the same word. All speakers of English, however, whether they be American, Canadian, Indian, Australian, or British, can understand all particular versions of "tent" as they are pronounced by each of these and other speakers, and they do not normally notice any difference between the [t] at the beginning of the word and that at the end, or between Mary's and Spike's [t]s unless these speakers happen to have a particular articulatory defect in producing this sound. From the point of view of psychological processing, this means that speakers must in some way "know" that all the varieties of [t] that they hear are in fact members of one and the same abstract class of sounds, and the class in this case is, of course, the phoneme /t/ (by convention, phonemic units are identified by the use of slashes, while actual sounds--i.e. phonetic units--are identified by the use of square brackets). Phonemes, then, do not exist in the real physical or acoustical world but only as abstract psychological classes or "ideas" in the minds of English speakers. But we also know as speakers of

English that all the variants of the sound [d] are significantly different from all the phonetic versions of [t] (because distinctions in meaning between pairs of words such as *tip* vs. *dip* or *try* vs. *dry* are recognized solely on the basis of these contrasts--that is, they constitute *minimal pairs*). It follows, once again from a psychological perspective, that speakers somehow unconsciously assign all the various [d]s they hear in different contexts and from different speakers to a different class from that to which they unconsciously assign all [t]s. We can say, then, that the phonemes /t/ and /d/ contribute to meaning differences in English since they represent distinct classes of sounds--classes, that is, which, following Saussure, are in opposition to each other.

Sets of underlying features:

It was at this point in the analysis that Trubetzkoy's endeavors became truly significant in the development of structuralism. The question he and other members of the Prague School asked was that of how differences which underlie these oppositions within the phonological system as a whole could best be characterized. They raised the question, in other words, of how the relations between units in phonological systems could be accounted for in the clearest and most economical way. They realized that phonemes could be further analyzed and reduced in terms of an even more detailed underlying system of distinctive features that were smaller in number than phonemes themselves (therefore leading to a simpler and more revealing analysis).

It was Trubetzkoy's insight that phonological systems should be understood not as mechanisms made up of independent phonemic units but rather as systems of phonemes constituting organic wholes in which all units were interdependent and were distinguished in terms of these underlying sets of features. According to this analysis, for example, in English the phonemes /t/ and /d/ are distinguished solely by the feature of voicing (/d/ is voiced ([+voice]) whereas /t/ is voiceless or ([-voice]) and no other property apart from this binary relation between them has importance for communication in English). Significantly, however, this relationship also exists between other pairs of sounds in English, including /p/ vs. /b/, /k/ vs. /g/ and /s/ vs. /z/.

This last observation leads to the conclusion that the voicing distinction is a central characteristic of English. Indeed, it underlies an important regular pattern in the language concerning the *stop* phonemes (/p,t,k,b,d,g/--i.e. those sounds made by completely stopping the air passage at some point and then allowing a plosive release of air) which come in neat regular pairs, each distinguished by voicing as follows:

	Bilabial		Alveolar		Velar
[-voice]	/p/	vs.	/t/	vs.	/k/
	vs.		vs.		vs.
[+voice]	/b/		/d/		/g/

We already know *how* each of these sounds are made (they are all stops). Once we have specified *where* they are made (the lips, the alveolar ridge and the velar region--the soft area behind the hard palate--are the places of articulation corresponding to the three columns respectively), we only need to specify whether or not they are voiced to identify each phoneme uniquely. We need, then, only three features to distinguish between six stops. In this way, the Prague School linguists successfully demonstrated that many natural language phonological systems, including that of English, could be reduced by way of this kind of analysis to no more than a handful of distinctive features.

The second important part of this type of analysis was that it led to the realization that the phonological systems of all languages are in fact *relativistic* systems in which certain sets of features underlie oppositional relations between elements. Accordingly, the sound $[p^h]$ (a highly aspirated version of /p/, in which lots of air escapes audibly from the mouth, as it would in the exclamation "Peter!") is "not phonemic" in English, for example, because it does not signify a different meaning from other types of [p] sound. In Thai, however,--to use a familiar example--the situation is quite different since in this language the word transcribed phonetically as [paa] means something *different* from the word transcribed phonetically as $[p^h aa]$ (the two words mean, respectively, "forest" and "to split"). This means that speakers of

Thai must be assigning the sounds [pʰ] and [p] to two *different* phoneme classes, namely, /pʰ/ and /p/. The significant point to note here is that both English and Thai share the *same* phonetic sounds ([p], [pʰ], and [b]), but that they are *in different structural and oppositional relations to each other* in the two languages. Where English distinguishes either [pʰ] or [p] from forms of /b/ (via a simple voicing distinction), an extra distinctive feature enters into the relationship in Thai such that a *triangular* pattern of oppositions exists between [pʰ], [p], and [b]--that is, there are three phonemes where English only has two.

English	Thai
[p], [pʰ] and other realizations of /p/ vs. all realizations of /b/	/p/ vs. /pʰ/ vs. /b/

The structuralist approach

The central purpose of this excursion into the work of the Prague School linguists is to illustrate what structuralist analysis of language is all about. The efforts of the Prague School linguists were devoted to demonstrating that the sounds of natural languages have significance only through their oppositional and distinctive relations to each other, and not by virtue of any "absolute" properties taken in isolation from this relationship. This led to a clear foundation for further structuralist analysis. It is easy to imagine the nature of the analytic trend which followed the early ideas of Trubetzkoy, a trend which is apparent in the work of another Prague School linguist, Roman Jakobson, and also in that of Chomsky, Halle, and other transformational grammarians. It is a trend towards greater and higher levels of structural abstraction leading in the end, indeed, to a point at which the phoneme is no longer a relevant concept. According to later structuralists, phonological systems can be described uniquely in terms of distinctive features without any reference whatsoever to individual phonemes.

Apart from simplicity and economy of description, analysis of language into distinctive features has some other important qualities. First, it clarifies the relations between elements, showing that their identity derives solely from their comparative relationships with other sounds. Second, such analysis shows the underlying regular patterning of the sound systems of particular languages. Third, it shows how different languages, while sharing some of the grounds on which particular distinctions are based, reflect different particular arrangements or patterns of organization between their phonemes. This latter realization, of course, has the further powerful entailment that individual languages actually draw upon a *universal* set of distinctive features and yet make different uses of such features. That is to say, different languages have different patterns of phonemic opposition even though they share many of the raw sounds selected from the pool which is common to all languages. The structuralist influence in this is, once again, the perception that all phonemic units *only have value within their particular systems of relativity to each other*, and it is this idea which still dominates structuralist perceptions about language systems. One of the consequences of this kind of analysis is that languages can be treated as if having an "objective organic" life of their own. In this way, structural analysis of language, the skeptic might observe, can proceed much like the classification of mollusks or other natural phenomena. As such, it represents perhaps the most extreme form of treating language as "scientific object."

3. Language is Innate

In *Aspects of the theory of syntax* Chomsky (1965) put forward the view that

>...the child has an innate theory of potential structural descriptions that is sufficiently rich and fully developed so that he is able to determine, from a real situation in which a signal

occurs, which structural descriptions may be appropriate to this signal... (p. 32)

Chomsky continued by outlining the characteristics of a "language acquisition device" (LAD) which was supposed to be the innate mechanism used for language learning.

Rationalism vs. empiricism

Chomsky's proposals about the LAD are clearly within a tradition of *rationalist* (or *nativist*) thinking following Descartes, as opposed to the *empiricist* position espoused by the English philosopher John Locke. Locke held the view that each child is born with a *tabula rasa* (or 'blank slate') thus having to learn language solely from experience, whereas Descartes argued that human ability for thought was God-given and present at birth.

Not surprisingly, Chomsky's rationalist perspective on language learning has come under some heavy fire, due in part to the ambiguity and untestability of the LAD hypothesis--there is simply no way anyone can finally establish just what mental equipment or "information" a human child is born with. The issue remains an important one, nevertheless, for if the rationalist position is correct, it implies that genetic endowment may exist in the form of certain universal underlying properties of language. It implies, in other words, that there may be a "universal grammar" underlying all natural languages on the basis of which children learn the particular rules of the language (or languages) they hear in their environments. The central idea is that children are born with a set of *innate universals* such that "learning is only a matter of filling in detail within a structure that is innate" (1965, p. 39). The hope of universal grammarians is that through the objective analysis of human languages the form of the grammar common to all of them will emerge (see above, and Chapter Five).

Innate universals

Chomsky has supported the case for innate universals in several ways. First, he has argued that although languages are idiosyncratic in the particular qualities of their systems they yet seem to share much in terms of the general principles of how things are arranged. According to Chomsky, this in and of itself demands an explanation in terms of universal endowment followed by "selection" by the child of the particular rules that apply to the language to which he is born. Chomsky (1967) has argued that the deep structures of languages are similar and that the rules that operate on them (in his grammatical theory, transformational rules) constitute a limited set of formal operations used across different languages. Second, Chomsky has emphasized that children learn the natural language of their environments *despite* the less than ideal language performances that they hear from those around them and, it could be added, despite the sometimes less than optimal conditions for language learning into which they are born. Chomsky argues that

> ...the child learns the principles of sentence formation and sentence interpretation on the basis of a corpus of data that consists, in large measure, of sentences that deviate in form from the idealized structures defined by the grammar that he develops. (1967, p. 6)

These characteristics of language acquisition and, in particular, concomitant phenomena such as the overgeneralizations children typically make during language learning (for example, the regularization of the irregular past tense form *write* to *writed*) seem to invalidate the empiricist notion that children learn language solely on the basis of their experiences of language around them.

Third, Chomsky (1967) has argued that language learning is independent from general intelligence since most children gain language competence despite huge differences in intelligence levels. This implies that language must be a *discrete* faculty, independent from other kinds of thinking (an entailment which has further implications for interpreting the relations between language and thought and for the description of universal grammar). Fourth, the speed and facility with which children learn language, Chomsky has argued, could only be based upon a specific and dedicated device such as LAD. He observes that

> ...the tremendous intellectual accomplishment [of language acquisition] is carried out at a period of life when the child is capable of little else, and that this task is entirely beyond the capacities of an otherwise intelligent ape. (1967, p. 4)

While no detailed model of the language acquisition device has yet been developed, the above ideas survive as the backbone of justification for Chomsky's rationalist theory.

4. Meaning in Language is Founded on Truth

Most of us would probably accept that there is a strong relationship between meaning and truth in our own expressions and in the statements of others. If Fiona, who lives in Seattle, phones Fred, who is in Chicago waiting for a flight to see her, and tells him that it is raining on the west coast, it is clear that in most cases Fred will assume that she is speaking the truth. Of course, she could be intending to communicate ironically, in which case Fred will most likely recognize this in her intonation pattern (given a good telephone connection) and assume she truly means the opposite. She could also be lying to him for some sinister purpose, but even if she were, the lie would not have the same effect or meaning if it were not uttered against a background in which she (and all others) are expected to tell the truth in simple statements such as *It is raining in Seattle.* Certainly, the weather reporters on the local television networks would be in trouble if they made the comment and it did not represent the actual conditions seen through the living room windows of the local population.

The construction of a theory of meaning has to start somewhere, and a good place would seem to be with explaining the interpretation of simple declarative statements like the one about rain in Seattle. It is possible that if a concise statement about how truth is crucial to meaning in simple sentences such as this, then ways could be found to extend the analysis to include other classes of utterances, such as questions or imperatives. The search for lawful relations between language, meaning, and truth, however, has proven to be fraught with difficulty, and it seems clear that it will continue to challenge philosophers of language for a long time to come.

Several different answers have been suggested to explain the relationship between truth and meaning in declarative statements. One suggestion, represented in *coherence* theories of meaning, has been that expressions such as Fiona's are true simply because they are coherent with other statements in English--such statements, that is, fit into a network of language expressions accepted as true because they are consistent with each other. Another suggestion, represented in *correspondence* theories of meaning, has been that such expressions are true because they correspond to perceptions about real-world events. A third solution has been suggested by *pragmatist* philosophers such as John Dewey, and it involves combining the notion of correspondence with that of empiricism. According to pragmatists, a statement is true when it both corresponds to events in the world and satisfies an additional empirical test of its veracity.

Tarski's proposals

Some particularly influential proposals concerning the relations between meaning and truth were put forward by a Polish philosopher, Tarski, whose ideas have been further developed by other philosophers such as Carnap, Davidson, and Quine within what has become known as the "semantic" theory of language and truth. Tarski's arguments can be used to characterize some of the central issues in the historical and continuing debate about the relations between language and logic.

Tarski started out by recognizing that the idea of truth crops up in many different contexts. For example, we can have true emotions in addition to true beliefs, and works of art can also have "inner truth." He describes his main objective, however, to be the limited one of coming to some conclusions about the relations between truth and objective *logical* systems, and this centrally involved looking in detail at the properties of declarative sentences and at how they are interpreted as being true or false. More specifically, Tarski undertook to clarify more formally the following explanation offered in the *Metaphysics* by Aristotle:

> To say of what is that it is not, or of what is not that it is, is false, while to say of what is that it is, or of what is not that is not, is true.

Tarski noted that Aristotle's formulation referred only to the type of sentences that say that something "is" or "is not," and therefore that it was not general enough to cover other types of declarative sentences (for example *Bush wears fancy ties.*).

A second way in which the formulation needed amending was by specifying the language to which it related. Clearly the utterance "Bush wears fancy ties" might be true in English, but could be judged neither true nor false if uttered to a monolingual speaker of Urdu. In other words, the sentence *Bush wears fancy ties* is true or false only in some communicative (English-speaking) context where it is meant and understood to mean that Bush does in fact wear fancy ties. In Tarski's terms, this can be stated as follows:

1. The sentence *Bush wears fancy ties* is true if and only if Bush wears fancy ties and
2. The sentence *Bush wears fancy ties* is false if and only if Bush does not wear fancy ties.

At this point, Tarski noted, his analysis had provided a partial definition of truth: He had defined truth or falsity for sentences of the kind *Bush wears fancy ties* and he had stated explicitly the conditions under which such sentences would be interpreted as true or false. Key to this definition of truth is the phrase "if and only if," which is a way of stating logical equivalence (that is, we are saying that *Bush wears fancy ties* is true when it is equivalent to his actually wearing fancy ties).

The expression on the left hand side of "if and only if" Tarski called the *definiendum*, or the sentence whose meaning is explained. The expression on the right hand side was called the *definiens*, or the explanation. Instead of the italics used above for the definiendum, Tarski used single quotation marks as follows, and it is important to notice that the two sentences concerning Bush's ties actually have quite different status from each other:

'Bush wears fancy ties' is true if and only if Bush wears fancy ties.

The left hand side occurrence should be paraphrased "the English sentence *Bush wears fancy ties*," where this sequence of four words constitutes the grammatical subject of the entire sentence (on both sides of "if and only if") but where *Bush* the man *alone* stands as the subject of the definiens on the right hand side. What it is crucial to understand here is that the formula contains two levels of expression. First, the entire sentence refers to a smaller sentence, i.e. the claim made in English *about* some state of affairs in the real world, and, second, (in the definiens), to the actual state of affairs which may or may not exist. Note also that the definiendum involves the description of things at a higher or "meta-" level; the definiendum describes the English *language* as it appears in the sentence, not the purported state of affairs in the actual world.

Once Tarski had reached the point of successfully dividing things between "linguistic" and "actual" states of affairs, it was then possible to generalize the formula to other sentences in English. All English sentences were designated "true" wherever the same schema could be replicated, namely, where it could replace the particular sentence on either side of the "if and only if" (equivalence) connective. If the letter p stands for any English sentence then the schema can be stated as

'p' is true if and only if p

and any declarative sentence which conforms to this formula is true.

The next question Tarski asked concerned how an "adequate" theory of meaning for all declaratives could be built from this basic axiom. He stated this concern as follows:

> The problem will be solved completely if we manage to construct a general definition of truth that will be adequate in the sense that it will carry with it as logical consequences all the equivalencies of [the above] form. If such a definition is accepted by English-speaking people, it will obviously establish an adequate use of the term 'true.' (1969, p. 267)

Tarski argued that generalizing the schema into a complete theory of meaning based on truth would be relatively easy if it were possible to identify and delimit the set of English sentences over which it applied. All that would need to be done would be to construct the finite list of such sentences, all of which submitted to the "'p' if and only if p'" formula, and then to connect them up with a string of *ands*. In this way a theory of meaning could be set forth in the form "'Bush wears fancy ties' is true if and only if Bush wears fancy ties *and* 'Mrs. Bush likes fancy ties' is true if and only if Mrs. Bush likes fancy ties *and...*" and so on until the final sentence in the list had been expressed. What we would finish up with would be one huge conjunction (the size depending upon the number of sentences included in the initial set). Tarski argued that all this could be stated in a much simpler way. The whole case of the concatenated sentences could be expressed by way of the general schema:

> For every sentence in the subset in English (or in any other chosen language), this sentence is true if and only if either this sentence (and any sentence in the set) is a real description of the state of affairs in the world (a general *definiens*) and this sentence is identical to the 'sentence' in the *definiendum*.

Some of Tarski's formal notation has been omitted in the above but it should be noted that all the latter schema really expresses is a generalization of the initial schema presented above to all members of a set of sentences (this could contain any number of sentences--a hundred, a thousand, or even a million or more) and that, as such, it represents an explanation of meaning in this particular *corpus*.

The next important step in the argument, however, was connected with Tarski's observation that although this generalization could be applied to a *limited* set of sentences in English, there is a good reason why it cannot be readily generalized to the *whole* language. The reason for this was (as we saw in the previous section) that language is dynamic, unpredictable, and has infinite potential for forming new sentences. Another reason was that the English language itself contains the word *true*, and that when this word is used in sentences this complicates things enormously by yielding insoluble contradictions. To make this point clear, Tarski referred to the "antinomy of the liar," a contradiction which can be illustrated in the following way. First consider the sentence:

(1) The sentence above beginning "Another reason..." is false.

We will call this sentence 's.' The next step according to the schema is:

(2) 's' is false if and only if the sentence numbered (1) is false.

This is equivalent to saying

(3) 's' is true if and only if s.

When we substitute the sentences in this formulation, however, the following contradiction arises:

(4) The sentence *The sentence above beginning "another reason..."* is true if and only if the sentence above beginning "another reason..." is false.

Since both the metalanguage (i.e. the language of the definiendum which is about English) and English expressions themselves contain the words *true* or *false*, then, it can be readily demonstrated that the schema will not generalize to the *whole* of English, since it does not work in cases where either of these terms enters the statement about reality that we wish to show to be meaningful and true. Another quick demonstration Tarski gave of contradictions such as this was by way of the case of an imaginary book in which the statement *The sentence printed on the next page of this book is true* appears on the first ten pages but page eleven carries the statement *The sentence printed on page one of this book is false*. According to Tarski, paradoxes such as this have, not surprisingly, produced sometimes fatal levels of torment in some logicians in the classical epoch!

Despite the sometimes amusing nature of such conundrums, however, Tarski identified their intractability as a serious problem. Indeed, he called such nonsense forms "a symptom of disease" in logical theory. The antinomy of the liar demanded resolution if the theory of meaning and truth so far developed was to be rescued. One solution, of course, would be simply to excise the word *true* from the English language, but this would work against any serious claim of generalizability for the theory.

Tarski's proposed solution to the liar paradox was based upon an extension and formalization of the idea mentioned above. It was to treat the language in the definiendum as a *meta-* statement. Truth, argued Tarski, is a *relative* phenomenon: It is relative to the language in which it is claimed, and we therefore need an analytic level that is objective and *independent* of particular languages in order to deal with the truth or falsity of statements expressed in them. This led Tarski to argue that the problem of truth could only be successfully approached from the perspective of a *hierarchy* of languages, where the one in which the statements being assessed as true or false (eg. the everyday English of "This sentence is false") was to be treated as an *object* of description (i.e. an *object language*, while the description itself was framed at the higher level of a *metalanguage*). According to Tarski's solution, then, the truth or falsity of sentences must always be expressed at a higher level than the object sentences themselves. In this way, the liar's statement "This sentence is false" when properly interpreted is really just the innocuous form "This sentence is false in the object language" (i.e. everyday English). The sentence is now non-paradoxical and unambiguous, since it is a sentence in the metalanguage and, as such, establishes the sentence in English to be simply false. When we say a sentence is true or false in a language such as English according to Tarski's proposals, then, we are essentially using a metalanguage to do so--we are discussing English as an object language. In this way, the liar paradox vanishes since it is to be interpreted as a metalanguage statement about another sentence in the object language; it is not eating its own tail.

The somewhat simplified account of Tarski's definition of truth has been presented *not* because it is the most widely accepted version of how meaning should be understood but, rather, to identify a particular line of reasoning which is significant for greater understanding of other contrasting approaches to meaning. In later discussions, we shall see that the truth-functional approach to meaning brings with it several intractable problems together with many detractors. Suffice it to say at this point, however, that others, in particular the American philosopher, Davidson, have enthusiastically adopted Tarski's attempt to build a theory of meaning on the rock bed of truth, and the line of reasoning outlined above, together with the search for a truth-functional explanation of meaning, continues today.

Summary

In this chapter, four ideas have been outlined, each of which reflects an essentially objective approach to the description of how language works. The first of these is that language is rule-governed, the second, that language is structured, the third, that language is innate, and the fourth, that language and meaning are founded on truth. In one form or another, these ideas emerge repeatedly in discussions of language theory, and they also have implications for practice. In the next chapter, we will turn to the other end of the analytical spectrum, to the analysis of language within the "subjective" tradition, a tradition which emphasizes the central importance of human intentions, intuitions, and feelings in language.

CHAPTER THREE

Fundamental Ideas about Language II: Language and Subjective Experience

> Language is our all-encompassing medium, almost certainly the oldest means of communication and expression, one which is both central to and pervasive in the realm of all human thought. It is the basis of whatever social cohesion we can attain. It determines in large measure the way we look at the world; it enables us to control it. It links the past intimately with the present and makes possible at least some continuity into the future....We need it to grasp things intellectually and to get others to do so. We cannot avoid it even when we talk about it. To a large extent, it defines our very humanity.
> (Morton Bloomfield: *Language as a Human Problem*, 1973)

Introduction

The four ideas to be introduced in this chapter share a concern with active communicative processing. Unlike the objectively-oriented ideas introduced in Chapter Two, these ideas all focus upon language-users and their thoughts and intentions during communicative interaction rather than upon the language system considered as a scientific object for analysis. In the subjective approach, language is treated as a phenomenon inseparable from the workings of human consciousness. The first of the four ideas is that language should be understood as *action* and *use* in *context*. The second is that language and *thought* are indistinguishable, that linguistic and cognitive processes are largely synonymous. The third is the idea that language and *culture* are inextricably bound, that they are *relative* to each other, and the fourth is that language is just one of many communicative *sign-systems*. Like the four objectively-oriented ideas introduced in the last chapter, the following ideas are also foundational to language education.

Four Subjectively-oriented Ideas about Language

1. Meaning Arises from the Use of Language in Context

A point Tarski recognized was that even if his truth-theory could be extended across the entire sentence output of a particular object language this still would not capture the mercurial nature of language in everyday use. This is evident in his suggestion that a truth-based theory of meaning would ultimately have to

> ...take account of the fact that many sentences vary in truth value depending on the time they are spoken, the speaker, and even, perhaps, the audience. (quoted in Hacking, 1975, p. 135)

Many theorists have sought to describe meaning from the opposite direction taken by philosophers of logic, and they have started out from the observation that speech gains some of its meaning from the context of its utterance. They take the position, moreover, that meaning rests just as much upon the interpretation of personal intentions, personal functions and goals, as it does upon truth or falsity as they are defined in logical systems. It will also be recalled that Tarski's approach to description included only declarative sentences. But how might we assess the "truth" of other types of utterances such as questions, imperatives, and other aspects of human expression? It does not seem reasonable, for example, to ask for the truth-value of "Does Yeltsin like Bush's ties?" or of "Take that tie off!" There seem to be many sentences which are neither true nor false. They certainly mean something, but neither require nor lend themselves to interpretation in terms of strict truth or falsity.

The problem of multiple meanings

Another motivation for rejecting the exclusive linking of meaning to truth is to be found by considering the many meanings that any one utterance can have on different occasions. Even the straightforward declarative utterances examined by Tarski can have many different contextually-dependent meanings. Consider, for example, the many possible interpretations of the declarative sentence *Yeltsin is on TV*. On different occasions, this could mean any of the following:

> *Come downstairs, the program is starting.*
> *Something's up--looks like there's an important announcement.*
> *Forget watching a movie--there are political broadcasts on all channels.*
> *Yeltsin is on TV right now.*
> *Yeltsin is on TV this evening.*
> *I can't go out tonight--got to study for my math class.*
> *Well I guess watching hockey is more entertaining than that!*
> *Yeltsin's resignation speech is on.*

The list of possibilities for the interpretation of just this one sentence, indeed, is endless. It is infinite in a way which parallels the infinity of sentences themselves, since there are infinite possible contexts for every utterance in a language. What follows from this, of course, is that sentence meaning is clearly dependent upon something more than its truth value (notice that the speaker above, in addition to the possibilities listed, could be lying or being ironic and yet still be meaning something). In particular, what we need in order to decode the sentence accurately on given occurrences of its expression is information about the situation in which it is uttered and about the speaker who utters it. The sources for this perspective on language are to be found in the work of various philosophers who have reacted against the truth-functional view of meaning in language, philosophers such as

Wittgenstein, Austin, Grice, and Searle.

Wittgenstein's language games

The reaction away from the truth-functional view of meaning is perhaps most emphatically represented in the work of Wittgenstein, who in the later part of his career disavowed the truth-functional orientation of his earlier work. Along with other logical positivists, such as Schlick and Carnap, Wittgenstein had argued in the early part of his career that meaning could only be described by way of demonstrating its adherence to the laws of logic. A story is told that the point of revelation to Wittgenstein of this earlier mistake came during a discussion with an Italian economist, Piero Sraffa. Wittgenstein was toeing (and towing) the logical positivist line when Sraffa got up, showed the philosopher a gesture of contempt used by Neapolitans, and demanded to know what the "logical form" of the gesture would be. By Wittgenstein's own recollection, this was the point at which he realized that meaning in language could not be captured simply by relating it to logical form (cited in Hartnack, 1965, pp. 48-49).

At the heart of the later Wittgenstein's thought is the idea that communication through language involves what he calls "language games." One of Wittgenstein's earliest repudiations of the attempt to describe language in terms of a logical calculus is to be found in his "Blue Book," which is made up of notes of lectures he gave at Cambridge University in the early 1930s. Here Wittgenstein called the logical approach to meaning "one-sided" and observed that "in practice we very rarely use language as such a calculus." He further observed that normal language use does not involve *conscious* attention to language rules and that to suppose that we do would be equivalent to believing that children play games "according to strict rules" (1958, p. 25). Wittgenstein also recognized that acts of *naming* things, the one type of act that philsophers typically concentrate upon in developing their theories of language, corresponded to only one of *many* language games played during communicative encounters. According to his later view, knowledge of language involved knowing how to play several different kinds of games, and language could only be understood in terms of these multiple options. Wittgenstein no longer saw language as a monolithic system of logical interrelationships, but rather as a composite of the many (indeed infinite) number of games that could be played. The man holding up his hand and saying "No admittance" was playing one game, while (to give a current example) the executive responsible for the slogan "The quality goes in before the name goes on" would be playing quite another. Wittgenstein held that such games (which variously involve acts of imposition, persuasion, and so on) were pervasive in communicative interactions and that the boundaries between them were not always clear. As one of his many analogical references to chess makes clear, he also recognized that interpretation is always context-dependent; at one point in time someone may wish to refer to the chess board in terms of its color patterns, while on another she may refer to it in terms of its squares--there simply is no absolute underlying object which will always be referred to in the same way. In short, Wittgenstein came to see words as *tools* and, as such, that they can be used in many different ways.

Speech acts

Three other philosophers, Austin, Grice, and Searle have also recognized the importance of *acts* of speaking, and they have taken the explanation of speech acts as the central goal for a theory of meaning. In *How to do things with words* (1962), Austin attacked the tradition of philosophy which took truth as the criterion for meaning on grounds that many declarative sentences are uttered without the speaker's intention that they be interpreted in terms of strict truth or falsity. The sentences Austin had in mind were forms such as

> *I invest you with the insignia of the Warthogs*
> *I hereby christen this yacht Bubbles*
> *I declare you insolvent*
> *I apologize*
> *I object.*

Utterances such as these are used to *do* things, and Austin called them *performatives*. The central characteristic of such performative utterances is that they function not to describe the objective world but, rather, to change the states of things in speakers' environments. When the president of the Warthogs organization places the cloak around the shoulders of a new member his utterance actually changes the status of the newcomer; it does not make much sense to ask whether the utterance is "true" or "false." Likewise, utterances such as "I object" or "I promise" each establish a new state of affairs and the conversation which included responses to these utterances of "true" or "that's simply false" would be patently bizarre.

Although performative utterances may not be true or false, however, they may certainly be communicatively successful or unsuccessful. The performative utterance "I warn you" issued to the Terminator by an unarmed opponent, for example, would not likely succeed in changing the status quo. Accordingly, Austin gave the names *felicitous* and *infelicitous* to successful or successful utterances, respectively, and then set out to define the felicity conditions under which performatives work. Some of the criteria for communicative success Austin came up with are as follows. First, some conventional acceptance of the performative must be in place (that is, for instance, there must be a conventional acceptance among all Warthogs that the utterance "I invest you..." does actually constitute an act of admittance). Second, the utterances must be contextually appropriate (as the warning to the Terminator is not). Third, execution of the utterance must be correct and complete. Fourth, the people involved must have the requisite intentions and willingness to respond to the speech act. Violations of speech act felicity conditions, then, result in breakdowns in communication. They run against conventional expectations rather than against truth, falsity, or "verifiability."

Just like the logicians, though, Austin (1962) aimed at a general theory of language and, indeed, *How to do things with words* builds up from the notion that there is a special class of utterances (performatives) to a position where performatives are treated as just one class within a general theory of language performance. Austin's final claim was that *all* speech centers on what he calls illocutionary acts containing both performative and simple declarative utterances as subclasses.

One of the main problems Austin faced in extending the theory, however, was providing clear criteria for the identification of performative utterances. For the theory to be watertight there was an onus on Austin to classify utterances in terms of their grammatical properties or in terms of the linguistic items which turned up in the various types of utterances he described. It is clear, however, that no one-to-one relation between various utterances and classes into which they fall can be readily established. Consider the utterance "I apologize," for instance, which is a performative act when a speaker walks into class late but is not one when she is responding to a stage director's request to relate her lines to her positions on stage ("I apologize, then I move over to Elvira, then exit pursued by a bear etc...."). The converse can also take place. I can utter something (for example the noun "Door!") in a manner which clearly serves the function of a performative utterance without it having any of the grammatical properties claimed to be required of such utterances, properties such as "beginning with I..." or such as "containing one of a special class of verbs called 'performative verbs'" (which include the verbs *invest, promise, christen*, and so on). In order to attempt explanation of the multiple (perhaps infinite) grammatical and lexical guises in which performative utterances could come, Austin invoked the concept of *illocutionary force*. "Door!," then, has a "force" when it is uttered on the basis that the full paraphrase "I order you to close the door" is conventionally understood to have such force in some context. Although there still remain some problems concerning the unambiguous interpretation of utterances, Austin succeeded here in initiating an interest in pragmatic language functioning as a whole, an interest which has developed into a major field within language studies.

Searle (1969; 1976) has worked on Austin's ideas and has attempted to develop them more formally into a theory of meaning that incorporates stricter definition of the original categories. In particular, Searle has suggested that Austin's felicity conditions are not merely external constraints but that they should be treated as integral to utterances. If a speaker promises to do something, then in order for this to materialize as a successful speech act Searle claims that several felicity conditions must be in place, including the condition that the speaker subjectively *intends* to follow up the promise, and *believes* both that he can satisfy the promise but that he wouldn't do it as part of the normal course of events (that is, the promise is a significant and meaningful commitment).

Communicative principles

It was Grice (1957) who first attempted to reconcile the truth-functional and pragmatic approaches to meaning. Grice drew a distinction between what he called "natural meaning," the meaning which resides in sentences themselves disembodied from communicative context (the sentence Yeltsin plays pinochle, for example has some resident meaning quite apart from how I might communicate something by uttering it on some particular occasion) and "non-natural" meaning. He accounted for this latter kind of meaning in the following formula (cast here in less formal terms than the original):

> A speaker means something when she makes an utterance if and only if, first, she intended the utterance to have an effect on her audience and, second, she intended the effect to occur simply because her audience recognized this intent.

This interpretation of meaning portrays successful communication as a complex event in which both (or all) parties share mutual knowledge of each others' communicative intentions. The most important part of Grice's dichotomy is its recognition that the first and second kinds of meaning are by no means necessarily in a one-to-one relationship. The resident meaning of a particular statement, that is, may have little or nothing to do with how it is actually *used* in some communicative context. The distinction between the two types of meaning permits all sorts of relations between sentences, on the one hand, and how they are used by speakers, on the other. These relationships range from those of a very direct kind to the highly indirect (indeed, contradictory) relationship achieved in irony (by saying "Oh, sure, Hitler was a real saint of a man," for example, I will be understood in most contexts to mean exactly the opposite).

Obviously, recognition of the complexity inherent in communicative situations demanded some further explanation of the nature of such complexity, and Grice (1975; 1978) later developed his description of communicative interaction by introducing some further influential terminology. First, proceeding on the belief that language-users generally work on the basis of some fundamental principle of co-operation in communication, Grice identified four basic conversational maxims which prescribe what speakers should do if they are to be successful. These were

(1) The co-operative principle:
Make your contribution such as is required, at the stage at which it occurs, by the accepted purpose or direction of the talk exchange in which you are engaged.

(2) The maxim of Quality
Try to make your contribution one that is true, specifically:
Do not say what you believe to be false.
Do not say anything for which you lack adequate evidence.

(3) The maxim of Quantity:
Make your contribution as informative as is required for the purposes of the exchange.
Do not make your contribution more informative than is required.

(4) The maxim of Relevance:
Make your contributions relevant.

(5) The maxim of Manner:
Be perspicuous, and:
Avoid obscurity.
Avoid ambiguity.
Be brief.
Be orderly.

It should be noted, however, that it may often appear that these maxims are not being followed in an *obvious* way. The following imaginary possibilities should make this clear. If Yeltsin's interpreter says to Bush, "We want to bring three extra advisors to the lunch meeting" it would appear that Bush has violated Grice's fourth and fifth maxims if he replies, "Fourteen lunches have been prepared." In fact, however, Yeltsin nods with approval when this is translated back to him, now comfortable in the realization that the appetite of Russian officials has been duly anticipated by the Americans. Yeltsin, of course, might also grunt in disapproval to Bush's reply, interpreting him to mean that there will be no modifications of the arrangements already made for fourteen officials. The point to be made here is that even though Bush's reply appears *superficially* (to an outsider) to violate the maxims, in fact Yeltsin's interpretation (either way) depends upon his knowledge that Bush, at a deeper level, *is* following the maxims; he is merely leaving out unnecessary information (since he knows Yeltsin can make a simple deduction) thus conforming to all of Grice's prescriptions. Whichever way he replies, Yeltsin has fulfilled *his* part of the conversational bargain, of course, by assuming that Bush is acting with his language in a principled way. Grice calls necessary inferences such as Yeltsin's "conversational implicatures." Implicatures, then, are based upon both the actual content of the utterance and upon the sets of expectations of co-operation that language-users bring with them to communicative exchanges.

Grice's observations about meaning, just like those of Austin and Searle, have been subject to further refinement and critical analysis. They represent, nevertheless, a stream of thinking which continues to be influential and useful in applied description and practice.

Contexts of situation

While the major contributions to the idea that language is "use in context" so far outlined have been made by philosophers, there is one other important stream of thinking that was originally initiated within the field of anthropology and later developed by linguists. The anthropologist who sparked interest in analyzing language in context was Malinowski, who worked on descriptions of societies in the Polynesian Trobriand Islands of the South Pacific. A major problem Malinowski recognized was that of translating Trobriand language forms into English. He argued that this could only successfully be accomplished if detailed information about the contexts of situation in which utterances were made (see, e.g. Malinowski, 1936). Malinowski observed that language was a mode of action in context, and that its use typically reflected social functions as well as simple descriptions of objects and events.

In supporting his view, Malinowski referred to various kinds of utterances in English which seemed to reflect the essentially functional nature of language. He noted, for example, utterances such as "How do you do?" and "Ah, so here you are," which seem to function to secure or reinforce social bonds rather than being meaningful in any sense involving paraphrase or translation to other terms. Malinowski referred to utterances such as these, which have a purely social and non-literal function, as *phatic* utterances.

Malinowski also noted that children learning languages use language as "active forces" or "utensils" to manipulate the world around them. He further believed that this was a feature of what he referred to (in keeping with the times) as "primitive" languages. He identified various kinds of functions in Polynesian languages and, in particular, he identified the *pragmatic* function, where language was interpreted to be a formal action to get things done, the *magical* function, where language was used to gain control over the environment, and the *narrative* function, where language was used to tell stories, to preserve the history of society.

The linguist who was first to embrace Malinowski's ideas about language functioning in its "contexts of situation" was a British scholar, J. R. Firth. During the 1920's and 30's Firth developed these ideas into a tradition of linguistic analysis sometimes referred to as the "London School." Firth's endeavors are continued now largely in the work of M.A.K. Halliday, who has developed categories of language functions the farthest (see Chapters Five and Seven).

Firth's main objective was to show how context of situation could (and should) be incorporated into the formal (Saussurean) description of language, to show, that is, how context of situation could be treated as a descriptive category just like words or sentences. He proposed that the following categories be introduced into linguistic analysis:

> A. The relevant features of participants, persons, personalities.
>   i. The verbal action of the participants.
>   ii. The non-verbal action of the participants.
>
> B. The relevant objects.
>
> C. The effect of the verbal action.
> (Firth, 1957, p. 182)

Firth argued that moving down from this higher level of analysis to lower levels, linguists could interpret meaning as represented at all these lower levels of structure (sentences, words, sounds). In this way, structural units were to be treated as phenomena related to each other across levels within a unified system (his theory is sometimes called "System Structure Theory"). Firth's account of linguistic systems was in terms of sets of choices that language-users make in particular contexts. *Context* interpreted at the highest level was the social context of situation, and at the phonological level it consisted of the phonological environment for the production of particular sound segments. An example of the latter kind of context might be that of /s/___ /r/ in English. Only certain phonemes can come between /s/ and /r/ in English. There are, in other words, some phonological constraints on the co-occurrence of phonemes in this context. The paradigmatic possibilities, the items which can be "slotted in" at this particular phonological location, are /k/, /t/, and /p/ (as in the words *scratch*, *stripper*, and *spritzer*, for example).

Although the terminology of the theory, as it has been developed by "neo-Firthian" linguists such as Halliday, is somewhat complex, the central process in neo-Firthian analysis can be summarized as follows. First, analyze the context of situation in which utterances take place (this could be a market, a church, or any situation whatsoever) and determine the function of the language uttered in the situation. Second, identify the units of speech uttered in context and show how sentences provide the next (structural-grammatical) level of context for the units that function within them (clauses). Continue the process for phrases, words and morphemes. Third, show how the phonological units of utterances function within syntax, yielding the actual substance of the sounds produced or heard (an example of this level of analysis appears above). The key characteristic of the model is that every part of the analysis is concerned with *intended meaning in context*. All levels of units, that is, are described in terms of their *function* in the overall context-dependent meaning. In Halliday's terms, each smaller unit is an "exponent" of the level of units next above it. In this descriptive theory, structural analysis is totally dependent on functional-semantic analysis. The functional approach has become especially influential in the description of child language acquisition. (A more detaile overview of systemic analysis appears in Chapter Five).

2. Language and Thought are Indistinguishable

In a trivial sense, it is fairly obvious that language and thought are closely related: When individuals speak or write, they are involved in making thought explicit, and the external linguistic forms of the thoughts bear at least some connection to the silent inner forms which precede them. Less readily answered, however, are the questions of whether *all* thought is linguistic in nature, and of whether children pass through a pre-linguistic stage of thinking before language and thought become connected. Although this is an expansive and complex area of debate, a good starting point is to be found in the tradition of Russian thinking about language and cognition first inspired by Vygotsky.

The Vygotskian perspective

In the collection of Vygotsky's papers published posthumously in the book *Thought and language* (published in Russian in 1934, and published twice in English translation; 1962, 1986), he summarized his major claims about the development of thought and speech as follows:

1. In their ontogenetic development, thought and speech have different roots.

2. In the speech development of the child, we can with certainty establish a preintellectual stage, and in his thought development, a prelinguistic stage.

3. Up to a certain point in time, the two follow different lines, independently of each other.

4. At a certain point these lines meet, whereupon thought becomes verbal, and speech rational. (1986, p. 83)

Vygotsky argued that the way in which "thought becomes verbal" was by way of *inner speech*, which he contrasted with outer, or social speech. He wrote that inner speech is "speech for oneself" whereas external speech is "for others." External speech is the "turning of thoughts into words" while inner speech is the reverse. Consequently, he argued, "the structures of these two kinds of speech must differ" (1986, pp. 225-226).

What Vygotsky had in mind when he referred to inner speech, then, was *not* the process of silently talking to oneself, nor was his reference to the inner language of Humboldt or the competence of Chomsky. Inner speech was, rather, an *underlying* form of language, distinct from outer and audible speech, and having its own characteristic structure and founded on pure "word meanings." According to Vygotsky, production of language forms for communication with others was grounded in the word meanings of inner language, and these abbreviated "predicate" forms, having no complex structure, "die as they bring forth thought" (1986, p. 249). The central idea here is that inner language forms serve as *prototypes* for what we want to communicate. Let us suppose, for instance, that Tom Brokaw notices that Diana is wearing a particularly grotesque hat. His first thought about this is simply in the form "hat" (or perhaps "hat!"), which, if he were not in a communicatively demanding situation might be sufficient to his own cognitive needs. When Tom actually has to fill in a few moments of prime time for several million television viewers, however, it is the *external* form of this cognition that he must produce. Here it will be necessary for him to identify not only the simple predicate form of the utterance but also the topic and (by way of intonation) his views of Royal taste and he will say, perhaps, something like "Well, Connie, what do you think of the new pink hat?" Vygotsky also referred to inner speech as "a dynamic, shifting, unstable thing, fluttering between word and thought, the two more or less stable, more or less firmly delineated components of verbal thought" (1986, p. 249). According to Vygotsky, children go through a stage in which thought patterns are pre-linguistic but then quickly move on to a stage, by way of the development of inner language, at which thought becomes fused with language and is defined in linguistic terms.

Vygotsky's view of the relationship between language and thought which was strongly opposed by Piaget, was developed within a tradition of thinking from von Humboldt in which language and *culture* were considered to be inseparable. Although it is worth considering these two relationships (i.e. the relationship between language and thought and between language and culture) apart for the purposes of analyzing their potential educational significance, they are in fact closely logically related to each other. For this reason, the following section should to some extent be treated as a direct continuation of the discussion.

3. Language and Cultural Identity are Inseparable

The argument that language and thought are closely related entails the view that speakers of particular languages within the boundaries of specific cultural groups will see the world in terms of the categories and characteristics of that language and, thus, differently from members of other cultural and linguistic groups. On this view, languages are considered to be distinct therefore not simply in terms of their particular grammatical or phonological systems, but also in the ways in which these systems affect the processes of organizing cultural environments and experiences. Humboldt argued that inner language served partly to impose categories on the unordered sensory information coming from the physical environment, and that speakers of different languages were, in effect, living in different worlds and thinking in fundamentally different ways from each other. Humboldt's ideas concerning these so-called *relativistic* aspects of language and thought were taken up in this century by the anthropological linguist, Whorf.

Cultural and linguistic relativism

Whorf was a anthropological linguist working on the description of American Indian and Eskimo languages. As a result of his observations of such languages, he developed some specific ideas about how languages are inseparable from the cultures in which they develop. Whorf's major proposals about language and culture are now known collectively as the "Whorfian hypothesis," or as the "Sapir-Whorf hypothesis" (in recognition of Sapir's professorial influence on Whorf at Yale University), and the hypothesis has two parts. The first part has already received some attention in the last section and is, namely, that thinking is *dependent* on language. This is now often referred to as the principle of *linguistic determinism*. The second part is really an entailment of the first, namely, the idea that individuals everywhere experience the world differently in accordance with the categories of their particular languages. This he called *linguistic relativism*. The idea is expressed particularly clearly in the following extract:

> The background linguistic system (in other words, the grammar) of each language is not merely a reproducing instrument for voicing ideas but is itself the shaper of ideas, the program and guide for the individual's mental activity, for his analysis of impressions, for his synthesis of his mental stock in trade. Formulation of ideas is not an independent process, strictly rational in the old sense, it is part of a particular grammar, and differs, from slightly to greatly between different grammars. We dissect nature along lines laid down by our native language. (In Carroll, ed., 1956, pp. 212-213)

Whorf supported this idea by claiming that individuals "cut up" the world according to the culture-bound conventions we learn as children and that

> ...every language is a vast pattern-system, different from others, in which are culturally ordained the forms and categories by

which the personality not only communicates, but also analyzes nature, notices or neglects types of relationships and phenomena, channels his reasoning, and builds the house of his consciousness. (ibid.)

Whorf argued his thesis about language by comparing Amerindian language to what he called "Standard Average European" (SAE), which included all standard European languages; English, French, Italian, German, and so on. He perceived the structures of Amerindian languages to be radically different from those of the SAE group, and provided examples of these differences at the levels of both lexis and grammatical organization.

Culture-bound lexical categories

At the lexical level, the most familiar example Whorf provided concerned the differences in categorizations of snow between Eskimo, SAE, and other languages. Whorf observed that Eskimos both recognize and label different kinds of snow--"slushy snow," "falling snow," "tight-packed snow," and so on, whereas Aztecs and speakers of English have a more general concept of snow together with a corresponding absence of linguistic differentiation to describe its more detailed characteristics.

Another example Whorf offered concerned the labeling of time in English and other languages. In English, we are able to pluralize the word *hour* in just the same way that we can pluralize *book*. In this way, we categorize time in much the same way as we categorize objects, and we might each readily say, for example, either I have ten books, or I have ten hours to complete the assignment. Whorf claimed, however, that this represented a very *particular* pattern of thinking about time, and that it was quite different from the treatment of time in Hopi. Hopi speakers do not treat time as a collection of objects, but rather as a medium in which *events* take place, so that the direct English translation of the Hopi word *pew'i* is not, according to Whorf, the verb *come*, but the phrase "eventuates to here," or "manifests itself here" (Whorf, 1956, p. 60). In contrast, as speakers of English, we categorize time much like we categorize other things, as "substance." In this way, we can easily refer to *moments* or *bits* of time as if they were pieces of an overall structure, whereas the Hopi see time in terms of "eventuating" cycles that have no direct connection with the behavior or categorization of objects. Whorf stressed that the Hopi think of time not as a string of separate time elements but as one *continuum* in which the events--prayer, singing, eating, and activities of preparation for events--serve as the major markers of time.

Another area of lexical contrast between languages which has received special attention following Whorf has been that of color differentiation. Gleason (1961) and others have argued that languages do not dissect the color spectrum into the same linguistically-defined categories. In the Shona language of Africa, for example, the word *cicema* covers the categories of green and yellow in English, while in the Bassa language the word *hui* covers all of purple, blue, and green in English.

Culture-bound grammatical categories

Perhaps the most intriguing part of Whorf's hypothesis concerns the relations between language and thought as they are reflected at the level of grammatical organization. At this level, Whorf's ideas amount to the claim that languages represent different *logical* ways of thinking about things in individual experience. In comparing Nootka to English, for example, Whorf argued that since the grammatical patterns are radically different from each other in the two languages, speakers of these languages must think in radically different ways. Whorf claimed that in Nootka, there were no parts of speech and that "...the simplest utterance is a sentence, treating of some event or event-complex" (Whorf, 1956, p. 242). The Nootka version of the English sentence *He invites people to a feast* has no subject-predicate relations but, rather, is made up of just one very complex word *tl'imshya'isita'itlma*, which Whorf analyzed as follows:

> [The word] begins with the event of 'boiling or cooking,' tl'imsh; then comes -ya ('result') = 'cooked;' then '- is 'eating' = 'eating cooked food;' then -ita ('those who do') = 'eaters of cooked food;' then -'itl ('going for'); then -ma sign of the third-

person indicative...[giving the whole word as above]...which answers to the crude paraphrase, 'he, or somebody, goes for (invites) eaters of cooked food. (ibid. pp. 242-243)

In contrast to the Nootka expression, the English expression (and the English language as a whole) embodies what Whorf called the "naïve" notion of actors who produce actions. He argued that this logical frame is so pervasive in English that speakers typically interpret even forms such as *I hold it* in terms of an actor and an action, whereas what such a form truly expresses (according to Whorf) is a state of affairs of things in *relation* to each other. Despite some well-recognized problems of Whorf's views stated in their extreme form, the idea of linguistic relativity continues to be a provocative one. The idea continues to have repercussions in such areas as multicultural education, since it seems to suggest, when interpreted in its "strict" form, that any one culture may be literally "unknowable" from the point of view of another, or that we are *culture-bound* by our languages.

4. A Language is Just One of Many Operative Sign-Systems

In Saussure's *Course* we find language defined as "a system of signs that express ideas" and we encounter the claim that:

A science that studies the life of signs within society is conceivable; it would be a part of social psychology and consequently of general psychology. (1974, p. 16)

Saussure called this new potential science "Semiology (from the Greek *semeion* 'sign')" and argued that linguistics, as a discipline, should be viewed as "only a part of the general science of semiology." We have already seen how this idea was interpreted within Saussure's larger programme for language studies and, in particular, how his further distinction of signs into signified and signifier provided the keystone for linguistic structuralism. Although it shares with Saussure its emphasis on the primacy of signs in language, however, it is in a parallel but distinct tradition of thought that the sign has received its most complete analysis. This is the tradition of semiotics.

The revival of semiotics

As Eco (1984) has demonstrated in a thorough analysis of the field, the roots of semiotics lie in classical and medieval thought. While there are now several "schools" of semiotics (in particular, it is possible to identify Russian and French lines of development) one of the most profound influences on current approaches within the "science of signs," has been that of the nineteenth century American philosopher, C. S. Peirce, who incorporated an analysis of sign types into what amounts to a radical theory of subjective knowledge.

Peirce's significance in the history of thought about signs is better understood by looking first at the words of the English philosopher, John Locke who in his *Essay concerning human understanding* (1690) argued that there were three essential kinds of "science" or knowledge. The first type concerned knowledge about matter and "things," and the second concerned knowledge about the "spirits." Concerning the third type, he wrote:

> The third branch may be called...the Doctrine of Signs, the most usual whereof being Words, it is aptly enough termed also Logic; the business whereof, is to consider the Nature of Signs, the Mind makes use of for the understanding of Things, or conveying its Knowledge to others. For since the Things, the Mind contemplates, are none of them, besides itself, present to the Understanding, 'tis necessary that something else, as a Sign or Representation of the thing it considers, should be present to it: And these are Ideas. And because the Ideas of one Man's Mind cannot immediately be laid open to the view of another; nor be themselves laid up any where, but in the Memory, which is apt to let them go and lose them: therefore to communicate our Ideas one to another, as well as record them for our own use, Signs of our Ideas are also Necessary. (p. 361; original punctuation and capitalization preserved)

Peirce's development of these basic ideas took several forms. First, he gave more precision to the notion of signs. A sign (which he called a *representamen*) was defined by Peirce as "something which stands to somebody for something in some respect or capacity" (*Collected Papers*, Vol. 2, para. 228). This simple-looking statement about the role of signs actually reflects a complex set of relationships between the sign (*representamen*), what it stands for (its *object*), the respect in which it stands for its object (its *ground*), and the individual to whom the sign means something (its *interpretant*). According to Peirce, then, the interpretant perceives things in terms of the *triadic* relationship between representamen, object, and ground.

Second, Peirce categorized various *kinds* of relationships between these elements of perception and interpretation. Not surprisingly, the terminology necessary for such categorization became voluminous, and Peirce generated sixty-six possible combinations of signs that he held to exist within the process of semiosis. The three most basic categories of possible relationships between a sign and its object, however, were the *icon*, the *index* and the *symbol*. The iconic relationship covered forms of direct resemblance between signs and objects such as may be found in the relationship between a painting and what it portrays (as interpreted by the viewer) or in mathematical equations, diagrams or metaphors. The indexical relationship was one of sequential or causal connection between signs and objects such as might be found in signs giving directions, or meaningful gestures representing information about placement in space or time. In the case of symbols, Peirce argued, there is no direct connection; the relationship is *arbitrary* and *conventional*. Symbols are what the interpretants use to express the relationships between signs and objects, and words are perhaps the best examples of such expression. Whereas a picture of a rose petal may be a direct *index* of a rose, and where a drawing of a rose and its functional parts may be *iconic*, then, use of the arbitrary sounds in "rose" will be *symbolic*. The complex system of sign relationships that Peirce described originates in the possible combinations of these classes; symbols, for example, can have indexes and icons incorporated into them and he wrote, indeed, that "the most perfect of signs are those in which the iconic, indicative, and symbolic characters are blended as equally as possible" (*Collected Papers* Vol. IV: para. 448).

Third, Peirce treated semiosis as a fundamental *logical* process and he defined logic, indeed, as "the science of the general necessary laws of signs" (Vol. II, para. 227). According to Peirce, then, even more fundamental than the axioms of formal calculi are the way things are subjectively interpreted through signs. Perception itself he considered to be "logical" in that even the most basic elements of cognition involve relations between things. On this view, there is nothing that is known that is not a relation of one kind or another through the process of semiosis, the process of interpreting signs. This logic of subjective knowing, it should be noted, is quite distinct from the truth-functional logics discussed in the last chapter.

Fourth, Peirce saw that these relations were *unlimited*. Signs can also be signs *of each other* in an infinite progression and knowledge, therefore, should be understood as a process of *translation* between signs and sign systems (a view which Jakobson, 1980, argues, incidentally, if it had been adopted would have constituted a notion of meaning "which no mentalist and no behaviorist could reject..." p. 34).

While Peirce's complex categorization of signs is often treated as his central contribution, it is really the latter two points which are of greater significance and which differentiate him from other thinkers. One danger of approaching Peirce's ideas is that they can be easily misinterpreted to amount to a formulation the character and scope of which correspond closely with linguistic structuralism. While there may be apparent lines of compatibility between Peirce's semiotics and later linguistic theory, however, (and this is especially clear in the correspondence between Peirce's and Saussure's views of linguistic symbols as arbitrary and conventional), the direction taken in Peirce's philosophy is really quite different. In particular, it should be noted that language, for Peirce, was only *one* semiotic code within a multitude of other codes interpreted through other channels of meaning. Language, therefore, could itself be understood in relation to these other channels of perception and interpretation. For Peirce, *everything* in thought involved semiosis and, as stated at the outset, the elaboration of this idea gives rise to a significant new theory of knowledge. It is Peirce's understanding of the processes of knowing through semiosis (rather than his detailed categorization of signs) which composes the most exciting and potentially influential aspect of his contribution.

If the relations in and between signs are conceived as "structures" then the question remains of their "location." Are these various and unlimited structures to be found "in the world" or are they to be found "in the head" or "in the mind"? Structuralist thinking as we contemplated it above strongly suggests that structures (such as those uncovered by structural linguists) are *independent* of the thinking of organisms which participate in structurally-organized behavior or, at least, that there is no *direct* relationship between the structures and their place in linguistic or perceptual processing. Peirce's analysis and understanding of the structures of signs, however, was radically different, and he argued that although sign structures can be thought of *partly* as independent entities, semiotic structure and thought were really one and the same thing: They were indissoluble and inseparable from each other. It should be noted, therefore, that this aspect of Peirce's thinking is consistent with the view that thought and language are inseparable. In Peirce's view, indeed, they appear to be synonymous. He claimed that "there is no element whatever of man's (sic) consciousness that has not something corresponding to it in the word" and that "the word or sign that man uses is the man himself." "Thus," he continued," my language is the sum total of myself; for the man is the thought" (Vol. V: pp. 313-314).

Another and more metaphorical way of viewing life as Peirce saw it might be that humans are adrift in a "sea of signs," the particular interactions between which and with which he becomes subjectively involved actually constituting his identity. Human beings, then, both constitute and are constituted by the process of semiosis; they exist at the locations of the particular sets of semiotic intersections they experience. This, it should be acknowledged, represents a far more profound view of the relation between structures, existence, and individual identity than the more limited analysis of structure to be found in the tradition of thinking grounded in the structural linguistics of Saussure. It represents nothing less than a potential explanation of "phenomena" themselves and, as we shall later see, for this reason bears close relations to developments in the field of phenomenology (see Chapter Nine).

Summary

In this chapter, four subjectively-oriented ideas about language have been reviewed. The first is that meaning arises out of use in context, the second is that language is inseparable from thought, the third is that language is inseparable from cultural identity, and the fourth is that language is a sign-system. The shared characteristic of these four ideas is that they each emphasize that explanation of language must involve taking into account the subjective experiences and intentions of language-users. This represents a significant contrast to the objectively-oriented ideas about language presented in Chapter Two, which treat language as a phenomenon that can be detached from communication. The final idea, the semiotically-inspired idea that language should be conceived as one of many sign-systems used for communication can be understood in one sense as being an attempt to reconcile the objective and subjective orientations to language, since signs apparently lie at the intersection of the worlds of objects and of subjective experience and interpretations. In the following chapters, language will be viewed from the perspectives of the various disciplines in a way which will expand the basic ideas so far discussed. The possibility of synthesis between the objective and subjective orientations is continued both in the more detailed analysis of semiotics in Chapter Nine and in the final discussion relating theory to practice.

CHAPTER FOUR

Language and Biology

If man (sic) is a natural creature and a product of evolution, it is reasonable to suppose that man's capacities as a knower are also a product of evolution. If we are capable of believing and knowing things, it must be because these capacities, and the organs in us or organization of us that are responsible for these capacities, *historically* performed a service that helped us to proliferate. (R. G. Millikan, *Language, Thought, and Other Biological Categories: New Foundations for Realism*, 1984)

Introduction

Superficially, it might appear that descriptions of the physiological bases for language processing should be both easier to develop and less ambiguous or abstract than descriptions of syntactic or semantic systems. After all, biology, it might be argued, being a "natural," as opposed to a "social" science has at its disposal strict empirical techniques and procedures which should yield detailed, incontrovertible and factual information about physiological functioning. When it comes to describing the relations between language and biological functioning, however, establishing the "facts" is far from easy, and the related issues are both complex and controversial.

There are several reasons why the relationship is such a challenging one to describe. First, while great advances have been made in describing human physiology, there is still much to be discovered about the relations between evolutionary development and language. In particular, it remains unclear whether the emergence of language should be viewed as *dependent* upon certain organic changes in the species or whether, to the contrary, language in some way played a *leading* or *causative* role in physiological adaptation. Second, contemporary discussion about language in relation to biology has become enmeshed in the continuing philosophical conflict between rationalist and empiricist positions on the innateness of linguistic abilities. In the end, then, what seems initially to be a relatively clear-cut area of knowledge turns out to be much less so.

Despite the sometimes esoteric nature of philosophical debate about linguistic and biological development, however, there have also been some relatively uncontroversial findings about the relations between human physiology, speech, and hearing. We will start with some of these less disputable findings and then move on to review some of the more contentious issues.

The Mechanisms of Speech

The Larynx

The human larynx is perhaps the most complex organ in the physiological chain involved in speech, and its evolutionary development provides important clues to how speech developed in our species. The larynx is located at the top of the *trachea* (or "wind-pipe") and is made up of cartilage, ligaments, and membrane. In the center of the larynx lie the *vocal cords* (or *folds*), which are two thin mucous membranes that are either brought together by the *arytenoid cartilages*, at which point they vibrate and make sound, or apart, in which configuration air passes freely from the lungs through the open space (the *glottis*) and into the higher *oral* and *nasal* cavities. The geometrical shape of the membranes when they are drawn together is three-dimensional and looks more like a pyramidal form than a flat two-dimensional disk on a horizontal plane.

The laryngeal mechanisms serve two main functions. First, they serve as the source of vocal sounds and, second, they serve to guarantee unhindered breathing by blocking off the trachea from unwanted intrusions and ensuring that all food and liquid is properly diverted into the esophagus, leading down into the stomach. Significantly, the detailed interaction between the larynx and the esophagus is unique in humans and its development to this point constitutes an intriguing part of the evolutionary emergence of speech.

Types of Physiological Control Producing Speech Sounds

Air passing through the larynx can be used to produce *voiced* and *unvoiced* sounds, depending on whether or not the vocal cords are drawn together and set in motion. If they are drawn together and set in vibration, voiced sounds are produced, while if they are drawn apart, air passes freely through the glottis and unvoiced sounds are produced. Further modifications occur to the air as it exits the body by way of the mouth (oral cavity) or nose (nasal cavity). It is possible to classify the consonant and vowel sounds produced in speech by way of the kinds of modifications made to the air stream as it exits the body. *Stops* such as the sound [p] are produced by completely *stopping* the air at the lips and then releasing it quickly to give a typically "plosive" sound. *Fricatives* such as [s] are produced by *partly* closing off the air stream to produce a characteristically high-pitched rush of what acousticians call "white noise." Vowels are formed by changes in the shape of the oral cavity: The high front vowel [i] found in the word *beat*, for instance, is produced when the jaw is high in relation to the palate of the mouth and when the highest point of the tongue is right at the front of the mouth, just behind the upper teeth. The mid back vowel [o], found in *boat*, on the other hand, is produced when the jaw is mid-way between its highest and lowest positions and when the highest point of the tongue is at the back of the mouth. With the addition of the distinction between *lax* and *tense* vowel sounds (i.e. the distinction between whether a vowel, such as [I] in *bit*, is produced with the muscles around the speech mechanisms relaxed, or whether it is produced, as in [i], with the same muscles slightly tensed), the parameters of *high vs. low* and *front vs. back* can be used to describe each vowel uniquely.

The following facts are crucial to an understanding of the central evolutionary changes which underlie human language. First, speech is produced during *exhalation*. Second, controlled pressure is applied to the column of air as it is exhaled. This pressure is produced both by muscles surrounding the lungs and by the closing of the vocal cords within the larynx. Third, the vocal cords are set in motion as the air is allowed to pass between them. Fourth, further intricate modifications are made to the air stream, notably by the tongue and by way of changing the shape of the oral cavity, in order to produce intelligible sounds. Taken as a whole, human speech represents stupendous feats of coordination of these various movements. The variety of sounds in languages, then, shows that humans are capable of a much higher degree of physiological control over the relevant organs than are other animals. These coordinated movements take place so rapidly that conscious monitoring of them is not normally involved, although conscious monitoring may play a function in language learning or remediation. The key question is how these coordinated capacities are developed in individuals on the basis of the phylogenetic changes in the human species.

Phylogenetic Development of Speech Mechanisms

Erect stance

If our own species is compared to the *pongidae*, the most advanced apes, several physiological distinctions that are significant to an understanding of human speech become apparent. First, humans are fully bipedal. This evolutionary development has led to a natural lowering of the brain within the skull, leaving more room for upward development of the cortex together with greater space and flexibility in the neck. Bipedalism is also associated with greater freedom of movement in the arms and hands, leading to the evolution of tool use, likely a direct precursor to language (which can be justifiably conceived as "symbolic tool use"; see Vygotsky, Chapter Nine, below). Second, our erect stance has led to a lowering of the larynx in the neck and a gradual elongation of the distance between the upper laryngeal mechanisms and the velum. A natural consequence of this has been that the portion of the neck and head that can be used to resonate any sounds made by the vocal cords has increased. In addition, this has provided the opportunity for making lower-pitched and more varied sounds than the relatively high-pitched transmissions of the apes. As men and women developed greater motor control of the musculature in the lips and tongue so, too, they developed the capacity to interfere with the streams of air as they are exhaled in the ways mentioned above.

The changing function of the larynx

Lieberman (1984) cites some of the more detailed analyses undertaken of the development of the larynx. In particular, the research of Negus (1949) suggests that all animals possess larynges having a common phylogenetic origin in a valve designed to protect the lungs from infiltration-- originally the infiltration of water in fish such as the lung fish. In a thorough anatomical comparison of the larynx in mammals and other animals, Negus demonstrated the logic of the evolution of the larynx from its original function as a breathing mechanism in fish. He argued that different species developed the larynx variously either to accommodate greater breathing capacity or to facilitate the making of sounds. According to his analysis, horses, for example, which are able to open the larynx to 114% of the size of the trachea, have more advanced laryngeal adaptation for breathing than primates, who are able to open the larynx to only 50% of the size of the tracheal cross-section. This makes horses especially suitable for the purposes for which they are typically used by humans, while the greater laryngeal restriction in primates increases their capacity to make more refined and distinguishable sounds (Lieberman, 1984, pp. 268-270). Lieberman (Lieberman, 1968a: Lieberman, 1984) has argued further that it is the additional adaptations in primates leading to downward sloping ribs and a corresponding ability of the intercostal muscles to impose control over expiration which provide another key precursor to speech (1984, p. 114).

Breathing and eating

Another interesting characteristic of the human larynx and vocal cords is their peculiar deficiency when compared to those of other animals when it comes to the interaction between breathing and eating. As Lieberman points out, Darwin himself noted that the lowered position of the apparatus in humans means that all food and drink has to pass over the trachea leading to some risk that such substances will find their way into the latter rather than into the esophagus. A clear comparison can be made between humans and chimpanzees: In the chimpanzee, the larynx lies directly behind the tongue and is much closer to the velum and nasal cavity than it is in humans. During breathing, the epiglottis and velum of the chimpanzee connect and overlap allowing food and liquid to pass around the sides of the laryngeal tube and into the esophagus while air continues unimpeded through the trachea. This means, of course, that chimpanzees can eat or drink and breathe through the nose at the same time.

These physiological characteristics of the chimpanzee are also present in newborn humans who, for the first three months of life are also able to breathe through the nose and suckle at the same time, thus reducing the imminent danger of suffocation. A simple self-test is sufficient to demonstrate that in human adults, due to the lowered position of the larynx and the absence of closure between the epiglottis and the velum, swallowing and breathing are mutually exclusive events. Lieberman argues, indeed, that the particular phylogenetic descent of the larynx in humans (paralleled to some extent by the ontogenetic development from babies to infants) represents a highly *un*ideal adaptation in comparison with other mammals. It is unideal since, while it benefits speech, it also means that "an error in timing can propel the bolus of food into the larynx with results that are often fatal." He associates this adaptation, moreover, with the "finding of cadavers in medical school dissection with a preserved piece of steak blocking the larynx" (1984; p. 281). All of the above forms part of Lieberman's argument that the development of speech in humans is the result of quite logical sequences of change in the course of the same natural evolutionary processes as those that governed phylogenetic development in all other species. This suggests that the development of language in humans should be regarded as a quite natural and logical part of evolutionary development, and *not* as a *sudden* or unpredictable arrival. This idea stands in opposition to the "innateness hypothesis" developed within the framework of Chomskyan linguistics, which rests on the claim that language is something "endowed" and "special" in humans.

Parallel adaptations

In his influential work *Biological Foundations of Language* (1967), Lenneberg made several additional comments contributing to our understanding of the development of the speech apparatus, although he appears either to have been unaware of or to have rejected the pioneering work of Negus. One comparison Lenneberg made between the physiological structures of humans and apes concerns the development in the former of stronger muscles in the face and lips than in the latter. In particular, he argued that the appearance in humans of one type of muscle, *risorius Santorini*, at the sides of the mouth permits much greater refinement of articulatory control. Concerning the resulting ability in humans to coordinate the muscles around the mouth, Lenneberg wrote that these muscles "make possible rapid and air tight closure and sudden explosive opening" that are prerequisite to speech (p. 37).

Concerning the larynx, Lenneberg cited the work of Fink and Kirschner (1959), who demonstrated that the shape of the laryngeal tube corresponded to an ideally efficient "nozzle" for the transmission of columns of air for sound production. As they put it, "[t]he exponentially curved surfaces (of the human larynx) constitute a horn functioning as an acoustic transformer...during phonation" (quoted in Lenneberg, p. 49). According to Lenneberg, this is a "morphological correlate" of speech, although both here and elsewhere in *Biological Foundations* he deliberately treated as spurious any conclusions that might be drawn concerning this and other correlates as "causes" of speech.

Evolution of the brain

From an orthodox evolutionary and comparative standpoint, the complex *central nervous system* (CNS), consisting of the brain and spinal cord appears to have developed from the simple cords of nerves in worm-like animals. The system developed from lower animals in a series of layers and each of these layers is associated with certain observable changes in behavior (although it should be kept in mind, once again, that a *correlation* between anatomical development and types of behavior in no way guarantees that the former is the direct *cause* of the latter).

The central function of the spinal cord in humans is to transmit information about the body to and from the brain. The spinal cord also governs involuntary reflexes (such as knee-jerks) in addition to movements under potential or actual conscious control. As the spinal cord enters the skull and merges with the brain it becomes thicker, at which point the *brain stem* can be identified. The brain stem is the earliest part of the brain to have evolved, and it contains mechanisms shared by all vertebrates-- mechanisms regulating more complex reflexes, such as the beating of the heart, the maintenance of stable temperature, and breathing necessary to life. Through the brain stem pass all the ascending and descending nerve fibers transmitting and receiving information to and from the brain.

The layers of the brain

Above the level of the brain stem, it is useful to divide the brain into three concentric anatomical and functional layers. Following Hilgard, Atkinson and Atkinson (1979) these layers, which gradually evolved, are a) the *primitive central core*, b) the *limbic system*, and c) the *cerebrum*. For present purposes it is necessary only to observe that the various mechanisms within the central core of the brain function to regulate more advanced forms of motor coordination (such as those exhibited in swimming, piano-playing, or speech), and that the limbic system, which evolved at the mammalian stage, functions to exert some control over basic instincts. While these lower systems may in some ways influence linguistic behavior, however, it is the cerebrum, with its surface of the *cerebral cortex*, which lies at the center of all higher mental processes and which has most to do with the development and utilization of language.

It is a well-known fact that the cerebrum is divided into two *cerebral hemispheres* which mushroom out from the brain stem and which are connected together by a bundle of nerve fibers known as the *corpus callosum*, through which information can be transmitted between the hemispheres. Viewed from the side, the structure of each hemisphere can be divided into four main *lobes*, (frontal, temporal, parietal, and occipital) and can be seen to have two dividing *fissures* (the fissure of Rolando and the Sylvian fissure). Another familiar fact is that each hemisphere receives and transmits information through the spinal column relating largely to its *opposite* side, although aural and visual information involves both hemispheres. (See Appendix A for diagram).

Cerebral dominance

It is now recognized that one hemisphere has usually gained *dominance* over the other. In right-handed individuals, the left hemisphere is dominant, whereas for left-handed individuals, the right hemisphere is often, although not universally, dominant. The process in the first ten or so years of life by which one hemisphere develops to a position of dominance is known as *lateralization*. It has been established that particular areas of the brain are directly responsible for controlling certain bodily functions, including those involved in speech. This idea lies at the core of traditional neuropsychological theories and is commonly referred to as *localization*. With these basic terms in mind, we can now go on to consider in more detail what is known about the specific relations between the brain and language functioning.

Language and the Brain

The Findings of Broca

In 1861, a physician named Paul Broca gave an address before the Anthropological Society of Paris which has influenced thinking to the present day about the brain. Researchers before Broca had argued that higher mental functions were associated with particular parts of the brain, and *phrenologists* had even argued that particular individual capacities could be located by feeling the shape of the skull. Broca's presentation was based upon his examination of one patient, a fifty-seven year old called Lebourge, whose only speech consisted of the word *tan*, although he largely understood the language of others. Examining Lebourge's brain at the autopsy, Broca found a cyst in the left frontal lobe, and from this finding he developed an argument about the course of the effects of the trauma on the patient.

In his presentation, Broca divided communication into two categories, linguistic and non-linguistic, and he also drew a distinction between *expressive* and *receptive* linguistic abilities. On the basis of these categories, Broca argued that Lebourge's deficiency had been limited to expression. In this way, then, a particular area of the brain was located and directly linked to a particular physiological function. An important entailment of Broca's argument was that concentration should be placed on the location in the brain of specific convolutions, rather than on its size and shape. Broca's analysis, furthermore, was consistent with a growing belief in the asymmetry of hemispherical functioning (i.e. the idea of cerebral dominance).

From later anatomical research on patients suffering from *aphasias* of various kinds, Broca (1865) suggested that in some cases damage to the left hemisphere could be remedied by transferring functional control to the right hemisphere. This reflected his discovery that, despite the location of "Broca's area" in the frontal part of the left hemisphere, *some* aspects of linguistic functioning were carried out under the control of the right hemisphere and, in particular, that the right hemisphere functioned prominently in the association of expressions to meanings.

Following Broca's presentation, work on aphasia expanded greatly.

Findings of other surgeons, however, included cases where patients suffered from lesions in Broca's Area yet apparently suffered no associated behavioral consequences. As Caplan (1987) notes, the period following Broca's pioneering work became somewhat confused and lacked a unified theory to explain the relations between sites in the brain and language behavior--the field became "data rich and theory poor" (p. 49).

The Findings of Wernicke

It was another physician, Carl Wernicke, who drew together many of the observations made during the decade of research following Broca and who provided a unified framework for thinking about them. In particular, Wernicke identified several types of aphasia and related them to different cortical areas. He suggested, moreover, that language processing involves the integration of several disparate but interactive brain systems.

The patients Wernicke studied in detail shared with Broca's patient a loss of expressive ability, but differed in the particular characteristics of language breakdown they exhibited. While they sounded relatively normal and were able to produce regular patterns of intonation, Wernicke's patients yet failed to communicate any consistent meaning. His patients typically articulated words which appeared to have been related in some way to their "target" utterances. These words, for example, might share a common vowel or other sound patterns with potentially meaningful forms, or might have some lexical association with suitable words. They amounted, however, to nothing more than "jargon" to those listening. One patient, speaking what has since been referred to as *jargon aphasia*, was found at the autopsy to have a brain lesion in the left hemisphere in a position further back from that of Broca's patient and extending into the parietal lobe. Wernicke's subsequent analysis of the localized function of this area was that it played a central part in the *association* of different forms of sensory and linguistic information. This led in turn to a series of deductions, the essential conclusion being that lesions in this relatively posterior part of the left hemisphere were linked to disruptions of *both* receptive and expressive processing of meaning. Wernicke further argued that the area (since known as *Wernicke's area*) was primarily responsible for bringing together the flow of information about language from memory and the mechanisms involved in the representation of meaning in articulated speech. It was the concept of "information flow" between centers of cerebral processing which was Wernicke's major innovation (Caplan, 1987, p.53). Wernicke subsequently made further predictions about a variety of damaging effects which could arise from combinations of lesions in Broca's and Wernicke's areas. He also distinguished between lesions in these centers and those found in the pathways linking them together.

Connectionism

Wernicke's theory of brain functioning is now known as the *connectionist* theory due to his idea that functions were the result of "connected" brain components. Research following Wernicke and, in particular, that conducted by Lichtheim (e.g. Lichtheim, 1885), continued to concentrate upon the identification of particular aphasic characteristics and their localization within particular components of the brain. Caplan (1987) defines some characteristics of connectionist theories. First, the faculties of reading, writing, speaking and hearing were believed to be physiologically discrete. Second, they were believed to be connected and interactive with each other. Third, the notion of brain "centers" emerged where each such center was conceived as "a single psycholinguistic faculty, associated with one major type of storage for linguistic items, located in a particular area of the brain (1987: p. 62). Caplan further points out that there was a decline in interest in the connectionist model over the earlier part of the century possibly, he suggests, due to disaffection with everything German.

Despite its erstwhile unpopularity, however, the connectionist model has been more recently revived by theorists such as Geschwind (e.g. Geschwind 1965; 1979), who has formulated many of the most familiar current notions about the brain. A useful crystallization of the recent connectionist position appears in Geschwind (1979), where he outlines the findings about the cerebral processing of language made on the basis of the earlier work of Broca and Wernicke.

The Orthodox Model of Brain and Language

The current orthodox connectionist model of language processing in the brain embodies the claim that the most basic underlying forms of language originate in Wernicke's area, and that these are then passed on to Broca's area, where they are processed to yield "blueprints" for the articulation of speech. As Geschwind (1979) points out, Broca's area is adjacent to the area of the motor cortex dedicated to control of the musculature of the speech apparatus, and it is to this motor area that the forms generated in Broca's area are directly transferred. Wernicke's area also functions in the comprehension of language since messages originally received in the auditory cortex are transmitted to it for semantic decoding (p. 111). If language input to the brain is in visual form, the connectionist model predicts that it will first pass from the visual cortex to the *angular gyrus* (directly behind Wernicke's area) where it is translated into auditory form before receiving semantic decoding in Wernicke's area. According to the model, the writing of words involves a reversal of operations along the same cortical pathways. As Geschwind points out, this basic connectionist model is consistent with a multitude of data collected over the last century from aphasic patients. Lesions in Broca's area, for example, have been found to disturb speech production while having negligible effect on comprehension, whereas trauma suffered in Wernicke's area disrupts language processing at the deeper levels of comprehension and meaning, thus likely affecting all aspects of linguistic communication (ibid.).

Another finding about the nature of aphasias supporting the connectionist model has been that damage to the angular gyrus effectively severs the links between the systems used in auditory and visual linguistic processing. This results in patients able to speak and to comprehend speech normally while being unable to write. In addition, it is now thought that reading requires translation into auditory form at the angular gyrus before processing for meaning takes place in Wernicke's area (Geschwind, 1979, pp. 111-112).

Geschwind cautions against treating the various connected brain sites as having absolute and fixed status. He elaborates this idea in reference to the many patients studied who have managed somehow to overcome trauma to the language centers in the brain by transferring them to other healthy cortical locations, locations either adjacent to or far removed from the traumatized sites. He notes in particular that many studies suggest that the areas directly surrounding Broca's area may "share its specialization in latent form" (p. 112). Other significant findings have been that many young children show complete recovery from lesion damage and that left-handers often make better progress than right-handers, a finding that leads to the conclusion that hand-dominance and language-dominance may be directly related.

Geschwind further outlines the now familiar description of hemispherical specialization consistent with the connectionist model. While the hemispheres are symmetrical in the way in which nerves from one side of the body feed into the brain hemisphere on the opposite side (*cross-lateralization*), he argues that they are "profoundly asymmetrical" in other respects (p. 114). According to Geschwind, the left hemisphere is usually the dominant hemisphere for language, while the right hemisphere is responsible for the processing of more abstract patterns, such as those found in music or art. Supporting evidence here is, for example, that patients with damage to the language areas in the left hemisphere are nevertheless often able to *sing* words and melodies. Patients undergoing left temporal lobectomies, moreover, while forgetting much linguistically-oriented information, can yet remember locations and faces, together with more abstract visual and auditory forms. Once again, however, Geschwind cautions against overestimating the degree to which the hemispheres are specialized, pointing to evidence that the right hemisphere may well have some "rudimentary linguistic ability" and that there are "doubtless many tasks where the two hemispheres ordinarily act in concert" (p. 115).

Alternatives to the connectionist model

Although the connectionist model, in which language processing is described in terms of the supposed connections between localized cortical centers, continues to have some influence, various theoretical objections have been raised to the approach at various times. Shallice (1988) refers to the early locationist theorists such as Broca, Wernicke, and Lichtheim as "diagram-makers" rather than "connectionists" to reflect their approach to drawing definitive pictures of supposed fixed orders of events in the brain (p. 6). In an extreme form of diagram-making, Lichtheim (1885) actually went so far as to include "concept-centers," wherein concepts were supposedly elaborated upon following the generation of "motor word representations" according to the Broca-Wernicke plan.

Shallice cites several lines of attack that were marshalled against the early theorists. First, the actual evidence for localized centers was argued to be tenuous at best. Marie (1906), for example, reanalyzed Broca's cases, finding the lesions to be actually far larger and less specific than Broca had claimed, and Moutier (1908) found patients who exhibited the same symptoms as the Broca's aphasics while having lesions in quite different locations. Following these anomalous findings, then, the psychological claims of the early theorists were treated with disdain and skepticism. Second, the psychological explanations provided by the diagram-makers for various syndromes were disputed. It was clearly questionable, for instance, whether the explanation that the agrammatical forms of Broca's aphasia were linked, as they claimed, to the "loss of motor images" of language. Third, it was argued that the general "theory-driven" method by which hypotheses were first set down and then attempts made to confirm them, led to an absence of rigorous "data-driven" empiricism, resulting in spurious description and justified skepticism. Head (1926) expressed such skepticism about descriptive circularity in the comment that "the more carefully the patient is examined, the less certainly his disorder corresponds to any preconceived category" (see Shallice, 1988; pp. 9-11).

Neurolinguistic Processes: The Research of A. R. Luria

One highly influential version of the connectionist model has been called the *process* model (Caplan, 1987, Chapter Seven). Although earlier connectionist theorists had held that linguistic elements may be stored at different cerebral locations, the process model adheres to the claim that all linguistic activity involves the interaction of *many* sub-components, even though such sub-components may themselves be specific and localized. The key figure in the development of this process-oriented view about language processing is the Russian neuropsychologist, A.R. Luria and, since his work has been and continues to be very influential as a foundation for *neurolinguistics*, it is worth examining his contribution in some more detail.

Language processing in a "shattered world"

Luria's detailed description of a single case, *The Man with a Shattered World* (Luria, 1975) provides a thought-provoking and concise introduction both to the complexities of the field of neuropsychology and to the types of behavioral and linguistic phenomena that require explanation. The patient, Zasetsky, whom Luria describes as the "real author and hero" of the investigation, suffered from the results of a bullet which entered his brain, and Luria's clinical notes cover twenty-five years of his life (p. 16). Fortunately for the field of neuropsychology, Zasetsky himself regained the ability to write and has provided history with his detailed notes on what it is like to attempt to recover from such a trauma.

Although suffering from great loss of memory, Zasetsky managed through much trial and effort to recollect parts of his past life. He came to a point in his attempted recovery where he was able to remember some details of his early school years, his teachers, his friends, and the town in which he grew up. He remembers, too, fighting on the western front against the Nazis, and waking up on an operating table, and how he had to begin reconstructing his mind. He describes the initial experience of a head wound that "seemed to have transformed me into some terrible baby" (p. 23). When he awoke, Zasetsky found he could not even recollect his own name. Luria found in his first meeting with Zasetsky that his patient was able to label some things correctly while being unable to label others--for example, his left and right hands. Luria also found that Zasetsky could list the months and seasons of the year in order, while being unable to state which season or month preceded the next. Luria's examination of Zasetsky's brain tissue revealed that the bullet had lodged in the parieto-occipital regions of the left hemisphere.

Luria's analysis of Zasetsky reveals his characteristic way of thinking about the place of language within a framework of *integrated processes*. Specifically, Luria concludes that language was "not simply a means of communication but a crucial part of the entire process of cognition" and that "[a]part from being a means of communication, language is fundamental to perception and memory, thinking and behavior." Language, in other words, "organizes our inner life" (p. 40). According to Luria's analysis, then, the damage to Zasetsky's brain should be understood to have disrupted not only his language processing but also his ability to integrate other interactive systems such as perception and memory. But as is clear from his ability to make notes or to reconstruct his life at all, Zasetsky's cognitive and linguistic processing abilities were not entirely obliterated. Luria associates this retention of ability to the absence of damage to the frontal portions of Zasetsky's brain. In contrast to patients such as Zasetsky, Luria had discovered that patients with damage to the frontal sections of the brain continue to be able to learn but unable either to form plans for the future or to impose control over their own behavior. Luria describes such patients, unlike Zasetsky, as having been "robbed of any possibility of a future" and as having "precisely what it is that makes a person human" (p. 41).

Luria categorizes Zasetsky's notes in terms of the particular types of problems he faced in reconstructing his shattered world. First, it is clear that Zasetsky suffered from problems involving the relations between language and *space*: He recorded how he could only pick out certain letters from words without being able to see anything else around them and how he often forgot where simple parts of his body, such as his shoulder or his forearm, were located. He also had problems grasping the meaning of spatial terms such as *right*, *left*, *up*, or *down* (p. 55). Second, Zasetsky knew that he had particular problems relating to the reading process. He described how he went up to signs on doors but that no matter how carefully he examined the individual letters he was unable to read them. His anguish is apparent in the following comments in his diary:

> I couldn't read a thing....I stood there as though rooted to the spot simply unable to understand why I couldn't read that sign. After all, I could see, I wasn't blind. But why was it written in a foreign alphabet? Wasn't someone playing a joke on me--a sick man? When I just look at a letter, it seems unfamiliar and foreign to me. But if I strain my memory and recite the alphabet out loud, I definitely can remember what the letter is. Learning to read means having some magic power, and suddenly I'd lost this. I was miserable, terribly upset by it. (pp. 61-63)

As Luria informs us, however, Zasetsky persisted with reading and eventually regained the skill through arduous re-learning by way of forming new associations between letters, sounds, and words. The "turning point" in Zasetsky's rehabilitation came with writing, which he suddenly discovered he could do relatively automatically:

> I finally picked up the pencil and after repeating the word *krov* [blood] a few times, I quickly wrote it. I hardly knew what I'd written since I still had trouble reading--even my own writing. (p. 69)
> I often have to stop and think about the first letter, but when it comes to me I have no trouble writing it. However, I often notice that I swallow or lose letters, or confuse those that are similar in sound--like k and kh, z and s....[o]r else I'll substitute a letter I've already used in a word and write *zozoto* instead of *zoloto*. (p. 70)

Zasetsky further described the tortuous route through sounds, to syllables, to complete words he sometimes had to take in order to write complete longer words. Later on in Zasetsky's progress, it remained the case that recalling words and their meanings represented a supreme challenge. He came to understand the meaning of many words only by constantly comparing objects with each other until the labels became clear, and he wrote that:

> Every word I hear seems vaguely familiar...except that it has lost meaning. I don't understand it as I did before I was wounded. This means that if I hear the word *table* I can't work

out what it is right away, what it is related to. I just have a feeling the word is somewhat familiar, but that's all. (pp. 91-92)

Zasetsky's case and normal processing

Luria's explanation of Zasetsky's linguistic problems includes the following points that may have great significance for a more general understanding of the neural normal processing of language. First, it was clear from Zasetsky's case that words contain many kinds of attributes--some shared across all their occurrences, and others specific to given instances. A billiard table, for example, looks somewhat like other tables but yet has many attributes that are specific to it--the green felt, the pockets, the pyramid of balls, and so on. The problem for Zasetsky, Luria suggests, lay in pulling out these attributes, in forming the associations between objects, events, and their contexts. Normal individuals are capable of detecting the distinguishing features of objects and events around them with remarkable facility and rapidity in such a way that they only have to exert mental energy over definitions when something is very unfamiliar or novel. Normal language processing, in other words, appears to rely on complex but highly automatic and fluent processes of *synthesizing* information, of relating visual and other sensory stimuli to their distinctive representations in language, for example. It is his inability to utilize these processes of differentiation and synthesis that Luria argues to be central to Zasetsky's condition. Luria states that

> ...the bullet that penetrated this patient's brain disrupted the functions of precisely those parts of the cortex that control the analysis, synthesis and organization of complex associations into a coherent framework (by isolating the essential features of objects perceived and retaining traces of language habits). (p. 97)

For Zasetsky, the processes which are so automatic in normal individuals had to be reconstructed at the cost of huge effort, and he had continually and monotonously to label objects, to keep the labels in mind (in short-term memory) while comparing them with other labels, and to revise and to learn his associations. Luria holds these associations to be precisely what enable normal individuals to build up and to access vocabulary (p. 98).

Second, Zasetsky's loss of capacity for processing using short-term memory meant that he typically "latched on" to the first or last words of sentences and, while attempting to decipher the meanings of these, often forgot the intervening words. Single words continued to have meaning for Zasetsky, but his short-term memory loss meant that both understanding and producing extended utterances were largely impossible for him.

Third, he was unable to grasp the logical and rhetorical relations between things in his attempts to read extended texts. Luria describes Zasetsky's constant problem in detecting the grammatical relations between elements in sentences; he had trouble with negatives, in relating subjects and objects to each other, and even with simple comparative sentences such as *An elephant is bigger than a fly*. From thousands of informal experiments on Zasetsky, Luria concludes that he was able to understand sentences in which the word order corresponds exactly with the sequence of actions described (sequences such as *Winter came...it grew cold...and snow fell*) but was incapable of dealing with more complex constructions such as propositions containing relative clauses. Luria's conclusion was that "his inability to understand the logic implicit in grammatical constructions was his chief disability" (p. 113).

Luria and the Russian tradition

A good detailed outline of Luria's more precise ideas about neuropsychological processing of language appears in Luria (1973), and it also serves to locate Luria's place within the tradition of Russian psychology following Vygotsky (see also, Luria and Yudovich, 1971).

Central to Luria's position is his rejection of the "narrow locationist" models of Broca, Wernicke, and those under their direct influence, in favor of descriptions aimed at explaining mental processes in terms of complex *functions* involving the interaction of many cerebral elements. Specifically, Luria disparages any notion that mental functions can be interpreted as the "functions of particular tissue" in the brain and revises the notion of function to associate it with the sum total of processes that go to make up any complex activity, such as digestion, respiration, or speech. The key idea here is that any such function requires the coordination of a *whole gamut* of underlying cerebral activity. According to Luria, then, analysis of mental processing requires detailed attention to a whole *system* of coordinated activity--activity, moreover, which can never be reduced to the contribution of any *individual* localized areas of brain tissue. Functions such as respiration or speech, Luria argues, must be understood as "complete functional systems, embodying many components belonging to different levels of the apparatus" (1973, p. 27). One key characteristic of functions is that they may be supported by *different* sub-systems, and Luria gives the example of respiration, during which the intercostal muscles may in some situations take over the function of the diaphragm, or vice versa. For Luria, then, analysis of complex functions involves understanding how they are *orchestrated* rather than how they are localized--although references to a plurality of different locations or sites may necessarily be involved.

Luria's revision of the notion of localization is closely tied to his analysis of complex higher mental processes, such as those involved in language use, as resulting from the gradual superimposition during the course of human development of mental action on simple manipulative movements. Like Vygotsky, Luria believed that mental action gradually takes over from physical action in a process of gradual symbolic internalization. Luria emphasizes, moreover, that human developmental processes are never "static," and that it is therefore to be expected that the activities which contribute to higher functions will to some extent "move about." In this way, the locations of particular functions actually *change* during the course of development, and any one apparent function may therefore result from dynamic and movable sub-systems (pp. 30-31).

Cortical "zones"

The matter of localization is treated in Luria's theorizing in terms of various cortical *zones*. The young child, according to his theory, thinks principally in visual terms and by *recollecting*. In adolescence, abstract thinking develops in such a way that the earlier more simple processes of perception and memory are "converted" into more complex analytic and *reflective* processes. According to Luria, this leads to "lower" and "higher" cortical zones, and lesions in the lower brain zones of a young child will have far more impact on basic cognitive processes than it will in the those of an adult, since the latter has developed higher levels which are functionally dominant over the lower processes. In adults, it is lesions in the higher zones that will have most impact on lower-level perceptual functioning (p. 33). The central task of neurological science, then, is to

> ...ascertain by careful analysis which groups of concertedly working zones of the brain are responsible for the performance of complex mental activity; what contribution is made by each of these zones to the complex functional system and how the relationship between these concertedly working parts of the brain in the performance of complex mental activity changes in the various stages of its development. (Luria, 1973, p. 34)

An important entailment of this position is that there can be no simple approach to the *symptoms* of neurological disorder. Luria insists that there can be no simple way of associating symptoms to localized areas, and that similar symptoms, indeed, may be related to quite different components of the complex cortical interaction that underlies them. Correct diagnosis, then, must rely on what he calls "complex structural analysis" (p. 38). The only sure way of building more secure neurological models is, according to Luria, by comparison of all lesions occurring in any localized focus in the cortex together with close analysis of how the characteristics of disturbances are changed by lesions in different locations.

In summary, then, Luria's approach rests upon resisting the temptation to search for direct one-to-one relations between individual cortical locations and mental processes and upon embracing, in its place, "the analysis of how mental activity is altered in different local brain lesions and what factors are introduced into the structure and complex forms of mental activity by each brain system" (p. 42). Luria's theory of brain functioning has, of course, been developed well beyond the outline presented here, but enough has been reviewed to give an idea of Luria's particular way of thinking about the neuropsychology of language. Luria's process model concentrates upon isolating and identifying cortical patterns underlying *interactive* language processes distributed across *various* interacting cortical locations. Perhaps most important of all is Luria's insistence on approaching the description of brain traumas affecting language armed with an accurate prior account of language processes themselves. This principle requires, first, that researchers come to the task with a secure notion about language *structures*, since it is only in this way that a clear account can be provided of the psychological processing of linguistic elements. In describing the neuropsychological history of Zasetsky, Luria (1975, p. 108) emphasizes his need for more accurate analysis of the linguistic characteristics of the patient's language production and reception; and it is this emphasis upon accurate description of the language system itself (an emphasis apparent as early as the work of Head, 1926) which underlies much recent work on aphasia and, specifically, the development of *neurolinguistics* as an area of concentration in its own right.

Neurolinguistics and Linguistic Aphasiology.

Culminating in the work of Luria, we have seen a gradual shift away from attempts to build theories of neuropsychological processing of language on the basis of analyses of the structure of the cortical areas and towards much greater concentration upon the characteristics of language output. Combined with the growing realization that the mechanics of the mind are extremely complex and can certainly not be descriptively reduced in any simple way to specific cortical "locations," this realization of the value of detailed analyses of linguistic structure has led to the emergence of the field of *neurolinguistics*. The work of Luria presaged an era in which, as Jakobson (1980) put it,

> ...the cardinal conclusion one may draw is the necessity of an ever closer cooperation between linguists and neurologists, a joint and consistent scrutiny which promises to open a deeper

insight into the still unexplored mysteries both of the brain and of language. (p. 98)

One important outgrowth from the core interest in the relations between linguistic processing and cortical structure within the general domain of neurolinguistics was the area now often referred to as *linguistic aphasiology*. To some extent, the focus of the latter differs from its parent discipline in that the emphasis lies firmly in the *linguistic* phenomena related to aphasia and to the specific revelations about language processing to which comparison between aphasic and normal language lead. It was Jakobson, a linguist whose work spanned both European and American schools of thought, who did perhaps more than anyone else to lay down the foundations of how the linguistic analysis of aphasia should proceed.

Jakobson's foundations for the analysis of aphasia

Reviewing his own earlier contributions, (e.g. Jakobson, 1968), Jakobson (1980) identifies several key principles for neurolinguistic analysis. First, he insists on a clear separation between the mechanisms of linguistic *emission* and *reception*. Speakers, he argues, quite unlike hearers, are free from probabilistic assumption. When a speaker utters the word "sun," for instance, he is not in a mode of thinking where the distinction between the homophones *sun* and *son* is an issue: This is only an issue for the hearer, who must decode messages according to his prior expectations about meaning and his assessment of communicative context. In the study of aphasia, Jakobson insists that these are two quite distinct kinds of language competencies, where the receptive capacity to decode meaning is to be considered "privileged" over emission, since there are so many cases where receptive capacities are developed while encoding remains impossible (pp. 100-105).

Second, analysis of aphasia should proceed on the basis of the clear and polarized types of the syndrome already known. It is from further detailed analysis of these relatively "pure" types that descriptions of more "mixed" types of aphasic disorder can be predicated (ibid.).

Third, the language data gathered must be of a wider and more natural kind than that comprising responses to doctor's questions. This latter type of response, Jakobson insists, constitutes a particular place in our verbal behavior and should not be interpreted to be the same as spontaneous speech. Neurolinguistics requires rich language data collected from aphasics across a variety of communicative situations.

Jakobson cites several studies he considers important to the development of neurolinguistic analysis among which is that by Goodglass (1968). In this study, a consistent pattern of aphasic treatment of several inflectional morphemes in English was found in that aphasic subjects retained the inflectional forms relating to the pluralization of nouns (e.g. several dream*s*) while typically losing inflections in utterances such as John*'s* dream (where *s* signifies *possessive*), and John dream*s*, (where *s* signifies third person singular verb agreement). In the normal acquisition of English as a mother tongue, meanwhile, children typically learn the plural formation first, the possessive form next, followed by the third person singular inflection. All of this suggests analysis in linguistic terms as follows: *dreams*, the first normally acquired and the last form retained by aphasics is simply grammatically "one word," while the possessive form is really a phrase (in the form "of John," "of Mary," and so on) and the third person agreement inflection has the underlying form of a full subject-predicate clause ("John dreams"). What we have here, then, is a neat description of aphasic loss in terms of degree of *linguistic complexity*, and the agrammaticality of aphasia can be seen closely to correspond with the levels defined by degrees of grammatical complexity. As Jakobson further points out, the first thing to be lost in agrammatic forms of aphasia is the complex ability for predication, for combining subjects and objects as co-modifying variables. This is an ability central to all forms of language processing beyond simple "this and that" references and which underlies the central human capacity for *displacement* (i.e. the ability to refer to things not present in time and/or space). The above example gives a good indication of the general mode of analysis in neurolinguistics, and the central notion underlying neurolinguistic analysis is that there must be a degree of *isomorphism* between linguistic structures (organized into levels of grammatical complexity) on the one hand, and neurological functioning, on the other.

Modularity

One other central assumption underlying neurolinguistic analysis is of great importance to neuropsychological modeling more generally and this is, namely, the assumption of *modularity*. A weaker form of this idea is simply that language is discrete from other cognitive abilities, that it constitutes a "module" separate and dissociated from abilities such as those underlying mathematical, musical, or artistic thinking. A stronger form of the modular hypothesis, however, is that language and language processing can themselves be further broken down into several modules or discrete subparts which maintain their own autonomous functioning. Following Fodor (1983), modules such as the "lexical," "syntactic," or "semantic" modules are suggested to be systems in their own right operating in hierarchical relation to each other; that is, any one module must operate on information input from lower, but not higher, modular levels. According to Blumstein (1988), however, the most recent view is that it is unlikely that localized cortical organization will directly reflect this hypothesized modularity of language structure and process. Recent findings about aphasia suggest that disabilities are not so neatly organized into modular-linguistic categories and "the mapping of discrete neurological structures to linguistic functions or language modules is not very promising" (p. 213).

Levels of Linguistic Analysis

Recent findings about aphasia have emerged at each of the levels of *phonology*, *lexicon*, and *syntax* (Blumstein, 1988). These findings have great significance for our understanding of language processing and of the relation between linguistic analysis and neuropsychology.

Phonological errors

At the phonological level of aphasic processing, an array of errors has been observed and classified. In particular, researchers have observed *substitutions* of phonemes for each other, *deletions* of phonemes or syllables, *additions* of extra phonemes, and *environmental* errors (which would include *Spoonerisms*, such as the famous "You have hissed my mystery lecture" for "You have missed my history lecture" together with other forms of *metathesis*, such as the ubiquitous "nucular" for "nuclear"). From data relating to each of these four categories and taken across a variety of languages, several general findings have emerged. First, the direction of phonological errors within aphasic subjects can be *predicted*; for instance, they replace target phonemes with substitutes that differ from the former in only one *distinctive feature* (for example the word *bit* is often replaced by the word *pit*, which is distinct from *bit* solely in the voicing distinction on the first sound--[p] is unvoiced, while [b] is voiced). Aphasics, moreover, generally lose processing control over the least stable features within the linguistic hierarchy, features having to do, for instance, with manner of articulation such as the distinction between *stops* and *fricatives*--before they lose control over highly salient features such as consonant vs. non-consonant sounds (Blumstein, 1988, p. 215).

Wider evidence shows that, while aphasia deeply disrupts phonological aspects of language processing, the disruptions yet still remain systematic and that no complete violations of the regular patterning of languages take place--aphasic patients do not invent new rules which are inconsistent with how phonetic and articulatory processes work naturally. As Blumstein puts it

> ...phonological errors in aphasia reflect patterns consistent with the view that the underlying phonological system of the patient is still governed by structural principles intrinsic to the phonology of language in general as well as to the particular language affected. (p. 216)

It has been found, however, that Broca's aphasics may suffer from disruption to the phonetic "timing mechanism," which governs fine features of articulation such as the exact time of the onset of voicing when a vowel follows an unvoiced consonant. From the perspective of neurolinguistics, this reflects a *phonetic* level of deficit that is quite distinct from the *phonological* deficits typical of Wernicke's aphasics. (It will be recalled from Chapter Two that the phonetic level of description concerns raw acoustic data, while the phonological level relates to abstract psychological classes by which raw data is organized for meaning.)

Lexical errors

At the lexical level, the most common observed deficit in aphasics relates to the ability to name things. Typically, many patients grope around for words or reduce their descriptions to weak general representational forms such as "thing." Several neurolinguistic explanations have been offered for this phenomenon, commonly called *anomia*. One is that objects are not perceived correctly and are therefore mislabelled. Another is that patients have inappropriate structural representations of words in their mental stores, and yet another is that while these representations may be correct, patients are unable to gain access to them in memory (ibid. p. 221). To date, the detailed linguistic evidence from aphasics has not permitted disambiguation of the underlying sources of impairment, although it is clear that the information itself has led to more sophisticated hypotheses about the systematicity of deficits. It seems to be widely accepted, moreover, that many of the lexical problems of aphasics can be most accurately described in terms of breakdown in processing the relations between words as they are described in linguistic semantics. Following experiments by Goodglass and Baker (1976) and by Grober *et al.* (1980), for instance, it seems that Wernicke's aphasics suffer from a reduced ability in forming associations between semantic classes of words--for instance they may lose the capacity to assign *orange* to its superordinate category *fruit*, and there is a direct relation between the loss of this ability and the ability to name relevant objects (e.g. "orange").

Syntactic errors

As might be expected, aphasic patients demonstrate a wide range of syntactic problems, especially in the reception and production of complex sentences. Analysis of aphasic disturbances in syntactic processing (disturbances falling into the class of syndromes generally referred to as *agrammatism*) is closely dependent upon the particular grammatical model used as the basis for classification of errors. As will be seen in the next chapter, the question of what might be "the best" grammatical description of sentence structure is still a very open one--and, indeed, the quest for such a model and the related arguments constitute the central and most voluminous debate about language in recent times. Some of the key findings about aphasics' processing of sentences are, first, that patients find it easier to process strings of words when the order of these words directly reflects the order of events described. For this reason, active sentences such as *The elephant hit the monkey* are far easier for the aphasic patient to understand than the passive transformation *The monkey was hit by the elephant* (Caplan et al., 1985). Aphasics also find sentences containing two action verbs much more difficult than those containing only one (ibid.). In their interpretation of these findings, Caplan *et al.* suggest that certain key constraints may operate in aphasics' sentential processing. In particular, they suggest that there are lower and upper bounds on the scope of the sentences that patients are able to deal with--they appear to be readily able to process Noun-Verb-Noun or Noun-Noun-Verb configurations (the lower bound of abilities) while unable to process forms where single nouns relate to more than one verbal form (the upper bound). What appears to follow from this is that aphasic patients retain a "basic parsing" capacity which operates on one verb and its subject and object at a time--and it is the conclusions patients draw as a result of this basic parse that governs their experimental response (i.e. they move the dolls according to this basic analysis, an analysis which works only part of the time). Other significant findings about aphasic sentence processing reveal that all deficits in syntactic processing may be due to various forms of impairments to *memory* (Baddeley, 1976, 1981; Carramazza et al., 1981; Saffran, 1985).

Syntax and word classes

Research into sentence production establishes that there is good reason to treat syntactic processing as a discrete part of the larger enterprise of language processing as a whole. English syntax involves the participation of several different classes of words and morphemes. One of several major distinctions that can be drawn between classes of words or word-elements is that between *content words* on the one hand (nouns, verbs, adjectives) and what are often called *function words* on the other (i.e. words such as prepositions, pronouns, and conjunctions). From a semantic perspective, the first of these two classes can be understood to be made up of language forms which bear the major part of the meaning in sentences, since they generally lie at the heart of the content contained in subjects and predicates, while the second class can be understood as the "glue-words" which bind things together in the formation of sentences. Function words have also been described as the "mathematical operators" in sentences, since they often act like the pluses, minuses, and other such operational mathematical symbols describing the relations between numbers.

Another and perhaps more significant characteristic of the distinction between content and function words in English is that content words can typically be modified in various ways. For instance, content words are modified by the addition of inflectional morphemes like those mentioned earlier, such as the plural, the possessive and, in the case of verbs, the third person singular inflection together with past tense and past participial inflections. In addition, content words can often be combined to make *new* words in the language (or neologisms). Two recent examples are *kidults*--for adults who fail to behave at their proper age-level--and *xeconophobia*--a word recognizing the economic factor underlying xenophobia for new immigrants into Canada. They can also combine with derivational forms which change their parts of speech (the noun *fantasy*, for example, combined with the morpheme *-ize* yields the verb, *fantasize*, and so on). English Function words, on the other hand, do not enter into such new combinations so readily, and they can be considered as closed classes of elements which are relatively stable over time, which are fixed in number (as opposed to the potential productive infinity of content-words) and which receive little or no modification--examples are the prepositions (e.g. *on, in, over, between*), the possessive adjectives (e.g. *my, your, their*), and the possessive pronouns (e.g. *mine, yours, theirs*). The interesting general finding in cases of agrammatism is patients' typical lack of control over the category of function words, together with their corresponding over-reliance on content forms.

One thing clearly emerging from the literature on aphasia is the dependency of the field upon analysis of the language system itself. What seems to be evolving in this area is a lively reciprocity between arguments about how best to describe language structures, on the one hand, and arguments about whether the "best" theoretical description of language structures provides the basis for the "best" description of agrammatical language processing, on the other. The field of linguistic aphasiology is one where many hypotheses founded in linguistic analysis are currently being contested, while many new and valuable questions are also being generated about what are the true psycholinguistic components underlying language processing.

Other Developments in Neurolinguistics.

Despite the patent limitations of the original suggestions about neurological functioning by Broca and Wernicke, it is amazing to see how ardently the questions they raised are still pursued, and how strong their influence on current theories remains. Cerebral dominance continues to be a major issue in neuropsychology and neurolinguistics, and numerous studies of war injuries in this century confirm the general finding that the left-hemisphere contains the principal mechanisms controlling both right-handedness and language in the majority of people, although many sub-groups of people have now been observed who do not conform in detail to all the original predictions. Some studies, for example, such as those by McGlone (1977, 1980) have focused on sex-differences in hemispheric dominance. One resulting suggestion is that differentiation between the hemispheres may be more clear in the case of right-handed men than women, although the results of Kimura (1983) suggest no such clear differentiation. In his review of the field, Caplan (1987, p. 352) identifies one of the major current questions about cortical organization as the "neurobiological" question of what determines lateralization of brain functions. One conclusion Caplan draws from all of the research on lateralization is that the phenomenon *is* organically and *not* environmentally determined: Specialized training in using the weak hand, or in literacy, or in the learning of second languages apparently has no significant effect on the basic distribution of dominant and non-dominant functioning within the hemispheres and, to date, evidence strongly suggests an unchanging *genetic* base for lateralization in each individual (ibid. p. 354).

Split brain research

Another development in the quest for further information about cerebral differentiation is to be found in the work on so-called "split brain" patients upon whom surgery has been performed to sever the *corpus callosum* connecting the right and left hemispheres, a radical operation which is performed only in rare cases to treat epilepsy.

Sperry (e.g. Sperry, 1966, 1968) has been a pioneer in this field and some of his major findings relating to language processing are as follows. First, split brain patients are typically unable to verbally identify pictures of simple objects when these are flashed to the right hemisphere, although verbal identification becomes possible when the same pictures are flashed to the left hemisphere. Although this provides clear and strong support for the localization of the major language mechanisms in the left hemisphere, the situation is really more complex, since patients are able to recognize pictures flashed to the right hemisphere in some way, as evidenced by their abilities to select with their left hands similar objects to those in the projected images *without* apparent verbal mediation. Second, a difference has been found between the hemispheric functioning and the *types* of verbal input to patients. Experiments have established that while following the flashing of simple nouns (names of simple objects) to the right hemisphere, patients are able to pick out named objects with their left hands. Following the presentation of verbs, however, there is no such recognition; when the verb *smile* was presented to the right hemisphere, for instance, no response followed, whereas patients typically displayed grins when the verb was presented to the left hemisphere (for a more detailed review of these experiments, see Springer & Deutsch, 1981; Gazzinga, 1983). Third, split-brain experiments have revealed that the writing ability of patients is maintained only in the right hand (controlled by the left hemisphere) whereas drawing is limited to the left hand. Fourth, however, many individual differences have been discovered in the functions assumed by each of the hemispheres, and experiments have revealed that the distribution of functions may be dictated in part by *individual* neurological history and by the apparent abilities of the right hemisphere to take on some supposedly typical left-hemisphere processing roles (Zaidel, 1978).

Split-brain experiments, then, while generally confirming left-hemispheric localization of language functions have also revealed many as yet not fully understood hemispheric effects. From these experiments it seems clear that hemispheric localization is not a simple matter and that the right hemisphere is likely to play a critical part in language processing--perhaps at the level of semantic, spatial, or emotional association and connotation rather than at that of speech production or syntax. It seems that language processing must normally be the result of lively and continual *interaction* between the hemispheres.

Neuroradiology.

Over the past decade, various technical advances have resulted in the use of *computerized axial tomographic* (CT), and *positron emission tomographic* (PET) scans leading to even more detailed pictures of the location of cerebral functioning than were possible with pathological-anatomical approaches and thus to greater potential refinement of the traditional locationist approach. In particular, advances in positron emission tomography have permitted researchers to view activity across the entire brain during its processing of set linguistic tasks. Essentially, PET scans involve the prior radiological labeling of substances in the body such as glucose or blood, followed by monitoring of the particular movements of these tagged substances as they take part in cerebral processing.

Montgomery (1989) provides a convenient review of some of the most recent findings using PET scans. Researchers at Washington University School of Medicine, for example, are currently studying images of subjects' brains in which various locations are seen to become illuminated during linguistic processing. One conclusion drawn from examination of such images has been, contrary to traditional thinking about the reading process, that words that are read need not be translated into auditory form before semantic decoding. By revealing precisely where cortical activity takes place, PET scans at the Institute purport to show that the visual forms of words can be fed directly either to the articulatory motor system (resulting in speech) or to the frontal areas of the brain which serve to analyze meaning, without first being processed within the area of the auditory cortex. When subjects are specifically asked to process rhymes, however, PET scans reveal the concomitant activity of the auditory cortex, leading to the general conclusion (consistent with Luria, above) that language processing involves "a number of component parts that can be added or left out depending on the nature of the task" (Montgomery, 1989, p. 60).

In this new research paradigm, direct injection of radioactive oxygen into subjects' bloodstreams results in detailed images of the brain showing the locations to which the blood naturally rushes during mental processing. Analysis of linguistic activity proceeds by superimposing pictures on one another and by subtracting one from another to reveal the centers of processing. Montgomery reports one experiment, for example, where a picture of brain activity is first taken as a subject stares at an image and is later subtracted from a picture of the same subject silently reading. The subtraction results in a third image showing a concentration of activity at the junction of the occipital and temporal lobes supposed to be at the core of word-recognition. Logically, this process of image subtraction, if extended to cover many cases, can be used gradually to eliminate individual differences in localization of processing and to build up a general picture of the cortical locations common to all language users.

One further consequence of contemporary PET scan research has been to challenge the traditional acceptance of Broca's area as a location specific to the motor processing language. PET scans have revealed that Broca's area is crucial to a wider range of motor processing and, moreover, that ungrammatical speech results only from a combination of trauma to Broca's area together with trauma to other cortical areas in front of it. PET scan results also raise questions about many of the earlier assumptions about neurolinguistic processing: Contrary to the traditional view that semantic meaning is inseparable from auditory processing, for example, researchers at the Washington Institute have found that when subjects are asked to name uses for nouns that are flashed to them (e.g. *drive, ride,* or *sell*, for *car*) the auditory cortex fails to light up, while three other areas (the right side of the cerebellum, together with certain clusters of locations in both the left frontal and middle cortex) are seen to be highly active. It should be recognized, however, that the fundamental logic of this new approach is grounded in and consistent with the earlier versions of locationism previously discussed. While the research is still in its infancy, it clearly promises to provide the basis for some more detailed testing of the traditional descriptions developed within the context of neuro- and cognitive psychology. It may provide a solid basis, moreover, for exploring the relations between linguistic and other types of cognitive functioning (mathematical, musical, aesthetic, and so on).

The Innateness Hypothesis

In Chapter Two the view of many contemporary theorists that language abilities are innate was introduced. It is now time to look at this claim in some more detail and within the context of the biological and neurological findings discussed above.

The Nature of Innate Capacities

As suggested in the last chapter, Chomsky is the principal representative of the position that language is innate, and the claim is embedded within a history of philosophical controversy about whether children are born with inherent powers of reasoning. Some philosophers, generally called "Rationalists," have claimed that they are, while others, called "Empiricists" have claimed that children are born with "blank slates" upon which all learning must be etched through environmental experience. The current debate, however, is really a more limited one than this. Few, if any, scientists would--or could--deny the strong influence upon learning and behavior exerted by genetic inheritance, and it is a generally accepted idea that normal children are born with *some* crucial genetically defined potential. The present argument, then, mainly concerns the exact nature of *what* it is children are born with which leads to their capacity for language use. It is generally accepted that humans are born with some kind of potential for symbolic creativity--even though it is also clear that such creativity will not be triggered in an environmental and cultural vacuum.

One of the major issues in current debate about innateness centers on the difficulty of describing precisely what is the nature of the representation of information in the genes (Block, 1981). Such precise description represents a formidable challenge since it demands explanation of the relationship between what is potentially stored in the genes on the one hand, and how what is stored functions to *cause* or lead to processes such as those involved in language learning within a given linguistic environment, on the other. In other words, resolution of the issue depends upon nothing less than an explanation of *genetic determination* itself. The explanation of genetic determination, moreover, demands some clear description of how genetic potential interacts with environmental variables and this, in turn, requires some clear separation between genetic and environmental contributions to behavior in any relevant situation (ibid.).

For and against Chomsky

In the Chomskyan model of language acquisition, it is held that children are born with what might be called a set of *universal hypotheses* about how language works and is put together. The young child is held to "operate" upon the natural language input she receives (be it in English, German, Chinese, or any other language) and from this input "selects" the *particular* grammar which is consistent with the more *general* form of grammar with which she is born. This more general form is now called *Universal Grammar*, a grammar which theorists claim, contains the fundamental rules and constraints of all known human languages.

An especially clear presentation of some common rebuttals to the Chomskyan position and of Chomsky's characteristic defenses appears in a published debate between himself and Putnam (see Block, 1981; pp. 292-361). To Putnam, the above view of the innateness of language remains vague, and the arguments used to support the innateness hypothesis appear both specious and empty. Taking first the argument that the ease with which children learn their mother tongues demonstrates specific innate language abilities, Putnam counters with the view that this is really nothing more than the vacuous assertion that humans have to be born with *something* in order to learn anything. Children's learning of language, he claims, can be explained in terms simply of the presence of "general intelligence," by way of which they are able to name objects. On this basis, children develop the capacities for understanding and producing more complex verbal or modal varieties of expression. According to Putnam, moreover, these abilities represent a natural extension from acts of naming things not requiring any specific endowed knowledge of the grammatical operations claimed by Chomsky to be at the heart of Universal Grammar.

Putnam, then, views language as a natural consequence of the fact that humans are in a sense "computing systems" born with a species-specific communicative interest in each other. On this view, there is no need to argue that children are born with detailed grammars but, rather, simply a need to recognize that they are born with general intelligence and, from this, the ability to follow some fairly simple and generalizable logical algorithms together with a natural desire to communicate (1981, pp. 295-6). Putnam's central accusation against the Chomskyan view of innateness is that it is unnecessarily elaborate, and he claims that there is no good reason to suppose that children's rapid learning of languages is anything more than the demonstration of the application of the endowed capacity from general intelligence to name objects and their relations. Putnam further refutes Chomsky's arguments concerning the *independence* of linguistic from other abilities by indicating that there are many problems solved by individuals on the basis of *general* and *multipurpose* learning strategies. Individuals, moreover, display many levels of learning ability; some become masters of chess, some can solve logical problems impossible for computers, and some learn the vocabularies of languages in greater depth than others. According to Putnam, however, it is simply not known exactly how humans do come to learn and, until learning processes are better understood, there is no justifiable principle upon which to separate the "innate" from the "learned." The evidence of individual problem-solving abilities seems to point in the direction of the innate presence of *general* heuristics for learning, but in the context of the observation of dramatic individual differences in learning and the absence of a full explanation of the nature of learning itself there is, according to Putnam, no justification whatsoever for partitioning linguistic from other abilities. In Putnam's words, this kind of theorizing "only postpones the problem of learning; it does not solve it" (1981, p. 298).

One of Chomsky's responses to Putnam is to turn the tables on him. While Putnam accepts the idea of the innateness of "general intelligence," Chomsky argues that he (Putnam) is no more able to describe such general intelligence in detail than others are of being able to describe exactly what is the nature of innate language abilities. If Putnam's refutation of Chomsky's claims about language innateness is to be grounded in the assertion that language abilities derive from general intelligence then, according to Chomsky, the onus also rests upon him to demonstrate with some precision just how language is related to abilities included within the domain of general intelligence. One of the crucial differences between them is that whereas Chomsky's view is that children are born with some specific information about what counts as a human language (i.e. some innate capacity properly to "select" the grammar of their mother-tongue on the basis of a set of universal constraints that work for all languages), Putnam's view is that grammars are properties of *languages* rather than being innate phenomena (1981, p. 351). This is so since he argues that languages are learned in just the same way as most other things--long after children are born. On this view, languages are considered to be systems much the same as those underlying mathematics, physics, or other areas of human ability and knowledge.

But *is* language really just like other modes of thought? Chomsky argues that it is not. In the first place, children learn language on the basis of sometimes "limited and rather evidence (i.e. the language forms of those they hear) and, in the second place, knowledge within areas such as physics involves the presence of "consciously articulated principles" and "verification," making them quite different cognitive domains from the learning of language. The acquisition of language according to Chomsky, then, is qualitatively different from the learning, say, of mathematics or automechanics, since all those activities that derive from general intelligence and not a specific language component are extremely sensitive to the way in which they are presented and taught to human learners: Humans are wholly dependent upon the nature of the "input" of information given by others (including teachers) in these latter domains, whereas with language, Chomsky claims, genetic endowment permits children to override whatever faulty language input may come their way and to approximate the ideal grammatical forms of their language. It should be noted, of course, that while most humans learn language, very few of them, in contrast to physicists and linguists, are able to state what the underlying rules of language are or how they might be formally tested. In disagreement with Putnam's point about children's postponement of language learning to a later stage, Chomsky points out that the question of the innateness of language is very similar to the question of the innateness of such abilities as binocular vision or that of being born with arms as opposed to wings. If, as Chomsky believes, language is innate, then the key challenge is to explain the quality of this innate capacity, and it is Putnam's focus on *learning* which is the pseudo-issue, the red herring. Chomsky's insistence upon the presence of innate universal grammar is further bolstered by more specific investigations of the rule-systems underlying natural languages to be discussed in the next chapter.

The crux of Chomsky's argument lies in the claim that language is something *special*: It is a specific capacity endowed in the form of a Universal Grammar. But how did such a capacity come to be established through evolution? It seems that, like Descartes, Chomsky believes that language capacity has arrived by way of some unknown force which is in some way *external* to normal evolutionary processes. According to this view, the capacity for language cannot be fully explained by way of the standard Darwinian model by which evolution takes place in multiple small steps--it is a unique, "God-given" evolutionary leap.

Lieberman: A Neo-Darwinian Position

One of the clearest lines of attack against the Cartesian-Chomskyan position on the evolutionary appearance of language has been provided by Lieberman, some of whose analysis of the phylogenetic and ontogenetic development of the biological prerequisites for language has already been discussed. It will be recalled that an essential part of Lieberman's argument is that human linguistic abilities bear close relations to certain neural mechanisms developed in other animals and that they are not the result of some hypothetical specialized "language organ" as the Chomskyan view implies. He traces one source of the neo-Rationalist position back to a letter of Descartes in which the philosopher claimed that language "belongs to Man alone" (quoted in Lieberman, 1984, p. 3). While the Chomskyan position takes language to be the product of abilities quite separate from those that underlie the thinking of all primates, Lieberman views language as being the result of some kind of logical evolutionary extension of these propensities for cognitive activity and, concomitantly, he also believes that human communication has much in common with that of other animals.

Evolutionary adaptation

In his interpretation of Darwin, Lieberman holds that while the model describes and predicts evolution to be made up of small peripheral organic changes it is nonetheless true that sudden leaps can occur, leaps which are, contrary to the Chomskyan model of language, yet clearly the product of logical evolutionary adaptation. Sudden "jerks" occur in evolution when one small change opens the door to a whole new set of adaptive possibilities. Lieberman gives as an example to support this view the development of the swimbladder in fish, an organ which originally served for flotation but which, once discovered to support the second function of breathing, served as the biological foundation for quite rapid evolutionary development of the lungs, leading to all sorts of further adaptations (1984, p. 9). Lieberman argues that evolution reveals what he calls "functional branch-points," and he cites the work of Negus on the larynx (see above) to support the idea of the adaptive spurts which have taken place when one organ has been found to support more diverse activities than those for which it was apparently intended.

Lieberman's central move against Chomsky's anti-Darwinianism, then, is by way of some revision of Darwin's theory to allow more rapid change following the onset of a new evolutionary branch or direction. His ultimate goal is to demonstrate that language can and, indeed, must be accounted for within the framework of standard evolutionary and bio-genetic theory. This approach entails the rejection both of Saussure's *langue vs. parole* and Chomsky's *competence vs. performance* distinctions since both count as Platonic *idealizations* about the underlying and independent "form" of language, idealizations away from the notion of language as being the direct result of evolutionary communicative adaptation. Lieberman summarizes the argument as follows:

> The trend of modern molecular biology in recent years has been to stress the genetic variations that make up natural populations. Human linguistic ability, insofar as it is based on innate information, must be subject to the same variation as other genetically transmitted biological traits. Thus there cannot be any speaker or hearer in a population who has the grammar of Chomsky's ideal speaker-hearer. The properties of the abstract average, if that is what we mean by the competence grammar or langue, can be determined only by studying the *variations* that typify the linguistic behavior of individual members of a population. Some biological properties of language may indeed be present in almost all 'normal' human beings, but we can determine what these central properties are only if we study the total range of variation in linguistic behavior. (p. 14)

On this view, then, language is no "magical idealization" but results, rather, from individual variations in symbolic behavior that are quite consistent with the general evolutionary propensity for adaptation.

A "distributed" model

Lieberman further contends that part of the human brain functions in much the same way as it does in lower animals, which have been found to make simple reactive associations a crucial feature of which is that they are *distributed* throughout the neural mechanism. Lieberman cites studies supporting a "distributed neural model" of memory in which events are stored as "traces" which extend throughout the neural circuitry and which are not confined to specific neural locations (p. 16, cf. Luria, above). According to Lieberman, this central core as it has been developed in humans shares much in common with those of other higher mammals; there is simply nothing like a specific neural center for language which can be identified in humans but not in their evolutionary predecessors. But there is clearly *some* kind of differentiation in humans which has to do with the capacity for speech, and this Lieberman identifies as "the set of peripheral neural mechanisms that structure the input-output levels of human language--speech, gesture, and facial expression" (p. 17). Lieberman argues that these later mechanisms are recent and peripheral specializations. In terms of a computer analogy, they are mere "add-ons" to the more fundamental neural system having much in common with those of other primates.

According to Lieberman, the form of distributed neural systems is such that they can adapt by way of generating new synaptic connections and resulting new pathways. In supporting this claim, he cites the fact that brains continue to function despite losing many thousands of neurons each day. They survive, therefore, by this pervasive and continuous formation of new pathways. To Lieberman, while there seems some justification for the "loose" locationist model at the center of current explanations of aphasia, the model consistent with most data is what he calls a "distributed-discrete" model in which specialized input-output features such as those involved in language (and which are the typical sites of trauma in cases of language breakdown) are localized but which "feed into a central general purpose distributed computer" (p. 34). According to this model, humans do possess innate mechanisms for the perception and production of speech signals, but these mechanisms are similar to mechanisms in other animals which function in calls and other communicative displays. Lieberman further claims that the innate specialized speech mechanism in humans have developed quite logically within the context of the evolutionary trend towards greater motor control. Motor control over language has evolved in much the same way as motor control over activities such as breathing and bipedal walking. At the heart of all human activity, according to Lieberman, lies the general neural mechanism shared by *all* animals allowing simple classification and response to the environment (pp. 22-35).

Speech and hearing

In contrast to the claims of Lenneberg, Lieberman argues that the human respiratory system underlying language ability shares much in common with the respiratory systems of other animals producing vocalizations. In particular, the anatomy of the lungs and the rib-cage in both apes and humans allow both species to control expiration in a way which lead to the ability in humans to structure the breath-groups of speech. This ability is a direct descendant of the development of the lungs and the larynx from the evolutionary arrival of the swimbladder in fish (1984; Chapter Five). Lieberman holds that the ability of humans to perceive and decode speech is very similar to other kinds of evolutionary "matching" of communicative processes. In the bullfrog, for instance, it has been discovered that neural mechanisms have developed which are specifically tuned to the acoustic properties of bullfrog calls. In humans, similar neural mechanisms apparently exist which are tuned to the complex formant structures and complex air movements produced in speech (pp. 132-136).

Explaining Chomsky's "critical period"

One characteristic argument put forward by the Chomskyan School to support the innateness hypothesis is that no other explanation other than the hypothesis seems possible for the sudden and miraculous spurt in which children learn the essentials of their various first languages. It is apparent that children in all societies acquire language between (roughly) the ages of eighteen months and three years, and unless sufficient language data is available to them at this critical time, and unless the environment for language learning is a positive one, children simply do not acquire language properly. In contrast to the very special human status accorded by Chomskyan theorists to the so-called "critical period" of language-learning in young children, Lieberman argues that this has much in common with other acquired phenomena in both humans and other animals, abilities such as binocular vision, visual acuity, and bird calls (pp. 214-225).

Relating animal and human communication systems

Finally, Lieberman believes that the apparent abilities of some apes to communicate with gestures and symbols demonstrates the presence of rudimentary linguistic behavior from which natural language has evolved. Chomskyan theorists, of course, arguing for the human specificity of "linguistic abilities," are committed to emphasizing the *differences* between human and animal communication systems. This argument depends, however, on providing a very clear-cut distinction between what counts as "linguistic" and what does not. Lieberman finds this boundary hard to define and questions, for instance, whether a child wanting a cookie from his mother and looking up at her and saying "guk" is in fact communicating in a "linguistic" or a "non-linguistic" mode (p. 227). Studies of the behavior of apes trained with American Sign Language demonstrate that they perform in a similar way to young human children, and it is Lieberman's contention therefore that a direct evolutionary line of development appears to exist between earlier modes of symbolization and natural language. It is likely, Lieberman claims, that:

> The initial steps toward the evolution of human language could thus have started with the hominoids ancestral to both human beings and apes. (p. 255)

Discontinuity vs. Continuity Theories

In contrasting the Chomskyan approach with that of Lieberman, Orr Dingwall (1988) identifies Chomsky with what is generally known as the "discontinuity" theory of evolutionary progress, supported also by Lenneberg and by Fodor, Bever, and Garrett (1974), and Lieberman with the opposing "continuity" theory proposed by Wilson (1978), according to which language has developed by the gradual refinement of traits in primates together with the gradual development of behaviors which were adaptively advantageous. It seems, further, that much of the apparent dispute between these two polarized positions rests upon the interpretation of the nature of language. The discontinuity theorists, as we have seen, are committed to a very "specialized" and narrow view of language--a view of language which stresses its formal, rule-governed and systematic nature--while the continuity approach maintains a far wider view of language encompassing gestures and symbols which do not readily submit to formal grammatical analysis.

In a further attempt to resolve the issue, Orr Dingwall returns to Darwin and to Darwin's description of sets of behaviors as "homologous." Essentially, homologies were understood by Darwin to be clusters of behaviors in closely related species which showed common characteristics and which could be traced back to some common ancestry. Analyzing the evolutionary nature of language in these terms, the relevant components of the homology are, first, *cognition*, the ability to deal with concepts, second, *coding*, the ability to link abstract concepts with sensor-motor representations and, third, *transmission*, the processes of sending and receiving messages (Orr Dingwall, pp. 281-284). This leads to some pertinent observations about the various manifestations of communicative behavior in primate species. First, if cognition alone were sufficient to stimulate language then apes should acquire it. Second, nonhuman primate symbolizations have much in common with aspects of human *paralanguage* rather than with speech (that is, with the systems of gestures and expressions which run parallel with speech but which are not part of it). Third, detailed comparison between the larynx in humans and apes reveals that they are "at best fractionally homologous" to each other (ibid. pp. 293-294).

Although Orr Dingwall takes Lieberman to task on several methodological points, he is in basic agreement with Lieberman about the nature of the attributes that are homologous and those that are distinct between humans and other primates. In particular, he cites research conducted at the Max Planck Institute for Psychiatry in Munich as providing further clues about the status of language attributes. In this research, which utilizes the technique of systematic electrical stimulation to a selection of brain parts taken from a range of higher and lower animals, various discrete levels of neural organization have been revealed to underlie communicative processes. The lowest area, located in the *medulla*, contains the basic motor neurons used in phonation and in making modifications in the pharyngeal region. Electrical stimulation of an area in the mid-brain of animals ranging from amphibians to higher primates resulted in communicative sounds typical of each species. At a higher level, the researchers have discovered two significant cortical areas; a developed motor area together with an area controlling communication within *conditioned* settings as opposed to mere innate signals. It appears from this research that primates other than humans utilize only the first two of these neurological levels, while humans are alone in utilizing the developed areas at the third level and within the neo-cortex. This evidence about species-specific homologies and distinctions, then, tends in general to support continuity approaches to evolution such as that justified and taken by Lieberman (although, as noted in the review of Lieberman, "continuity" need not necessarily imply the absence of small evolutionary leaps at points of critical mass in adaptive momentum). But like Lieberman and in contrast to Chomsky, Orr Dingwall finds no reason for supposing language to be entirely the *de nuovo* creation of humans (p. 306).

Summary

In this chapter, an attempt has been made to cover the basic territory of knowledge and dispute concerning the biological nature of language. A number of physiological facts are known, such as the workings of the articulatory system, and the comparative structure of the human larynx in relation to the structures of those in other animals and primates.

Despite the presence of considerable scientific knowledge about the biology and physiology of language, however, one of the most pervasive disputes in the area of language studies is really at heart a philosophical one continued through from Plato and Descartes, a dispute concerning the merits, on the one hand, of an "idealized" notion of language such as that developed in the work of Chomsky and, on the other, a more naturalistic and Darwinian view of language as bearing close (and therefore very "unideal") relations with the communicative abilities of our evolutionary ancestors. The dispute has ramifications both for the formal analysis of language and, intersecting with this, for the formation of pedagogical principles, since belief or otherwise in the "special" human status of language has some effect on how it is studied and taught.

CHAPTER FIVE

Grammars

It is reasonable to regard the grammar of a language L ideally as a mechanism that provides an enumeration of the sentences of L in something like the way in which a deductive theory gives an enumeration of a set of theorems.... Furthermore, the theory of language can be regarded as a study of the formal properties of such grammars, and, with a precise enough formulation, this general theory can provide a uniform method for determining, from the process of generation of a given sentence, a structural description which can give a good deal of insight into how this sentence is used and understood. In short, it should be possible to derive from a properly formulated grammar a statement of the integrative processes and generalized patterns imposed on the specific acts that constitute an utterance. (N. Chomsky, *A Review of B.F. Skinner's "Verbal Behavior*," 1959)

Introduction

Chomsky's review of Skinner's *Verbal Behavior*, quoted above, stands as one of the key documents for identifying the issues and concerns of contemporary grammarians. As can be seen from the quotation, Chomsky's thinking at this time went far beyond the mere rejection of Behaviorism, with its insistence on interpreting language in terms of stimuli and reinforcements and with its parallel insistence on viewing utterances as "chains of habits." Chomsky's comments mark a new age in language analysis and in the understanding of what a grammar is, an age in which grammars are no longer considered to be mere descriptions of regularities in languages, but rather as "theories" of language designed to reveal its fundamental nature. The precise details of how grammatical rules are best described and of how communicative processes and grammatical structures relate to each other are still matters of debate, but Chomsky's demonstration of the inadequacy of any behaviorist account of language, and his parallel development of the foundations of *transformational-generative* grammatical analysis (henceforth TGG), have substantially altered the agenda for linguistic analysis. In this chapter, we will explore the nature of grammatical analysis following the Chomskyan paradigm-shift. The first part will look in more detail at Chomsky's arguments for transformational grammar and at the nature of what he called "standard theory," the model outlined in *Aspects of the theory of syntax* (1965). Second, we will trace some of the main developments in grammatical theory founded on Chomsky's original formulations. Third, some alternatives to the North American generative approach to grammar will be considered.

Standard Theory: The "Aspects" model of 1965

Grammar as Theory of Language

As anyone who was taught grammar in high school before the 1970s knows, the study of grammar and language up until this time was underwritten by a strong sense of *prescriptivism*. The purpose of studying grammar lay in learning how to conform to a "standard" set of rules of speech and writing in ways which would guarantee a socially positive response. Grammar textbooks were full of terms adopted from Latin grammars, terms such as "gerund," or "mood" or "strong vs. weak" verbs, and lists of "verb tenses" often appeared including "simple present progressive," "future perfect," and so on. When it came to the analysis of sentences, the approach was generally one of identifying various kinds of phrases and clauses and dividing sentences into "simple" vs. "complex" categories (see, e.g. Smart, 1959).

While the prescriptive approach to grammar may have shaped at least the more formal language behavior of generations of school students, from the perspective of enhancing knowledge and understanding of *language* it had many shortcomings. In particular, the pervasive classifications of things upon which such grammars were based (classification procedures referred to by several names, including *constituent analysis* and *parsing*) did little to explain the *general rules* by which language is organized, and this detailed classification, moreover, did little to *simplify* the description of language. But the continued use of Latin terms following its widespread use in the Middle Ages tended to encourage this proliferation of terms and categories in ways which actually obscured the patterning of English. It has since been realized that the descriptive terms used for Latin, with its rich inflectional system to reflect changes in tense, mood, voice, person, number, and case, are largely inappropriate to the description of English, which has only a limited number of inflections surviving from its earlier history, and which now depends upon a richer system of syntactic ordering rules to compensate from this reduction of complexity within its morphological system.

Properties of a truly descriptive grammar

In *Syntactic Structures* (1957), Chomsky, following the inspiration of his teacher, Zelig Harris (1951), essentially overthrew both the prescriptive approach to grammar and the behaviorist approach to language by demonstrating their *descriptive* inadequacies, their inability to "explain" anything of significance about the shared system of rules by which humans communicate. The main ideas in *Syntactic Structures* relating to this rejection of prior approaches to grammar can be summarized as follows.

First, Chomsky claims that grammarians should be concerned not just with the specific description of individual languages but, rather, with the description of the commonalities that underlie *all* languages (p. 11). In this way, the grammar of a particular language like English is viewed as "selecting" a set of rules that are unique to it from a larger set of rules from which all languages make similar "selections."

Second, a grammar of a language ought to make quite specific what will be included as *grammatical* as opposed to *ungrammatical* utterances. In order to achieve this end, what is needed is to demonstrate how a given grammar guarantees that if its rules are followed only grammatical utterances will result. Another way of putting this is to say that a set of grammatical rules should *generate* all and only the grammatical sentences of a language. Native speakers are the best judges of whether the output of such a grammar is, indeed, grammatical (p. 13).

Third, the term "grammatical" needs to be disjoined from the term "meaningful." As Chomsky points out in reference to his famous sentence *Colorless green ideas sleep furiously*, grammaticality is not always guaranteed by meaningfulness, but solely by the correct syntactic ordering of elements: The above sentence is largely meaningless, but nonetheless grammatical, while **Furiously sleep ideas green colorless* and several other possible concatenations are clearly both ungrammatical and meaningless (p. 15). (The custom of using asterisks to mark ungrammatical forms will be used throughout this chapter). There is something to be explained about language, then, that *is* purely grammatical in nature, and no complete theory of language should fail to account for this.

Fourth, in order to explain in some way just how the grammatical sentences of a language are formed (as opposed to the ungrammatical ones) a grammar must be *simpler* and *more general* than the language itself. In order to satisfy this criterion, a grammar must be something other than merely a mode of assigning sentences to various classes or creating lists of inventories which, together with their associated terminology, may actually turn out to be more cumbersome than the language they attempt to rationalize. From a technical standpoint, this leads to recognition of a highly significant principle in grammatical analysis, one partly recognized by linguists prior to Chomsky, but which he exploits to its fullest in TGG. This principle is, namely, that grammatical description requires the inclusion of *several independent levels of analysis* (p. 18). In order to simplify the description of sounds, for instance, it will be necessary to show how they are distributed in relation to a broader level of analysis, that of word-structures, and in order to simplify that of word-structures, it will be necessary to show

how these, in turn, are distributed in relation to ordering rules. The necessary levels for grammatical analysis, then, are at least those of syntax, morphology, and phonology. It does not get us very far to take any one of these levels independently of the others and merely to exhaust the possible occurrences at this one level. What needs to be demonstrated, in contrast, and what will lead towards the goal of revealing the rules of how grammatical sentences are generated, is just how these levels interact with each other, how they constrain each other to lead to grammatical options.

Sixth, language is not *finite* in its extension, but *infinite*, and this is another reason why no classificatory approach to grammar, no matter how exhaustive, can ever in principle be complete. What needs to be demonstrated is not just how sentences that language-users may happen to hear or produce conform to a set of grammatical rules, but how the grammar of a language permits the construction of an *infinite set* of grammatical utterances *in principle*. This is only possible, of course, if the grammar does indeed incorporate several interacting levels of analysis (see above) in such a way that elements at any one level are free to recombine within the constraints of levels above them (pp. 20-22). Chomsky's argument at this point is cast in terms of analogies to various types of language "machine" which might be utilized by a grammar. He rejects any "finite state" machine which exhaustively iterates sentence "states" for the language, any machine which works only in a strict linear "left-to-right" order in which one linguistic element (say, *the*) predicts the occurrence of a subsequent element (say, *giraffe*) and so on for each syntactic construction. As Chomsky states, "English is not a finite state language," and for this reason, a grammar needs to reveal just how the infinite variety of past and future utterances is wrought out of the finite forms in languages, namely, the building-blocks of their phones, phonemes, and morphemes. (There are other very good psychological reasons for rejecting the left-to-right model as the basis of language processing; see Lashley, Chapter Six).

The six points outlined above collectively lead towards a characterization of grammar which is quite different from those which preceded Chomsky's insights. They lead to an idea of grammar as a theory of language which is capable of predicting all and only the grammatical utterances in a particular language such as English. The best way of seeing how all of these criteria can be satisfied is to see how they are combined, expressed, and extended in the standard model of TGG developed on the basis of *Syntactic Structures* (1957), and more fully described by Chomsky in *Aspects of the Theory of Syntax* (1965). Following the publication of *Aspects*, many versions of this "standard" theory have been developed by linguists, varying more in terms of particular notations chosen than in terms of the foundations Chomsky had established. These versions have been developed at the same time as other grammars incorporating quite substantial amendments and changes to the original theory, some of which will be mentioned later. One representative expression of standard theory is to be found in the grammar developed by Marckworth and Prideaux (Edition 4, 1978), and this grammar will now be used as a basis for exploring the standard TGG model further.

Outline of a Standard Transformational-generative Grammar

The several levels of linguistic analysis referred to above are expressed in the grammar as interacting components which work together to generate the grammatical sentences of English. The first of these components is a set of *phrase-structure* rules, which serve to produce the basic hierarchical (or "tree") structures of sentences.

Phrase-structure rules

Technically, this component is a set of instructions to create all the kinds of tree-structures which underlie grammatical English sentences: Hence, they contain some of the most basic grammatical constraints in the language. The first of these rules is the instruction to rewrite S (sentence) as NP + VP (noun-phrase to the left of verb-phrase), which is really just another re-expression of the traditional rule "every sentence is made up of a subject and a predicate." Phrase-structure rule 1 yields the first part of a sentence tree-diagram:

1. S ---> NP + VP

is the instruction to produce:

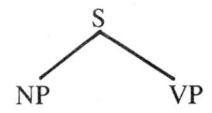

```
        S
       / \
      NP  VP
```

The phrase-structure rules continue this process of tree-creation by breaking down NP and VP further into a succession of possibilities as follows (where VP = verb-phrase; V_i = intransitive verb; V_t = transitive verb; AUX = auxiliary system; TNS = tense; DET = determiner):

2. VP ---> AUX + V
3. V ---> V_i
   V_t + NP
4. AUX ---> TNS
5. TNS ---> {PRES, PAST}
6. NP ---> DET + N + NO
7. NO ---> {SING, PLU}

The above set of seven rules is, of course, only a first approximation, and it will lead to the generation of only a very limited set of structures. It demonstrates in priniciple, however, just how the basic level of the analysis of the constituent structures of English can be accomplished by way of a set of instructions that are prior to and independent of other levels. The above phrase-structure rules will already generate a number of structures such as the following, all of which underlie simple grammatical sentences in English:

Example a.

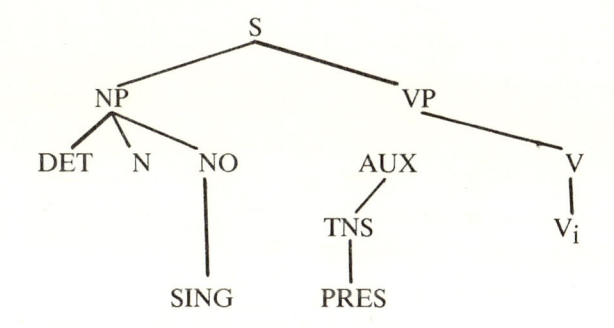

```
           S
         /   \
        NP    VP
      / | \    \
    DET N  NO   V
           |    |
          SING  Vᵢ
         AUX
          |
         TNS
          |
         PRES
```

(Tree for Example a: S → NP (DET N NO[SING]) VP (AUX[TNS[PRES]] V[Vᵢ]))

Example b.

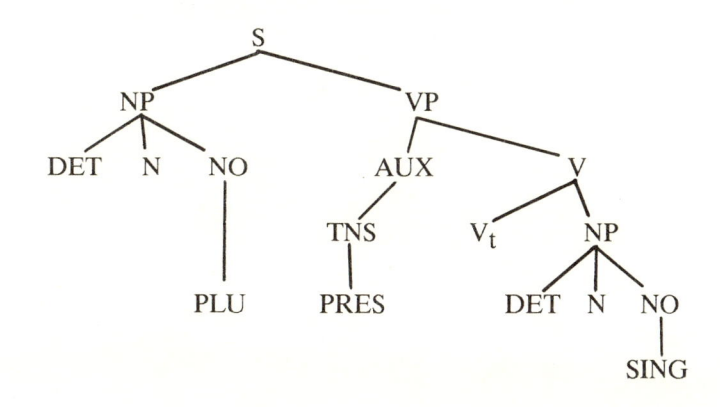

(Tree for Example b: S → NP (DET N NO[PLU]) VP (AUX[TNS[PRES]] V (Vₜ NP (DET N NO[SING]))))

Example c.

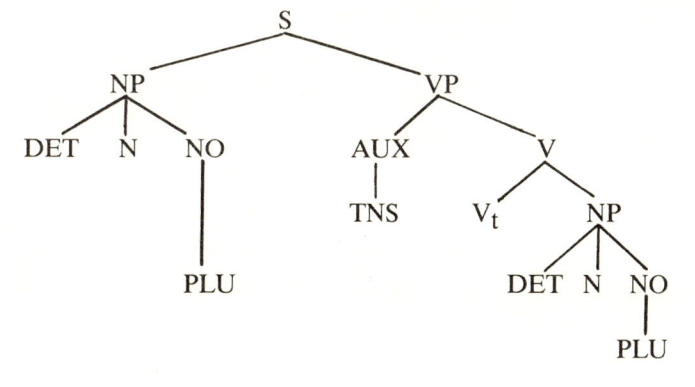

(Tree for Example c: S → NP (DET N NO[PLU]) VP (AUX[TNS] V (Vₜ NP (DET N NO[PLU]))))

The lexicon

The next component is the *lexicon*, which contains all the morphemes and words in the language. In a complete grammar of English according to the *Aspects* model, the lexicon would contain the entire inventory of morphemes and words including their subcategorizations into types. Nouns, for instance, would be subcategorized into "human" ([+HUMAN]), "animate" ([+ANIMATE]) and so on, and verbs would be similarly subcategorized in ways which show which nouns with which they co-occur. The following, however, is an initial version of such a lexicon that can serve to demonstrate how the phrase-structure rules and lexicon are combined in a TG grammar:

Lexicon:

DET(ERMINERS) —➤ {the, a}
N(OUNS) —➤ {cat, whale, sailor, aardvark, etc.}
V_i —➤ {smile, dance, breathe, etc.}
V_t —➤ {chase, entertain, hit, etc.}
(After Marckworth & Prideaux, 1978, p. 3)

The phrase-structure rules and the lexicon combine to form the *base* of a standard model TGG. When the base is put into operation to generate any particular sentence in the language, its output is called a *base phrase marker*, otherwise known as the *deep structure* of the sentence.

The process of generating the deep structure of a sentence can be demonstrated by extending one of the above example structures. Let us say that we had started out by attempting to write the deep structure of the sentence *The cats eat the cheese.* The structure given in example b above would then be the correct output from the phrase-structure rules alone. The lexical items *the*, *cat*, *eat*, and *cheese* would then be inserted from their appropriate locations in the lexicon, and the complete base phrase-marker (i.e. deep structure) would be as follows:

Example d.

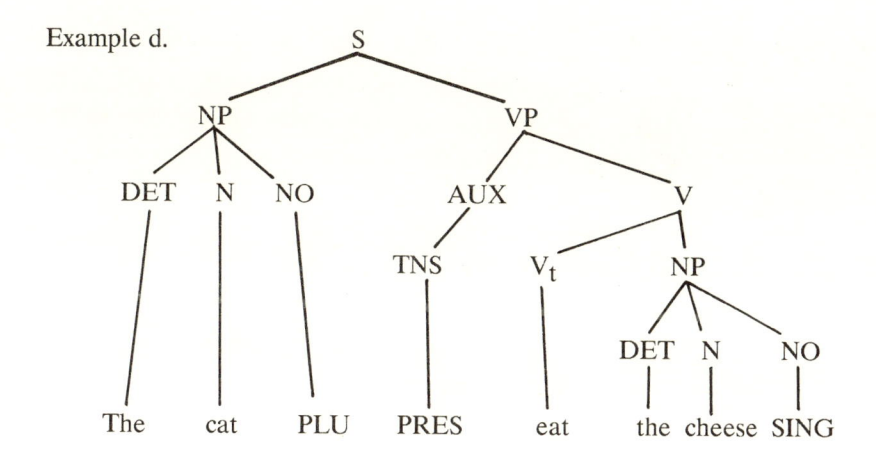

```
                    S
         ┌──────────┴──────────┐
        NP                     VP
    ┌────┼────┐         ┌──────┴──────┐
   DET   N   NO        AUX             V
                     ┌──┴──┐       ┌───┴───┐
                    TNS   Vₜ              NP
                                      ┌───┼───┐
                                     DET  N   NO
    │     │    │      │     │         │   │    │
   The   cat  PLU   PRES   eat       the cheese SING
```

Up until this point in the description of a sentence of English, TGG is not substantially different from the constituent-structure approaches which preceded. The use of tree-diagrams, of course, makes the structural description particularly clear, but the grammar fragment so far presented is in fact very similar to earlier grammars in principle and, even more significantly, it is not in the form presented above capable of satisfying Chomsky's criterion of being able to generate an *infinite* set of sentences in order to reflect the generative property of a natural language. It is really how the grammar is extended and refined from this point on that makes TGG so innovative and powerful when compared to earlier models.

Transformational rules

The first innovation comes with the addition of the *transformational component*, which takes the deep structure as input and which contains a set of rules that will bring any sentence from its deep structure to its *surface structure* (i.e. the form of the sentence as it is used in communication). The transformational rules are founded on Chomsky's key observation that grammatical description should capitalize on the fact that individual sentences actually belong to *families*, and that they can be viewed as variants of *kernel sentences*, which are the basic forms shared by all the members of a given sentence family set. Taking the same example sentence, the following set of related sentences can then be described:

Kernel sentence (simple active affirmative declarative):

The cats eat the cheese.

Transformationally related sentences:

The cats don't eat the cheese. (Negative)
The cheese is eaten by the cats. (Passive)
The cheese isn't eaten by the cats. (Negative and passive)
Do the cats eat the cheese? (Question)
Don't the cats eat the cheese? (Negative question)
The cats eat the cheese, don't they? (Tag question, negative)
The cats don't eat the cheese, do they? (Tag question, affirmative)
It is the cats which eat the cheese. (Cleft sentence, subject)
It is the cheese which the cats eat. (Cleft sentence, object)
It is the cheese which is eaten by the cats. (Cleft, passive).

Instead of describing sentences as if they were grammatically and semantically unique, as earlier grammarians had tended to do, Chomsky utilizes the relations held between sentences in sets such as the above to reveal the essential syntactic rules by which each one is guaranteed to be grammatical. This simplifies the grammar enormously, contributing to its descriptive power, since all of the sentences in a given set can now be related to the *same* underlying deep structure, the structure which will most closely approximate that of the underlying kernel sentence which provides the centerpiece of the group. The general function of the transformational component is then to provide a succession of changes to the original base phrase-marker, each of which produces a new, transformed, phrase-marker, which will ultimately yield the correct grammatical surface structural form. In the case of deriving the sentence *The cats eat the cheese* there is, of course, very little to be done by the rules in the transformational component. The string of elements (called the *underlying string*) found at the bottom of the tree-diagram (see example d, above) is in almost its final correct grammatical form. The underlying string *The cat PLU eat the cheese SING* does, however, require *some* further work; in particular, *PLU* and *SING* need to be removed and, more importantly, agreement between the subject noun and the transitive verb needs to be guaranteed. If the sentence to be derived were *The cat eats the cheese*, having a singular subject, then the grammar would have to ensure placement of the third person singular inflection (/s/) on the verb *eat*. In this case, it is equally important that the verb not take this morpheme in order to agree in number with the plural subject. This basic matter of subject-verb agreement has to be dealt with, along with many more complex matters, by the transformational rules, and the two rules required to achieve this end can be used to illustrate the general form of the transformational component.

Each transformational rule contains two clear parts. The first, called the *Structural Description* (SD), is the part which "looks at" a tree-structure in the course of a derivation, while the second part, called the *Structural Change* (SC) is an instruction to transform the structure found into the new structure required for grammatical surface structure. Transformational rules must also be *ordered* with respect to each other, since they strongly affect each other. A good illustration of this might be the case of passive sentences, in which, for example, it is very important to change the order of noun-phrases *before* conducting any form of verb agreement: If we were deriving the sentence *The cheese is eaten by the cats* for example, then the verb *be* must agree with *cheese* and not *cats* to produce a grammatical sentence (**The cheese are eaten by the cats* is clearly ungrammatical) and so *The cheese* must be taken from its original deep-structural positioning in *The cats eat the cheese* and shifted to the front of the verb *before* verb-agreement takes place.

In the case of deriving our first example, *The cats eat the cheese*, only two transformations are required. The first of these is:

$$\text{SD:} \quad N \begin{bmatrix} \text{SING} \\ \text{PLU} \end{bmatrix} \text{PRES}$$

$$\text{SC:} \quad 1 \quad\quad 2 \quad\quad\quad 3 \quad == \quad (\text{"transform to"})$$

$$\phantom{\text{SC:}} \quad 1 \quad\quad 2 \quad\quad \begin{bmatrix} -Z \\ -\emptyset \end{bmatrix}$$

Expressed in everyday English, this states the following: Structural Description: If the base phrase marker contains a Noun (N), followed by a singular marker (SING), followed by a present tense marker (PRES), then carry out the following structural change; Structural Change: Leave the noun as it is (1 transforms to 1). Leave the singular or plural marker as it is (2 transforms to 2). If the noun is marked singular, then change PRES to "-Z" and if it is marked plural, then change PRES to "-$\emptyset$" (this precise instruction reflects a *bracketing* convention in which the squared brackets used around SING, PLU/-Z, -$\emptyset$ are understood to mean that the upper element in the top row must be paired with the parallel member in the lower row). The operation of this transformational rule now produces another tree-diagram which is one step away from (i.e. "higher than") the original deep structure (see example d. above):

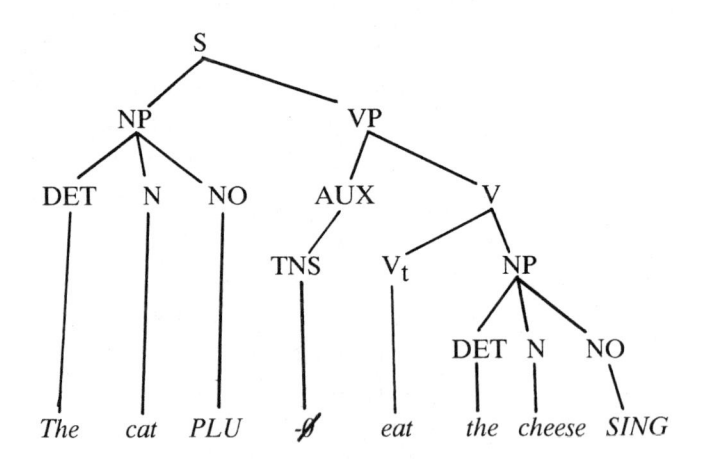

```
                    S
              /           \
            NP              VP
          / | \           /    \
        DET N  NO       AUX      V
         |  |   |       / \    /   \
         |  |   |     TNS  Vt NP
         |  |   |      |    |  / | \
         |  |   |      |    | DET N  NO
         |  |   |      |    |  |  |   \
        The cat PLU   -∅   eat the cheese SING
```

In the Marckworth-Prideaux grammar being followed here, the transformational rule which accomplishes subject-verb agreement in this way is ordered as number 10 of 20. One further transformation is clearly required for the complete derivation of our example sentence, one which now takes the marker "-∅" and places it to the right hand side of the verb *eat*. (The need for this movement is perhaps clearer in a case where the root verb form actually has to take a third person singular inflection, as it would in *The cat eats the cheese*.) The transformation which accomplishes this serves to shift the affix (and all other affixes which occur in more complex verb-phrases) from the left to the right of the element they modify. Stated in this way, the transformation encapsulates a powerful generalization about the relationships between all the elements in the English verb-phrase. The transformation is stated as follows:

    T: Affix shift

        SD: Af   Vb
        SC: 1   2 ⟹
             null   2 + 1

    CONDITION Vb = V_i or V_t; Af = TNS

This states that if the tree contains an affix (defined in the condition as TNS) next to a verb (in this simple grammar, this is either an intransitive or a transitive verb, but it will also include other auxiliary verb forms in more refined versions of the grammar), then take the affix and hop it over to the right of the verb. The resulting tree-diagram for our example sentence following this transformation is as follows:

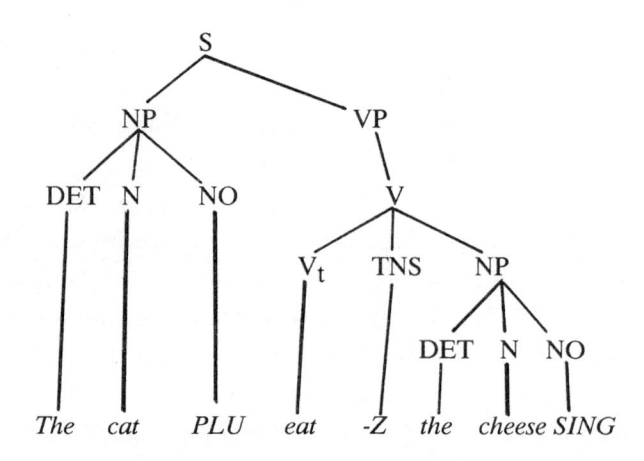

```
                    S
              ╱         ╲
           NP             VP
         ╱ │ ╲             │
      DET  N  NO           V
       │   │   │        ╱ │ ╲
       │   │   │       Vt TNS NP
       │   │   │        │  │  ╱│╲
       │   │   │        │  │ DET N NO
       │   │   │        │  │  │  │  │
      The cat PLU      eat -Z the cheese SING
```

The final section of the TGG is called the *morphophonemic component*, and this functions to take the final output string from this tree (i.e. the elements *The cat PLU eat -Z the cheese SING*) to its unadulterated surface form, the original sentence *The cats eat the cheese*. The morphophonemic rules are a set of rules which take the morphemes as input and predict the phonological shape of the utterance and they include instructions, for example, to place a voiceless plural form (/s/) on the end of *cat* following its voiceless final consonant stop (/t/).

The addition of recursion

The over all form of a "standard" transformational-generative grammar is summarized in the following diagram:

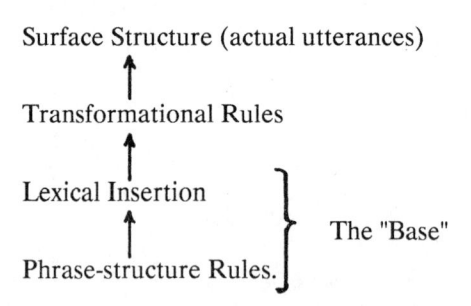

Surface Structure (actual utterances)
↑
Transformational Rules
↑
Lexical Insertion   ⎫
↑   ⎬ The "Base"
Phrase-structure Rules.⎭

As previously stated, the grammatical rules so far referred to are relatively simple and undeveloped. In order to represent the power of standard-theory TGG to generate an *infinite* range of sentences, it is necessary to introduce one further very important modification. It will be recognized that the first version of the Marckworth-Prideaux grammar presented above is actually still only capable of generating or deriving a limited, *finite*, set of sentences. Since the lexicon includes all the nouns and all the transitive and intransitive verbs in the language (this is symbolized by the three dots at the end of each category), this will be a very large set of sentences, but it will be a set, nonetheless, that is limited to just a few simple types of syntactic structure (sentences containing a subject noun-phrase with either an intransitive verb or a transitive verb together with its noun object).

How will a more complete grammar deal with the derivation of more complex sentences such as *The medal that was worn by the athlete who had won the race impressed the crowd*? The answer lies in the realization that any *complex* sentence such as the above is composed of several simple sentences which can each be described by a simple set of grammatical rules. In this case, it can be seen that the simple sentences are 1) *The medal impressed the crowd* (the matrix sentence) 2) *The athlete wore the medal* (in passive form) and 3) *The athlete had won the race*. A more complete grammar, then, must reflect the process by which the presence of two identical noun-phrases in two separate simple sentences is recognized, leading to the use of a *relative pronoun* (such as *that* or *who*). Having replaced the second identical NP with a relative pronoun, the grammar must then embed the entire relative clause within the matrix sentence. The set of rules that accomplishes this differs from the initial set presented above in that it must provide for the process of *recursion*, by which the grammar, during the process of generating a simple matrix sentence, can always return to its beginning to create the individual simple sentences that become the basis for relative-clause formation. Chomsky realized that this property of recursion could be written into the phrase-structure component by including the S (Sentence) symbol on the right hand side of the rules as well as in its initial position. Since it is noun-phrases that form the foundation of relativization (i.e. relativization is triggered by the presence of two identical noun-phrases in two simple sentences) the obvious location for the embedded sentence is immediately to the right of NP in the phrase-structure rules, as in phrase-structure rule 6, below, which reads "rewrite NP as Determiner plus Noun plus Number, plus an (optional) S(entence):

1. S → NP + VP
2. VP → AUX + V
3. V → $\begin{Bmatrix} V_i \\ V_t + NP \end{Bmatrix}$
4. AUX → TNS
5. TNS → $\begin{Bmatrix} PRES \\ PAST \end{Bmatrix}$
6. NP → DET + N + NO (#S#)
7. NO → $\begin{Bmatrix} SING \\ PLU \end{Bmatrix}$

The addition of this optional S-symbol (#S#) on the right-hand side of rule 6 is crucial to the grammar, since only now is the criterion of being able to generate an infinite set satisfied. It is easy to prove that it will now achieve this criterion, since it is evident that the grammar will now generate just one sentence which is infinitely long (even though such a sentence would be incomprehensible due to constraints on human memory). The idea of recursion, an idea borrowed from mathematics, is an extremely significant and powerful addition to the grammar, reflecting the productivity of languages in general. With the addition of recursion (and some other less important additions, such as a *passive* trigger, permitting generation of *worn by the athlete*, and of *perfective aspect* in the verb-phrase to yield *had won*), derivation of the complex sentence *The medal that was worn by the athlete who had won the race impressed the crowd* is now possible. The deep structure of this sentence (where some structures have been conventionally abbreviated using triangles) is:

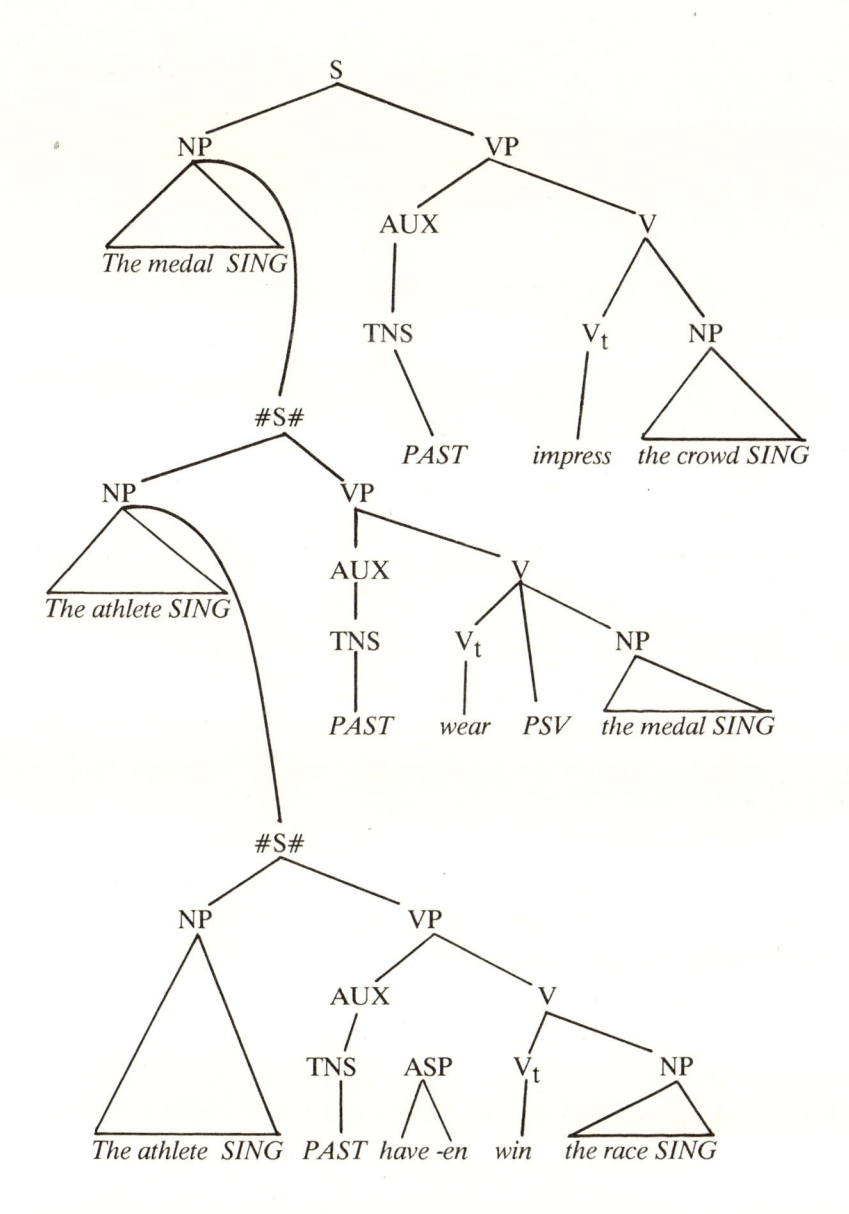

```
                            S
                   ┌────────┴────────┐
                  NP                  VP
                 /  \              ┌───┴───┐
               /_____\            AUX       V
            The medal SING         |      ┌─┴─┐
                  │               TNS    Vₜ   NP
                 #S#               |     |   /\
              ┌───┴───┐           PAST impress /__\
             NP       VP                    the crowd SING
            /  \    ┌──┴──┐
          /_____\  AUX     V
       The athlete  |    ┌─┴──┬────┐
         SING      TNS  Vₜ        NP
                   |    |       /\
                  PAST wear PSV /__\
                              the medal SING
                        │
                       #S#
                    ┌───┴───┐
                   NP       VP
                  /\      ┌──┴──┐
                 /__\    AUX    V
                         / \   ┌┴┬──┐
                       TNS ASP Vₜ  NP
                        |  /\  |  /\
                       PAST have -en win /__\
                                    the race SING
         The athlete SING
```

This deep structure will now be presented to the transformational component which, working in a series of *cycles* starting from the most deeply embedded sentence (*The athlete won the race*), will bring the sentence to surface structure. In the first cycle, then, the transformational rules will operate to produce:

(All higher structure remains the same)

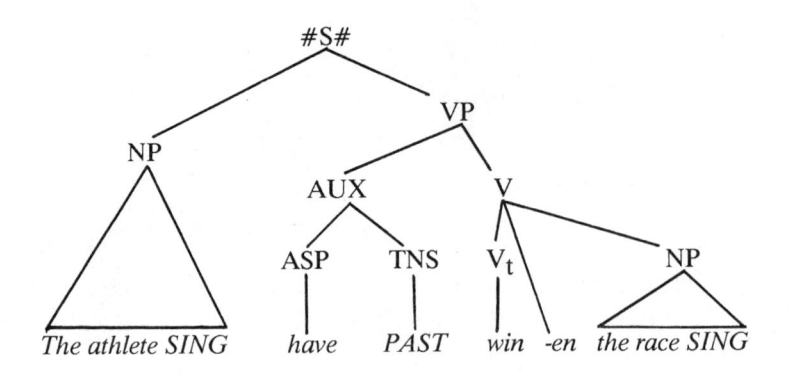

```
                    #S#
                   /   \
                 NP     VP
                /  \   /  \
               /    \ AUX   V
              /      \ / \  /\
             /        ASP TNS Vt  NP
            /          |   |  |   /\
    The athlete SING  have PAST win -en the race SING
```

The second cycle of transformations now operates on this most deeply embedded sentence together with the next higher one. At this point, the structural descriptions which trigger the relativization transformation come into play since *two* identical noun-phrases can now be recognized (i.e. *the athlete SING* in *The athlete SING PAST wear the medal SING* and *the athlete SING* in *The athlete SING have PAST win -en the race SING*). The relativization transformation replaces the second of these identical noun-phrases with WH -PROh, where WH is a symbol for any relative pronoun, and where -PROh adds the information that the noun to be pronominalized is *human*, as opposed to being in some other category such as *inanimate* or *concrete*. This latter information is necessary in order for the later morphophonemic rules to select the correct pronoun in surface structure (i.e. *who* in this case, as opposed to *that* or *which*). The output from this second cycle is:

(All higher structure remains the same)

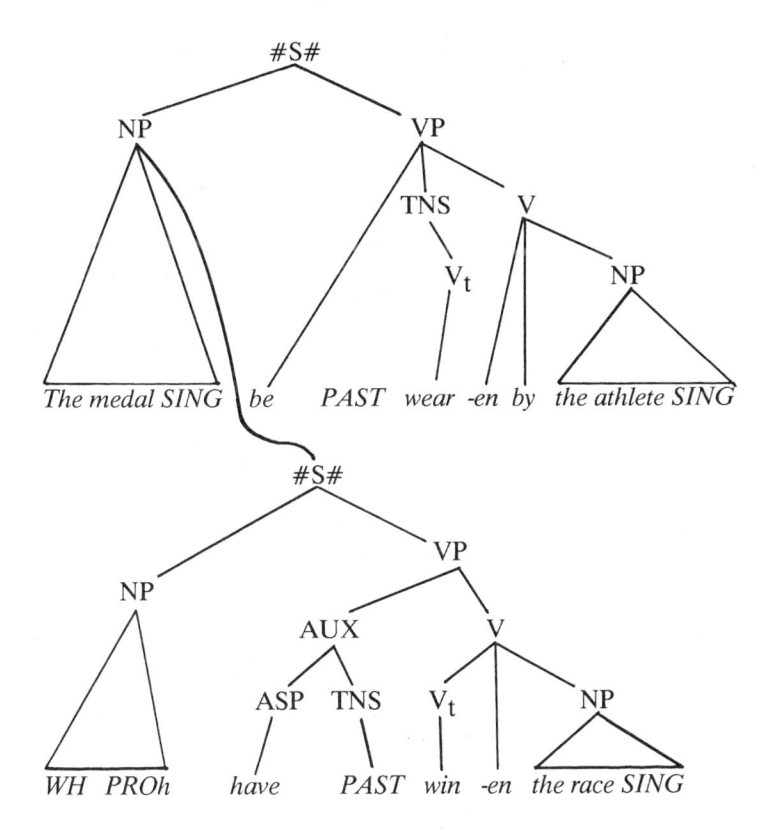

```
                    #S#
                   /    \
                  NP     VP
                 /|\    /|  \
                / | \ TNS    V
               /  |  \  \   /|\
              /   |   \  Vt  | NP
             /    |    \  |  |  /\
    The medal SING be PAST wear -en by the athlete SING
                    |
                   #S#
                  /    \
                 NP     VP
                /|\    / \
               / | \ AUX   V
              /  |  \ / \ /|\
             /   |  ASP TNS Vt  NP
            /    |   /   \   |  /\
       WH PROh  have  PAST win -en the race SING
```

In the third cycle of this derivation, the transformational rules "see" the entire sentence from the most deeply embedded relative clause up to the matrix. The two equal noun-phrases now recognized by the structural description of the relativization transformation are *The medal SING* in *The medal SING PAST impress the crowd SING* and *The medal* in the now transformed *The medal SING be PAST wear -en by the athlete SING*, and the final output tree-diagram is as follows (where *WH PROi*) stands for the inanimate *medal*, later to become *that*):

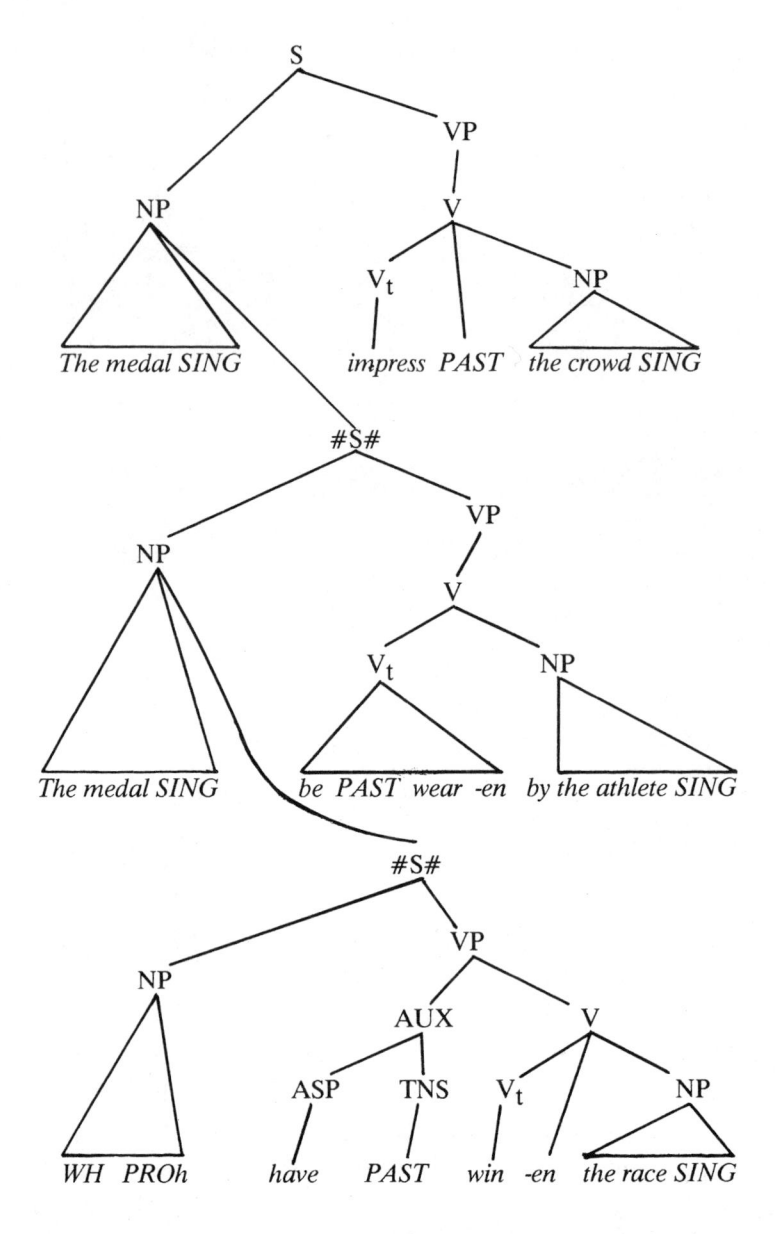

```
                          S
                    ╱         ╲
                  NP            VP
                ╱    ╲           │
               ╱      ╲          V
              ╱_____╲      ╱  │  ╲
           The medal SING    Vₜ   │   NP
                             │    │   ╱╲
                          impress PAST  the crowd SING
                                  │
                                #S#
                               ╱    ╲
                              NP     VP
                             ╱  ╲     │
                            ╱    ╲    V
                           ╱_____╲  ╱ │ ╲
                        The medal SING Vₜ  NP
                                      ╱╲   ╱╲
                                  be PAST wear -en  by the athlete SING
                                        │
                                      #S#
                                    ╱      ╲
                                   NP       VP
                                  ╱╲      ╱ │ ╲
                                 ╱__╲   AUX    V
                              WH PROh  ╱ ╲   ╱  ╲
                                     ASP TNS Vₜ  NP
                                      │   │  │  ╱╲
                                    have PAST win -en the race SING
```

The final result of the operations in the base of the grammar and the transformational component is the *final-output string*, which is the string of the terminal elements in the above tree-structure: *The medal SING #WH PROi be PAST wear -en by the athlete SING #WH PROh have PAST win -en the race SING #impress PAST the crowd SING.* At this point, all the basic syntax needed to produce the grammatical sentence we started with has been completed, and it only remains for the morphophonemic rules to bring the string to its final phonological form. In this case, morphophonemic rules will replace *WH PROi* with *that*, will replace *WH PROh* with *who*, will produce the correct past participles of the regular and irregular verbs (*impress PAST* becomes *impressed*; *win -en* becomes *won*; *wear -en* becomes *worn*), and they will also remove any remaining redundancies such as the *SING* markers to yield *The medal that was worn by the athlete who won the race impressed the crowd.*

Further transformations

The above example has been given to demonstrate the nature of a relatively advanced version of a standard transformational-generative grammar. There are, of course, many rules not covered here that are contained in such a grammar. In a more complete version of the grammar the phrase-structure component will contain optional rules for adding adverbial clauses (enabling sentences like *In the auditorium, the medal that was worn by the athlete who had won the race impressed the crowd*) and for rewriting the main verb into several other subtypes (including *ditransitive* verbs like *give*, capable of taking two noun objects, as in *Mary gave John the book*, and verbs with particles which either separate, such as *look up* or *switch on*, or which do not, such as *look at* and *seek after*). The phrase-structure rules will also contain complete specification of the English verb-phrase, which contains *progressive aspect* (be -ing) and *modal verbs* (*will, would, can could,* etc.) in addition to what has already been mentioned. The transformational component will contain additional rules for the formation of relative clauses, as well as rules for the formation of *negation, questions,* and all possible combinations of the two. It should also be noted that English permits the generation of many grammatical sentences which *reduce* relative clauses by deleting the relative pronoun and any following version of the verb *to be* in such a way that the above example sentence *could* reach surface structure as *The medal worn by the athlete who won the race impressed the crowd*, in which case an optional transformation will delete the *WH PROi* yielding *that* in the original example. Notice, however, that the grammar must be (and is) sensitive enough to various kinds of relative clause formation that it will not produce **The medal that was worn by the athlete won the race impressed the crowd*. Indeed, the deletion of relative pronouns is only grammatical in English in limited cases where the pronoun is a) followed immediately by the verb *to be*, or b) is followed immediately by a noun-phrase (as it is in *The rabbit that the cat chased escaped / The rabbit the cat chased escaped*).

The transformational component is well able to specify these additional options in very economical (or *parsimonious*) form, further illustrating the conciseness, power, and generalizability implicit in the entire grammatical model. On first encounter, a TGG may seem to be a somewhat complex instrument. When compared to earlier grammars, however, TGG has far greater power, capturing in a limited number of rules the entire range of sentence structures in a language. In this way, a TGG is far more *explanatory* than any prescriptive model could be, since it reveals the underlying grammatical rules that are unconsciously known and followed by fluent native speakers. Since it is capable of demonstrating what rules are followed, moreover, it provides a rich base for considering what is happening when they are *not* being followed or when they are being changed in some context or other.

Some descriptive advantages of TGG

The publication of *Syntactic Structures* (1957) and *Aspects of the Theory Syntax* (1965) not only changed the technical nature of grammatical analysis but also the nature of the questions considered relevant in the construction of grammars. Standard theory, of course, did not provide all the answers to these questions, but it provided the basis upon which many subsequent controversies have been discussed. In addition to the theoretical richness of the new model, however, it also made many more mundane aspects of the analysis of English significantly clearer. In the analysis of the verb-phrase, for example, the traditional Latin categories that had been superimposed on English were replaced by a much simpler and more relevant analysis in which only two tenses appear (*past* and *present*) marked on the first element of any verb-phrase, together with a watertight ordering rule represented in the following strict sequence: {TNS (Modal verb) (Perfective Aspect) (Progressive Aspect) (Passive Voice) Main Verb} (where regular brackets enclose optional elements). This precise and appropriate specification for English is instantiated in the phrase-structure and transformational rules of the grammar.

Other analytical advantages arise from the central distinction between deep and surface structure found in the model and, in particular, the grammar is readily able to show not only how the same deep structure may give rise to the generation of a family of surface structures, but also how *syntactically ambiguous* sentences have one surface structure but more than one deep structure. An example here might be a sentence like *The victim was found by the hospital*, in which *hospital* might be interpreted either as "a building" or as "people who work in the building" (i.e. paramedics or, less likely, nurses). These two interpretations are intimately connected with two quite different deep structure trees:

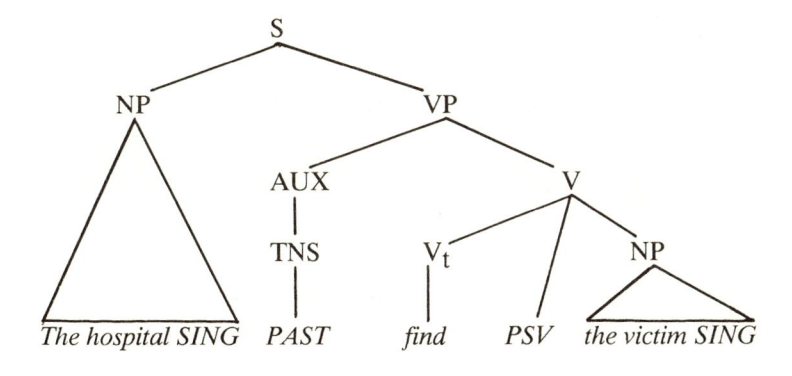

Deep structure a)

```
                         S
                   ┌─────┴─────┐
                  NP           VP
                  △        ┌───┴───┐
                          AUX       V
                           │    ┌───┼───┐
                          TNS   V_t     NP
                           │    │       △
            The hospital SING  PAST   find   PSV   the victim SING
```

Deep structure b)

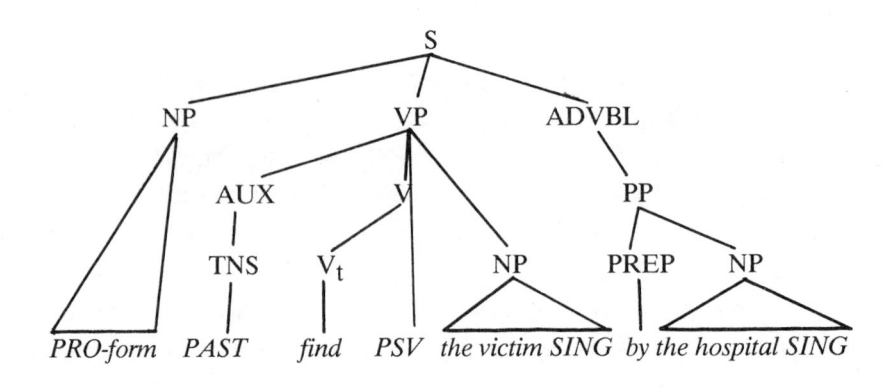

```
                              S
                  ┌───────────┼───────────┐
                 NP          VP         ADVBL
                  │     ┌─────┤            │
                  │    AUX    V            PP
                  │     │   ┌─┴─┐        ┌──┴──┐
                  │    TNS  Vₜ  │       NP   PREP   NP
              PRO-form PAST find PSV the victim SING by the hospital SING
```

Deep structure a) represents the structure underlying an interpretation of the surface structure in which the hospital is understood as a human agent for the action of finding the victim. Deep structure b) shows an alternative interpretation in which the agent is actually not known (for this reason, the agent is represented by a PRO-form), but where the victim's body was found in the general environment of the hospital building. Deep structure a) represents a full passive structure while b) represents a *truncated* passive (i.e. a passive where the agent is unknown and is "deleted" in surface structure) together with an adverbial phrase with a preposition and a noun-phrase. No grammar prior to TGG came close to explaining structural ambiguities like these with such clarity. The positing of two principal levels of syntactic structure, then, led the way to a more insightful description of how interpretation of sentences relates to their alternative underlying structures.

Developments Following Standard Theory

In the early sixties through to the seventies, many sometimes acrimonious conflicts arose concerning the nature of language and how grammars should reflect this nature. There is insufficient space in a chapter such as this to follow these conflicts in great detail, and readers are referred to Newmeyer (1986) for the most complete historical overview of the period. It is possible, however, to present a general outline of some of the most important debates that have followed in the wake of Chomsky's innovations. The theory which is the most direct descendant of TGG, and which is now most widely accepted, is called *Government and Binding* (GB) (following Chomsky, 1980, 1981). The development of GB, however, needs to be understood in light of some other earlier debates about the form grammars should take.

Generative Semantics

Even before the publication of *Aspects*, debate had been developing about such matters as the ideal form that deep structures should take, and about the nature and specification of transformational rules. The most important issue of all concerned the relationship between syntax and semantics. It seemed to theorists such as Katz and Fodor (1963) that the "deeper" theorists went in describing sentences, the more involved they were destined to become with meaning and, therefore, that grammars would have to reflect the involvement of meaning in native speakers' production and understanding of sentences. To return to the above example, *The victim was found by the hospital*, it is evident that the structural ambiguity illustrated is in fact inseparable from the interpretation of the single lexical item *hospital*. The deep structural differences presented in the above examples, then, are intimately connected in some way with the *lexical* interpretation of *hospital*. Ideally, a grammar should reflect this connection; the derivation of the sentence through the grammar, in other words, should reflect the interaction between the perceived meaning of *hospital* (as either "building" or "agency") and the syntactic structure of the sentence. From this perception about the centrality of the interpretation of lexical meaning, it can be argued that deep structures should be grounded in such meaning, and that the syntactic structures described during the course of derivation should be closely dependent on such *semantic* preliminaries. The arguments put forward by Katz and Postal (1964) were, essentially, that the base of the grammar should be *semantic*, rather than syntactic, in nature, and that the distinction and the interface between syntax and semantics should be clarified.

In order to reflect this centrality of semantics, Katz and Postal proposed that lexicons of the type outlined by Chomsky (and similar to the one outlined in the examples above) be enriched in the form of elaborate *dictionaries*, containing not only definitions of words but also complete information about their potential syntactic relationships with other words and a further analysis into their semantic components. To use the best-known example of a proposed entry, the Katz-Fodor dictionary would include the information for the word *bachelor* that it can represent either a *human*, who has his or her first university degree, or a *human male* who has never married, or a *young human male* who served under the standard of a knight. It could also represent a *young male animal* (i.e. a fur seal without a mate). These complete dictionaries were to be supplemented by a set of *projection rules* which work upwards from deep structure to regulate the formation of appropriate syntactic structure. To return to the previous example, the formation of the ADVBL structure would in this way result from the projection of rules predicated on the complete information given with *hospital* in the dictionary: Since *hospital* would have the prior interpretation of "building," this would trigger the correct adverbial clause formation during derivation leading to the appropriate (and unambiguous) reading of the sentence. According to this model, then, the syntactic form at the surface would essentially be a function of the rich semantic information given in the dictionary and of the interaction between this and the projection rules.

The Katz-Postal Hypothesis

One point which appeared to lend support to the proposals of Katz and Fodor concerned the nature of transformations. Ideally, it seemed that transformations, if they were purely *syntactic* in nature, should not change the meaning of a sentence between deep and surface structure. In *Syntactic Structures*, transformations had worked on kernel sentences to produce negative and questions forms, which clearly bore different meanings at the surface from that suggested in deep structure. It was questionable, too, whether passive sentences are exactly identical in meaning to their active transforms instantiated in deep structure. It was Katz and Postal (1964) who proposed what is now referred to as the "Katz-Postal Hypothesis," namely, that in order to keep syntax and semantics unconfounded in grammar transformations *should* preserve meaning. This gave further credibility to the idea that all the meaning elements of a sentence should be accounted for in deep structure and *before* syntactic transformations take place.

The above proposals of Katz, Fodor, and Postal, formed the basis of *generative semantics* (GS), in which context it became the central task to search for even deeper and more abstract levels of semantic analysis as the foundation for grammar. One casualty in this search was Chomsky's original idea that lexical information should be inserted at the level of the formation of the deep structure. It turned out, indeed, that complete specification of semantic information began to *erode* rather than to demonstrate any clear distinction between syntax and semantics. It had been argued, for instance, that a fully-specified semantic analysis of the verb *thicken* in a sentence such as *John thickened the sauce* would have to be in a form something like *thicken = cause to become thick*. Similarly, the underlying semantic analysis of *John killed Bill* would be *John caused Bill to die* (see Newmeyer, 1986, p. 91). McCawley (1968), indeed, proposed that the dictionary entry for *kill* should be even more decomposed as follows:

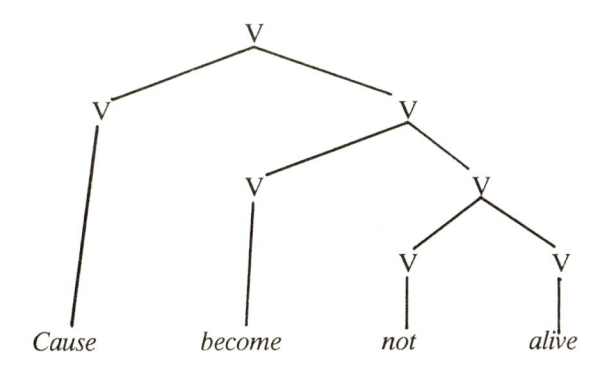

If even lexical entries could be decomposed in this way and realized in tree-diagrammatic form, then, and if there was every reason to suppose that semantics and syntax were ultimately interactive (as the Katz-Fodor projection rules had suggested), then Chomskyan deep structure appeared to be redundant.

The generative semanticists argued that semantic representations should merge directly into transformations, and that they should all take the same basic form of a sequence of operations on hierarchical structures leading to grammatical (and meaningful) output. In this analysis, any idea that a sentence could have two or more deep structures was, of course, no longer tenable.

The objective of the generative-semanticists to decompose lexical elements led in the end to a collapsing of the traditional notion that there were separate parts of speech, such as verbs, nouns, adjectives, prepositions, and adverbs. By the end of the 1960s, they had become convinced that there were only three necessary categories for grammatical analysis, namely, noun-phrases, verbs, and sentences: Given recognition of just these elements and the extremely rich dictionary entries for nouns and verbs, they believed that everything else could be developed from this information. This led, ultimately, to the belief that the deepest level of all was that of "natural logic," in which they had much in common with the logical positivists (see Chapter Three, and Lakoff 1974, p. 162).

Case Grammar

Working at the same time as the generative semanticists, Fillmore (1966, 1968, 1971) proposed that underlying sentence structures should contain information about the *thematic relations* between elements, information missing in Chomsky's *Aspects* model. He observed, for example, that in Chomsky's model all prepositional phrases were treated in much the same way and that the grammar at no point revealed that their contents actually reflect quite different roles and relations to other parts of sentences. In this way, phrases such as *in the garden, near to New York, on the following afternoon,* and *by the Terminator* are all treated as syntactically equivalent, even though the first one expresses the *location* of some action, the second expresses *direction towards* a location, the third expresses the *time* of some action and the fourth describes the *agent* of an action. There are several languages, such as Russian, German and Finnish, in which case relations, following the influence of Latin, are clearly marked in surface structure. Modern German, for instance, uses *nominative* case inflections for subjects, *genitive* inflections for expressing possession, *dative* inflections for indirect objects or the objects of certain prepositions, and *accusative* inflections for direct objects. In German, determiners, pronouns, and adjectives must all agree, moreover, in their expression of case. English, however, does not express case relations in surface structure so ostensibly, and case endings remain only in the pronoun system, where *she* (nominative) is contrasted with *her* (accusative and dative) and so on. Fillmore realized, however, that the relations themselves were still very much a part of English sentences and that they both could and should be captured in underlying structure. For English, Fillmore (1971) proposed the following cases:

>   a. AGENT
>   b. EXPERIENCER
>   c. INSTRUMENT
>   d. OBJECT
>   e. SOURCE
>   f. GOAL
>   g. LOCATION
>   h. TIME

He argued that if lexical elements were fully specified for the case relations in which they could participate, then surface-structural syntactic relations could be predicted from this. In the lexicon, a verb such as *see* would be specified to take both an *object* and an *experiencer*, while the verb *show* would be specified as relating to potential *objects*, *experiencers*, and *agents* (i.e., more informally, "things shown," "organisms seeing what is shown" and "showers of the things"). These underlying lexical constraints would then form the basis for ensuring that the appropriate case relations are established in syntax, yielding grammatical forms such as *The astronomer (AGENT) is showing the children (EXPERIENCERS) the moon (OBJECT)*, and not anomalous forms such as **The moon is showing the astronomer the children*, or **The astronomer is showing the moon the children*, which would both be blocked since they do not reflect appropriate case relations in English.

In Fillmore's case grammar, grammatical syntax was underwritten by the elegibility of lexical items to enter into certain limited kinds of logical relationships with each other. The approach shared much with generative semantics in its appeal to a semantic, rather than a purely syntactic base for grammatical analysis, while it differed in choosing the logic implicit in case relations as its foundation rather than the "natural logic" sought after by the generative semanticists.

Chomsky's Responses and Later Developments

The central dispute between the generative-semanticists, case-grammarians and Chomskyans was about the level or levels at which meaning should be accounted for in grammar. Chomsky's original proposals suggested that higher levels of the model, including transformations, still had some effect on the meaning of sentences, while opponents of the *Aspects* model all for one reason or another argued that meaning must be entirely accounted for *before* syntactical grouping and ordering take place. Several linguists supported Chomsky in rebutting this latter idea, however, demonstrating that many aspects of meaning were established only in the higher levels of sentence generation. Jackendoff (1969), for example, by demonstrating the clear meaning difference between pairs of sentences like *Many arrows did not hit the target* and *The target was not hit by many arrows* reasserted the idea that the passive transformation does have semantic impact. It is also clear that various transforms of certain negative expressions affect the scope of negation, as in *Not much shrapnel hit the soldier* vs. *Much shrapnel did not hit the soldier* (Jackendoff, 1969, pp. 222-225). Gradually, it became clear in a more general sense that all sorts of things in addition to transformations, including sociolinguistic and contextual variations of one sort or another may affect the surface meaning of sentences, variations which could not possibly be completely represented in the lexical or sub-lexical terms no matter how rich their specification. This realization brought about the swift overthrow of the generative-semantic model and a reassertion of Chomskyan analysis.

The central problem recognized by all sides in the debate was that of where to include semantic interpretation in grammar. In the standard theory, all meaning was supposed to be accounted for in the base, but it became clear that transformations such as passive did not merely preserve the meaning given in the base but altered it in significant ways on the way to the surface. Even clearer instances of how meaning is altered above the level of deep structure came from closer examination of the processes of *nominalization* and *pronominalization*, the processes of forming noun-phrases and pronouns standing for noun-phrases. As Jackendoff noted, the scope of negative modifiers often changes through transformations, and this kind of effect was also noticed in a range of syntactic structures. Take, for example, the sentences a) *Rustlers steal cattle*, and its passive transform b) *Cattle are stolen by rustlers*. Here, it is clear that *Rustlers* in sentence a) receives a wider scope, or "generic," interpretation ("all rustlers") which its instance in b) does not (where *cattle* is generic and *rustlers* is not). The sentences c) *Sheila feeds her cat* and its passive transform d) *Her cat is fed by Sheila* illustrate how the passive transformation does not maintain the intention in deep structure that it is *Sheila's* cat that she feeds and not a cat having a wider scope of possible ownership. In both these cases, it seems that moving what was a deep-structural object into subject position in surface structure affects its scope. The solution to these kinds of problems appeared to be to continue allowing transformations to perform their valuable role, but to supplement the grammar with both rules which determine the semantic *roles* of lexical elements in deep structure and rules which determine matters of scope and pronominal reference at the surface (Chomsky, 1970).

Extended standard theory

One result of this new set of additions in what became known as *extended standard theory*, was that grammars became more *modular* in structure. It became even clearer than it had been at the time of the *Aspects* model that a grammar is best conceived as a set of discrete variables and that a grammar gains the power of generation largely from the interactions between these discrete variables or components. Further close analysis of syntactic structures in English also led to greater simplification of transformational rules: In particular, cumbersome operations like those presented in the initial examples above, involving recognition of two identical noun-phrases as a basis for triggering relativization, or the inclusion of dummy PRO-forms to be deleted by transformational rules, were all greatly simplified by placing greater detail in the base of the grammar. It was realized that several of the operations that had been kept separate in standard theory actually contained many common elements and constraints (e.g. all forms of embedded clause in English behave in much the same way involving movement of a WH-form to the initial boundary of the clause). Once greater specification had been included in the base of the grammar it became possible to see the very general constraints on the movements of lexical items in sentences and to simplify transformational rules in forms such as "move-NP" or "move-WH."

This greater modularization of grammar and the parallel simplification of rules actually began to shift the foundations of grammatical theory once again. Rather than continuing along the path of providing satisfactory descriptions of individual languages, the way was now open to even greater explanatory power through the identification of *universal* properties of grammar. During the development of extended standard theory, there was a growing realization that in order to achieve the ultimate task of a grammatical theory, explanation of the *competence* of native-speakers to follow the grammatical rules of their languages, it would be necessary to specify how they acquired the specific grammatical rules of these languages on the basis of their innate capacity to learn a language. Ideally, then, describing the grammar of any individual language would be a matter of demonstrating the relationship between the particular grammatical rules of that language and those of the *core* grammar with which all humans, presumably, are born.

Government and Binding Theory

When the dust finally settled from all the debates about the inadequacies of standard theory and about the role and place of semantics in grammar, the new theoretical descendent which emerged and which has since gained the most general support was the theory of *Government and Binding* (GB) (Chomsky, 1980, 1981). The GB model incorporates the results of many separate theoretical discussions which took place between the mid-sixties and the early eighties and, as suggested above, it is closely associated with the search for universal properties underlying all languages. It is less easy to provide a concise overview of GB than TGG for several reasons. First, the theory is still under development, and there are therefore many individual differences in notation and approach. Second, and more importantly, the fundamental objective in GB is no longer the accurate description of particular grammars, but rather to explain nothing less than how grammatical rules are distributed across languages in general and how they are learned. GB theory brings together a number of key ideas and proposals, each of which needs to be understood in its own right for the model as a whole to make sense. These key ideas and their concomitant grammatical components are reviewed in the following sections.

Major Contributing Ideas in GB Theory

Universal Grammar (UG) and individual grammars

If we accept that all humans are endowed with some natural capacity for language, a capacity on the basis of which they are able to learn the grammars of the particular languages they first encounter (and second or more languages later), then it is reasonable to see the grammatical rules of these individual languages in terms of specific *constraints* on the universe of linguistic possibilities. To take an example, it is true to say that all languages are capable of generating complex sentences much like those involving the process of relativization in English (illustrated in the references to standard theory, above). Other languages achieve the same end, but they may select quite different devices to achieve it. It makes some good sense, then, to look at things from an almost opposite perspective from how things were viewed in standard theory, where the purpose was to describe how the relativization transformations "construct" the syntactic ordering out of the finite forms contained in the base, and to recognize that the formation of relative clauses in all languages involves some sort of *movement*, and that what is significant about each separate language is that it permits only certain kinds of movements and forbids others. Language learners, according to the theory, learn such general constraints on their language *without* hearing ungrammatical input. This means, then, that such constraints must be an inherent feature of language in general and that knowledge of them is in some sense innate.

Logical form rules

As suggested in the previous discussion, the major changes introduced since the early *Aspects* model have to do mainly with the treatment of *semantic* phenomena. In standard theory, it was assumed that all semantic information was contained in the base (although it was later realized that transformations did not always preserve this meaning). In GB, as a result of the many arguments demonstrating that semantic interpretation cannot be restricted to the base, the entire notion in standard theory that meaning can be decomposed into lexical elements (such as [+human], [-animate] and so on) is abandoned in favor of a set of *Logical Form* (LF) rules which do the job of interpreting such matters as the scope of modification referred to above. The former schism between deep and surface structure is now reduced to a distinction between *D-structures* and *S-structures*, related to each other by a very different set of transformational operations. Logical form rules, then, apply to the S-structure level output. Given an S-structure such as *Everyone loves her mother*, the LF rules will interpret the sentence in one of two possible ways; either as [For all x [x loves x's mother]] (equivalent to "Every woman loves her own mother") or as [For all x [x loves her mother]] (equivalent to "Every person loves some other specified person's mother") (following Horrocks, 1987, p. 97). In this way, it can be seen that the LF rules serve to provide necessary further disambiguation at the level of what was formerly called surface structure; they interpret sentences at the surface in ways which fully clarify the logical relations between subjects, objects, and other sentential elements, and in ways that were not included in the earlier model. Parallel to the LF rules is a set of *Phonological Form* (PF) rules to give sentence strings their final phonological shapes.

Simplified transformations

If the general function of the LF and PF rules following the formation of S-structures is clear, what are the grammatical operations by which sentences arrive at S-structure? This question can only be answered in relation to the theory of Universal Grammar that is so closely related to GB analysis. As previously stated, an assumption underlying UG is that all languages involve various kinds of constrained movement of elements in the formation of grammatical sentences. In its most general form, this universal grammar rule might be written simply as "Move-α," a rule which underlies all individual grammars. Every child is born with knowledge of this general movement rule but has to learn what the precise *values* of α are for her own first language. In English, it is clear that the values for alpha will include noun-phrases, which can be moved around verbs in various limited ways (for example, the switching of NPs in the formation of passives), relative pronouns, which must be shifted to the front of clauses that they modify, and adverbial clauses, certain of which can be moved to the beginning or end of sentences. What remains to be described in the grammar of English, then, is of far less complexity than that contained within a TGG, since the alpha rule assumes much of the necessary information. The result is a transformational component which is simply a list of the values of alpha for a given language.

This simplified form of the transformational component is now supplemented by some further modifications in the lexicon. In standard TGG, the phrase-structure rules contained elements like V_t (transitive verb) which rewrite adjoined to the left of object NPs (V ----- V_t + NP), together with lexical information that included formulae stating the basic syntactic frames of verbs (e.g. part of the entry for a verb such as *catch* would be {V, +

[----NP, PP]}, to show that *catch* can enter into structures such as *The police caught the robber in the supermarket*, while for *state*, a parallel entry might be {V + [-----S]}, to show that the verb appears in constructions such as *The police state + that the robber was drunk*). It will be recognized just from these examples that there was considerable *duplication* of information in standard theory; the phrase-structure rules establish, for instance, that transitive verbs take noun objects, while the lexicon essentially restates this information for each separate verb. In GB theory, all of this information is collapsed in a series of projection rules which specify and "project" the syntactic units into which a given element fits to all levels of grammatical description (cf. Katz & Fodor, 1964, above). One of the results of introducing such projection rules is to greatly reduce the scope and complexity of phrase-structure rules: If syntactic structures can be projected directly from lexical elements, there is little reason to have a *separate* component working on these structures independently.

X-bar theory

The formulation of the projection rules depends on another theoretical component in GB, namely, that of $\overline{X}$ ("X-bar") theory, a theory developed during the 1970s. $\overline{X}$ theory recognizes that each language has a characteristic way of constructing its phrases. In English, for example, verbs typically come before objects in the verb-phrase, prepositions precede their objects, and adjectives precede the nouns they modify. In other languages, lexical items cluster in different ways; in French, for instance, adjectives most often follow rather than precede nouns, in German, verbs are mostly shifted to the end of verb-phrases, while in Japanese, both verbs and prepositions follow their objects. $\overline{X}$ theory provides a basis for describing these kind of very general rules languages follow in the formation of their phrase-structures.

In describing these formation rules, $\overline{X}$ theory incorporates the claim that every syntactic structure has a *head* of some kind, a linguistic unit which provides its core and around which all else is organized. In the noun-phrase *the beer*, *beer* is the head noun, while in the verb-phrase *drinks the beer*, *drinks* is the head verb, and in the adjectival phrase *blind as a bat*, *blind* is the head adjective. In all these cases, the total phrase ($\overline{X}$) is said to be a *projection* from its head (X): $\overline{X}$, then, expresses the constraints on the kinds of relations that the given X (particular nouns, adjectives, verbs, etc.) can have with other elements; it expresses the possible syntactic groupings, the possible constituent structures, into which the head can enter. In the lexicon, each noun, verb, adjective, adverb, and preposition is specified for the type of complement structure it takes. Each item will have an *argument* which is a constituent which goes with it obligatorily, the most obvious example being a noun-phrase object for a transitive verb. The $\overline{X}$ is this first level of constituent structure; the combination of *shovel* and *the snow* is a $\overline{V}$ ("V-bar"), the combination of *man* and *about town* is an $\overline{N}$, and the combination of *generous* and *with money* is an $\overline{A}$:

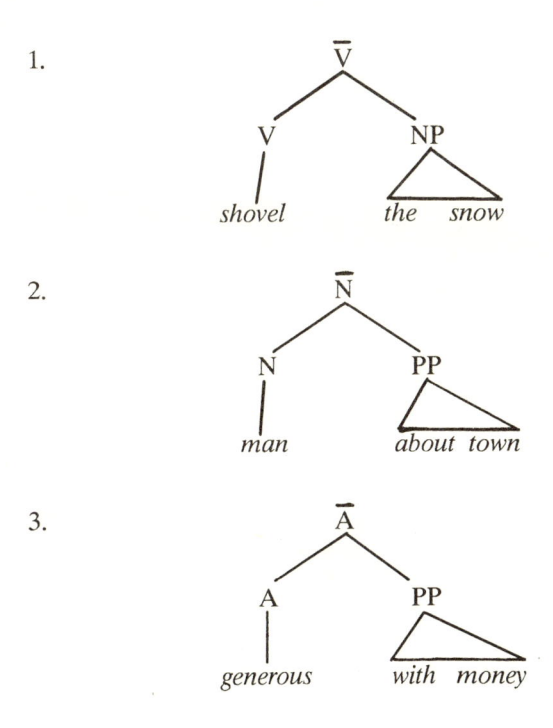

1. $\overline{V}$ → V (*shovel*) NP (*the snow*)

2. $\overline{N}$ → N (*man*) PP (*about town*)

3. $\overline{A}$ → A (*generous*) PP (*with money*)

Each of these basic $\overline{X}$ forms, though, can itself be combined with other items in what is called its *maximal projection*. Each $\overline{X}$ structure can be supplemented in certain ways by *specifiers* and *modifiers*. In this way, *man about town* can be specified by the determiner *the*, *generous with money* can be specified with *extremely*, and *shovel the snow* can be further modified by *around the garage*. In each case, this leads to higher-level X ("two-bar") structures. The general form of these higher level structures is given by the diagram:

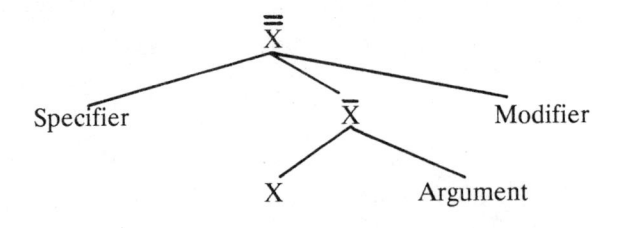

```
              X̿
           /     \
          /       \
    Specifier    X̄       Modifier
                / \
               X   Argument
```

(following Sells, 1985, p. 28)

The X structures for each of the above would then be:

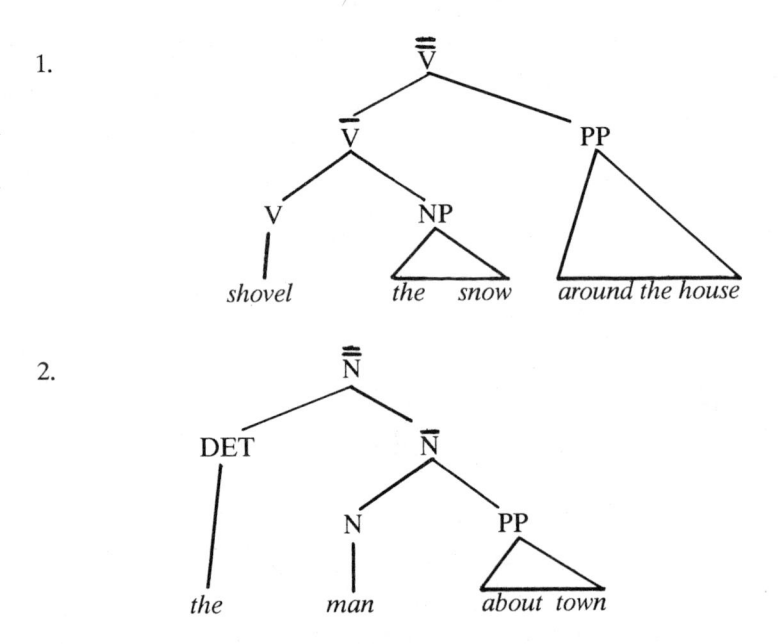

1.
```
            V̿
          /    \
         V̄      PP
        / \     /\
       V   NP  around the house
       |   /\
    shovel the snow
```

2.
```
            N̿
          /   \
        DET    N̄
         |    / \
         |   N   PP
         |   |   /\
        the man about town
```

3.

```
              Ā
           /     \
         Deg      Ā
          |      /  \
          |     A    PP
          |     |    /\
      extremely generous with money
```

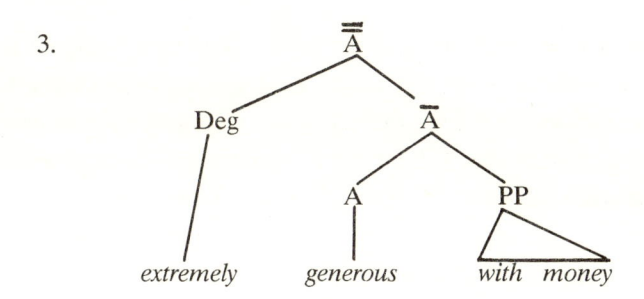

The central point in all this is that these complex X̄-structures are projections from information originally given in the lexicon about the relationships into which items can enter. Essentially, syntactic structures are created in the model out of the rich information given in the base of the grammar about *heads* and about the complements they take. The fundamental tenet of GB is that

> ...representations at each syntactic level are projected from the lexicon, in that they observe the subcategorization properties of lexical items. (Sells, 1985, p. 33)

This essentially obliterates the function of transformations which take one form as input and change it into another form as output: In GB, items contain their full syntactic identity in the base and carry this identity with them throughout.

Theta theory

X theory alone, however, will not account for grammatical syntax. It will not on its own solve the problems of scope of modification referred to above, nor will it on its own guarantee proper syntactic ordering always takes place. For complete sentence analysis, further semantic information of various kinds is required. The theta theory provides particular information about the *role* relations into which lexical items enter, information which is included within the *argument structures* of the heads. Typical roles to be included are those of *agent*, (the subject of a verb that acts in some way), *patients*, (recipients of actions), and *locations* (where something happens). In the case of the verb *shoot*, then, the complete lexical entry will assign the verb a subject agent, will assign to the NP object complement the role of patient ("something that is shot") and the PP complement the role location ("where the shooting takes place"). The Θ-criterion thus ensures that each separate constituent structure is assigned just one of these roles, guaranteeing, for example, that NPs are properly distributed (*The hunter shot the snake* but not **The snake shot the hunter*) and that no verb receives more than one agent (**The hunter was shooting the gun by the soldier*).

Government

As its title suggests, the role of *government* in GB is crucial. In general terms, government can be defined in terms of the constituent structures in which particular groups of elements are syntactically controlled. Hence the structure V_t + NP, for instance, is governed by the category that brings the two elements together (i.e. the node-label above them in tree-diagrams, namely, V) and the various permissible structures in noun-phrases are governed at the $\overline{N}$ level. It is necessary to specify government in grammar so that modifiers only modify within these local structures and cannot modify elements that are in structures found elsewhere in sentences. It is by way of the general property of government that both the subcategorization specifications of heads in the lexicon and the assignment of theta-roles take place.

Government is expressed in GB theory in terms of *constituent-commands* (*c-commands*) which define the particular relationships found in tree-structures. There has been some argument over the precise details of the operation of c-commands, but the generally accepted idea is that each type of head governs the other "sister" items within the same constituent structure (i.e. the other items dominated by the same node). Apart from ensuring, for example, that a transitive verb is followed in a verb-phrase only by certain structures (an object noun-phrase) and with no intervening complement structures, c-commands also obligatorily assign a case marking to each noun-phrase. Hence both verb and preposition heads automatically assign *objective* (or *accusative*) case to any subsequent nouns within the same structure:

```
       VP                              PP
      /\                              /\
     /  \                            /  \
    /    \                          /    \
   V ------> (object) N       Prep ------> (object) N
```

It is a requirement in the grammar that all nouns be assigned some case. Although each noun is not originally marked for case in the lexicon, it must pass through a *case filter* which moves it into an appropriate syntactic relationship where its case is clear (thus guaranteeing its structural integrity). In this way, the noun-phrase *the cat* will move into various relationships assigned by the case filter and requiring the addition of various associated elements as needed (the *meow of the cat*, illustrates *genitive* or *possessive* case assignment requiring *of*, while *gave the cat the milk* requires *dative* case assignment which would also permit the syntactic structure *gave the milk to the cat*).

Binding

Relations between noun-phrases are not just limited to those within constituent structures, and other kinds of relations are set up in both *anaphoric* and *pronominal* reference which go beyond the bounds of individual phrase-structure constituents. *Anaphors* are noun-phrases within a sentence which must be interpreted to have identical reference, good examples being the use of *reflexive pronouns* in sentences like *Sheila thought herself to be industrious*, where the anaphors are *Sheila* and *herself*. Other kinds of pronouns are less constrained in their reference than reflexives, and sentences like *Jerry thinks he is a butcher* or *Anita believes she is a kind person* demonstrate that pronouns can often be interpreted either as being co-referential (with Jerry or Anita in these examples) or as referring to some other person or object. A third category, known as *R-expressions* (*referential-expressions*) includes all other cases of reference in which noun-phrases can *not* be co-referential, as in sentences like *Sheila likes Anita's sense of humor* or *Donald has bought his son a pogo-stick*, in each of which two people are mentioned who cannot possibly be identical. Binding theory is a component of GB which works to establish exactly what are the correct relationships between noun-phrases in terms of their reference. Three rules relate to each of the three aforementioned categories: the first is that anaphors must be co-indexed within their constituent category, the second is that pronouns must be freely indexed in their constituent category, and the third is that R-expressions must be freely indexed everywhere. The effect of these binding rules is to ensure that co-referential noun-phrases (i.e. anaphors) appear in their correct positions, that pronouns that are not intended to be co-referential with other noun-phrases are appropriately indexed (e.g. *her* in *Sally's mother picked her up* is barred from referring to *mother*).

Alternative approaches

As suggested at the outset, any review of GB is necessarily somewhat fragmentary in nature. The above overview of the central ideas in GB, however, well reflects the theoretical direction taken by many theorists over recent years in the study and description of grammars. It might reasonably be claimed that GB theory has more to do with linguistic philosophy than with grammatical description per se, since its concern is so clearly the formulation of universal principles as opposed to clear and accessible descriptions of language such as English.

The main competitor to GB has been *Generalized Phrase-Structure Grammar* (GPSG), developed from original proposals by Gazdar (1982). One central difference between GPSG and Chomskyan-inspired models is its complete abandonment of a transformational component in favor of a fully-specified set of phrase-structure rules. Another competitor has been *Relational Grammar* (RG), following Perlmutter and Postal (1977), which was developed on the basis of many observations about the importance of various types of hierarchical dynamics discovered in languages. It was found in all languages examined, for example, that when noun-phrases are relativized the relative clauses are always raised to the same position in the matrix sentence as they were before the process took place; objects cannot become subjects nor can subjects become objects. Observations like this about grammatical relations became the basis of relational networks such as the following one for the sentence *The chocolate was eaten by Maxine*:

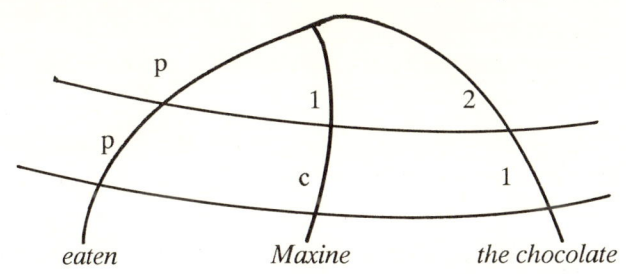

At the highest level in this network, the predicate *eaten* is complemented by the subject, *Maxine* (1) and the object, *the chocolate* (2). At the next level, *the chocolate* assumes the subject role (1), while *Maxine* no longer bears a grammatical role. The noun-phrase bearing her name has become a *chômeur*, a term derived from a French word meaning "unemployed." The original grammatical role of *Maxine* is usurped at the second level of the network by the former object. The central purpose of grammatical rules in RG is, then, to change *relations* between elements rather than to operate directly on structures, as they do in TGG or GB (see Newmeyer, 1986, pp. 215-218). The other major competitor to the GB framework is *Lexical-Functional* grammar (LFG), which revives the claim that everything in syntax should (and can) be derived from lexical information (e.g. Kaplan & Bresnan, 1982).

According to Newmeyer, in 1986 the distribution of allegiance to the theories so far described was about 66% to GB, 20% to GPSG, and the remainder to RG, LFG, and all other frameworks combined. It might be concluded from this that very little work has been conducted on grammar other than in the North American generative framework. This, however, is not the case, and this chapter will conclude with at least some brief mention of two types of grammatical analysis pursued by British linguists. The first type is identified in the work of Quirk, Greenbaum, Leech, & Svartvik (1972) (see also Quirk & Greenbaum, 1973; Leech and Svartvik, 1975). The second is found in the framework of *systemic* grammar developed in the tradition following Firth (1957) and Halliday (1961).

Traditional Grammar Revised and Extended

At the beginning of this discussion, it was suggested that Chomskyan grammar represented the overthrow of traditional, and especially prescriptivist, approaches. As we have seen, the results of this paradigm-shift in the study of language led to a period of rich theory-building in which the objective of providing descriptions of individual language such as English was largely superseded by the quest for universal truths. The rejection of traditional prescriptive grammars, however, has produced something of a void in the construction of grammars that are accessible to a general audience and that can be used as a basis for deciding what grammatical rules should be followed on given occasions.

Quirk et al. have gone some way to filling this void by writing a grammar of English which avoids the pitfalls of prescriptivism through the provision of a rich descriptive basis for such decision-making. While their approach is largely taxonomic and, unlike that of Chomskyans, one which is predicated on a single ("surface") level of language structure, Quirk et al. provide clear motivation for their analytic categories, and they present numerous supportive examples for their analysis with relatively uncluttered explanations of the grammatical patterning of English.

It is in the Quirk et al. grammar, and not in either a TGG or a GB manual, that it would be easier to look up almost any point of English grammar, ranging from the distinction between verb-types to the formation of *restrictive* vs. *non-restrictive* relative clauses. This latter distinction, indeed, is one that was very difficult to capture in a generative grammar due to its inseparability from complex surface-structural aspects of scope of modification. In the case of a restrictive relative clause, the clause is restricted to the noun-phrase it modifies; it serves to enrich the description of this noun-phrase in a way which "identifies" it more explicitly. In *The camel that is standing by the corner of the pyramid is photogenic*, the relative clause

(*...that is standing by the corner of the pyramid*) refers only to one particular camel: Looking across the sandy expanse at a plurality of camels, a prospective photographer is able on the basis of this restrictive relative clause to select this particular camel for attention. In *Doctor Who, who has visited two galaxies in the past year, is tired*, however, the relative clause is non-restrictive; it is a parenthetic comment about the Doctor and, indeed, it might be applied equally to any other crew members he may have travelled with. Quirk and Greenbaum (1973) state that *that/which* is the more likely pronoun to be used in restrictive relative clauses, reflecting the independence of such clauses from the essential or personal aspects of their antecedents. In this way, speakers of English are more likely to utter the sentence *The waiter that is serving the table over there..*, (although, as they point out, *The waiter who...* is also possible) than they are to say, in the case of a non-restrictive relative clause, **The waiter, that also served us last week....* They further explain that non-restrictive relative clauses might be thought of as fulfilling the same function as *coordinators*, since a form such as *Then Hans saw the house, which stood in a grove* can be paraphrased as *Then Hans saw a house, and the house stood in a grove*. This analysis serves to clarify the essential distinctions between restrictive and non-restrictive relative clauses; non-restrictive clauses are parenthetic in nature, providing additional, conjoined, but non-essential information about the antecedent noun-phrase, while restrictive relatives provide more essential and fully-attached information about antecedent noun-phrases (see Quirk & Greenbaum, 1973, pp. 382-383). Paradoxically, the scope of non-restrictive relatives, while wider than that of restrictive relatives actually provide more personal information about the subject than does the restrictive relative, even though its scope is narrower; the comment about the crew could equally well be attached to other crew-members, while the information about the camel "at the corner of the pyramid" could not be similarly attached to other camels).

The kind of presentation found in the Quirk et al. grammars has the clear advantage of allowing the inclusion and interpretation of all sorts of semantic information in the discussion of syntactic categories, an advantage not present in stricter and more mathematically-based generative grammars where, as we have seen, the inclusion of semantics continues to be wrought with technical obstacles of various kinds. While the *Contemporary Grammar of English* stands as a more *encyclopedic* and convenient reference to the grammar of English for a general audience, a reference which is likely to be of more *direct* use to teachers and their students, it should be noted that it fails to capture many of the simple and powerful generalizations found, say, in TGG. A good example concerns the matter of the permissible deletion of relative pronouns already referred to in the context of TGG, above. Concerning the optional deletion of relative pronouns in restrictive relative clauses, Quirk & Greenbaum state that "provided the relative pronoun is not the subject of the relative clause...a further option exists in relative clause structure of having no relative pronoun at all" (1973, p. 381). Their examples of sentences where pronoun-deletion would be blocked include the following two forms:

1. The boy that is playing the piano....

2. The table that stands in the corner....   (p. 380)

But while the deletion of the pronouns in *The boy is playing the piano...(is talented)* and *The table stands in the corner (is clean)* produce forms that support their case, they fail to note the acceptability of *The boy playing the piano is talented*, thus failing to capture the generalization that where a relative pronoun is followed by some auxiliary form of *be* (as it does in all *be + ing* and *be + en* structures) then it is also obligatory to delete this *be*-form along with the pronoun. If this extra rule is followed, it is quite possible to delete subject relative pronouns in embedded clauses and their proviso (quoted above) becomes invalid. The entire grammatical matter is handled with maximal simplicity and accuracy within TGG by way of the following component part of the transformational rules for relativization:

WH-BE Deletion (Optional)

$$\text{SD:} \quad \#\text{WH} \quad \text{PRO} \quad \begin{bmatrix} \text{be TNS} \\ \text{NP} \end{bmatrix} \text{X}\#$$

$$\text{SC:} \quad 1 \quad\quad 2 \quad\quad 3 \quad\quad\quad\quad ==\!\!>$$

$$\quad\quad\quad \text{null} \quad \text{null} \quad \begin{bmatrix} \text{null} \\ \text{NP} \end{bmatrix}$$

This rule states, briefly, concisely, and with complete generalizability across English, that where there is a relative pronoun (WH PRO) followed by the verb *be* in an embedded clause (as in, e.g., *The squirrel that was climbing the drainpipe stole the coconut*, then if the pronoun (*that*) is deleted, then the subsequent *be* must be along with it in order to ensure a grammatical sentence (*The squirrel climbing the drainpipe...* and not **The squirrel was climbing the drainpipe stole the coconut*). The other possibility contained in the same rule is that when WH PRO is followed directly by a noun-phrase (as it typically is where the relativized noun-phrase was an object in the embedded sentence, as in *The monkey that the tiger chased had fleas*, formerly *The monkey #the tiger chased the monkey# had fleas*) then this WH PRO alone may be deleted to produce *The monkey the tiger chased had fleas*.

This direct comparison between standard TGG and the Quirk et al. grammar reveals that while the latter may be more sensitive to certain contextual and semantic aspects of the grammatical categories in question, it is the former which more accurately captures the purely syntactic aspects of relativization.

Systemic Grammar

The continuous integration of semantic and syntactic criteria in grammatical theory evident in the Quirk et al. grammars is characteristic of the British tradition of grammatical analysis more generally. While the mathematical-logical orientation of TGG has been especially popular in North America, the British tradition has its roots in the work of J. R. Firth, who stressed the importance of analyzing all language in terms of its *contexts of situation* (see Chapter Three, above). His work is often discussed under the headings of "Firthian linguistics" or the "London School" (Langendoen, 1968; Davis, 1973). The work of Firth, who died in 1960, has been continued and elaborated by Halliday (e.g. Halliday, 1961) and others, and it is currently pursued by a group of British scholars (see, e.g. the collection of articles in Fawcett & Young, 1988). The central characteristic of the theory lies in the relating of linguistic elements (phonetic shapes, words, sentences) to situations, on the assumption that the grammatical forms these elements take are governed directly by extralinguistic aspects of these situations.

According to Firth, the broadest context in which language is to be analyzed is the culture in which it is embedded. All language behavior is viewed as exhibiting some *functional* characteristic within this broad cultural context and within the narrower contexts of situation. In order to describe meaning, Firth analyzed contexts into various factors. Unlike all other grammatical theories so far reviewed, however, the process following the categorization of contexts does not involve pre-established grammatical categories such as *noun*, *verb*, and so on. Rather, these categories are intended to emerge *from* the contextual analysis, an idea very much in keeping with Saussurean principles (see Chapters Two, Nine). The overall design of systemic analysis is as follows:

1. Cultural context
2. Situational context in 1.
3. Syntactic context in 2.
4. Morphological context in 3.
5. Vocabulary context in 4.
6. Phonetic context in 5.
7. Phonetic terms in 6.

(After Firth, 1957, pp. 26-27)

As suggested, the most direct descendant of Firth is Halliday, who has clarified and extended Firthian principles into a fully-fledged, functionally-based, theory of grammar. Halliday (1976) summarizes a more developed version of systemic grammar in six points as follows. First, grammar is based on *choice*; speakers of a language continually make distinctive choices from a range of options, options constrained by what has already been said and by contexts of utterance. The grammar of a language, then, "can be represented as a very large network of systems" (1976, p. 3). Entries into the network can be made in various ways and at various levels, and simultaneous options are possible. Given that a *clause* is to be uttered, for instance, the speaker simultaneously makes choices about *transitivity*, *mood*, and *theme*, which govern, respectively, the nature of the subject-object relation, whether the clause will be *declarative*, *interrogative*, or *imperative*, and how the topic will be expressed.

Second, description of the actual clauses and sentences uttered is to be thought of as "a list of the choices that the speaker has to make" (ibid., p. 4). Since the system-network contains all possible options, description of utterances in its terms specifies all necessary features and also shows how different utterances relate to each other. In some correspondence with TGG, sentences such as *John threw the ball*, *Did John throw the ball?*, *The ball was thrown by John*, and so on, will naturally be related in sets, although in systemic grammar, such utterances are viewed as sets of speaker-options.

Third, grammatical structure is to be generally conceived of as "a mechanism whereby the speaker realizes or makes manifest the choices he (sic) has made" (1976, p. 4). These options are then "realized" as structures.

Fourth, these realized structures are of two types: those that are "minimum-" and those that are "maximum-" bracketed, where minimum brackets enclose simple constituents (NPs and so on), and where maximum brackets contain constituents conforming to larger syntactic ordering rules. Cast in tree-structural terms, each of the nodes that dominate these bracketed structures represents a point of grammatical choice. At this level of systemic selection, speakers also make choices about topic and focus and so if, say, in an utterance like *Fred likes eggplant*, a speaker wants to emphasize that it is *eggplant* he likes (and not squash, for example) then a specific structure will be assigned. In a normal, or non-contrastive, utterance of *Fred likes eggplant*, *Fred's* existence is "given," while *eggplant* is identified as the significant new information. In systemic grammar, the structural differences associated with the distinction between given and new information is reflected in the distinction between *themes* and *rhemes*. Part of the speaker's structural responsibility is the assignment of what is the theme and what is the rheme in any utterance, and this assignment partly determines constituent structure membership (ibid., pp. 4-5).

Fifth, structures can also be labelled according to their structural *function* or their *class*. The structure of an utterance may reflect its function as describing an actor-process-goal or actor-action-object relationship, or as presenting a theme-rheme comment, and so on. *Class* choices involve selection of particular elements within phrase-structures, and these will largely follow from functional decisions (ibid., p.6).

Sixth, systemic grammar must indicate just how these choices are realized in structural terms. In this way, the grammar will be filled with explanatory "realization statements" taking various forms: Indicative expressions will be accompanied by statements to the effect that their subjects must be present, and imperatives by statements that their subjects will be absent. Other kinds of statements will make it clear what roles are assumed by individual elements; a noun, for example, might operate as both agent and object.

As might be expected, the fuller specification of the details of systemic grammar becomes complex (see Halliday, 1976). Enough has been presented, however, to indicate the general characteristics of the model, a model which is simultaneously structural and social-psychological in nature. Halliday has likened language processing to a "fugue" (1976, pp. 24-25) in which speakers must orchestrate many levels of decision-making, levels which it is the objective of systemic grammar to capture. Recent analyses in the Firthian and Hallidayan tradition attempt to capture grammatical options in terms of complex flowcharts (see, e.g., Fawcett et al., 1988). In general, there is a continuing insistence in the systemic approach to grammatical analysis in the integration of meaning, function, and structure, within descriptions based on language processing. This contrasts with North American generative approaches, in which, as previously suggested, there has been a tendency towards greater modularization of grammatical components. While the generative approach is accepted far more widely, systemic analysis provides an alternative which may be more readily interpretable, for instance, in contexts of teaching and learning, where the function of utterances is of primary concern.

Summary

The work of Chomsky (1957, 1965) represented a paradigm-shift in the study and construction of grammars. Chomsky viewed a grammar as a theory of language which went some way to explaining why some utterances are grammatical and others are not so. In order to reflect the intuition of native-speakers about the grammatical sentences of their languages, a grammar should reveal in principle the underlying set of grammatical rules by which such sentences are generated. The specification of these rules should be as economical as possible in order for a grammar to maximize its power and generalizability.

The theory developed by Chomsky to meet these criteria was known as transformational-generative grammar, and it involved the combination of several independent sets of rules which carried sentences from their "deep structure" to their "surface structure." In the base of the grammar, composed of the phrase-structure rules and the lexicon, the fundamental constituent structures of sentences were created in the form of tree-diagrams. This deep structure was then fed into the set of transformational rules in the grammar, which operated on the kernel sentence form of the sentence in order to yield a grammatical variant. A passive sentence, for example, would start in deep structure as an active kernel sentence, and then the transformational rules would make the necessary changes. Finally, the sentence would be passed through a set of morphophonemic rules which would yield its ultimate phonetic shape.

Chomsky's "standard" theory of 1965 was followed by a great deal of controversy and debate. In particular, there was concern over the absence of semantic criteria in the grammar, and the generative-semanticists attempted to remedy this situation by developing deep structures which were semantically-based and from which all surface syntax could be projected.

This entire project came to an end, however, when it was discovered that not all semantic information could in fact be included in deep structure, since matters such as the scope of modification appear to be surface-structural phenomena.

During the seventies, Chomskyan linguists worked to extend the standard theory in a variety of ways. In the early eighties, many of these developments were combined within the new framework of Government and Binding. GB theory is intimately related to Universal Grammar, to the search, that is, for universal laws underlying all natural languages. One central observation has been that languages behave in similar ways with respect to the movement of constituents into their correct syntactic order. The central logic of GB is to demonstrate just how individual languages constrain these universal laws of movement and, concomitantly, to simplify grammatical description considerably. The rich transformational component in TGG has now been replaced by far greater semantic and logical detail both in lexicon and at surface-level description. At heart of GB is the notion that syntactic detail can be largely predicted within the limited domains in which modifications of various kinds are governed (within noun and verb phrases, for instance) and in terms of which constituents must bind together.

In Britain, a rather different approach has been taken to grammar from that in North America. British linguists have tended to emphasize the integration of semantic and syntactic criteria in all aspects of grammatical description. The approach is apparent both in the traditional grammar of Quirk et al. and in the arguments of systemic linguists following Firth. While the *Contemporary Grammar of English* provides a detailed and useful reference to English, however, it lacks the simplicity and power of generative grammars. Systemic grammarians attempt to describe language in terms of the complex options speakers pursue, options which simultaneously involve decisions at the grammatical, modal, and functional level. This approach may have special appeal within educational contexts, due to its foundation in the social-psychology of communication. It is the generative-linguistic framework of Universal Grammar and Government and Binding theory, however, which has captured the attention of the majority of contemporary linguists. This represents a direct extension of the discussion initiated by

Chomsky (1965) about the relationship between grammar, innate language capacities, and language acquisition.

CHAPTER SIX

Language and Cognitive Psychology: The Processing of Linguistic Structures

> Communication with language is carried out through two basic human activities: speaking and listening. These are of particular importance to psychologists, for they are mental activities that hold clues to the very nature of the human mind. In speaking, people put ideas into words, talking about perceptions, feelings, and intentions they want other people to grasp. In listening, they turn words into ideas, trying to reconstruct the perceptions, feelings, and intentions they were meant to grasp. Speaking and listening, then, ought to reveal something fundamental about the mind and how it deals with perceptions, feelings and intentions. Speaking and listening, however, are more than that. They are the tools people use in more global activities. (Clark & Clark, *Psychology and Language*, 1977)

Relations between Linguistics and Psychology

There are really three phases that should be identified in the modern relationship between the formal study of language, on the one hand, and the investigation of psychological processes, on the other. The first phase lasted approximately from the middle of the nineteenth century to the early twentieth century, the second from that point to the onset of the work of Chomsky in the fifties, and the third is the phase of investigation inspired in one way or another by Chomsky's innovations.

The First Phase of Investigation

In the last part of the nineteenth century the general focus on language was rather different from what it is now, being a focus on the historical (*diachronic*) rather than the current (*synchronic*) dimension. What engaged nineteenth century scholars was not so much how individuals communicate through language but, rather, how languages originated and by what historical processes they have developed. The pivotal figure in the history of the *psychology* of language, however, was Wilhelm Wundt who, in the tradition of von Humboldt, was more interested in questions of the relation between language and consciousness than he was in how language evolved or how different languages compared with each other. Wundt was especially concerned with *apperception*, a term he used to refer to the span of focussed consciousness as humans attend to the world around them. Apperception was to be contrasted with *perception* in that the former referred to the *inner* world of the mind in which *associations* are built up which have a direct affect on cognitive experience whereas the latter referred to processes dominated by *outer* events (Blumenthal, 1970). Wundt argued that the associative mind had a life of its own, a life which could only be explained in terms of the atomic structures of thought. And this line of argument, not surprisingly, led him to be interested in language and, in particular, how language is stored in the mind and how it thereby plays an central role in the structuring of conscious experience.

Introspections and associations

Wundt relied in his psychological experiments on the now totally outmoded method of *introspection*. He trained his subjects in an attempt to make them rigorous in the analysis of their own sensations, reactions, and linguistic associations as the basis for understanding their mental structure. Despite the doubts raised about the reliability of this kind of approach, there were several ideas generated in Wundt's laboratory that remain interesting to us today. In particular, his idea of sentences as *holistic apperceptions*, and not merely as sums of associations, is a productive one, and it is an idea that bears close similarity to the ideas about language espoused within a more recent psychological model of "simultaneous vs. successive processing" (Das et al., 1979). Wundt expressed this idea as follows:

> The sentence...is not an image running with precision through consciousness where each single word or single sound appears only momentarily while the preceding and following elements are lost from consciousness. Rather, it stands as a whole at the cognitive level while it is being spoken.
> ....From a psychological point of view, the sentence is both a simultaneous and a sequential structure. It is simultaneous because at each moment it is present in consciousness as a totality even though individual subordinate elements may occasionally disappear from it. It is sequential because the configuration changes from moment to moment in its cognitive condition as individual constitutes move into the focus of attention and out again one after the other. The claim that the sentence is a 'chain of word concepts' is as psychologically untenable as that it is merely a 'chain of words.' On the contrary, it is the dissection of a totality present as a whole in consciousness. (Wundt, 1912, quoted in Blumenthal, 1970, pp. 21-22)

It was not Wundt's theory of holistic apperception and language, however, which most greatly influenced those who followed him. It was, rather, his reliance on the empirical method and his use of the data of subjective verbal associations which led directly into the dominance of Behaviorism in the analysis of language during the second phase.

Despite the fact that Wundt is generally referred to as "the father of psycholinguistics," it seems that he was actually pre-dated by the work of the British psychologist, Francis Galton both in the search for associations and in the introspective method by which they were sought. In 1880, Galton published the results of an experiment in which he had simply written seventy-five words on slips of paper, kept them for a few days, and then recorded the connections of ideas that they stimulated when he looked at them again. He recorded the ideas and classified them into three groups:

visual or other imagery of past events; the emotionally-involved reenactment of events or attitudes; and verbal ideas, including names, sentences and quotations. The proportions of responses in each of the three categories were, respectively, 33, 22, and 45 per cent, and he wrote in the journal, *Brain*, that

> It would be very instructive to print the actual records at length, made by many experimenters, if the records could be clubbed together and thrown into a statistical form; but it would be too absurd to print one's own singly. They lay bare the foundations of a man's (sic) thoughts with curious distinctness and exhibit his mental anatomy with more vividness and truth than he himself would probably care to publish to the world. (1880, p. 162)

Marbe's Law

In 1901, two experimenters, Thumb and Marbe, reported a study in which they had elaborated upon Galton's ideas by exploring the structures of the verbal responses of a group of subjects to specific and organized linguistic stimuli. Thumb and Marbe read out ten family relation terms ("father," "sister," and so on), ten adjectives, ten pronouns, ten adverbials of place, and ten adverbials of time to their subjects whose responses were noted, together with the time of delay between stimulus and response. The experimenters found that the responses, while not identical between subjects except for a few pairs such as "brother-sister" and "father-son," clearly reflected a propensity to respond in certain word classes: Kinship terms were met with kinship terms, nouns were followed by nouns and adjectives were followed by adjectives. Some paired associates (i.e. pairings of stimulus word and subject response word) occurred more frequently than others, and in classical behaviorist manner this was interpreted to mean that subjects responded in terms of the *habit-strength* of the bondings they formed between stimulus and responses words. Thumb and Marbe went even further to establish what became known in psychology as "Marbe's Law" by showing that frequency of subjects' responses bore a direct relation to their response times; the more frequently occurring response items (eg. "sister" to "brother") were also the subjects' *fastest* responses, while the least frequent responses were the slowest. All of this established a bedrock of research into stimulus-response association and, of course, strengthened the credibility in general of the growing idea that language behavior was largely a matter of empirical learning centered on habit-formation. Many other studies were conducted along the same lines in the same era which further intensified the growing faith in measurement of verbal association and habit strength in one form or another as the key to scientific knowledge about language behavior and, indeed, about how language behavior supposedly varied across cultures (for a succinct review of these many studies, see Hörmann, 1979, Chapter 6).

The Second Phase of Investigation

Behaviorism

The second phase of work on the psychology of language, the era of Behaviorism, reached its climax in the work of B.F. Skinner. The behaviorist approach to the description of language was crystallized in Skinner's book *Verbal Behavior* (1957). Building on the half-century of work on behaviorist principles, including the work of Pavlov and many others on animal learning and behavior, Skinner developed a theory of language behavior predicated on the triad of *stimulus*, *response*, and *reinforcement*. In Skinner's analysis, all that should be considered in attempting to explain language interactions are the audible events. In the context of Skinnerian Behaviorism, there was no reason--indeed, it would be a serious mistake--to speak of "thoughts" or "ideas" "in the mind" behind or beyond the words uttered themselves. All language behavior in this analysis, then, is seen to be no more and no less than the interplay of stimulus conditions and the sound-utterances they give rise to, or "cause."

Skinner outlined two major types of responses. The first, called *mands*, (from com*mand*, de*mand*, and so on) were a class of response occurring in certain stimulus conditions which involved directing action in others. Mands are "elicited responses" which apparently occur spontaneously but which, in fact, according to Skinner, are inseparable from the stimulus conditions in which they occur. *Tacts* (from con*tact*), the second type, were viewed as "emitted responses" or "operants," and these were of special interest to Skinner since, just like the pecking of a pigeon or the routines of a circus animal, they could be brought under control through deliberate conditioning. Tacts were direct verbal responses to stimuli: A person responding "Delicious!" to his host's red wine would be, according to Skinner, "tacting," and this response will then typically be *reinforced* (or otherwise) by the further positive or negative responses of those present in the immediate environment. With some reason, Skinner believed that verbal behavior, particularly that of children, just like the behavior of intelligent animals, could be *shaped* by the deliberate manipulation of levels of positive reinforcement (verbal approval, confirmation, and so on). While there is reason to believe in some very limited contexts (including, perhaps, that of trying to establish communicative interaction with severely language-delayed or autistic children) that language behavior can in some ways be shaped in this manner, and while a few experiments, such as those of Verplank (1955) and Greenspoon (1955) did show that the responses of college students can to some extent be modified by the amount of approval they are given, Skinner's theory simply failed to account for language behavior *as a whole* and the theory met with a somewhat ignominious defeat at the hands of Chomsky (1959) (see also, Chapter Five).

The Third Phase of Investigation

Chomsky's rejection of Behaviorism

The third phase begins with the fall of Behaviorism, the re-emergence of Rationalism as opposed to Empiricism in language theory in the work of Chomsky, and the rise of Cognitivism as the dominant mode in psychology. In his review of Skinner's book (cited at the beginning of Chapter Five, above), Chomsky undermined any attempt to explain language on behaviorist foundations. He ridiculed the idea that responses were always under the direct control of stimuli and that a response, say, to the image of a red chair, could possibly be predicted: One person's response might be "red," while another's might be "chair," while those of others might be "how much?" "ghastly!" or "what's *that* doing there?" If all these (and myriad other) responses are possible from the same stimulus, how could unique stimulus-response bonds ever be established? It turns out, indeed, that any analyst in the Skinnerian mode finds she must actually deduce what a stimulus might be *from* the response given, thus leading to vicious circularity. In this way, the so-called stimulus to the response "ghastly" would be constructed as some situation in which the chair violated the aesthetic expectations of an individual, while the response "red" would have a quite different set of stimulus conditions. A second line of attack concerned the lack of apparent explanatory power in Skinner's theory. Chomsky accused Skinner in his use of *apparently* scientific terms such as stimulus and response of creating the mere "illusion of a rigorous scientific theory with a very broad scope" (Chomsky, 1959, p. 30). As the above illustrations demonstrate, Skinner's behaviorist account of language was simply too limited to account for the complexity of communicative interaction. Indeed, it was inadequate even to explain the basic knowledge that a speaker of a language has about the relations among elements in utterances. The realization of this kind of inadequacy led into the third phase of thinking about the psychology of language, the phase of modern psycholinguistics.

The field of psycholinguistics

From the behaviorist perspective, all human action, including those actions which go to make up linguistic performance, are understood to be habit-driven. In terms of utterances, this meant that the behaviorists essentially saw sentences as *habit-chains*; that is, as sequences of linguistic units bonded together by their probabilities of co-occurrence just like strings of paired associates. According to the behaviorist analysis, then, if I utter the sentence "The Penguins are going to win the Stanley Cup," then, I speak it as the result of certain social stimulus conditions which trigger certain "habits" of expression (even though I have never actually stated this before and I really think, to the contrary, that the Calgary Flames are going to do it).

Second, the word *penguins* is claimed to follow *the* and the word *win* follows the word *to* and every other item follows every other item according, once again, to the strength of the habitual bonds between them, the strength of which is supposedly predictable in terms of their frequency of occurrence.

Linear vs. hierarchical processing

Some time before Chomsky's rebuttal of the behaviorist view of things Lashley (1951) had already indicated some of the severe limitations of any account of language processing which denied *internal* planning on the part of the language user and which viewed sentences as strict linear events in which individual words related exclusively to their sequential precursors and were predictable in terms of habit strength. Lashley argued that there were several types of evidence that we are in fact constantly planning things in advance during speech, and that we are evidently able to see well beyond the scope of a word and its *immediate* linear partners in a string of elements. If this is so, of course, it provides counter-evidence against Behaviorism both at the particular level of demonstrating that the view of sentences as habit-chains is untenable and, at a more general level, by demonstrating that mental processing (or "mind") is a constant mediator in language use, and that language behavior cannot possibly be just the result of stimulus-response conditions and empirical learning. A first type of evidence for this comes, then, from the fact that in sentences such as *Are the bishop and the actor on good terms?* the correct use of *are* could be possible only if the speaker had already planned the entire sentence and had realized the need for *number agreement* in the verb form *prior* to articulating the two noun-phrases (*the bishop* and *the actor*). Under a Skinnerian analysis in which sentences were understood to take place in strict left-to-right order, it is difficult to see how such types of agreement could take place.

A second type of evidence comes from the kinds of errors people typically make during language performance. Noting some of his own typing errors, Lashley (1951) gave the example of typing *wrapid writing* (for *rapid writing*) to illustrate a large class of errors involving the articulation of elements *prior* to their proper position in expressions illustrating, once again-

-albeit through mistakes--our propensity for looking ahead to later language material in the midst of expression (Lashley, 1951, reprinted in Blumenthal, 1970, pp. 183-193). These kinds of errors also occur during speech in spoonerisms (*Our queer old dean* for *Our dear old queen*, and so on) and, as Lashley pointed out with a now well-used example, they also occur during the comprehension of speech. His example was the sentence *Rapid righting with his uninjured hand saved from loss the contents of the capsized canoe*, in which it will be noticed that, from the hearer's point of view, *righting* is homophonous with the far more frequently-occurring *writing*. As Lashley pointed out, the intended interpretation of the word (i.e. the correct choice from the homophones) had to wait until the end of the sentence (where *canoe* provides the key). In this way, the utterance has to be kept in memory for a significant time and the hearer must also then be able to skip back over the intervening material in order to "insert" the correct meaning. None of these activities were permitted within the strict left-to-right constraints of Behaviorism (1951, ibid).

Generativity and productivity

An even more famous sentence than Lashley's "canoe" sentence, was Chomsky's *Colorless green ideas sleep furiously*. In addition to his use of this sentence in arguments about syntax (see Chapter Five), Chomsky also used this sentence to illustrate several points about language that were in direct conflict with the behaviorist account of processing. First, it is an expression that is unlikely to have been uttered before Chomsky thought it up and therefore cannot be the result of conditioned learning through past communicative encounters. Second, the fact that it is grammatical (although meaningless), and that speakers can judge it as being grammatical, means that speakers of a language such as English must have much more going for them than mere sets of habits: They share knowledge about the *underlying structure of their language*. The kinds of arguments that Lashley, Chomsky, and others put forward in the fifties and sixties, then, laid the basis for the fusion of the formal study of language on the one hand, and the investigation of cognitive psychological processing on the other. In short, the rejection of

Behaviorism came with the establishment of a paradigm shift to a completely different set of assumptions about language processing. First, language-users were now assumed to be conscious, active, and creative processors who share with others a fundamental knowledge of the rules of their language and whose language behaviors are not simply determined by their prior learning and experiences: language-users, in other words, were now believed to exercise choices and to make plans during communication and to have as much potential for changing conditions through language as for being changed by them. Second, language processing could not be understood to be merely *linear* in nature. The fact that speakers, as the above examples show, must mentally "leap around" their expressions in order to make things agree with each other and in order to conduct the occasional necessary disambiguations (eg. *righting* vs. *writing*) means that processing is at least partly *hierarchical* in nature. The hierarchical units of information used in syntactic processing were, of course, neatly expressed in Chomskyan grammars (units such as noun-phrases, verb-phrases, and so on; see Chapter Five), and here grammatical theory fit very well with parallel work in cognitive psychology, in which the term *chunks* was used to describe such hierarachically-ordered units of knowledge in language and perception more generally (Miller, 1956).

It was with the overthrow of Behaviorism and the growing alliance of linguistics with cognitive psychology that the birth of modern psycholinguistics took place. Shortly after the birth of the field, however, theorists and researchers realized the need to deal with a difficult foundational problem, namely, the question of whether linguistic units correspond in any precise way with psychological units.

The question of the psychological reality of linguistic descriptions

As we have seen (see Chapter Five), Chomsky (1957, 1965) viewed the grammar of a language as being much more than a mere exhaustive classification or description of linguistic items. He conceived of grammar as nothing less than an explanatory theory of a universal human phenomenon, namely, that of language learning on the basis of a set of universal grammatical rules. A grammar was to describe the *competence*, or internal knowledge, of a group of speakers. Although the issue of the reality of linguistic units had been debated for some time before Chomsky, the development of the notion of a grammar as an explanatory theory of language raised the question to a new level of significance. Traditional linguists had analyzed English and other languages into their levels of phonemic, morphemic, and syntactic units, sometimes without much concern for whether these units were the ones actually known, intuitively or otherwise, by normal speakers. In the nineteen-sixties the time had come to put the question of psychological reality to the test.

If transformational grammars were truly direct representations of speaker knowledge, then it was quite reasonable to suppose from a psychological point of view that more complex transformations would take longer to process than less complex ones. It will be recalled that the major components of standard transformational grammars were, first the *base*--the combination of the phrase structure rules and the lexicon, second, the transformations on the output from the base and, third, the morphophonemic rules which provided the instructions for realizing morphemes in their correct phonological and phonetic form and which brought sentences to the form of "surface" utterances. Viewed as a series of processes in which speakers engaged, it initially seemed quite reasonable to predict that the formation of sentences which involved transformations such as *passive*, *negation*, and *question* would take subjects longer than simple active statements in which the syntactic order established by the phrase structure rules need little or no transformational change before reaching the surface. The hypothesis that the psychological complexity of utterances could be measured by the number of grammatical rules used in processing was called the *derivational theory of complexity* (DTC) (Fodor, Bever & Garrett, 1974).

The derivational theory of complexity

One typical early investigation into the relations between transformational grammar and mental processing was the experiment conducted by Miller, McKean, and Slobin (reported in Miller, 1962). The researchers presented their subjects with two columns of written sentences. In one column, subjects would find a *kernel* sentence (i.e. a sentence in simple active form similar to how it would appear in the base of a grammar before being transformed in some way), and somewhere in the other column there would appear a transformed version of the sentence. In one column, for example, might appear the kernel sentence *Jane liked the old woman*, while in the other column there was the sentence *The old woman wasn't liked by Jane*, a sentence involving both passive and negative transformation on the original. The task of the subjects was to match sentences to each other, and the experimenters exhaustively measured the time it took for them to find related pairs of a) kernel sentences and their passive transforms b) kernels and negatives c) kernels and related negative-passives d) negatives and passives e) negatives and negative passives f) passives and negative passives. Predictions were that the pairings involving only one transformational operation (i.e. a, b, d, above) would as a group take less time than those involving two transformations (all the others). The findings were consistent with the predictions, appearing to lend support to a psycholinguistic model in which grammatical and psychological complexity were isomorphic.

In 1964, Miller and McKean conducted another version of the experiment using tachistoscopic presentation. Here, sentences were flashed to the subjects and they were required to perform given transformations-- *negative, negative-passive*, and so on. On completing the transformations in their heads, subjects pressed a button to reveal a search list from which to select the answer. This method revealed the same kind of results. Subjects' processing times matched the complexity of the transformations required by the experimenters. The data seemed to suggest, further, that complexity could be measured by simple addition; the time taken to process two transformations (*negative* and *passive*) was nearly equivalent to the addition of the times to process each transformation individually (negative plus passive), an apparently strong indication that psychological and grammatical "distance" were one and the same thing.

While these and other experiments (e.g. Gough, 1966; Savin and Perchonok, 1965) in one way or another all confirmed the derivational theory of complexity, however, later experiments began to undermine it. When

Bever, Fodor, Garrett, and Mehler (1966; reported in Fodor, Bever & Garrett, 1974) required subjects to determine which of a series of tones that they heard just before a sentence was presented was the same as a tone presented immediately after the sentence, they found no differences in the times taken to complete the task when the sentences were varied for transformational complexity. According to the derivational theory of complexity, subjects should have taken longer to make decisions about the tones when they processed intervening sentences such as *John phoned the girl up* (vs. *John phoned up the girl*) and such as *The bus driver was fired after the wreck* (vs. *The bus driver was nervous after the wreck*) since the first type requires a transformation moving the particle (*up* of *phone up*) and the second requires passivization following the deep-structural form "X fired the driver..." (reported in Fodor, Bever, & Garrett, 1974). Fodor and Garrett (1967) further found that the addition of adjectives to sentences did not bring corresponding increases in complexity as measured by subjects' processing times. This was especially damaging to the derivational theory of complexity since, in standard transformational grammar, each adjective in a sentence required transformational derivation through the complex process of *relativization*: In this way, the sentence *The pompous general returned from the bloody fight in the barren desert* should involve the presumably time-consuming combining of a string of elements in deep structure that would look something like the following; *The general--the general was pompous--return from the fight--the fight was bloody--in the desert--the desert was barren.*

In addition to the gradual accumulation of unsupportive findings, it became clear in the late sixties and the seventies that any attempts to establish any *direct, one-to-one*, or *isomorphic* links between transformational grammars and mental processing were doomed to failure on other more commonsensical grounds. Fodor, Bever, and Garrett (1974) argued, for instance that it was just as reasonable to propose that complex sentences involving many transformations might take longer to process due not to transformational complexity per se, but to the fact that the transformations typically destroy the clarity of the basic kernel-sentence forms, simply making them more obscure and less logically clear. It was, after all, the case that transformational grammar made maximal use of such kernel sentences as the starting points for analysis solely because they were simple. They argued, therefore, that any apparent evidence for the derivational theory of complexity such as that provided by the early experimenters was spurious: There was no more reason to believe subjects' longer processing times had been due to transformational complexity than to the obscuring of clear meaning.

Finally, Fodor and Garrett (1967) had demonstrated that certain types of sentences are clearly *easier* than their counterparts, even though they are transformationally more complex. An example of such a pair of sentences might be *The first shot the tired soldier the mosquito bit fired missed* vs. *The first shot fired by the tired soldier bitten by the mosquito missed* (reported in Fodor, Bever, and Garrett, 1974). It is quite clear that the addition of the passive transformation in the second version (*bitten by the mosquito...*) makes the sentence easier to process and to understand. For all these and other reasons, there was overwhelming evidence by the mid-seventies that neither grammarians nor psychologists could hope to establish any simple one-to-one correspondence between transformational-grammatical and mental processes. This leaves open the intriguing question of precisely how language users *do* conform to grammatical regulations--as they certainly for the most part do. The rejection of the derivational theory of complexity strongly suggests that the kind of relationship between speakers and Chomskyan grammars is a very indirect one. The "output" of a speaker and a grammar may be largely consistent, but the processes by which each yields grammatical sentences appear to be different.

Psychologically realistic grammar

An important step in the debate about the nature of grammars was initiated by Bresnan (1978, 1982), who argued that it *was* possible to write psychologically "realistic" grammars *if* Chomsky's limited notion of language competence was replaced by greater recognition of what actually goes on in language use as the basis for the construction of grammatical categories. The key problem with the derivational theory of complexity lay, of course, in demonstrating that the *transformational* process had any psychological reality, and so Bresnan and others developed the alternative grammar, known as *Lexical-Functional Grammar* (see also Chapter Five), which abandoned the complexities of transformational rules in favor of more complexity at the *lexical* level. In standard TGG, relations between elements in sentences--elements such as subject and object noun-phrases or between particles, verbs, and object nouns--were defined and understood in terms of the transformational relations between individual sets of sentences predicated on one simple active kernel. In Lexical-Functional Grammar, it was claimed that all this essential information about the relations between syntactic elements was stored not in some specialized mental component devoted to transformations but, rather, in the same place as the meaningful content of language was stored; with words, in what has often been called the "mental lexicon." This lexical encoding, it was argued, was much more intuitively realistic in terms of language processing than any transformational mechanism. Bresnan's grammar still contains a distinction between "deep" and "surface" structure, but now the deep structure contains *logical* information which leads to the correct arrangement of things at the surface. If we take the sentence *The tanker dumped the oil*, then, it is Bresnan's claim that the psychologically-real underlying form of the verb will include information about the semantic and syntactic frames in which it could occur. Thus the form would be something like *DUMP: verb; subject is an agent* (i.e. one who performs the action); *object is a patient* (i.e. one who receives the action)." Another lexical entry would exist in the grammar for the verb *dumped* as it appears in the passive version of the same sentence; *The oil was dumped by the tanker."* Here the lexical entry would be something like *DUMPED: object is an agent: subject is a patient.* Similar types of entry would exist for all items.

The crucial difference between this arrangement and that in traditional transformational grammars is that, in keeping with what realistically goes on in everyday communication (and with the later findings concerning the Derivational Theory of Complexity, see above), we should not expect passive expressions necessarily to take any longer than active expressions. In Bresnan's formulation, the surface structural distribution and the relations between elements is known immediately, the lexical item in question has been traced in memory. As speakers of English, we know immediately, for instance, that the verb *dump* requires certain support around it in order for it to make any sense; it must have a subject (clearly identified or implied) and something must actually be dumped (an *intransitive* realization of the verb is extremely unlikely--*President Bush dumped...* requires *Quayle* as object). We also, of course, know many other things about any such verb in English; *dump* can be used with both *animate* and *inanimate* and both *human* and *non-human* objects (although it requires an animate human or non-human subject). A central point to realize here is that *just from this knowledge alone* (and certainly without the cumbersome processes of transformations): We can immediately construct syntactic distribution in surface structure--the information we have retrieved from memory about *dump*, for example, brings with it the whole frame of syntactic elements in which it exists in its active or passive realizations. Second, this is a far more psychologically-realistic way of describing things than are the theoretical alternatives. Functional-lexical grammar puts words, morphemes, and lexical meaning right at the center of language processing, making syntactic structure *subordinate* to meaning, an arrangement which makes some of the negative findings in relation to the derivational theory of complexity more readily understandable. The above account of Bresnan's innovations is, of course, somewhat simplified and has been included to establish a central controversy about psychological reality and linguistic description. More detailed accounts of the theory appear in Bresnan, 1982; Sells, 1985; Horrocks, 1987).

The controversy over the psychological reality has been dealt with at some length here since it has been and will continue to be truly foundational in the field of psycholinguistics. In the rest of the chapter, however, we will turn from foundational issues to some of the major experimental findings about language processing at the levels of comprehension, speech, reading, and writing.

Major Experimental Findings

Comprehension

The mental lexicon

One important area of investigation in experimental psycholinguistics has been that of how language users "store" words and morphemes and of how these elements are organized in memory. A considerable challenge faces researchers attempting to describe the structure and nature of the mental lexicon (elsewhere also referred to as the "mental dictionary," Glucksberg and Danks, 1975, or the "internal lexicon," Carroll, 1986, since it is clear that languages such as English contain many homonyms and synonyms, and that words can mean many different things in different situations. The natural variability of linguistic signs strongly suggests that any viable model of storage will contain complex possible interconnections between the lexical items in mental storage, complex in that the items are stored not only with their simple dictionary-level definitions, but also with information about their *extended* or *associated* meanings.

Katz and Fodor (1963), working within a theoretical-linguistic orientation, argued that lexical items must be organized *hierarchically* and in terms of distinctive features. This means that items are integrally linked to others in terms of the features they share or do not share. In this analysis, the item *animal*, for example, is organized within the kind of tree-structure typically found in a biology textbook where the category *living things* is broken down into *Animals* vs. *Plants* and where *Animals* further branches out into *Mammals* vs. *Non-mammals*, and so on. At the time, this model, which reflected the parallel analyses in phonology and, as we have seen, in syntax, was very influential (see Chapters Two and Five).

Questions soon arose, however, about the *psychological* viability of description by way of hierarchical distinctive-feature systems, and several crucial problems were identified with this approach in relation to the explanation of mental processes. First, there is the problem of the categories chosen as the nodes within the tree-diagrams: Is there any good reason, for instance, to select the features *Feline* vs. *Canine* instead of *Domestic* vs *Wild* in the organization of descriptions of animals in the system? It seems that for one purpose the former, while for another, the latter choice of terms might be preferable. In any case, it is clear from a psychological perspective that *both* organizations would have to co-exist in some way and that *different* modes of lexical organization may well be triggered by different contexts and communicative situations. Second, having chosen the features, how can the theorist justify their particular hierarchical ordering in relation to each other? In some semantic tree describing "occupations," for example, would it be best to choose gender (i.e. *Male* vs. *Female*) as a superordinate category over *Profession* or vice versa? Such choices as these clearly have considerable impact on the resulting form of tree-structure but, once again, appear to have no well-motivated basis. One danger from this, of course, is that the structure may well turn out to be an artefact of the theorist's own imagination and not a viable description of *general* properties of semantic processes at all. The Katz and Fodor analysis, then, while providing a valuable alternative model to that of an everyday dictionary, failed to capture the complexity and variability of mental associations referred to earlier.

Associative meaning

What, more precisely, were the elements that were missing from a linguistically-oriented account of semantic structure and which would need to be included within a psychological model? One element was clearly that of *associative* meaning, a type of meaning, as we have seen, that had fascinated psychologists from the time of Wundt. A number of psycholinguists, including Trier (1934), Porzig (1934), Bousfield (1953) and Jenkins and Russell (1952) became especially interested in the *fields* of associations apparently built up in the mind, where fields were understood to be conglomerations of stored associations having their own internal dynamics. An illustrative study was that by Deese (1962) in which he attempted to define the precise structures of such mental semantic fields.

Deese's attempt to explain the structure of these semantic fields more precisely relied on the idea that the meaning of a word-stimulus could be understood as the sum total of associative responses to that stimulus. If two words yield identical responses, then they would by this definition have the same meaning and "two stimuli overlap or resemble one another in associative meaning to the extent that they have the same distribution of associates" (1962, p. 163). In his experiments, Deese presented his subjects with sets of stimulus words that had already been established to have associative links with or to be in the same semantic field as each other. One such set included the words *moth, insect, wings, bird*, and so on, which had been found to be associative responses to the word *butterfly* by Kent and Rosanoff. Subjects were required to give responses to each of the stimuli and then the frequency of occurrence of these responses was calculated. In particular, Deese was able to calculate the overlap of meaning shared by the items by observing, for instance, how many times the word *fly* occurred in responses to both *moth* and *insect*, and in terms of how many times they occurred as responses to each other. In this way, Deese built up a large matrix comprised by what he called "coefficients of similarities" between the stimulus words in the field. Finally, he subjected the matrix of coefficients to a *factor analysis*, a statistical analysis which finds out how everything is intercorrelated in the data. Looking at the four mathematically-derived factors that emerged from the data, Deese argued that one of them represented "animal creation" (including words such as *moth, wing, insect, bird*), another one represented inanimate objects (*yellow, flower*, etc.), another one represented animate items (including *wing, fly, bird*), and the fourth, another group of inanimate terms arranged in a bipolar manner. In this way, Deese gave the notion of semantic field some objective rigor and any word within a field could supposedly be given a precise measured profile in relation to other items.

Deese had demonstrated that the ways in which words are used to refer to things (i.e. their *denotative* meanings) were connected with the ways in which they relate to each other (i.e. in their *associative* meaning). A further aspect of how words might be related to each in the mental lexicon was explored by Osgood, Suci, and Tannenbaum (1957), who looked at the relations between words and *feelings*, at what is known as *connotative meaning*. In order to find out how their subjects felt about various words, Osgood et al. asked them to respond to words on a *semantic differential scale*. This technique, still used by marketing researchers, involves asking respondents to judge where a given word falls on a number of bipolar scales comprised, at each end, by two adjectives. Examples of such scales are *happy........sad, strong.......weak, cold.........hot, slow.......fast*, which might used for the analysis of, say, the word *music*, and subjects responded by filling in their feelings about music in terms of the scales provided: They might, for instance, rate music as being "sad, strong, cold, and fast." Using factor analysis, these researchers claimed they could reduce connotative meaning to three underlying scales--*good vs. bad, active vs. passive*, and *strong vs. weak*, dimensions that they called *Evaluation, Activity*, and *Potency*. One of the major problems with the analysis, however, is that the dimensions that serve as input into the analysis are pre-constructed and are not therefore free from the subjectivity of the experimenters themselves. Despite this limitation, the semantic differential technique did much to establish that emotional responses and the associative interconnections between words due to them would have to be taken into any complete account of meaning in the mental lexicon.

Computer-based psycholinguistic models

This linguistically-inspired view of the mental lexicon led to the work of Collins and Quillian (1972), who combined the idea of the hierarchical organization of distinctive features with knowledge about computer memory in order to create a testable psychological model. In their model, the words in the mental lexicon are connected to each other by two kinds of "pointers." One kind of pointer represents *property relations* between elements; *dachshund* would be marked as a member of the class *dog*, and *dog* a member of the class *animal* and so on. In this analysis, the sentence *A dog is an animal* was called a *superset sentence*, since it defines a set-member in terms of a set name higher than itself. Sentences such as *A dachshund has small legs* would be called a *property sentence*. On the basis of computer program design, where replication of information is avoided at all costs, Collins and Quillian constructed the pathways in the model on the basis that no information would be stored in any one location. In this way, properties common to all dogs (for example, that they have legs, tails, and that they bark) would be stored only with the category name *dog* and not repeated at the hierarchically lower node *dachshund*. What follows from this way of arranging things is that economy of information storage is wrought at the expense of time taken to process that information, since it means that processing the word *dachshund*, for instance, will involve travelling up the hierarchical network to find information stored with *dog*. Collins and Quillian constructed experiments founded on an entailment of all of this, namely, that the time needed for a subject to decide whether or not a given sentence was true should be a direct function of the number of paths travelled in finding the relevant information. The sentence *A dog is a dog* should be verifiable very quickly, since it does not require any "travelling" about the network, while *A dachshund is a dog* should involve one path and *A dachshund is an animal* should involve two. The experimenters found that subjects did indeed take longer to verify statements in proportion to the number of paths taken in hierarchical processing. Later researchers, however, forced amendments to the hierarchical processing model, by demonstrating that humans do *not* process the internal lexicon in exactly the same way as a computer, and that we appear to store at least some information at several locations on the basis of whether it is useful and on the basis of whether it helps in the *speed* of processing, rather than on the strict basis of economy of storage (Conrad, 1972).

While the idea that the lexicon involves hierarchical storage remains a powerful one, many problems have emerged with hierarchical distinctive-feature analysis, suggesting that, at the very least, hierarchical analysis of the mental lexicon needs to be supplemented by other forms of analysis.

Lexical items in context

All the previous models of lexical processing were founded on words taken out of context. More recently, it has been realized that much of what words mean depends upon the circumstances in which they are uttered and comprehended. One clear finding has been that when subjects are asked to access particular words provision of the correct context makes the task easier (Stanovich and West, 1983), and the effect of context is even greater on difficult low-frequency words than it is on familiar high-frequency ones (Stanovich and West, 1981). In a study of subjects' processing of ambiguous words, Swinney and Hakes (1976) found that they could provide contexts which helped the subjects to disambiguate words easily. In order to provide a disambiguating context for the word *bug*, for example, they wrote the following short passage containing a number of other verbal clues leading to one particular interpretation:

> Rumor had it that, for years, the government building has been plagued with problems. The man was not surprised when he found spiders, roaches, and other bugs in the corner of his room. (quoted in Carroll, 1987, p. 169)

In another parallel passage and using similar means, Swinney and Hakes biased the context towards the *electronic* meaning of *bug*. They found in all cases that words that were disambiguated by context in this manner took the same amount of time to process as normal unambiguous words thus demonstrating, once again, that retrieval from the mental lexicon is significantly affected by surrounding circumstances and cannot be treated as just some disembodied or machine-like process. Psychologists have often referred to parts of processing which derive from the higher level of context *top-down* processes, while those processes which derive from the lower level of words themselves (or sub-parts of words including phonemes and morphemes) *bottom-up* processes. While the earlier experiments, then, can be said to have concentrated only on bottom-up processing, these later findings concerning context strongly suggest that the processing of words involves *both* top-down *and* bottom-up processing, a characteristic which may well be true of language processing taken as a whole. This idea underlies many processing models developed throughout the eighties and still being developed in the nineties.

Remembering sentences and text

No one familiar with research into memory for sentences could continue to believe, if they ever did so, that individuals store and recall exactly what they hear. Far from having passive "slates" onto which is inscribed every detail of the language we hear, it appears that we are active at every stage of the process: What we hear is actively filtered and generally altered in some way both as we record it in and as we retrieve it from memory. Once again, these facts about memory appear to dispel the behaviorist myth that there is no *mediation* between input and output, and they also suggest that human modes of processing are quite different from those of machines (such as computers), which tend to record things far more accurately.

Memory for gist:

Inspired by Chomksy's distinction between deep and surface structure, Sachs (1967) conducted an experiment to see how her subjects would remember some target sentences that she embedded in longer pieces of text. In a passage about the invention of the telescope by Lippershey, for instance, she targeted the sentence *He sent a letter about it to Galileo, the great Italian scientist*. Sachs also wrote three other versions of this target sentence to add to the original one for a total of four from which the subjects were to choose what they thought was the sentence they had heard when they listened to a recording of the passage. The three additional sentences were, first, a passive version, *A letter about it was sent to Galileo, the great Italian scientist*, second, a formal transformation, *He sent Galileo, the great Italian scientist, a letter about it* and, third, a version which actually changed the meaning of the sentence, *Galileo, the great Italian scientist, sent him a letter about it*. Now if subjects remembered the passage verbatim, they would clearly choose the correct sentence; that is, the sentence in the exact surface-structural form that it was found in the original text. If, on the other hand, they did not record or remember this exact surface form but, rather, processed for the meaning or *gist* of the passage, then they would be about as likely to remember any of the other sentences in the set which were mere transforms of the target sentence (and which, therefore, shared its deep structure) as they were the original. By the same token, however, the subjects should, of course, not choose the sentence that contained altered meaning, since they would find this inaccurate and anomalous in terms of the information they had heard. Sachs found this to be the case: Subjects confused the three sentences that bore transformational relations to each other, while correctly rejecting the semantically inaccurate version. The effect became even more clear as Sachs increased the delay between presentation of her passages and the time of subjects' recall. The experiment neatly captures the idea that for most of the time, individuals listen for the gist of what they hear rather than attempting to record all the detailed phonemes, morphemes, and prosodic features in the input. Of course, there may be individual differences in how much detail is remembered, and there are certainly times, such as those when telephone numbers or names have to be remembered, when we switch modes to some extent and make a deliberate attempt to record things in detail. In general, though, and in most communicative circumstances, it appears that we quickly discard surface structural details in favour of semantic content.

Propositional processing:

Other researchers have proposed that we concentrate on remembering essential *propositions* in text. Kintsch (1974), in particular, has argued that discourse is stored in propositional form, where propositions consist of a predicate and one or more, and where information is included about how propositions relate to each other in hierarchical structure. Meyer (1975) also proposed that text was stored in terms of hierarchically-ordered sets of propositions. Both of these models were important in that they yielded precise descriptions of the structures of texts on the basis of which the originals could be compared in detail to subjects' responses in various experiments. It was soon found that the number of propositions contained in a text correlated precisely with the length of time taken to process it (Kintsch and Keenan, 1973; Kieras, 1981), and a series of studies firmly established that higher-order propositions are recalled better than lower-level subordinate propositions (Kintsch et al., 1975; Thorndyke, 1977; Meyer, 1975; McKoon, 1977).

Constructive memory:

Another well-known experiment by Bransford and Franks (1971) adds a further crucial piece of evidence about storage and memory of sentences. Bransford and Franks devised a set of complex sentences based on the same simple propositions:

1. *The ants were in the kitchen.*
2. *The jelly was on the table.*
3. *The jelly was sweet.*
4. *The ants ate the jelly.*

The set of complex sentences was generated from this group of simple ideas so that there experimental items containing *three* ideas (e.g. "The ants in the kitchen ate the jelly which was on the table."), items containing *two* ideas (e.g. "The ants ate the sweet jelly.") and items made up of one idea (e.g. "The ants ate the jelly."). The subjects heard 24 of these sentences, interspersed in such a way that it would be difficult for them to "count" the ideas in their heads. Bransford and Franks then presented 28 test sentences to the subjects, some of which they had heard, but most of which they had not. Included in this test set were some sentences containing *four* ideas, a level of complexity not included in the original set. In keeping with their predictions, the experimenters found that subjects *thought* they had heard all the sentences. They were largely unable to distinguish between those sentences that had been originally presented and those that were in the test set, and the effect was greater the more complex the sentences: Subjects confused sentences containing three ideas more than those containing two or one. Most impressive of all was the finding that subjects were most convinced that they recognized the sentences containing *four* ideas. All of this suggests that individuals not only discard surface structure in favour of remembering ideas, as Sachs had found, but that, in addition, they perform *constructions* in memory, bringing ideas together in more complex bundles than they were in original presentation. Other experimenters have suggested, further, that when we recall information we often *add* things to it (Bregman and Strasberg, 1968), that we use all inferences available to us, and that we tend to do so in ways which fit in with our view of "normality" (Turner and Rommetveit, 1968).

Schema-theory

Many of the ideas about memory for sentences and prose taken up by later researchers actually derive, however, from the earlier work of Bartlett (1932), work in which he lay the groundwork for many of the later experimental findings and, indeed, for what has become known as "schema-theory" in the area of research into reading (see below). In his book *Remembering*, Bartlett included reports of several informal experiments he conducted within a wide-ranging discussion of the nature and consequences of constructive memory. Bartlett gave a particularly convincing demonstration of how we typically elaborate on things in memory by way of a North American Indian story he presented to some British readers. The story concerned a young Indian man returning to his village, Egulac, and relating a trip up a river where he and his companions met with some ghosts, and where he was apparently wounded. The passage ends:

> He told it all, and then he became quiet. When the sun rose he fell down. Something black came out of his mouth. His face became contorted. The people jumped up and cried. He was dead. (Bartlett, 1932, p. 65.)

In explaining the changes that readers made when they were asked to reproduce the story in their own words, Bartlett referred to processes of *sharpening, leveling,* and *rationalizing*. One subject, for example, sharpened the story to include reference to the Native having been shot with an arrow, a fact not mentioned, and added at the end that the Native "writhed and shrieked" as he died. The same subject also rationalized the passage by such additions as that the friends of the Native were "filled with terror" at his condition. The reader also leveled the text by omitting certain details that he apparently thought unimportant. Putting all these kinds of evidence together, Bartlett concluded that both listeners and readers typically approach stories with prior *schemata*--that is, with sets of *expectations*, based on their own experiences of what is likely to be included. Constructions, then, do not seem to be merely random in nature, but seem to reflect the biases of individuals who alter things in memory to normalize them to fit in with their own thoughts and *ideas*. This was a finding that provided a rich context not only for experiments on memory such as those reported above but also for further research into how the *cultural background* of individuals partly provides the substance of individual schemata: It has been found consistently that our expectations are partly based on what our culture has led us to believe happens in the world. The development of all these ideas in what is now known as *schema-theory* has had great impact on research into reading and writing (see below).

Speech

Less is known about how speech is produced than about how it is understood for the simple reason that the precise origins of the process are largely unknown. It is clear that speech involves some type of planning and that we have to some extent to know what it is we are going to say before we say it, but the details beyond this are much more difficult to decipher and a number of intriguing yet basic questions remain. Do we always know *all* of what we are going say, for instance, and does the representation of what we are about to say take on the exact shape of the utterance itself, or is it, as the psychologist Vygotsky suggested, in some kind of "inner" or "prototypical" form?

Evidence of planning: speech errors

One of the clearest indications that we do not simply generate representations of utterances and then "read them off" some kind of inner screen as we speak lies in the pervasiveness of speech *errors*. Errors can be of several types. *Shifts* involve the swapping of sounds (also called *metathesis*) as in "She's swelling sizzle sticks" for "She's selling swizzle sticks." *Exchanges* involve swapping two words or morphemes, as in "Grandpa receilinged the plaster" for "Grandpa replastered the ceiling." *Anticipations* involve bringing one or more sounds forward in the utterance (strongly suggesting that we typically look ahead at least to some extent), as in "I'm going to sow you the seashore" for "I'm going to show you the seashore." Other types include *perseverations* (repeating an earlier sound later), *additions, deletions, substitutions,* and the *blends* familiar in elementary school, such as "dreaping" and "sleeming" for *dreaming* and *sleeping* (Fromkin, 1971; Shattuck-Hufnagel, 1979; Carroll, 1986. Garrett (1975) concluded that speech errors, in general, tend to involve confusions of sounds occurring in similar environments and that, even though they are errors, they tend to conform with the phonological laws of a language. The central finding has been that, collectively, they represent *systematic* changes to the intended stream of utterance and as such suggest the presence of constant speech planning.

According to Fromkin (1971), planning utterances involves six stages: identification of meaning; selection of syntactic structure; generation of intonation contour; insertion of content words; formation of affixes and function words (i.e. addition of prefixes, suffixes, and what are sometimes called the "glue-words" of the language, such as prepositions, pronouns, and conjunctions); and specification of the phonetic shape of the utterance. In terms of a transformational-grammar, what Fromkin suggests is that we work from the deepest level of structure, the level at which the most basic elements of meaning are stored, up to the most superficial level--the level of actual sounds. Speech errors appear to support this layered model of planning since they appear to exist at specific levels and not to involve any more than one level at a time. In the examples above, for instance, "sizzle-sticks" for "swizzle-sticks" involves only the phonemic level, while "receilinged the plaster" involves only the morphological level, and so on. Fromkin also used the examples of "frish gotto" for "fish grotto" and "blake fruid" for "brake fluid" to demonstrate the autonomy of phonetic segments in planning and processing: If we did not separate out clusters such as "gr" or "fl" during processing, then they would, of course, move around as whole units in erroneous output. Garrett (1975) provided further support for the autonomy of linguistic levels and planning stages in speech by demonstrating that errors involving sounds tend to take place within the framework of adjacent words, while most word-level errors take place within clauses. Errors with morphemes or entire words only occur at the level of whole utterances, and Garrett argued that all of this supports a scheme such as Fromkin's in that word errors seem to be tied to the deepest level of processing, the formation of meaning and basic syntax, while errors with sounds appear only *after* basic syntactic units--clauses and phrases.

Combined processes in speech

An especially interesting integrated approach to speech production is taken by McNeill (1987), following the inspiration of Vygotsky (1962, 1978). According to McNeill's analysis, speech should be viewed as "linguistic acts" producing "symbols" that have the following four main characteristics: First, utterances (symbols) are affected by their contexts; second, they are in contrast to other utterances; third, they are affected by thought; fourth, they can be generated spontaneously, without specific external stimuli. McNeill claims that speech involves the simultaneous engagement of two different types of thinking. The first of these is *syntactic-linear* thinking, which involves the sequential organization of speech segments, and the second is *global-synthetic*, or *imagistic,* which involves the forming of analogical connections between things. He believes that speech comes about through the synthesis of these two forms of thought and, further, that the unraveling of speech involves the continual "unpacking" of gestures and images. He argues that during communication gestures sometimes "take over complexity" from speech, while on others the reverse is true and speech takes over complexity from gesture. The crucial point here, supported by some experimental evidence is that speech and gesture are always closely related in communication. They apparently share the same underlying expressive roots and freely support and exchange with one another during speech production. McNeill (1985) provided evidence for the interchangeability of linguistic and gestural forms during speech by using a *delayed-auditory-feedback* (DAF) technique. In his experiment, subjects heard their own voices slightly delayed (by about the length of one syllable), and he found that subjects who produced few or no gestures under normal speaking conditions yet began to gesture under the DAF condition in an apparent attempt to compensate for the linguistic simplifications forced by the intrusion of the delayed feedback. McNeill (1986) provided further evidence for the close relations between gestures and language in a study in which subjects replaced information first presented in visual and gestural form with purely linguistic forms when they were later asked to recall this information. It appears, then, that gestures may constitute a very fundamental part of speech. All of these ideas bear close relation to what Vygotsky (1986) had intended earlier when he wrote of "inner speech."

In studying hearing and comprehension it is at least clear what the nature of the input to processing is, while, as previously stated, one of the intransigent difficulties of all research on speech is that researchers cannot simply go into the mind and search for the presence of inner symbols. McNeill suggests, nonetheless, that the *indirect* evidence to support the notion of inner speech and symbolization is strong. In a videotaped narration, for example, a narrator produced a complex groping gesture at the word *finds* while articulating the phrase *and finds a big knife*. Here, then, it seems reasonable to infer that the inner symbol out of which the rest of the phrase was unpacked was *finds*. The complex gesture, which included the picking up of the knife from behind the subject, apparently contains the "intrinsic value" of the word (not completely unpacked through the syntax). Like Vygotsky, then, McNeill views *finds* as a typical example of the kind of short-form inner "predicates" that underlie speech formation. In complete contrast to the Chomskyan interpretation of deep structure, in which syntax is considered to be prime, McNeill's model suggests that such brief predicate forms of inner speech, packed with images and gestures, are prior to syntactic processing. All the mental operations that come with inner predicate forms go to make up its *sense*, and sense will be partly individualistic and context-sensitive in nature.

To summarize McNeill's model, it suggests, first, that consciousness is punctuated by inner symbols, which are the matter of thought itself. There are presumably modes of thought which do not involve translation into surface-structural form (either at the level of inner talking-to-oneself or at the full level of externalized speech), and these modes are constituted by and inseparable from inner-language predicates. These predicates themselves involve various kinds of mental activity and, in particular, the fusion of linguistic processing with imagery. An inner language predicate comprises, then, both information about grammatical relations--about whether the verb *find* for example, accepts a subject and an object and so on--and about what kind of actions, or gestures, it supports. Second, all of this information and all of the related types of mental processing are contained within this "nucleus" and out of this speakers "unravel" sentences in linear form through time. This unraveling, moreover, often gives rise to communicative expressions which involve *both* gestures and linguistic forms in a mutually supportive relationship. Language, indeed, is *itself* viewed as a form of gesture. Speech, then, is a matter of the continual renewal of these predicates in the speakers mind, influenced as they are both by situational events and by other language uttered during exchanges, followed by the continual unraveling of what is contained in the predicates through language and gesture. Although this neo-Vygotskyan model remains to be fully tested and justified, and in the absence of unequivocal scientific techniques, it provides a rich and intuitively reasonable way of thinking about speech production, together with a set of intriguing hypotheses for further exploration.

Interactive processing

One further trend in thinking about language processing is that which links *both* of the processes so far discussed, which views the processes of listening-comprehension and speech production as closely related to each other, as it does processes of reading and writing (see below). Experimental studies by Studdart-Kennedy (1987) and by Porter (1987) both support this idea in several ways. First, it appears that when we listen to a speaker we in a sense *rearticulate* the sound patterns of what is being said as part of our process of comprehension. Second, this process of rearticulation is so basic as to be automatic. Third, and most important, and what follows from the first two points, a *common code* appears to underlie both listening and speaking--a code which includes the phonetic elements utilized in both activities.

Reading

Reading, like listening and speaking, involves the integration of many different kinds of mental acts, and the history of reading theory is largely a history of debate over exactly what kinds of acts these are and how they exist in relation to each other, debate over which come first and last, and which have priority over others. Like language theory in general, reading theory went through a Behaviorist phase during which visual symbols were treated strictly as conditioned stimuli, paired with phonic entities, and in which reading took place in strict left-to-right sequential order. The objections raised by Chomsky to this kind of approach to language are also pertinent to reading, and later theorists have realized that the processing of written text involves recursive looking back and forth just as much as it does strictly linear movement. Reading, indeed, when compared to listening and speaking, affords *more* opportunity for recursive processing, due to its characteristic permanence on the page, a permanence which greatly facilitates memory and therefore the readers' abilities to move around text.

Until fairly recently, there was a tendency to view written language as merely the secondary by-product of spoken language. It was assumed that spoken forms preceded written forms both phylogenetically during the evolution of language and that they were also prior to writing in everyday language usage. But is this view justified? Isn't it possible that early drawings and cave-paintings might have actually acted as stimuli *to* vocal noises which then became gradually systematized by way of cross-reference to the visual signs? No one, of course, can settle such a dispute easily, but it seems at least a plausible suggestion that the two systems were, like speaking and listening, *interactive* with each other during the phylogenetic development of language. Certainly, written language has influenced the nature and content of spoken language by way of its aforementioned capacity to capture descriptions of events in time: One culturally-central feature of written language is that it provides a historical medium in which all sorts of records can be passed on. Unlike the oral transmission of myths, such as those told from generation to generation by the Norse and the Greeks, writing has a permanence and totality about it that is quite different. In general, written forms, unlike spoken forms, and because they are more permanent, require *more* processing than spoken forms--they involve visual (or tactile) *and* auditory processing (although some theorists argue that some readers are able to move directly from written symbols to interpretation of meaning), and they appear to involve more *conscious* types of processing; the terms *skimming* and *scanning*, for example, have been used to refer respectively to the types of reading we engage in when just looking to see what articles are contained in, say, a newspaper, and the type of more intensive reading we consciously do when we are looking for particular information.

The variety of reading models

Over the past two decades, psycholinguists have debated many particular aspects of the reading process. Even by the mid-seventies, indeed, there had been so many reading models proposed that some even questioned whether trying to establish any *one* theory of reading was a worthwhile project (Gibson & Levin, 1975). There have also been many types of models, including *information-processing* models, which view the reading process in terms of a number of sequential "boxes" leading from "input" to "output," and *analysis-by-synthesis* models, which view the formation and testing of hypotheses as the central processes in reading.

Perhaps the best-known of this latter type of model is that of Goodman (1967), who put forward the idea that reading is a "psycholinguistic guessing game." Goodman demonstrated clearly that different readers reveal different kinds of errors, or *miscues*, when they read: Good readers make errors in oral reading that show that they are always making hypotheses about the *meaning* of the text, while poor readers' miscues suggest that they are concentrating on lower-level aspects of texts, such as the sounds of words. In this way, an example of a sophisticated erroneous reading of the word *freight* might be "cargo," whereas production of "fright" or "fate," words which merely look or sound like the target word--would demonstrated less sophisticated reading since they obviously interfere more with over all comprehension. Goodman's "guessing-game" model has been influential in establishing that good readers are *active* processors of text who are constantly trying to make sense out of things by hazarding productive guesses about what authors intend. In keeping with work in other areas such as listening comprehension, some theorists have argued that the process is primarily *bottom-up*, and that it centrally depends upon skills like being able to break up strings of phonemes and morphemes (Shankweiler & Liberman, 1972), while others have argued that reading is essentially a *top-down* process proceeding from the extraction of contextual meaning (Smith, 1971). More recently, it has been realized that *both* of these types of processing must be at work during reading. The interpretation of small segments, including individual sounds and morphemes, depends in many ways on what the general context of meaning is around them, while this context of meaning, in turn, is partly built up from these small elements which combine with elements in memory and experience. Debate continues, though, on the relative importance of the two types of processes and while Swinney (1979, 1981), for example, has stressed the autonomy of lower-level processing by showing experimentally that *both meanings* of ambiguous words appear to be triggered during reading, no matter what the context. While this may be true, however, it seems that even if two meanings of ambiguous words are triggered at first, at some stage in the process the reader has to choose the relevant one, and many other theorists have concluded that top-down processing is the final arbiter of meaning. In contrast to those who have stressed the priority of either bottom-up or top-down processing, Rumelhart (1977), Perfetti, (1985) and many others, have argued that the processes are *interactive* in nature, and that both types of processes proceed *parallel* to each other in reading. According to Perfetti, reading involves at the lower level the continual encoding of basic propositions contained in the text and continual cross-referencing of these propositions with mental "models" of what the text is about. According to parallel processing models such as this, comprehension of text only comes when a *threshold* of information as achieved by way of these two approaches: it is almost as if meaning arises only when pressures are exerted from several different psychological sources at the same time.

Schema-theory and reading processes:

The term schema-theory (following Bartlett, 1932) has been used to describe a number of top-down reading models which stress the importance of various aspects of background knowledge during reading. It has been shown, for example, that our knowledge of one type of schema called scripts, which covers what we know about typical sequences of events (such as what goes on in restaurants, churches, schools, and so on) governs our expectations about what will happen in texts and, this, in turn, governs the way in which such texts are processed. Such knowledge includes understanding about how characters are motivated and about how causes and effects are related to one another (Schank & Abelson, 1977). Other researchers have concentrated on schemata about the structure of information in texts and, in particular, it has been found that reading is affected by whether or not stories conform to expected patterns. Western stories generally have a constant type of underlying structure containing a beginning, including a statement of the setting of the story, a middle in which the action is developed in fairly predictable ways, and an end where a problem or situation is resolved. Some researchers have gone so far as to suggest that children in our culture actually develop schemata conforming to what they call story grammars which then influence their story-reading (Mandler & Johnson, 1977; Stein & Glenn, 1979). Stories written according to typical and expected structures are generally processed more easily and remembered better. Cross-cultural studies testing recall for stories from different cultures (and thus associated with particular sets of expectations for subjects from particular cultural groups) have also demonstrated that when readers find the structure they most expect (i.e. that in their own culture) they process more easily and remember text better (eg. Carrell, 1983; Piper, 1985a). Instructional procedures that emphasize the importance of developing these types of schemata in young readers have been proposed by Pearson and Johnson (1978), as have procedures for encouraging learners to develop the metacognitive ability to provide semantic maps for themselves in order to enhance perception of textual relationships (McNeil, 1984).

Reading, literacy, society

The feature of cultural permanence and the function of writing to maintain and develop culture through history and literature brings with it a new dimension of discussion about language, and many current explorations of reading view it as inseparable from the general context of *literacy*. This has also meant that recent developments in reading theory have been naturally integrated with discussions about cognitive and social development and, of course, education. There is an increasing realization, moreover, that psychological descriptions of reading are also inseparable from the social matrix of literacy, and it has been forcefully pointed out that being able to read and write is like belonging to a "club" of literates from whom illiterates are largely excluded (Smith, 1988). It is also now recognized that children's chances of academic success in schooling (and therefore their subsequent career chances) are crucially influenced by the level of literacy of their parents and, in particular, by whether reading materials are readily available and by whether parents model reading and engage in discussing stories with their young children (Wells, 1986). Being able to read, then, significantly changes an individual's socio-cultural scope, and this is likely to be an even more powerful effect in the future, given the explosion of information that is encoded in written form and society's increasing dependency upon it. The educational and cultural centrality of written forms and of the processes of reading, then, mean that, far from being merely a way of recording speech, written forms truly have a life of their own in that through the process of reading they significantly change both the language competence and the lives of individuals.

Any full discussion of the psychology of the reading process now includes recognition of the strong influence of the *social*-psychological factors connected to literacy. No better example of how such factors and reading success are related could be found than in the experiences of the many adults in our societies who for whatever reason were not fortunate enough to grow up in a literate environment. What works against the acquisition of reading skills in school or, later, as an adult is not any fundamental psychological defect but, rather, the *shame* and feeling of rejection that comes from not being a part of the club. Reading, then, cannot be thought about simply in terms of *any* single psychological theory, no matter how complex or interactive, unless it is able to account in some way for these social aspects of what it means to read and write.

Writing

Like reading, writing processes are highly affected by their sociocultural contexts and, like reading, writing can be undertaken for many different purposes. Children brought up in a literate environment quickly learn to exploit writing and the permanence it gives to their thoughts, and they soon become able to satisfy various needs in writing stories, poems, messages to others, diaries, and even recipes (Berko-Gleason, 1989). As children get older, they manage to create longer and more complex texts, and it seems clear that the development of writing skills, just like that of reading skills, is inseparable from the development both of thinking in general and, through the attainment of literacy, from the development of social identity.

Writing processes

Like reading, the permanence of written script also allows types of psychological processing not permitted during the quick ebb and flow of spoken language. Good writers constantly edit what they have written and constantly refer back recursively to previous text in order to organize their subsequent writing. Writing typically takes place in an even more extended time-frame than reading, and part of the process of writing may include extensive breaks for periods of speculation or inspiration.

One further observation that has been made about written language is that it is more *decontextualized* than oral language--it is *monologic* rather than *dialogic*. In other words, writing cannot depend on all the contextual cues that typically support spoken communication, contextual cues including not only situations but also expressions, gestures, and intonation patterns. This means that writing generally has to be far more complete and correct in form than speech in order to compensate for this absence of contextual input; the writer has to create both the message *and* its context if the reader is fully to understand the intended meaning. This also means that there is more "psychological distance" between the sender and receiver of writing than of spoken discourse (Scinto, 1986, p. 57). Over all, then, it is clear that writing may be the most demanding of all the language skills. As a result of its decontextualized nature and the corresponding need for the inclusion of additional information of various kinds, writing is generally more complex than speech and it depends upon grammatical structures such as relative clauses and other complex embedded forms in ways not so typical or necessary in oral communication.

Cultural and social aspects

Given this additional complexity and the higher demands made by written language, it is not surprising that although even very young children can write in *some* form or another, and even though they can use writing in functionally different ways, there is a considerable lag between their spoken and written expressive abilities. For this reason, Vygotsky (1986) has argued that writing and speech are quite different psychological functions. Several theorists have suggested that learning how to write comes about only in the act of symbolization itself: At some stage, children realize through their early copying or scribbling that the marks on the page actually set up correspondences to other things, that they *stand for* things in the real world, and this is the precursor to more advanced writing (Werner & Kaplan, 1963; Humboldt, 1836; Scinto, 1986). Both Vygotsky and Luria have emphasized the point that such conscious use of symbolic forms comes about only from *cultural* pressures on the emerging writer. These psychologists have also emphasized that the developmental point of conscious realization of symbolization leads to quite new forms of interaction between the child and the world of symbols around her and to which she may contribute, interaction which lays the foundations for education (Vygotsky, 1962; Luria, 1978).

As previously stated, writing, like reading, is deeply culturally and socially embedded, characteristics which make writing inseparable from the educational processes by which it is largely shaped. For this reason, the most important work on the writing process over the past few decades appears to have been done by educators and by researchers who have taken into account the inseparability of psychological processes in writing from their cultural and social contexts. Information-processing approaches, which tend to focus on writing processes divorced from the cultural and developmental matrix in which writing takes place have tended to be less satisfactory than those analyses that have started from a consideration of cognitive development, literacy and schooling.

As an alternative to information-processing models, Scinto (1982, 1986) has developed a model of writing which is centered on social functioning and which draws upon a background of Prague School rather than transformational linguistics. Scinto starts by defining *text*, the product of writing, as

> ...a functional unit of complex meaning, an extended predication that involves the elaboration of ensembles of sentences by a process of composition and concatenation. (p. 109)

He continues the definition by identifying in very general terms what the principal processing steps in writing may be:

> This process of composition requires the generation of a unifying schema (i.e., an underlying goal-directed communicative intention), the organization of the meaning...into appropriate information units, and the concatenation of these units through the integration of semantic, pragmatic, and metapragmatic systems of the written language into a coherent linear surface form. (ibid)

Scinto further claims that texts are *coherent* in that their internal units are in relations of *dependency* to one another, and so this means that writing involves close attention to the binding of ideas to each other. The fundamental units of a text that must be woven or bound together in this manner are sentences. (It is interesting to note that while we typically *write* in sentences, we do not normally *speak* in them, which is why I have generally used the term *utterance* in referring to speech.) At a level of structure that is intermediate between sentences and the whole text is another level of organization containing what Scinto calls *combinatorial text modules* that serve to organize sentences into the logical and topical units, or "sentence clusters" going to make up the text. One of the central processes of writing is that devoted to the construction of *thematic progression*, by which the organizations of sentence clusters are themselves arranged in ways which articulate the intended meaning. A central part of this process is the way in which writers repeat *themes* in different sentences in order to guarantee that readers can follow the main line of thought, while these themes are given different *rhemes* (i.e. predicates or modifying ideas) in each sentence within a given cluster. In the above ten or so sentences, for example, the repetition of the idea of "psychology of writing" has served to maintain the theme, while each sentence has one or more rhemes that further develop ideas about this theme (see Scinto, 1986, pp. 110-111).

It has already been suggested that writing is a highly *conscious* activity, and Scinto's description of how texts are put together helps us to understand why this must be the case. In developmental terms, this means that children can only master the writing process if they are *aware* of the necessity to create textual order. Writing, indeed, as it is acquired during schooling may bring with it the larger psychological consequence of establishing individuals' mediation and control over their own lives. It may stimulate the construction and development of an inner world of thought and action necessary to social survival. Scinto argues, too, that there is a close correspondence between children's writing development and their attainment of cognitive stages as they were described by Piaget (1958).

The reading-writing relationship

Several researchers have indicated the close relationship between writing and reading, suggesting that writers read their own output for several purposes. One purpose is that of distancing themselves from their own work to see what the writing looks like from their readers' points of view, and another is to monitor the clarity and organization of their writing (Perl, 1980; Rose, 1980).

Flower and Hayes (1981) developed a model in which both reading and writing depend upon three elements: the task environment, long-term memory, and the process of planning, translating, reviewing and monitoring. They suggested that the processes of planning engaged in by readers and writers are identical, that they are each active in generating ideas and in superimposing organization on texts, and they are each limited by similar constraints on what can be stored in short-term memory. Flower and Hayes (1981) argued that writing, like reading, also involves the continual formation of *goals*--goals of extracting or of creating meaning, some of which evolve *during* reading and writing.

Tierney (1983) reported an interesting series of experiments in which subject writers were required to write to target readers a set of instructions to assemble a model and in which both the writers and readers were required to think aloud as they constructed and interpreted each other's intentions. He found, for instance, that if writers concentrated on specific attributes of objects they were describing in their writing then the readers, too, tended to concentrate on these attributes. Both writers and readers seemed to be aware of the relative importance of attributes without any specific mention of their function in description. It was also clear from the experiments that the writers often assumed the roles of readers, and they frequently commented on their own levels of success in being clear in their instructions. Readers acted as writers by criticizing the texts and adding or clarifying things where they thought necessary, thus demonstrating that reading to some extent involves the *re*writing of texts to fit in with reader expectations and needs (an observation about processing which is entirely consistent with previous comments about schema-theory and normalization). All of this suggests that a central part of the psychology of writing, like that of speech, involves the making of *plans* for constructing comprehensible texts, and that writers and readers enter into relationships in which such plans are both conventionally understood and acknowledged. It is likely that different kinds of plans exist for different kinds of texts, and it is also clear that good writer-readers are highly sensitive to their particular audiences (Crowhurst, 1980).

Summary

We have seen in this chapter how meaning lies at the center of all language processing and how this, in turn, means that processing is, contrary to the claims of behaviorists, largely non-linear in nature. Language use more typically involves such processes as planning, searching for gist, recursive checking, and reconstruction in memory. It also involves role-switches between speaker and hearer and between writer and reader.

One key difference between reading and writing, on the one hand, and speaking and hearing, on the other, is that the former are significantly more deeply embedded in cultural and social learning and achievement. For this reason, it is impossible to capture the complex processes of reading and writing in any tight psycholinguistic rules or formulae since they are not motivated merely by the need to communicate information of various kinds but also by much deeper cultural needs to create new forms of literature, to stretch the imagination, to impress others, to share in social and aesthetic pleasure. As Rosenblatt (1978) and others have pointed out, writing and reading engagements may be looked upon as *transactions*, and transactions are largely active and to some extent unpredictable. In the case of literary engagements, it seems clear that writers may engage in almost inconceivable levels of complexity or even ambiguity; they may in many cases not even be aware of the levels of ambiguity they create. In addition, the interpretation of text may be different for different readers and across different historical periods. Any attempts to capture the processes of writing within any simple communications model, then, in which the success of texts is measured by the degree of correlation between author intention and readers' interpretation would seem to be doomed to failure. In short, only certain aspects of reading and writing can be described by traditional psycholinguistic methods. The reasons for this become clearer as we venture further into the territory of sociolinguistics and the philosophy of language.

CHAPTER SEVEN

Language in Culture and Society

We tend to think of language exclusively as a communication device, but it is more than that. If it were not, we should all be speaking with the same tongue. Looking back through super-tribal history, it is easy to see how the anti-communication function of language has been almost as important as its communication function. More than any social custom, it has set up enormous inter-group barriers. More than anything else, it has identified an individual as a member of a particular super-tribe, and put obstacles in the way of his defecting to another group. (D. Morris: *The Human Zoo*, 1969)

Introduction

Although there had been great interest in the relationship between language and cultures in the work of von Humboldt and other linguists who saw language as a creative force developed within social communities, this orientation to language was largely absent in the work of both the nineteenth century philologists and the twentieth century structuralists. We have seen in Chapter Five how transformational-generative linguists, although apparently accepting von Humboldt's invitation to recognize the creative aspect of language but yet interpreted this within a highly mathematical framework which essentially isolates language from its communicative functions. The "data" used to support transformational theory, it will be recalled, are "grammaticality judgments" or the abilities of native speakers to decide whether isolated segments of language--usually individual sentences--presented to them by linguists in formal circumstances do or do not correspond to the grammatical rules of the language. While such judgments can provide important clues to the mathematical aspects of linguistic structures, and while transformational rules do indeed reflect an *aspect* of linguistic creativity, it has seemed clear to many other linguists and language researchers that true linguistic creativity is a much broader phenomenon than this, one driven by fundamental social and communicative purposes. Many different kinds of analysis have been undertaken on the basis of this assumption, including that of sociolinguists, ethnographers, and discourse-analysts.

Sociolinguistics

The central task of sociolinguists has been to identify the many elements in language-use which signal social identity of various kinds, signals which given by speakers both unconsciously and consciously and which play a crucial part in the structures of communicative interaction. No two individuals, of course, speak in exactly the same way, or have exactly the same vocabularies and intonation patterns. In general, however, speakers in all languages belong to groups of speakers who both articulate and recognize a common *dialect*. The study of such dialectical variations has been a central theme in sociolinguistics and has led to many valuable insights into the pervasive relationships between language variation and social identity.

Dialectology

It is commonplace knowledge that individuals from different locations in the United States, Canada, Britain, or any other English-speaking location are likely to recognize differences in each others' speech patterns. Sociolinguists have long been interested in studying such differences as these in order to discover the details of the language variations and their relation to language styles or dialects. Dialects are language varieties used by discrete social groups, groups formed either by geographic location, by ethnic background, or by other social factors, such as socio-economic status (or "class").

Regional dialects

The familiar recordings John F. Kennedy's speech illustrate one of the major structural differences between English dialects, namely, between those dialects which have a strong "r-coloring" in /r/s following vowels and those which do not. In a historical news recording, for instance, Kennedy is heard stating that he is looking for a job in government and has just finished his degree at Harvard. The recording reveals no sound of the /r/ in either of its written places, where the /r/ sound would certainly be clear in a speaker from Missouri, New Mexico, or indeed, from almost anywhere else in the United States except New England. The situation is a little simpler in Canada, where all speakers exhibit r-coloring and in Australia, where they do not. In Britain, where both varieties have their roots, the situation is more complex. While the dialects of London and the central South of England are "r-less," those to the west, north, and east have various manifestations of r-coloring.

Dialectical variations such as these result from a combination of historical and geographical factors which dialectologists attempt to describe. It is clear that mountain ranges and rivers are among the geographical features which have tended to make English-speaking groups discrete, although the conservation and development of dialects is, of course, a social phenomenon, one which takes place when people *feel* part of a community and not one that is a simple consequence of location. Dialects, in other words, seem to be a function of the desire of a community to protect close relations between language and cultural identity. Sociolinguists proceed by marking maps of countries or areas with *isoglosses*--lines which describe the boundaries of speech varieties that have developed in regions over time.

Pronunciation and accent differences

Many dialectical differences have to do with *pronunciation* and *accent*, where the latter may be defined as "the cumulative auditory effect of those features of a person's pronunciation which identify where he (sic) is from, regionally or socially" (Crystal, 1985).

Findings about pronunciation in speech communities in the United States have been numerous and they concern matters such as the formation of particular vowel and consonant sounds and the degree to which r-coloring (i.e. the sound produced when /r/ is enunciated with the tongue pulled back slightly in the roof of the mouth) is represented. The word *wash* is pronounced like "warsh" in South East Ohio and Kentucky, but without any r-coloring in other areas such as Chicago, New Jersey, Tennessee, or Massachusetts; the word *roof* rhymes with *push* in Chicago, but not in the other places; *greasier* sounds like "greazier" in Tennessee, and like "greashier" in Kentucky; the word *oil* sounds like "oyal" in Chicago and Massachusetts, more like "all" in Kentucky, and like "erl" in New Jersey. Other well-known differences across the United States involve various pronunciations of the vowel *a* as in *marry* (in some areas *marry* is homophonous with *merry* and *Mary* while in other places it is not) and the vowel *o* as in *cot* (which in some areas is the same as in *caught*, and other areas, not) (see McManis, Stollenwerk, & Zheng-Sheng, 1987, pp 351-352).

In Britain, where the distinction between dialects having strong r-coloring and those not having it (i.e. so-called "r-less" dialects) originated, the distinction still persists so that in the North, West and East of England strong r-coloring can still be heard, while in most London speech r-coloring is absent. There are many other significant differences, too, relating to how the vowel normally spelled with the letter *a* is pronounced. In North America, the vowel in *grass* is almost always the same as that which a given speaker will produce in *hat*. In England, however, these two vowels will be coordinated in both Midlands and Northern dialects, while they will be differentiated in London, where the vowel in *grass* will be the same as that in *car* and where the vowel in *hat* will be the same as that in *cat, bat, match,* and so on. Anyone seeing any of the many versions of George Bernard Shaw's play *Pygmalion* (or its musical version, *My Fair Lady*) will know, too, that the *Cockney* dialect of East London contains numerous unique pronunciation effects, perhaps the most salient of which is the replacement of the *t-sound* in words like *butter* with a *glottal stop* (the sound that might be typically produced at the very beginning of a long "Aaaah!" exclamation. American and Canadian speakers, of course will produce the characteristic *flap* sound in the same environment, making *butter* sound much like "budder."

Compared to either the United States or Great Britain, the accents in Canada are relatively homogeneous. A sound that American and other humorists have often capitalized on, however, is that produced by Canadians in words like *house* or *about*, which to other ears often sound like "hoose" and "aboot." These latter renditions are in fact slight exaggerations of what actually happens in the Canadian pronunciation of these words, which is a phenomenon that phonologists have called *Canadian raising*; the first part of the diphthong is actually "raised" slightly (i.e. the jaw-position is slightly higher than it would normally be). This only happens before *voiceless* consonants (such as the *s* in *house* or the *t* in *about)*, however, so that the vowel sound in *lout* is audibly different from that in *loud* in most Canadian speech. The *degree* to which this raising takes place differs, though, and it is much more audible in the speech of those growing up in the Ottawa Valley in Ontario than in the speech of those growing up in other parts of Canada.

Morphological variation

While many of the most obvious dialectical differences involve pronunciation or accent, however, sociolinguists have also recognized distinctions at both the morphological and syntactic levels. Among examples at the level of morphological variation could be included the extended use of the third person singular present tense marker (*-s*) in some Northern British and Welsh English dialects in first and second persons, as in *I wants* or *You thinks*, and so on, or the use of *been* to mark the *present perfective* form (as in *I been know you*, meaning "I've known you for a long time") in the Philadelphia region in the United States. If as my wife did, you grew up in Missouri and later found yourself studying on a prestigious campus on the

East Coast of the United States, you would have soon learned to put your groceries in a *bag* and not a *sack*, while if you had come from certain areas in Pennsylvania or North Carolina, you would have learned to use *bag* instead of *poke*. In Canada, a *sofa* is often called a *Chesterfield*, while in certain areas of the Mid-western United States, it is called a *davenport*; *couch* appears to be universal. A skunk is a *polecat* in much of the Ozark hills in Missouri and Oklahoma.

Some of the differences between words used for the same things by British and American speakers are well-known, and they include *cookies* vs. *biscuits*, *bonnet* vs. *hood* (of a car), *boot* vs. *trunk* (of a car), *lorry* vs. *truck*, *lift* vs. *elevator*, *pay rise* vs. *pay raise*, and so on, and while *knocking someone up* is a quite innocent matter of waking someone in England, you had better not announce that you are going to do this to someone early in the morning in the United States! In England, distinct from American usage, the word *fag* is used colloquially for a cigarette, or to designate a junior boy in a private school given menial tasks to do for others more senior than himself.

Canadian English speakers have developed over the years a fairly extensive vocabulary of their own, much of it contributed by way of Native Indian expressions. In Canada, a *Calgary redeye* is a drink (an acceptable mix of beer and tomato juice), a *Chinook* is an adopted Indian word meaning a warm wind blowing from the Pacific over the Rocky Mountains and on to the Prairies, a *gaspereau* (from Canadian French) is another word for herring in Atlantic Canada, a *jinker* is a Newfoundland gremlin, and *screech* is a Newfoundland rum. Australian English is also replete with its own terms for things, including *pommy* (Englishman), *Sheila* (any woman), *Bruce* (any man), and *barbie* (barbecue), as well as colorful expressions such as *as scarce as rocking horse manure*.

Syntactic variation

Syntactic variations between dialects are less common than those at the previous levels, which is not surprising since changing the order of elements in speech is consistent with major changes in both productive and receptive processing that are more typical of different *languages*. Some examples include the verb-phrase rules of *Black English*, which yield forms such as *He done gone downtown to get him a car*, where *done* replaces *have* as the auxiliary verb and the tendency of speakers in Southern Missouri to intensify adjectives with the pre-modifier *right*, as in *That's a right nice pie*, and *He's a right fine guy* (in which all the *i* vowels, incidentally, will be pronounced much like a lengthened version of the *a* vowel in *bad*).

Some of the major differences between American and British English at the morpho-syntactic level found by Strevens (1972) are as follows. First, there is a difference in the past participle of *got*; where British English has *got*, *gotten* is the more typical form in North America (as in, for example, *I think she could have got(ten) the chance to compete*). Second, the use of the verb *have* is different in several constructions. In Britain, the question form of *Have you an umbrella?* is quite common, while in North America it is much more common to say *Do you have an umbrella?* This latter form is present in British English, but is only used to ask if someone continuously possesses something over a long period, as in *Do you have a large house?*, *Do you have children?*, *Do you have warts?* and so on. Instead of *Do you have...?* British speakers are more likely to say *Have you got...?* when asking for something in an immediate time frame. Strevens also notes some interesting differences in the use or non-use of prepositions in British and American dialects. Where Americans say *I'll check that out*, British speakers say *I'll check up on that*. Where Americans talk *with* other people, British speakers talk *to* them, and while you can *call on* friends in Britain, you can't *visit with* them as you can in North America. American speakers are able to delete certain prepositions that British speakers can't, moreover, and can *write him* (vs. *write to him*) or *want out* (vs. *want to get out*) (Strevens, 1972, p. 52).

The challenge of defining "dialect" precisely

All of these various dialectical differences, then, gradually develop in a language like English as people migrate to new territories where they establish communities with particular interests and needs, and where their new experiences give birth to linguistic additions and modifications which are then reinforced in intra-group communication. Although the above examples are all typical of what sociolinguists refer to in describing dialects, however, the *precise* definition of the term *dialect* has been notoriously difficult. The most common criterion used to distinguish between dialects, on the one hand, and languages, on the other, has been that of *mutual intelligibility*, the criterion based on the idea that if two speakers can understand each other they must be speaking the same language no matter how different their particular dialects might be whereas if two speakers cannot understand each other then they must be speaking different languages. Unfortunately, concise as this criterion might appear, it is not so easy to defend in practice, since many North Americans, for example, cannot readily understand people speaking in a heavy Scottish accent and many southern British speakers cannot understand a dialect of English called Geordie spoken in the dock area of Newcastle. On the other hand, there are areas of the world such as the border between Norway and Sweden or the Dutch- and Flemish-speaking Netherlands where, despite the presence of two supposedly distinct languages, speakers can in fact understand each other. Dialects, then, should be viewed as *overlapping* language systems which are held together by certain core features, including most of the sounds, most of the words, and just about all of the syntactic rules. Key changes in syntactic form, together with substantial phonological and morphological independence that constitute a separate language should be detectable from the comparison of *any* of the dialects from one language with any of those from the language to which it is being compared. Intelligibility, however, is a somewhat dangerous comparative criterion, especially given the abilities of humans to understand so much on the basis of knowledge of even a few words from another language, even though these may exhibit unfamiliar ordering or pronunciation. *Dialect*, then, is a theoretical term useful when making comparisons relative to particular linguistic situations. The fact that in the end *no* speaker shares *exactly* the same speech or language forms with any one else and that we each have our own individual dialects (called *idiolects*) makes it clear that dialects really exist in a vast *continuum* across languages without having *rigid* boundaries between them.

Dialects and the Consolidation of Social Identity

Interesting though dialectological analysis of language forms is in isolation from human psychology, the whole topic becomes far more significant when related to that of human feelings and behavior. As has already been suggested, dialects do not just develop on purely geographical grounds. If they did, then differences would presumably dissolve in the presence of later patterns of migration and in that of the mass media, which should tend to homogenize language patterns. The opposite appears to be true: Not only are the dialectical characteristics of the Welsh, the Irish, Nova Scotians, Bahamians, Iowans, or of thousands of other groups apparently resistant to change, but there is also evidence of the continuing process of dialectical variation and consolidation all around us. It is especially clear in the development of vibrant new forms of English in the Caribbean, India, Africa, and Australasia. The maintenance and development of dialects, indeed, may be the clearest example of the *productive* characteristic of language referred to by von Humboldt, Chomsky, and others. The driving forces of this productive expansion lie in the dynamics of localized group membership. Even the ardent attempts of the nineteenth century philologists failed to reveal the origins of language itself, and no one is yet sure how dialects and languages have developed and distributed across nations and cultures in the way that they have, although it seems highly likely that the processes of cultural identification found in dialects lie at the core of these larger historical movements. While feelings and reactions can lead to the consolidation of dialectical variations, they can also lead to feelings of *exclusion* (of members of different dialect groups) as well as *inclusion*, and it is at this point of recognition that sociolinguistic analysis of forms merges with the study of the social psychology of human behavior, and where geographical differences merge with social pressures of various kinds in their affects on language.

Variations due to social strata

One of the clearest illustrations of how social pressures affect speech can be found in the ideolectical variations associated with what has been called *style*. Joos (1967) identified five styles of English that are chosen by individual speakers according to different expectations associated with differing social situations. These styles, he calls the "styles of the five clocks" on the basis that American speakers typically "correct" their clocks if they find they are "out of time" with those around them.

Individual speakers, according to Joos, freely move between these five styles, although any move of more than one either way is likely to be perceived as "anti-social" by any other witnesses to the move. The middle of the five styles is called *consultative*, a style used in normal everyday interaction with strangers and in which the speaker supplies suitable background information and participates continuously with the hearer. Joos argues that since this style is "hard work," we typically try for greater social interaction with new people we meet in order to make things easier. For this reason, we may soon switch to a "lower" *casual* style that is reserved especially for friends, acquaintances and insiders. Two ways of achieving this casual style are by way of *ellipsis* (i.e. by way of leaving out inessential and formally correct linguistic forms--Joos gives the example of changing *I believe that I can find one* to *Believe I can find one*) or by way of *slang*. In addition, there are *codes* connected to casual speech within particular dialects which, today, might include the inclusion of such forms as *O.K. yeah, for sure*, and so on. Casual style can become *intimate* style when the need for any kind of public "information" is no longer present. The main characteristics of the intimate style are that it is created within a sub-group, such as a family or a small group of friends, incorporating its own special names and abbreviations, forms that would not immediately be understood by outsiders until they had been included within the group. Moving up the scale to *formal* style, Joos argues that this is characterized by lesser participation than consultative style, a feature which becomes necessary when the communicative group reaches six or more. Typical examples of formal style, then, might be found in the language of legislatures or parliaments. It is closely associated with various kinds of *ritualistic* behavior, such as waiting for turns and making formal requests to speak. *Frozen* style is even more formalized and might include the language of ceremonies, initiation rights, or legal situations. It is interesting to speculate that there may be some parallel between Joos' stylistic spectrum, which ranges from involvement by the subject (*intimate* style) to withdrawal of the subject and submission to the framework of objective language codes, on the one hand, and the subjective-objective characteristics of language theories, on the other.

Register

Variations in style that individual speakers make according to context have generally be discussed under heading of *register*. Our abilities to relate what we say and what we expect from others in the various communicative contexts in which we engage demonstrate that we are all to some extent "sociolinguists," although our mercurial changes of style may not always be consciously monitored. A university lecturer, for example, might ask a student at the back of a classroom if "they would mind very much if they closed the window" while at home might be heard saying "jeez, shut the window, would ya!" Such occurrrences reflect our general awareness of the contexts of our utterances and of the types of social relationship into which we enter at different times of the day.

Changes of register include changes of *field*, *tenor*, or *mode*. *Field* refers to the "topic-area" of a given communicative encounter: The field of a hospital will typically yield an entire lexicon of terms that are likely to pervade hospital communication and the same is true for a myriad of domains ranging from, say, classical music, to Cajun cooking. *Tenor* refers to the particular social relationship identified in the communicative exchange within a given field of discourse. Within the hospital field, for example, a range of possible exchanges between a doctor and a nurse might exist such as the following: "Nurse Adderley, do you think you could possibly pass the forceps over there on the counter--the ones by the electrocardiograph," "Nurse, could you pass the forceps over there on the counter," "Christine, pass the forceps please," "Chris, forceps," or "Forceps." Here, the tenor ranges from *unfamiliar-formal* to *familiar-informal*, showing the interaction between style, situation, and language form.

It is also interesting to note, of course, just how sensitive we can sometimes be to the way in which someone speaks to us. As Grice points out in the context of discussing *felicity conditions* (see Chapter Three), we seem to have certain *expectations* not only about the contents and structures of messages in terms of the imparting of information but also in terms of the stylistic medium in which communications are framed. Hence, the first of the above alternative forms might well be interpreted by Nurse Adderley or an onlooker familiar with the doctor as nothing but patent obsequiousness, as evidence of over-attention to the new employee. On the other hand, the simple "Forceps" might also be interpreted as rude language behavior, and as assuming a level of familiarity on the doctor's part that lacks regard for individual nurses. The possibilities for interpretation are endless in different contexts, and the point here is that the tenor of communications plays a pervasive part in how messages are formulated and interpreted. *Mode* refers to the physical means by which messages are transmitted and received and, in particular to the codes of speech and writing. Writing is the code which is more typically used for formal or more elaborate discourse, reflecting levels of educational training (Montgomery, 1986, pp. 101-107).

Speech vs. writing

While speech contains pauses of various kinds, is accompanied by gestures and facial expressions, and is, as we have seen, always directed to some specific social setting, writing is stable, permanent, and relatively self-contained. Speech offers more opportunity for stylistic variation and communicative flexibility, while writing provides opportunities for precision and detailed thought. In general, writing is more formal than speech, and where choices exist about how a message might be delivered, these two modes offer significant alternatives. For this reason, it is often good advice in institutions "not to put things on paper if you don't have to" (since it may stick around to haunt you) while, on the other hand, if you are a good manager with a personnel problem you want to solve, you are probably best advised to *talk* to the employee thus allowing, perhaps, for the free-play or negotiation of tenor within the particular field of discourse.

"Standard" dialects: Dialectical variation and social prestige

As has already been suggested, dialects are strongly related to the social psychology of "exclusion" and "inclusion" by way of which people establish and feel that they are members of particular social groups. Speakers of a dialect can to some extent be considered to be an *in-group*, feeling all the cohesion and exclusiveness that such group-membership can bring.

Much of the clearest evidence of in-group-out-group distinctions and behaviors relates to the presence of so-called "standard" dialects, perceived by many speakers of a language to be central or "most correct" when compared to the "satellite" dialects around them. In all of the major English-speaking countries there have developed dialectical variants that are considered "standard" in this way, and therefore as being socially prestigious. The presence of a standard is perhaps most evident in Britain where, unlike the United States, Canada, or Australia, accent is still used as an immediate sign of social status and where access to higher education and professional status is still strongly affected by accent in its correlations with prior schooling, family background, and geographical location. It also seems to be the case, however, that certain dialectical developments are taking place in Britain, and it is no longer true that "BBC English," or "Oxbridge," or the "Queen's English," or "Received Pronunciation," as the standard dialect has variously been called, is accepted as marking social superiority as it once was. One good illustration of how the dominance of these forms of "standard" British English is being slowly eroded can be found, first, in the number of reporters on television speaking with vibrant regional accents. This was noticeable, for example, during the reporting of the 1991 Gulf War on CNN, where Irish, Midlands, and Northern British accents were all heard. A second illustration can be found in the lack of conformity between the accent of the Princess Of Wales and those of other members of the Royal Family. This is not the time or place for a complete analysis of the princess's speech, but suffice it to observe that her speech patterns have come to reflect those of modern London rather than those of the traditional aristocracy. This is apparent in both her intonation patterns, which generally conform to *consultative* and *casual* styles in Joos's terms, rather than to *formal* or *frozen*, (perhaps bearing a close relationship to her popularity). A quick comparison between the varieties of /o/ produced by the princess and the queen also reveals that the vowel is much more "open" and rounded in the speech of the former while being more "closed" and diphthongized in the speech of the latter (and of many other "privileged" British speakers). It is Britain, though, where the idea of a "standard" English still has greatest currency and where it has the most immediate and recognizable effects on social groupings and employment opportunities. This situation is likely to continue as long as there is an education system divided between private (i.e. "Public") and state schools.

In the United States, television provides a ready source of data about the status of accents and of "standard" American English (SAE). It is still the case that the news-anchors all speak a very similar dialect to each other, one which might be considered "standard" American English. On the major networks there are, for instance, no accents from the Ozarks or from South Carolina or from Texas, and it would probably be considered strange if there were. In Canada, too, newscasters speak in homogeneous dialectical patterns, although there is much less variety of accent and dialect across the country as a whole upon which to draw. In North America as a whole, there is a much looser connection between accent and social status than there is in Britain, and this is not surprising in the contexts of meritocratic as opposed to class-based democracies.

Despite this relative homogeneity of dialects in North America, sociologists have nevertheless found that North American speakers of English *are* aware of certain social properties of dialects and that they may even make stylistic changes in order to accord with perceptions about "prestigious" forms. The interaction of social and regional factors in American English has been noted by Labov, for example, who examined the forms of r-coloring used by inhabitants of New York when speaking to people from other parts of the country. The standard view of the New York dialect is that, like that of Boston and the Kennedys, it is r-less in such a way that, for instance, there will be no r-sounds in "Park the car" or "Help the poor on Fourth Street." Labov hypothesized, however, that inhabitants of New York add r-coloring when they perceive that they are speaking to people with higher social status whose accents include such coloring. In this way, they "borrow prestige."

One group of language-users who exhibit such borrowing is that of salespeople, who constantly come into contact with customers from all over the country. Labov hypothesized that salespeople at up-market stores such as Saks Fifth Avenue would produce more r-coloring to accord with the status of their up-market customers than would salespeople at middle-ranking stores such as Macy's to accord with their customers and that salespeople at down-market S. Klein would make the least changes. In the study, an interviewer played the role of customer and approached salespeople at each of the three stores with a deliberate strategy to illicit the phrase "fourth floor." For example, the interviewer might ask "Where are the women's shoes?" to illicit the response in a given store. He would then elicit a repeat version by uttering "Excuse me?" (Labov, 1972, pp. 43-50). Labov found support for his hypotheses: At Saks, thirty percent of the sales staff interviewed had developed permanent r-coloring, while at Macy's only twenty and at S. Klein only four percent had. Another thirty-two percent of the staff at Saks, moreover, had apparently developed variable r-coloring to suit different contexts of interaction with customers. The conclusion was that r-coloring in New York is positively correlated with perceptions of social prestige. Sometimes, individuals even appear to *hypercorrect* their speech to accord with social expectations, and the words *opera*, or *idea*, or *coda* might all receive final r-coloring in order to reflect additional "prestige." (Akmajian et al., 1990, p. 236). These instances result from more-or-less deliberate manipulations of the language and are, of course, quite distinct from the socially insignificant appearance of inter-vocalic (i.e. between-vowel) r-sounds typically heard in British English speech, as in "Linder and I bought a Honder Accord" (for *Linda and I bought a Honda Accord*). Labov's findings, moreover, indicate the extreme *complexity* of interaction between speech changes and social prestige such as those evident in the language of salespeople. One indication of this complexity is that, in contrast to salespeoples' perceptions of their customers, it never seems to have been the case that the r-*less* accents of the Kennedys have been perceived as anything *but* prestigious.

"Sub-standard" Dialects

There is little doubt that people will continue to "pick up" on each others' accents and will continue to make judgments about them on this basis. Sometimes such judgments may in fact be positive, and sometimes speakers will even modify their own accents in accordance with those around them. Taken together with other changes of style and idiolect, this seems to suggest that humans are somewhat chameleon-like in their linguistic behavior. Where judgments about other accents become negative and potentially damaging, however, is when they are associated with other judgments such as those about *educational background* or *moral character* or *social class*. Up until the work of Labov, it was widely assumed, moreover, that certain dialects (or, indeed, languages) were more "primitive" or "simple" than others. Nowhere were these ideas more roundly challenged and defeated than in Labov's pioneering sociolinguistic research into Black English and his discovery that, even though a dialect such as Black English might involve substantial changes to the verbal system or to the lexicon, these changes did not involve simplification but, rather, alternative complexity. Discrimination against Blacks has been partly reinforced over the years by this myth of dialectical simplicity and especially by the idea that Black children speak "substandard" English in schools. Over the past three decades, a good deal of research has been conducted that demonstrates the error in this way of thinking.

Black English

It was Labov, once again, who in a series of studies established that Black English has just the same complex kinds of rules as White English or, for that matter, as any other language or dialect. One feature of Black

English Labov studied, for instance, was the use of the verb *to be*, the present tense forms of which are often dropped or, to use a more strictly linguistic term, "deleted." Typical forms in Black English might be *He fast, We goin' downtown, She not worried, She always goin' to the store,* or *You on television,* in all of which, when compared to the "standard," it appears that some form of *be* is missing. Re-writing the utterances, however, demonstrates that this deletion of *be* is by no means some random or "ungrammatical" omission but that it is, rather, merely evidence of a logical extension of a grammatical rule followed in the "standard." In another dialect, these utterances would be *He's fast, We're going downtown, She's not worried, She's always going to the store,* and *You're on television.* It can be seen that the deletions in Black English occur at precisely those locations where the other dialect(s) permit *contraction* of forms (e.g. *he's* from *he is*). Labov pointed out that this was, moreover, an *exact* correspondence, and that it would be no more possible in Black English to say *That's what they* as it would be in other dialects to say *That's what they're* (as opposed to *That's what they are*) (Labov, 1969, quoted in Akmajian et al., 1990, p. 239). What is common to both dialectical forms is that they allow some kind of *reduction* in specific syntactic locations: Black English differs from other dialects only in the extent to which this permission is granted.

In addition to the case of the verb *be* in both its uses as a *main* or as an *auxiliary* verb, there are also some interesting correspondences in the rules underlying contraction or deletion of other auxiliary verbs. Hence, where other dialects can make the following kinds of contractions--*I have done it* to *I've done it, She will bring the Mercedes* to *She'll bring the Mercedes, He would be mad if she crashed it* to *He'd be mad if she crashed it,* and so on--in Black English even further contraction is possible to *I done it, She bring the Mercedes,* and *He be mad if she crashed it.* Once again, the rule in Black English is grammatically regular and reflects a process which it shares in common with other dialects of English and, indeed, with other languages in general (McManis et al., 1987, pp. 101-105).

Forms of negation provide another interesting source for dialectical comparison. In Black English, the forms *She doesn't know anything* and *He doesn't like anybody* would be typically realized as *She don't know nothing* and

He don't like nobody, suggesting to many, particularly to pedantic educators, that Blacks are "illogical" since they use double-negation. On further examination, however, it appears that the rules are quite regular and follow a well-established pattern: In "standard" dialects, *some-* changes to *any-* when negation is present (*She knows something* vs. *She doesn't know anything*) just as *some* changes regularly to *no* in Black English. Both changes are grammatically regular, and it could well be argued that Black English merely marks negation *more clearly* than other dialects, having discovered a rather economic way of expressing negation without the need for extra morphemes or complex alternations. Such economization has been and continues to be at the heart of diachronic language change and is responsible, for example, for the gradual simplification of the pronominal system (e.g. from *thee*, *thou*, *thy*, and *thine* to the current system of *you*, *your*, and *yours*, with its neutralization of singular and plural forms) just in the same way as it is for the reduction of *not + any* to *not + no(t)*. Following this, it should be realized that the utterance *He don't know nothing about nothing*, then, only seems "illogical" *when* it is compared in a formal way to the form *He doesn't know anything about anything*. To the prescriptivist, it no doubt seems that if someone "knows," then they must know "something" and that they cannot possibly (logically) know "nothing." To the speaker of Black English, it might be coherently argued, the idea that if someone "knows" then they must know "something" is obvious, trivial, and can be assumed in communication. The grammatical "slot" that is used in other dialects for the alternation between *some-* and *any-*, then, can be used for *emphasis* and, possibly, for *style*--a style which is also evident in the repeated semantic content of *He killed him dead*. The main point of all this is that, as sociolinguists have repeatedly found, there is really nothing in any of these or countless other examples that can be used to support the idea that Black English is in any way different in nature from any other dialect in terms of its grammatical complexiy. It is a vibrant, productive dialect which has the same sophisticated potential for communicative intricacy as other dialects and which partly serves to express the identity of a cultural group.

As with other dialects, it is especially important when dealing with Black English to remember that dialects are not static and, indeed, that they contain many sub-varieties. Black English is not entirely consistent even across the city of New York, not to mention the differences between speakers living in Boston or California. Speakers of Black English, moreover, are just as likely to make register changes in differing social contexts as speakers of any other dialect of English. It is an unfortunate fact that much of the stigma attached to Black English comes from its quite erroneous comparison with *non-colloquial* "standard" American English. If Black English were compared with *informal* varieties of English--in other words, if *style* were held constant in the comparison--many of the supposed "sub-standard" forms of Black English would be seen for what they really are, instances just like those in all languages, of *familiar* and *informal* language developed for purposes of *social* interaction and group consolidation. Any stigma that might be associated with any dialectical variant is, in the end, founded on *social* grounds, and is patently irrational on any supposed grounds of *linguistic* inferiority. It also fails to recognize the entire nature of language variation and change.

Social stigma and educational response

But despite all the attempts of sociolinguists, educators, and others to establish the equality of Black English with other dialects, it remains true that there *are* social distinctions that are drawn between Black English, and now other informal dialects such as Hispanic English, on the one hand, and "standard" forms on the other, and that these social distinctions have great impact on individual development, freedom, and choice. Nowhere is this more apparent or of such social and educational significance than in the comparison between these informal dialects of English and the forms of English institutionalized and maintained in the "professions," the forms of English encoded in literature, in the law, and in all the pursuits typically represented within the universities. It is here that what has always been a problem for educators becomes a particularly acute dilemma since, although educators are drawn towards valuation and respect for the language varieties that students bring with them to schooling, they are also drawn by the responsibility of ensuring equal opportunity for entry into commercial and professional life. There is little question that informal varieties of Black or Hispanic English, grammatical, complex, and expressive though they may be, will close doors into the professions. Cast in simple terms, then, there would seem to be two possible solutions: Either a Black student who wishes to gain access into professional life must completely sacrifice her English, and with it her culture, in favor of adopting "standard" forms, or she must learn how to cope with *two* distinct dialects. From a social-psychological perspective, neither of these alternatives is an easy one. Complete obliteration of her Black English will put a student in much the same position as a bilingual student who might be required to forget, or *subtract*, her entire cultural background in favour of *assimilating* into a given culture, while learning an *additional* dialect means that she will be forced into forms of *code-switching* between Black English and the language of the professional system, a type of activity which can place stress on her sense of identity. This is a dilemma which is not easily resolved, and which will have to wait for its resolution on unpredictable changes in social stratification in relation to language use. If there is one dialect which tends to remain stable, however, it is for obvious reasons that in which legal, medical, and other formal institutional codes are inscribed, and it seems reasonable to predict therefore both that the concept of a "standard" will continue to exist and that many students will want to acquire it. At another extreme, others will no doubt continue to feel that acquiring the "standard" is associated with too high a cultural price.

Language, Class, and Social Codes

The term *class* is one that is used rather loosely, in both formal and informal ways, on both sides of the Atlantic but which generally refers to groups of people who are similar in socio-economic status and who exhibit similar behavior patterns and have similar beliefs and interests. The term crosses national dialectical boundaries and, for instance, the category *working-class* will include speakers from all over the United States, Canada, and Britain. Accordingly, both Black English in the United States and the Cockney dialect of East London in Britain are naturally associated with the working-class as opposed, say, to the "professional" class. In the United

States and Canada, in keeping with more meritocratic systems, the term *class* seems to be used almost exclusively to designate socio-economic status, while in Britain, as has been suggested before, class is still associated with birth and schooling as well as with wealth and success. The problems of analyzing linguistic differences due to class are especially trenchant since, while the analyses of sociolinguists and other researchers may be acceptable within the framework of larger historical and social forces, the analysis of class seems to involve subjective judgments. The dangerous aspects of constructing sociolinguistic arguments about class became especially evident in the research of the sociologist, Bernstein (e.g. Bernstein, 1958, 1962), who proposed some distinctions between the language varieties of London schoolchildren which were largely class-based and which had ramifications for their social and educational identity. These proposals were also highly influential in educational circles in the United States.

Bernstein: Restricted vs. Elaborated Codes

Early on in his theorizing, Bernstein wrote that:

> Working-class speakers do not merely place different significances upon different classes of objects, but their perception is of a qualitatively different order. (1958, p. 160)

It was clear that his idea of "qualitative difference" was not the value-neutral one espoused, for example, by Whorf (see Linguistic Relativity, above), since

> Working-class speakers show a preference for *descriptive* rather than an analytical cognitive process....The content of [working-class] speech is likely to be concrete, descriptive, and narrative rather than analytical and abstract. (1962, p. 33)

Bernstein's key distinction was between *elaborated* codes (the codes of middle-class children) and *restricted* codes (the codes of the working-class), where the two were held to be "qualitatively different" in terms of their levels of planning and their cognitive complexity. In a nutshell, he argued that working-class children spoke a form of language which restricted them to developing only simple concrete concepts and which held them back from abstract thinking, with which they are supposed to have "difficulty" (1970 p. 29).

Despite considerable and understandable opposition to these ideas, including that of Labov, Bernstein did not change his ideas all that much and even at the end of the period of this theorizing, he wrote that

> In contrast to the working-class speaker, the middle-class speaker proceeds to individualize his meanings, he is differentiated from others like a figure from its ground.... The 'I' stands over the 'we,' (1972, pp. 140-141)

suggesting, in other words, that members of working-class cultures were less able to individuate (i.e. to experience their individuality) than were members of the middle-classes.

Now it is not surprising that, along with those who were ready to adopt Bernstein's distinctions, there were others on both sides of the Atlantic who strongly rejected the idea that working-class people were any less capable of abstract thinking than anybody else (Rosen, 1973; see also Atkinson, 1985). Apart from any substantial difficulties there might be with the distinction, there were also clearly *political* and *educational* drawbacks of working from a basis such as this, from which the logical implication was to "rid" working-class kids of their restricted code and move them on to elaboration. One problem lay in Bernstein's terminological distinction between "abstract" and "concrete" thinking, a distinction he tried to support by the somewhat spurious evidence, among other things, of the number of pauses in the speech of members of each group: Since middle-class speakers apparently paused more often, Bernstein concluded that this showed that they spend this time "summarizing," "abstracting," and "generalizing" (1962, p. 42).

"Abstract" vs. "concrete" thinking

What *is* the difference between "abstract" and "concrete" thinking in any case? Bernstein and his co-researchers, including Lawton (e.g. Lawton, 1968) were unclear on this point and unable to distinguish between speech which reveals thinking "beyond the here and now" or which simply contains abstract terms such as "beautiful," "loneliness," or "intuition." Despite the sometimes vitriolic opposition to Bernstein's theory, however, it must be remembered that he was by no means a conservative thinker seeking to intensify class distinctions or to justify compensatory educational programs for the working-class. On the contrary, Bernstein's intentions were to *improve* education for all students, and he saw himself more as a descriptive sociologist than as an educational politician. In keeping with this realization, several more sympathetic reviews of Bernstein's ideas have appeared over the past few years, reviews which reveal that his work, if taken as an investigation of *style* within *dialect* may have much of value to say about language variation (Montgomery, 1986; Atkinson, 1985).

Some of the kinds of distinctions Bernstein observed in transcripts of the speech of working-class and middle-class subjects can be observed by way of a few examples. A typical example of elaborated code speech is to be found in the following, in which a male speaker is being interviewed about his various roles in life:

> Interviewer: What d'you think makes for job satisfaction?
> Subject: (laughter) erm (pause) I think that's always an impossible question to answer because it all depends very much on the individual (pause) what the individual wants out of life (pause) but I think (pause) there's got to be a vital interest (pause) erm (pause) the job's got to be interesting enough to (pause) maintain your interest in the job. (Adapted from Montgomery's transcription, 1986, p. 123)

This can be contrasted with the following comments on the same topic by a restricted code speaker:

Subject: I'll tell you a little tale (pause) erm when I was on the furniture (pause) on the furniture removals (pause) I was a foreman (pause) I - over all the lads chaps there (pause) anyway erm (pause) things were going along smashing you know er (pause) the firm started to build up you know and erm (pause) he wanted to break into the shipping you know (pause) business you know that was shipping immigrants abroad you know (pause) so I said oh I know about that I said er if you want to have a go have a go so er (pause) we started that and I started doing all these jobs and everything you know....
(Adapted from Montgomery's transcription, ibid., pp. 123-124)

According to Bernstein's theoretical distinctions, the speech of these British subjects can be distinguished on grounds of the relative *abstractness* of the first extract when compared to the second. The first speaker mentions "questions that are impossible to answer," and he seems to be at great pains to establish that he is an *individual* with his own views of things--an individual, too, who fits into a *general* scheme of things ("life") and in which the general concept of work must be evaluated. The second speaker, on the other hand, concentrates on relating his own specific experience in the form of a personal narrative, or "tale," and the constant repetition of *you know*, which contrasts with the *I think* mode of the first sample, according to Bernstein, reflects a much weaker sense of self and a continuing invitation to the listener to give credibility to what is being stated.

In general terms, the contrast between the two language varieties can be summed up by saying that while the elaborated code variant is characterized by a tendency to make *generalizations* about things, the restricted code variant reflects an opposite tendency towards *particularizing* things. These opposing tendencies are associated in Bernstein's analysis with "abstract" vs. "concrete" styles. In keeping with a more sympathetic reading of Bernstein, what he intended to explore and ultimately to explain was just how these two variants emerged and *not* merely to use them as class stereotypes. Bernstein viewed the codes as representing two modes of *social formation*, or ways in which individuals typically relate to each other in their families and in society as a whole. He argued that a further distinction could be made between *positional* or *closed* social relationships, on the one hand, and *open* or *personal* relationships, on the other. In the first type of relationship, family positions and roles are relatively strictly defined; fathers, mothers, siblings, all know what their roles are and what others' expectations of them are, and they conform to these. In this social formation, there are a great many shared assumptions, against the background of which communication takes place. In the open kind of social formation, roles are supposedly less strictly defined, more individual experimentation with roles is permitted, there are fewer shared assumptions about how things should be, all of which means that communication involves both more *negotiation* in general and more individual expression and persuasion.

A sympathetic interpretation of Bernstein's work, then, takes his primary intention to have been the exploration of two types or modes of social existence, modes which had ramifications for language use and for understanding the general relationship between language styles and social group membership and not to have exacerbated class distinctions. Interpreted in this more benign way, Bernstein's analysis represents a valuable springboard for the analysis of the whole relationship between language and cultural identity. Bernstein can be interpreted as a leading *structuralist* analyst since, like other structuralists such as Levi Strauss, he was concerned with describing the basic elements and contrasts in language conceived of as *social systems* (see *structuralism*, Chapter Two; Atkinson, 1985, pp. 5-7, 57-60). It is unfortunate--although Bernstein himself could perhaps have done more to extricate his theory from the nets of his critics--that the two social modes became synonymous with the two social *classes*. The idea that there *are* socially-based language codes, however, remains an intriguing one which, when divorced from notions such as "abstractness" or "individuality," which are all too readily correlated with claims about "ability," "intelligence," or "creativity," and so on, may contribute much to the understanding of dialects, styles, and language variation in general. Bernstein's theory, together with the reactions against it and the ensuing defence, themselves constitute an informative sociolinguistic episode, demonstrating just how strongly defended may be the right to maintain language varieties.

Language and Communication

Communicative Competence

A major turning-point in thinking about language and society came with a forthright rejection of Chomsky's notion of competence by the sociologist D. H. Hymes (1971, 1972). While Chomsky's ideas about linguistic competence had been centered on the "ideal speaker-hearer" who knows the grammatical rules shared by his speech community and who remains "unaffected" by constraints of situation and memory (1972, p. 3). Hymes argued for a definition of competence which *included* knowledge about social as well as purely grammatical aspects of language. Following Hymes, this version of competence is now generally known as *communicative competence*.

Reassessing "performance"

The realization that knowledge of language must involve something more than knowledge of grammatical rules rests in part upon a reconsideration of what is involved in language *performance*. While recognizing the distinction between the labyrinth of abstract rules shared but not explicitly known by all speakers of a language (Saussure's *langue*) and actual speech occurrences, with all their peculiarities and "erroneous" or "unideal" forms, Chomsky has persistently promoted the former over the latter in terms of their importance for language theory. But *is* performance really so peripheral as Chomsky has suggested, or does it involve more than the mere superficial working-out of forms generated through the underlying grammatical system?

It seemed clear to Hymes and others that performance was by no means a superficial or trivial aspect of language behavior and that in order to be successful communicators, speakers and listeners have to use a wider range of knowledge than that of their grammars. They have to know, for instance, about how to express things in ways that relate them to contexts or, indeed, when to remain silent (which doesn't apparently require any grammatical knowledge whatsoever), and they have to know how to interpret the performances of others in ways which take account of just how *un*ideal many expressions are.

In developing his broader definition of competence, Hymes paid respect to the theoretical integrity of Chomsky's ideas about competence as they were worked out within the framework of transformational grammar, but Hymes' own thoughts about competence were developed in a tradition of thinking which places cultural symbolism or *semiosis*, rather than grammar, at the center of communicative interaction. According to this more general view of competence, communication involves the continual use of culturally-based presuppositions and truth-values, and meaning is always *situated* in some context and emerges only from the dynamic interpretation of events or ideas. While the elements of language such as phonemes, morphemes, or grammatically well-formed phrases and sentences are viewed from this perspective as being relatively *static*, language performance is considered to be dynamic and social in nature and to be central to the entire communicative process; far from being "secondary" to competence, performance is viewed as the dynamic process by which the purely referential aspects of linguistic expressions, including the dictionary senses of words, are integrated with other channels of information. These parallel channels include those of shared cultural knowledge, elements of situations, and also *paralinguistic* features such as facial and other types of gestures which accompany speech (Saville-Troike, 1982, pp. 23-25). Part of this newly-defined communicative competence involves, moreover, speakers' knowledge about language variation phenomena such as dialects and the other regionally- and socially-based aspects of language discussed above.

Strategic competence

A further component of knowledge included within communicative competence has been identified particularly clearly in the area of second language-learning and the realization that speakers of a foreign language can gain great benefit from the conscious use of certain communicative *strategies* in order to make things easier for themselves and others (see e.g. Savignon,

1983). The use of such strategies has been discussed under the heading of *strategic competence*. Such speakers can adopt quite deliberate communicative strategies such as asking people to repeat utterances for them, for example, or asking them to speak a little more slowly in order to facilitate comprehension. They may also resort to gestures and facial expressions to help them to interpret their intended meanings.

Strategic competence is also a necessary part of communicative competence for those communicating *with* second language learners and, indeed, for all language-users having to make deliberate communicative adaptations for other groups of speakers. What seem to underlie successful communication with speakers of other languages are forms of *empathy* between communicators, forms of empathy which lead both sides in a communicative exchange to do everything in their power to interpret each other's intended meaning. In the case of communication between first and second language learners, these adaptations might involve various kinds of disambiguations on both sides achieved by way of probes, checks, and re-expressions of things until satisfactory interpretations are possible. The adaptations made by the fluent first-language speaker in such exchanges have been discussed under the heading of *foreigner talk* (following Ferguson, 1971, 1972). This kind of empathy, an ongoing and dynamic understanding about intended meaning, is also crucial in exchanges between children and adults, and the special language adults sometimes use with children has been discussed under the headings of *motherese* and *baby-talk* (Ferguson, ibid.; see also, Arthur et al. 1980).

A further interesting aspect of strategic competence is that it may even involve acts of deliberate "incompetence" in such circumstances, for instance, when a second language learner realizes that not being optimally fluent might reap rewards in sympathy, as well as additional attention and help from others, or where a speaker of another dialect of English realizes that her ability to emulate a Scottish accent perfectly is, if exercised, not likely to endear her to her Scottish hosts. In other situations, too, sophisticated speakers realize that it may be in their best interests to sound a little *less* competent than they truly are in order to reduce the risk of threatening those around them. It will be noted that all of these observations about the broad nature of linguistic competence are highly compatible with *speech act* theory and with the general idea of the necessity for sympathetic *cooperation* and adherence to *felicity conditions* developed more by philosophers than by sociologists (see Chapters Three and Eight).

Language Functions

Another idea that is compatible with both the socially-oriented notion of communicative competence and with speech-act theory is that language-users are constantly engaged in *functional* behavior. Every instance of communicative language use can be interpreted as reflecting some functional orientation on the part of a speaker (or writer), as reflecting some need or purpose intended to have certain direct or indirect affect on the listener.

It is quite easy to see how every utterance might be interpreted in terms of the communicative functions it embodies. A doctor telling a patient to cut fat out of his diet, for instance, and describing the gory consequences of continuing both to over-eat and smoke, is clearly functioning to warn her patient in a way which will change his behavior. A university professor delivering a lecture on nuclear fission is clearly functioning as an informer to her students, as a describer of scientific information, while most of Eddie Murphy's output functions to entertain his audience.

Halliday's analysis

Many theorists have attempted to categorize the central functions expressed in language, but probably the clearest and most widely accepted presentation has been that of Halliday, (see also Chapters Three and Five). Halliday's typology of language functions is especially clear in relation to his theory of how children learn their first languages, and he proposes that the learning of language is fundamentally inseparable from the learning of how to use language in these functional ways. Halliday views seven central functions of language as "models" that children have in their minds of how language can be used: Language is, for the child, "a rich and adaptable instrument for the realization of his intentions; there is hardly any limit to what he can do with it" (1973, p. 10). First among these is the *instrumental* function, in which the child expresses through language her need to accomplish things in the immediate environment--to get things done. When a five-year-old shouts out "I want a drink" or "That's my piece!", then, or even when she merely screams or grunts in a certain way, she demonstrates her knowledge that sounds and gestures can be used to change things to her advantage--or at least that she can have a good shot at changing them to her advantage.

A second function that children quickly learn is that of the *regulation* of others and, in particular, regulation of themselves by parents and teachers. In using language to control children, adults provide children with models of how they can begin to control others, including their peers and their elders. Examples of regulatory language used by adults might include "You just make sure you thank Aunt Jane for the cookies" or "You do that one more time and it'll be your room for the rest of the day" or "Do you think it would be a nice idea to keep the glue on the tray?" Children quickly learn to emulate these kinds of orders and requests in organizing the behavior of others (as any parent knows who has forgotten a promised present or trip, or who has not brought the right brand of cereal home).

Closely related to this regulatory function is that of *interaction*, involving the use of language to develop and maintain social relationships with others. The presence of social in-groups and out-groups has already been mentioned in relation to dialectical variation and, in addition to developing close social relationships with other family members, children who are socially successful also learn how to speak the same varieties of language as those of groups they want to join or continue belonging to. Just like dialectical groups, all social groups to some extent gain consolidation from shared language use, preferring to use terms or ways of saying things that identify individuals either as group members or outsiders. The particular forms of language used are not important (they are, indeed, arbitrary, in the Saussurean sense) and might range from the use of a funny accent during play to the use of a specific form such as Pig Latin: What matters within the bounds of interactive functioning is that language is being used relatively consciously as a means of achieving a desired closeness to and identification with others.

Halliday's fourth function is the *personal* function, involving use of language to identify the self independently from group membership. According to Halliday, children learn who they are as individuals partly from the effects their speech has on others--effects which, in turn, shape the growth of individual personality.

Fifth, there is the *heuristic* function of language, or the use of language to find out things about the world, to make tests to see if things are as they appear to be, and so on. Children habitually ask a lot of questions and, (consistently with what Bernstein found before him), Halliday stresses the importance of this function in the child's ability to succeed in school. Articulate children appear not only to know how to use questions effectively and how to ask further logical questions following responses, but they also seem to have a metalinguistic awareness that there are "questions" and "answers" and that these play a central role in learning.

Sixth, there is the *imaginative* function, where language is used partly to play. Poems, riddles, rhymes, songs, and word games would all come in the rubric of imaginative language, and all of these activities essentially explore the nature of things beyond the parameters of the everyday world and extend language to the expression of new meanings and new experiences. Finally, there is the *representational* function which children learn later, especially during formal schooling, as a mode of informing others about things by way of accurate descriptions of structures or events (Halliday, 1973, pp. 11-17).

Problems facing a functional analysis

According to the functionalist viewpoint of Halliday and others, then, language is at its root functional, and can be analyzed into categories of functional behavior. But while the general contention that language and social functioning are closely related seems incontrovertible, several analytical problems related to the functional theory of language use should be identified. One such analytical problem with language relates to the question of just how *conscious* speakers typically are of their language functioning--do functions, in other words, exist in a one-to-one relationship with conscious intention? It seems clear, for instance, that the doctor might not consciously conceive of her diatribe on polysaturates as a "warning" at all but merely as a dispassionate description of facts having much in common with the lecturer's on fission. On the other hand, the lecturer might be unaware of how her lecture is actually functioning to inform a group of students how to build a bomb or another group how to protest against nuclear energy. Functions, then, are slippery phenomena.

Second, when it comes to the analysis of actual speech events, it is often difficult or impossible to decipher exactly what *is* intended. If we take the simple example of an utterance such as "People who like apple pie also like cats," we can see that this might express a purely *representational* function, or that it might serve to include people in a group of those who are like-minded (*interactional* function), or it might serve to describe a *personal* point of view. It could even be *regulatory* in being uttered as a warning to a sub-group of allergic apple-pie-eaters to maintain their distance from others. Of course, it would be inconsistent with a functional theory of language to separate such an utterance from its *context*--indeed a central tenet of the theory is that all linguistic-functional activity is context-bound.

But there is a further difficulty which is not resolved even by carefully relating functional analysis to communicative contexts, and it is that speakers may often produce utterances which express more than one function at the same time. Even if we were to restrict the context of the above, say, to that of a party at which the host has the intention of pawning off some unwanted kittens from the litter her Persian Blue has just had (where "People who like apple pie also like cats" is uttered to a group of people with their forks in the apple pie) the functional interpretation may not be clear. The *prior* functional intent of the host may be *regulatory* in that she is trying through artful analogy to persuade one of the pie-eaters to take a cat, but at the same time the utterance is also likely, of course, to express a *personal* function. It may also be partly *interactional* in reinforcing her relations with others, and may also even be partly *heuristic* in her intention to see just what kind of response she gets. In summary, there appears to be something of a *boundary problem* associated with functions--a persistent problem of determining exactly where they begin and end, even though Halliday apparently realizes that functions can indeed be multi-layered and "polyphonal" in adult language use. This, indeed, may be a central quality by which adult speech can be differentiated from that of children (Halliday, 1978). It is possible, moreover, that we are all such artful dodgers when it comes to speech that a functional focus actually *changes* during the course of utterances as we receive feedback from those around us or from other aspects of contexts. For this reason, the more precise analysis of what happens *during* discourse and within the processes of social interaction has also provided an important focus of sociolinguistic research.

Discourse Analysis

The "game" of communication

When two or more individuals communicate, be it through the medium of speech or writing, a great deal more is typically going on than the transmission of messages. As Wittgenstein observed, language use is rather like a "game" in which the players interpret each other continuously and dynamically and meaning emerges at least partly from the success with which the game is conducted. To take the basic example of two people talking to each other, it is clear that in addition to merely transmitting and receiving information, they have to *coordinate* their communicative activities--certainly, they cannot speak at the same time as each other and they must also pay due regard to the shifts of opinion and topic effected by each other if they are to stay in communicative touch.

There is an old British Vaudeville routine which underlies this point. In the routine, one drunk is trying to get to Wembley Stadium (a major sporting venue) while a second has phonological problems with his companion's slurred speech, a routine which neatly demonstrates violation of the fundamental principles of coordination of interpretations:

> Drunk 1: Where's Wembley? (...'Wednesday')
> Drunk 2: No, today's Thursday. (...'thirsty')
> Drunk 1: So am I, let's go an' 'av a drink...

It might be argued, perhaps, that the routine is extremely *well* coordinated at the level of the underlying functional needs of the participants, but as a piece of coordinated discourse, it lacks the kind of attention to detail that is normally the case in successful discourse. Coordination problems occur whenever people cannot hear each other properly, or when they cannot understand each other for any other reason or. Indeed, problems may occur when one speaker wants to prevent another from saying what he is saying. Generally, these problems can be overcome by certain conversational "gambits" or "plays" which restore communicative integrity, and this, once again, shows that speakers do in fact know how to play a rather complex "game."

Ethnographic descriptions

Several ethnographers of communication have set out to define more precisely what the rules of the game of communicative interactions are like. One thing they have established is that one of the most basic parts of the conversational game involves *turn-taking*, the ability of the participants to decide when it is time to speak, when to let the other person speak, or when it is appropriate to interrupt, and so on (Sacks, Schegloff, & Jefferson, 1974). Sacks et al. observed that speakers typically *plan* for alternations between them, that they keep "overlapping" talk to a minimum, that they are able to negotiate smooth and seamless "transitions" between each other's speech, and that turns can vary in their order and length. They concluded from this that turn-taking "allocations" are clearly made during the course of communicative exchanges, and this is particularly evident in cases where more than two speakers are present, when quite explicit choices of who has the next turn can often be observed. In addition, speakers have various methods by which they can *repair* any trouble caused either by two speakers speaking at the same time or by any violations of turn-taking.

On further examination of the system by which conversational turns are taken, Sacks and others found that speakers must listen carefully for the right moments to enter. This is no easy or simple matter, since turns may take the form of almost any length of utterance ranging from single words to extended discourse units. In addition, turns can be signalled by any of the participants in a conversation (possibly even in the form of a gesture from a non-speaking participant) or they can be the result of a speaker simply taking the initiative in the context of silence. They suggested a set of nested rules of the game by which turns are taken: First, the current speaker may in some way overtly select the speaker to follow (either by asking a question, or naming her, or some facial expression and gesture, for example), following which the second speaker is then obligated to take his turn. Second, if the current speaker does not select the following turn-taker in this way, and there is a break, then the first speaker to enter has the right to the next turn. Third, if this chance for an entry into a turn is not taken, then the first speaker has the right to continue.

Role-playing and conversational "moves"

All of these observations about conversational turn-taking make it clear that the game conducted by speakers is largely one of *role-playing*. Just as in the case of a game like volleyball, there is a "server" in a conversation, and fast decisions have to be made, and signals given, concerning who is to be the next in contact with the ball, decisions that are partly governed by the established rules of the game and partly by the opportunism and abilities of the players. Concerning the actual "serving" part of conversation, Schegloff (1968) observed that speakers make *openings* which direct the nature of the ensuing discourse. Following analysis of telephone conversations, he found that openings had basic structures that he called *summons-answer* sequences. In the case of a telephone call, the summons is the bell ringing itself, but in other cases it may be almost any instance of communicative need; arrival in a (helpful) secretary's office, for instance, is generally a summons to the secretary to acknowledge the arrival and to ask what the person wants. The summons is immediately followed by some kind of answer or response and, together, the summons and the response form what Schegloff called an *adjacency pair*. What happens next following the identification of the receiver is, in the case of a telephone call, that the caller is bound to identify herself also. Conversation, then, may be viewed as a continual chain of summonses and answers that are bound to each other by underlying rules of mutual obligation. The initial sequence in a sense "locks" the participants into a relationship which is both conversational and social in nature.

Adjacency pairs may not just be of the summons-answer kind, and Sacks, Schegloff, and others have shown how *greetings* also come in pairs with appropriate responses (*returned* greetings), how *offers* require *acceptances* or *refusals*, how *thanks* require *acknowledgements*, and how *apologies*, *complaints*, *challenges*, or *compliments* also have their own responses. It can readily be seen just how strongly these responses are required by considering the violations of the conversational game that take place without them. If, for instance, you say "Hi" to someone and you are pretty sure that they have both seen you and heard you and yet they turn their head away and continue on without breaking stride, you may rightly feel offended. You may rightly conclude that the behavior on the part of your ex-friend is *deliberate*. Indeed, it is a perfectly reasonable culturally-based deduction that there must be some *reason* for this violation of the adjacency principle; perhaps you are wearing the same designer shirt or, less trivially, it has been discovered that you and not your friend are to be the next district manager. The point is that, as a conversational role-player, you can clearly recognize the breach of conversational convention. You are therefore fully justified in searching for an explanation of the violation. To the ethnographer, this kind of recognition and response captures the true nature of language as it both contains and is constrained by the social and cultural codes which underlie the rituals of conversational interaction. To take another example, if an individual apologizes to someone he works with, then he has good reason to suppose that the person to whom he makes the apology will be complicit in patching things up. If the apology is just not good enough, however, and does not match the severity of the transgression, then it is perhaps entirely appropriate for the person to whom the apology is offered to deliberately withdraw from the engagement and *not* to accept the apology. In either case, once again, the conversational *meaning* is constructed out of the particular moves that are made in the game and, at a more detailed level, out of the particular ways in which the invitations to form adjacency pairs are either accepted or rejected. The turn-taking system as described by Sacks, Schegloff et al. provides a rich model for understanding how conversational meaning emerges: It emerges *not* only from what is directly stated or even from what is indirectly stated, but also from the relations between what is said and the framework of expectations and social rules in which things are said. Meaning, in addition to having representational and functional elements, is also *negotiated*.

An ethnographic perspective on language, then, stresses the centrality of social and cultural knowledge and negotiation which seems in many respects to have a kind of "grammar" of its own, even though this is of a quite different kind than that conceived within structural or Chomskyan linguistics. Further details of the systematic *routines* of interaction that are typical in conversation, or of how *openings* or *closings* or *requests*, *questions* or *answers* are actually dealt with have been provided in a number of studies (for a good review of such studies, see Clark, 1985).

Establishing topics

Perhaps even more complex than the rules and inferences relating to the "game" of conversational exchange is the question of how topics, having been established, are developed and maintained, and this involves a further interaction between social and *textual* sources of information. As Sacks (1971) observed concerning the nature of conversational topics, "...it is a general rule about conversation that it is your business not to tell people what you can suppose they know" (cited in Coulthard, 1977, p. 75). It is also true that what is chosen as a topic for discussion among speakers is partly a function of who and where they are: You do not talk to somebody you are meeting for the first time about your irrational fear of snakes, nor do you generally choose to talk about your skin-disease in an elevator packed with strangers. When a speaker introduces a topic, then, it is clear that she is generally constrained in a number of ways. It is also clear that she must have some idea of *significance* in her mind if she is to produce anything conversationally interesting or appropriate to those around her--things must be "newsworthy" if they are to get serious attention (Coulthard, 1977, p. 76).

In the examples related to turn-taking given above, the constraints were of such a kind that the speakers *must* obey them if ordered conversation is to take place. At the level of topics, too, there are obligatory constraints: Unless you are acting in a soap opera or melodrama, you *have* to tell your parents you're getting married, you *have* to tell your (current) husband that you're pregnant, and he *has* to tell you he's lost his job. All of these kinds of information, just like turn-taking role plays are part of the fundamental fabric of cultural and social expectations by which we all live. But there are other constraints on topics that are less strict than these. They are constraints, nonetheless, and they have to do with such matters as what is considered "newsworthy" or not. There is an underlying principle in conversation that a speaker must provide *new* information, although this must bear close enough relationship to *old* information for it to make sense. This has been referred to as *given-new* contracting (Clark & Clark, 1977).

In almost every communicative situation, there are clear expectations about what is *relevant* and what kinds of information are to be exchanged. Sometimes, there are extremely tight social constraints placed on what will be talked about as in the case, for example, of the expected responses following the dialing of an emergency phone number. In social interaction more generally, these constraints may be much more relaxed, covert, and difficult to define, but they are still clearly present. Conversational moves such as asking the check-out person at the local supermarket for advice about a relative's neurosurgery, lecturing a speaker of English as a second language on the details of given-new contracting, or talking to a university president about the problem your cat is having adjusting to a new brand of litter would all constitute violations of this contract (and, in the last case especially, of a number of other conversational guidelines besides). They would do so by failing to identify topics which the listeners could engage in. At the other extreme, a tennis novice explaining to Boris Becker how tennis balls can be made to spin in various ways through differing forms of racquet contact would also violate the convention by failing to identify topics about which the listener knows more (and therefore is more likely to be treated as an invasion of privacy than as interesting new information).

Sacks (1971) also observed that good conversations, once founded on acceptable topics, involve a certain amount of topic *changing*. What seems to happen in many conversations is that when a topic is presented it is generally accepted by other speakers, who then speak to the topic in their own terms gradually redefining and sometimes modifying it completely, a process which may have much in common with the processes of normalization observed by schema-theorists (see Chapter Six). It appears that speakers need to work continuously to establish exactly what the topic *is* and what it means to *them*, and this sometimes leads to certain kinds of conversational "drifting." When things get out of hand, language-users have various ways of getting back to a level of interaction in which the topic *is* sufficiently shared and they re-establish the *coherence* of the discourse. One of the most fundamental principles by way of which speakers keep on track in discourse is that of analyzing what is being said in terms of the question "Why is that being said now and to me?" (Sacks, 1971, cited in Coulthard; see also Brown & Yule, 1983, p. 77).

Analyzing speech interaction

Discourse analysis is a field of study that has been influenced not only by the ethnographic perspective, the perspective that stresses the relationship between language and social role-playing, but also by the perspectives of speech act theory and pragmatics (see Chapters Three and Eight). The general purpose of the field of discourse analysis has been to develop ways of describing the choices and the related events that take place in actual communication. Discourse analysts conduct research on the actual data of everyday speech interaction. This task is a formidable one, since it necessarily involves the subjective involvement of those analyzing communicative situations and transcripts, and it may also involve introspective judgments by the actual participants.

Perhaps the most difficult of all aspects of communication rules to capture is how *emotions* play their part in the formation of exchanges. It seems clear that communication *does* involve continual emotional involvement of one kind or another, and emotional reactions are pervasively connected with the *judgments* we make during conversations, judgments both about how to continue our own participation in the game, and about the people we are speaking with. All the above examples of adjacency-pairing or of the misappropriation of topics, naturally involve feelings and judgments; spurned greetings, or the introduction of eccentric topics are both likely to have consequences for the participants. This is also true, indeed, of variations due to dialect and register.

Goffman: Discourse channels and signals

The theoretical model which perhaps draws all of the various aspects of conversational interaction together is that of Goffman (1976), who has suggested that communication in any cultural context includes the following elements: the presence of adequate two-way acoustic messages; the presence of *back-channel* feedback through which speakers become aware about the status of their speech, whether or not it has been adequately received and interpreted; the presence of *turnover signals*, indicating the turn-taking junctures; the presence of potential *pre-empt signals*, by which the flow of conversation can be interrupted and redirected; the presence of *framing capabilities* by which communicators can separate such phenomena as asides or jokes or ironic comments from the central stream of meaning, the presence of Gricean norms (see Chapters Three and Eight); and the presence of other constraints such as background noise or the presence of other listeners which, although they may not be part of the central communicative exchange yet have an effect on its nature and effect.

If these "universal" constraints exist in communication, though, Goffman argues that there are a number of additional constraints that are even more closely tied to cultural background and expectations. These he calls *ritual* constraints. Once a channel has been opened up for communication to take place, for example, it seems to be a ritual constraint, at least of Western societies, that the communicative "space" is filled with something. In England, this becomes especially evident in the pervasive chit-chat about the weather in elevators (i.e. *lifts*) or at bus-stops, or just about anywhere. The weather seems to fulfil some kind of *filler* role such that if there is an empty communicative slot to be filled, and if there is no other more pressing topic (which would have to be something fairly dramatic like the outbreak of war), then it will suffice. Following a suggestion by Malinowsky, the term *phatic* has been used to cover this kind of language, whose main function is simply to maintain social discourse, rather than to signal any real interest in the topics mentioned. To a lesser extent, speakers also appear to "fill" conversational slots more generally with remarks that will simply "keep things going" even though they do not have any new information to contribute. Goffman's point is that in our own cultures we have a right to *expect* certain kinds of communicative interaction to take place and we have learned to marshal our skills accordingly. In the alternations within adjacency pairs, for instance, we are emotionally involved and generally prepared to engage in the rituals of exchange. Others have noted just how the absence of knowledge about how these rituals are enacted in another culture can lead to *language shock* in outsiders. This is especially clear in the case of second language learners (see Hatch and Long, 1980).

Language and the Formation and Maintenance of Cultural Identity

Linguistic Protectionism

Several examples have been given of how language is related to recognized social structures such as dialect, class, or ethnicity. In the case of Black English, for example, it is clear that this particular dialect serves both to consolidate an in-group and to some extent to exclude the dominant White group around it although, as has been pointed out, the dialect itself contains sub-varieties that are formed on the basis of the same socio-cultural dynamics. The recent development of *rap* in music, from *rapping* in street discourse, further reinforces these aspects of dialectical identity, and there are many other examples of how specific forms of language are developed and maintained as part of the "protection" of a given culture. One of these is the historical development of *pidgins* and *creoles*.

Pidgins and Creoles

Pidgin languages and creoles originated in the need to simplify languages in order to facilitate communication between trading partners. During the colonial period when traders visited the coasts of Africa, the Caribbean, and other groups of islands in the Atlantic and Pacific regions, it became clear that neither of the two cultures apparently wanted to invest the time and energy to learn the language of the other. Accordingly, they protected their positions by resorting to these simplified or intermediate forms, even though the language of the colonizing party was the one which supplied most of the root morphemes, as in the cases of English, French, and Portuguese pidgin languages. The word *pidgin* is itself an adaptation of a Chinese word meaning "business," and the word *creole* once referred to White colonists from the tropical colonies, applying only later to the slaves from these colonies (Traugott & Pratt, 1980). The latter term is now used to refer to forms of language which have developed over time *from* pidgins, and which have become stable language varieties in their own right, learned by the children of pidgin-speakers.

It has sometimes been assumed that pidgins and creoles, since they are apparently simpler in some respects to the languages upon which they are based are, in a similar way to certain dialects, "degraded" or "debased" linguistic forms. But while it is true that pidgins do simplify grammar in two important respects (they all but eliminate inflections and they accomplish syntactic complexity by way of conjunctions rather than embedded clauses) it should not be assumed that they are incapable of complex reference or expression. This is evident in a story spoken in a variety of West African Pidgin English spoken in the Cameroons:

> som boi i bin bi fo som fan kontri fo insai afrika, we i bin get plenti sens. i pas king fo sens sef, sow in neym bin bi sens-pas-

king. king i bin feks plenti, ha i bin hia sey, dis simol-boi i di kas eni-man fo sens.

The translation of this into English runs as follows:

There once lived a very clever boy who lived in a beautiful part of Africa, where he gained great wisdom. He was smarter than the king himself, and so was called "wiser-than-the-king." The king was very annoyed when he heard how this boy was outwitting everyone. (Traugott & Pratt, 1980)

In the rest of the short story, the king decides to try to outwit the boy by getting him to cut his hair and then demanding it back. It is the boy who outwits the king, however, by feeding some chickens as he cuts the king's hair and then demanding the feed back in return for the hair.

At the phonological level, the linguistic features that stand out in the pidgin English are the avoidance of complex consonant clusters, the devoicing of word-final stops to accord with the pattern of the local language, and the avoidance of the voiced and voiceless "th" sounds in English (later in the story "domot" and "mof" replace "door-mouth" and "mouth," respectively). At the morphological level, there is an absence of inflections and an apparently less rich system of relative pronouns than in English (the story contains "where" and "so" but no personal relative pronoun). But it is equally clear that some grammatical relations that are established by other means in English are by no means absent in this version of West African Pidgin English. The Pidgin-English *aspectual* system is particularly impressive, in which *don* expresses that an action has been completed (as in "i mof don lok"--"his mouth locked open--he was completely dumbfounded") while *di* expresses incomplete-continuous action (as in "ha i di kot-am"--"as he was cutting them"). Creoles have developed with special vigor in areas such as many of the Caribbean and Pacific islands where, in addition to a lack of opportunity or interest in learning the language of the colonizers, there has also been little subsequent access to the colonial language. Eventually, pidgins have often developed into stable Creoles, becoming full languages in their own right and it has been argued, moreover, that the *process* of creolization may be central in the development of languages over the course of history (see, e.g. Bickerton, 1975, 1977).

Decreolization

In cases where contact was maintained or strengthened between a colonizing and colonized community, such as that of Jamaica, there is evidence of *de*creolization, or of development towards the language of the colonizing power (English). Even though there has been some convergence with English, however, it is equally clear that there is a strong opposing tendency in many Jamaican and other Caribbean English speakers to differentiate their own language forms from the other forms of English around them. In this process, there is a re-emergence and re-assertion of Caribbean identity within the new post-colonial circumstances in which Creole speakers find themselves. As in the case of West African Pidgin English, Caribbean Creole embraces some evident grammatical simplification of English, replacing the lost regularity with other means for complex expression. Many of the changes found in the Creole forms parallel the kinds of changes that have taken place in English in its development from Anglo-Saxon. English has lost a great many of the inflections that were present up until the time of Chaucer, and Jamaican Creole has merely continued the same process further. Hence, Jamaican Creole has dropped the plural morpheme (*-s*, *-es*) (as in "dem addah girl" for "those other girls"); has dropped various markers used in the expression of past time (as in "mi go yeside" for "I went yesterday" or "mi don sliip" for "I have finished sleeping"); has dropped the markers for *present progressive* (as in "whey you a go?" for "where are you going?"); and has dropped the possessive inflection ("di man hat" for "the man's hat") (Montgomery, 1986, p. 82). This kind of grammatical simplification is a general process of language development and is in no way correlated with any lack of semantic complexity--what is lost in inflectional complexity is made up by way of new syntactic ordering and, of course, by contextual interpretation.

There are some important correspondences between the situation of Black English in Britain and the United States in that speakers of Jamaican

Creole in Britain, just like those of American Black English dialects, find it difficult or impossible to get work. On the other hand, competence in these dialectical forms is central to group membership and acceptance. In both Jamaican Creole and Black English speaking or "chatting bad" is an established sub-cultural skill and is used among other things to exclude or "freeze-off" outsiders. Hierarchies within a group may also form on the basis of levels of adeptness with the language variety. The most extreme case of how a language variety may be developed and reinforced in a way which both consolidates an in-group and excludes an out-group may be that of *antilanguages* such as that of Polish prisoners (called *Gryperska*) or perhaps even that of *CB Radio* slang (Montgomery, 1986). In antilanguages, users deliberately *relexicalize* the language to make it unintelligible to others and to challenge the authority of outsiders. As all of these cases seem to indicate, those aspects of language which serve to identify individuals within groups can also be viewed as part of a competitive market for channels of communication. It is almost as if, in analogy to channels, bands, or wavelengths in broadcasting, language-users within particular socio-cultural groups such as those discussed above need to "clear their own spaces" for communication. The close bonds between language and identity, then, with their markers of social inclusion and exclusion, are also reinforced by the continual need to invent specialized meanings that guarantee the exclusiveness and impenetrability of certain kinds of information. As such, they may have close connections with human territoriality.

Language and Gender Identity

While pidgins, creoles, and even certain aspects of dialectical variation are relatively conscious in degree and allow forms of choice, there are other forms of language variation which, while they serve in a similar way to maintain and reinforce social distinctions, are much less conscious and far more subliminal in nature. Some of the best examples of how this kind of relationship between language and identity is established can be found in the literature on language and gender, an area of increasing interest in the context of feminist sociology and language analysis.

The most obvious and superficial differences between the language of women and men have to do with the use of pronouns and the use of the morphemes *man* and *woman*. Phrases such as "Should anyone forget his pencil," or "A person entering should sign his name in the register" demonstrate a predominance of masculine terms in the language made especially clear by their following the supposedly neutral pronouns *anyone*, *someone*. Various attempts have been made to replace the pronouns *he* and *she* with other forms, such as *tey*, *co*, *thon*, and *person* (Crystal, 1987, p. 46). Equally familiar are cases of the inappropriate usage of terms like *chairman* or *salesman* for female personnel, terms which have been widely changed to *chairperson* and *salesperson*, or of terms like *waitress*, *stewardess*, or *actress*, which have been objected to on grounds that the feminine suffix (*-ess*) tends to perpetuate the idea of female subservience, a distinction which is no longer warranted in a world of redistributed work roles. Other evidence of masculine bias can be found in common expressions such as "the man in the street" and "Mankind" as well as claims such as "Man is the most intelligent primate" or "God made Man in his own image," all of which seem designed to suggest that women were either absent during the course of human history, indistinguishable from men, or of little literary or cultural significance. The apotheosis of this kind of language may be another example provided by Crystal--"Man, being a mammal, breastfeeds his young" in which a male writer seems incapable of acknowledging even quite basic distributional and biological facts (1987, p. 46).

Phonological differences

These masculine biases that appear to have developed over the social history of English can be viewed as stereotypes of women and of the societal relationships that are generally supposed to hold between the sexes. In addition to these relatively subconscious and habitual ways of expressing things with a masculine bias, however, sociolinguists have also found that there are even deeper differences in the manners or styles exhibited in the speech of women and men. A study in Montreal, Canada, showed that women in Quebec pronounce the French articles *il*, *elle*, *la*, and *les* with a much more pronounced /l/ sound than men (Sankoff & Cedergren, 1971) while a study in the United States showed that women stay with more standard pronunciation of /r/ following vowels than do men (Anshen, 1969). Similar small but regular differences have been found in other languages such as Bogoras and Bengali, and in the American Indian Gros Ventre language (Bodine, 1975). It has also been found in American English that girls are more likely to fully complete the pronunciation of all *-ing* forms, while boys are more likely to replace the velar nasal ending (*-ng*) with "*-in*'" (Fischer, 1958).

Lexical differences

Instances can readily be found of how gender differences are reinforced at the level of the lexicon. In English, for example, it has been estimated that there are ten times the number of words to describe promiscuous women than promiscuous men, clearly reflecting the pervasive sex stereotyping in our culture (Crystal, 1987,). Not only are there more such words, but the words for females are far more pejorative in nature (*slut*, and *whore*, for example, are far less salutory than *gigolo* or *Don Juan*). The use of male pronouns in English and other European languages is also significantly greater than that of female pronouns, and the expression *The teacher should never turn his back on the class* is much more likely, for example, than *The teacher should never turn her back on the class*, even in an environment where there are more female than male teachers. As King (1991) points out, not *all* languages are like English, French, German, or Italian in their continual expression of gender differences: Neither Mandarin Chinese nor Tagalog, for instance, make a distinction such as that appearing between *he* vs. *she*, *il* vs. *elle*, or *er* vs. *sie*. On the other hand, Tegulu, a language spoken in India appears to lead to even greater dangers of linguistic stereotyping than English in that its pronouns distinguish between male forms and forms used in relation to "anything else including females"; hence *waadi* refers to a male human while *adi* might refer to a woman, a shoe or any other (inanimate) object (King, 1991, p. 17).

A good example of just how deeply-rooted lexical gender distinctions can become in a language is provided by the Chinese writing system, which perpetuates female stereotypes first generated many centuries ago. Although in speech the widely-used noun *ren* is gender-neutral, meaning *people*, the writing system still incorporates many characters which are far from neutral. The character for *woman*, for example, is still drawn in the shape of a "serving woman" on bended knee and with outstretched hand. The character for *man*, on the other hand, is composed of signs for "power" and "field," reflecting men's original place as masters of their domains. In addition, there are many instances of complex characters for words having negative connotations which combine the pictogram of *woman* with other forms: The character for *greedy* contains the figure of a woman together with one for a forest (originally signifying women's alleged desire for multiple possessions) and the character for *vicious* combines the woman figure with that for *work*, having the connotation that "a woman's place is in the home" and she gets "out of hand" if she escapes from this situation. The character for *husband* is made up of the figure for *person*, on top of which is superimposed the figure for *sky* and then a line "even higher than the sky," thus reflecting the supreme importance of male spouses in the universal order of things. The servile woman figure also appears in the characters for all other Mandarin words marked for female gender, including *waitress, mother, hostess, daughter, sister,* and *concubine*. In parallel with English, Chinese, moreover, emphasizes the offence to women by having both *biaozi* ("bitch") and *biaozi yang de* ("son-of-a-bitch"). In both English and Chinese, then, even when a male misbehaves, there is the underlying suggestion that this is still the responsibility of a woman! (See Appendix B for related examples of Chinese characters).

Genderlects: Women and men in contrasting discourse worlds

It has recently been suggested that all the surface-structural gender distinctions that appear in languages such as English may be due to the separate *sub-cultures* in which men and women play out their roles and, therefore, that male-female discourse should be approached in the same manner and with the same kinds of hypotheses as interethnic discourse (see below), and that "male-female conversation is cross-cultural communication" (Tannen, 1990, p. 42). According to this view, and consistently with the Whorfian Hypothesis (see Chapter Three, above), these sub-cultures are seen to be related to different world-views based on female vs. male patterns of socialization.

Tannen, perhaps the most enthusiastic proponent of this view of gender effects in language (Tannen, 1982, 1986, 1990) has attempted to identify some of the defining features of what she terms *genderlects* (the different "dialectical" forms spoken by men and women). Tannen does not identify the salient differences between genderlects as being so much at the level of phonological or morphological features, however. Adopting some of the terminology of Goffman (see above), Tannen has put forward the controversial idea that men and women typically relate to each other through quite distinct (male vs. female) *frames of reference*. She claims that there are substantial differences in the ways in which men and women communicate both within and across the gender-groups and, in particular, that members of each sub-group frame their expressions in terms of different sets of cultural assumptions. For this reason, men and women often misunderstand and misinterpret each other's discourses and the *metamessages* within them (1990, pp. 28-36).

According to Tannen, women are tuned to a world of discourse in which the central purpose of language is to seek and establish a sense of *community*, a sense of *intimacy*, *connection*, and *mutual commitment* (1990, pp. 23-30). Men's language, on the other hand, may be more tied to a world in which *hierarchy* and *competition* are more salient and in which utterances are often directed towards establishing *status* (ibid.). Since these two discourse worlds are quite different, it is not surprising, Tannen argues, that women and men so often misunderstand each other, and she presents many examples in an attempt to support her point.

One example is of a male colleague, who responds to a message from his publisher requesting his precise location during the period in which his book is being produced by likening the publisher to a "parole officer." She contrasts this with her own very positive (female) response to a similar letter. While she sees such a letter as reinforcing her feeling of importance, of being needed, she surmises that her male colleague's response reflects the feeling of being "framed as both controlled and inferior in rank by being told to report one's movements to someone" (p. 39). Another example concerns how men and women supposedly react to and talk quite differently about divorce. Tannen argues that women define the resulting "freedom" from their partners in a quite different way from men: For women, "freedom" signifies an escape from the need to worry about their husbands, while for men, it signifies a more general escape from the confines of the institution itself, leading to less "claustrophobia" and "fewer responsibilities" (p. 41). In a third example, Tannen argues that female professors tend to take up university careers on the basis of a strong motivation to teach or to "join a faculty" (thus revealing a substantial commitment to *service* and *community*), while male professors are more motivated by freedom and independence from the kinds of hierarchical pressures found in commercial institutions (thus revealing their deep-rooted views of the world as an essentially hierarchical environment) (pp. 41-42).

The development of gender differences

These two views of the world, which underlie both how members of the other gender are understood and how they are responded to, are at least partly established during the period of child development, when girls and boys already demonstrate quite different patterns, respectively, of *intimate-cooperative* vs. *hierarchical-competitive* interactions (Tannen, 1990, p. 43). By high-school age, the patterns are apparently clearly established, and Tannen offers some discourse analysis of transcripts from the interactions of grade 10 girls and boys in their own gender groups. She quotes a girl called Sally, who is empathizing with another girl, Nancy, who is called home early by her mother from a class excursion. Sally tries to make Nancy feel better by letting her know just how sympathetic all the other girls had been:

> I thought it was kind of weird though, I mean, one minute we were going out and the next minute Nancy's going, "Excuse me, gotta be going."...I didn't know what was going *on*, and Judy

comes up to me and she whispers..."Do you know that Nancy's going home?" And I go, "What?" I go, "Why?" She goes, "Her mom's making her." I go, "Ah." She comes back and goes, "Nancy's left." Well, I said, "Well, that was a fine thing to do, she didn't even come and say goodbye." (quoted in Tannen, 1990, pp. 54-55)

According to Tannen, Sally's entire effort here is to "confirm Nancy's feelings of distress." Boys, in contrast, are apparently intent on establishing hierarchical relationships and each others' status even when they are also demonstrating concern for each other. In an extract of grade 10 boys' speech, one boy responds to another's concern about a girl by saying "I'll never understand that" and laughing, and both boys typically change the subject in accordance with their *own* needs and interests. If boys express feeling or concern, other boys in the conversation often apparently make comparisons between these levels of feeling and those of themselves or others: It is almost as if there is a competition to see who can demonstrate they feel the worst (ibid. pp. 55-57).

Remaining questions

Tannen's argument is in many ways persuasive, although while the kinds of discoursal events she describes seem to be accurate, the question remains of whether all of the differences are due to *gender* per se, rather than to *personality type*. Men and women, moreover, appear to do a great deal of role-switching in various contexts which a *static* analysis of genderlects may not capture. Many of the interpretations and misinterpretations she describes also appear to occur *within* groups of men or women, and it seems relatively easy to provide counter-examples to Tannen's examples where the *opposite* roles to the ones she suggests are taken by either sex. Tannen has successfully raised the question of how the language of men and women reflects the gender-based subcultures into which all humans are born, however. Future research may reveal that the qualities of genderlects themselves vary significantly according to the dominant cultures in which they are observed.

Language in Cross-cultural Interaction

Perhaps the most common occurrences of all in which the relationship of language, identity, and culture are put to the test are those where communicative interaction takes place across national, racial, or other cultural boundaries. In the modern post-colonial world, there are more and more instances of such interaction, especially between immigrant second language learners and members of host cultures or, as in the case of Belgium, Switzerland, or Canada between citizens from differing indigenous ethnic groups. The case of Canada presents a particularly interesting context for the analysis of cross-cultural interaction since it demonstrates just how politically volatile issues of language and culture may become.

Cross-cultural Linguistic Issues in Canada

Since the population of French-speaking Quebec represents about one quarter of that of Canada, it is not surprising that there should be strong territorial feelings about the English and French languages. Currently, there is a vibrant and sometimes acrimonious debate about the Canadian "Official Language" policy, which incorporates the assertion of equal rights to education in English or French for children in all Canadian provinces.

While some provinces, such as New Brunswick, have accepted the tenets of the policy enthusiastically, others, especially the Western provinces, have gradually come to realize that provision of such English-speaking educational rights, together with translations into French of all governmental and legal materials, presents an administrative and economic burden. One further source of tension lies in the realization that in many of these provinces, the number of French-speakers has been overtaken by that of speakers of other languages, such as Cantonese, Mandarin, Russian, German, and Italian. In Canada, then, it appears to many that the right of English or French-speakers to learn *two* official languages now supersedes the rights of other Canadians to learn either *one*. In short, there appears at present in Canada to be a somewhat uncomfortable relationship between official French-English bilingual policy on the one hand, and multicultural ideology, with its insistence on equal rights for all sub-cultural groups, on the other (Piper, 1989, p. 162).

It has also been pointed out that the political instantiation of "two founding races" (i.e. the English and the French) in various constitutional documents only reinforces what Porter (1965) referred to as the *vertical ethnic mosaic*, by which Canadian society is ranked according to ethnicity with priority in educational and professional access going to these two groups. For these and other related reasons, issues of language and cultural identity have become linked in Canada in socially and politically fundamental ways, putting any initiatives towards cultural or linguistic preservation at odds with any parallel initiatives towards equality of educational and vocational opportunity.

"French" vs. "English" Canada

In addition to generating the uneasy situation described above, Official Bilingual policy seems to have done little to alleviate tension between English and French Canadians themselves, and the Quebec Separatist Movement continues to gain strength. A very strong sense persists in Canada of the distinctions between the English and French languages and cultures. Something of this sense is apparent in the following extract, taken from a submission in a 1986 competition in which young Canadian writers were asked to express their feelings about living in an officially bilingual country. The passage is taken from a short story entitled "Waiting for Claudine," in which Claudine, a young woman from Quebec talks to her host while staying in Vancouver.

> "Do you like French?" she [Claudine] asked as we reached the sand.
> "How do I know? I can't understand it."
> "No. I mean do you like the sound of French?"

"No."
"But why?" She was extremely surprised by my response.
"It's too fast. You run all your words together."
"It's not true! French is beautiful. It is music. It's smooth... English is so rough."
"If you don't like English, why are you here?" I retorted, almost too quickly for my own liking.
"To be anyone in this world one must speak English. You are lucky to live here."
I had never considered myself lucky before. "Why don't you move here then?" The idea was distasteful, but I was her host, so I kept the conversation going, and asked.
"Oh, it's not my place, I'm French, not English."
"What difference does it make?"
"All the difference. We are opposite."
"Opposite?"
"Yes. You are on top and I am on the bottom. But we French make up for that in other ways."
I was dumbfounded by her words. She, the raven, felt that I was on top. "What are your ways?"
"We have our own dance and music. We have invented a unique language. On St-Jean-Baptiste Day we drink and eat tourtière and we praise the Virgin Mary that we are French and we are family." (quoted in Piper, 1989, pp. 169-170)

Another extract from the submission of young Anglo-Canadian expresses his cultural antagonism towards French lessons.

In English schools, French is laid out on the black slab,
Like well polished soapstone in highway boutiques, without craft.
It is spoken once a day, slowly
Like a prayer or a spell.
Many say it should be spoken
Other than it is. Do not believe it.
Were this true, then we are better sculptors,
Better players in our chalk dust,
Than God. (ibid. p. 170)

Overlaid on top of all these tensions connected to language and cultural identity in Canada are the claims of aboriginal people to *their* language rights. The current situation in Canada, then, well illustrates just how pervasive and significant these relations can be.

Cultural identity and language education

Not surprisingly, Canada has also been home to some pioneering research into the educational aspects of culture and language. Ever since the days of early work on the foundations of immersion language learning (e.g. Gardner and Lambert, 1959), a strong relationship has been recognized between cultural variables, on the one hand, and levels of *motivation* to learn a second language, on the other. Students of a second language are clearly better motivated and more successful when their second language (and culture) are treated *additively*, as opposed to *subtractively* (Lambert, 1975; Gardner, 1979). In subtractive education programming, the focus is on elimination or *extinction* of the first languages and cultures, whereas in additive programming, second languages and cultures are viewed as valuable additions to the backgrounds that students bring with them to their learning. It is now widely recognized that motivation and self-esteem in most second language students can be enhanced more readily by way of an additive approach. Severe erosion of the self-esteem based on secure first-language and first-cultural identity is now recognized, moreover, to lead to unacceptable levels of *culture-shock* (Furnham and Bochner, 1986). Perhaps the most extreme form of subtractive bilingual education continues to occur, however, and this is the deliberate *submersion* of immigrant students in mainstream high-school classes for which they have insufficient linguistic or cultural preparation. In these all-to-frequent cases, rather than systematic *immersion* in their second language, students are virtually "dumped" into regular classrooms where, without sufficient second-language training, they face demanding curricula and an unsympathetic peer group (for a more detailed discussion of this issue see e.g. Piper, 1985).

Interethnic communication

Work by Gumperz and his colleagues (e.g. Gumperz, 1982) has established that, even where second language learners have made considerable progress, features of their language may lead to communicative difficulties or, worse, to adverse reactions in first-language speakers. These kinds of effects were made very clear in a now well-known BBC documentary called *Crosstalk* (1981), in which interactions between Asian-Indian immigrants to the United Kingdom and various British officials were filmed. In one incident, an Asian English-speaker is heard rejecting a bank form he has been given by a male teller by saying "No, it's the *wrong* one!" (with a strong accent on *wrong*). This and other intonational effects in the immigrant's speech accumulate in a way which clearly offends the bank teller, causing him to respond abruptly. In another incident, the Asian immigrant to Britain is seen applying for a job in a college library. Here, the interchange between interviewers and applicant falls apart due to the quite different cultural expectations on either side about how information should be presented at an interview and about "what should be said." To the interviewee, it seems quite appropriate to tell the truth, namely, that he wants *any* job that he can get. To the British interviewers, it seems that the applicant should at least *appear* to have a particular interest in the institution to which he is applying. Not surprisingly, the immigrant fails to get the job due to these different cultural perspectives.

Both of the above are good examples of the general kinds of difficulties that may occur in cross-cultural communication, difficulties that may be due to relatively superficial features of intonation or to deeper-level culturally-based conceptual differences. In all cases, the perception of others *through* the kinds of language they use is fundamental to individual judgment. In more benign cases than those recorded in *Crosstalk*, cross-cultural communication can be more sensitively *negotiated* by way of *repairs* and what have been called "self-righting mechanisms" (Sacks, Schegloff, & Jefferson, 1974). At the other extreme, superficial features of language such as stress and intonation, just like skin-color, clothing, or even smell, can be used as a basis for prejudicial or discriminatory behavior. It remains true in many societies that even quite fluent, yet accented, second-language speech can be used as a basis for excluding people from jobs, property-ownership, or from sub-group membership in general.

Summary

The relations between language, culture, and society are ubiquitous, and they are closely related to individual feelings and behaviors. Sociolinguists have demonstrated that dialects, although hard to define precisely, continue to develop and to support cultural group identity. Dialects identify not only the location of a speaker's childhood but also play a strong part in the identification of class membership, especially in relation to the so-called "standard" dialects of given languages.

Apart from dialects, however, it is clear that various language codes exist which reflect social groupings, codes such as the "open" vs. "closed" formations described by Bernstein, the antilanguages of counter-cultural groups, or those which underlie gender distinctions. Communicative competence theory has done much to establish that language use is based not solely on grammatical knowledge, but also on other types of social and strategic knowledge as well. Halliday's analysis of language functions reveals, moreover, that language is always used for some purpose, even though the exact nature of such purposes may not be immediately evident during communication. Discourse analysts and ethnographers have shown how the complex "game" of language communication involves many sorts of role-playing maneuvers, including those concerning turn-taking and establishing and maintaining topics.

The most general finding of all is that language is intimately connected to feelings of human identity, whether this identity be founded on gender, ethnicity, class, or "race." The whole matter of language and culture is inseparable, moreover, from both political and educational decision-making. As current experience in Canada suggests, political and educational ideologies may often be at odds with individual opportunities and freedoms. Finally, language often signals cultural attributes which can lead to negative interpretation, prejudice, or discrimination. Language, just like other markers of cultural identity, can be used to include or exclude individuals from social groups of all kinds.

CHAPTER EIGHT

Language and Philosophy

Most questions and propositions of the philosophers result from the fact that we do not understand d the logic of our language...All philosophy is 'Critique of language'... (L. Wittgenstein, *Tractatus Logico-Philosophicus*, 1922)

[P]hilosophy has, as its first if not its only task, the analysis of meanings,...the theory of meaning...is the foundation of all philosophy, and not epistemology as Descartes misled us into believing. (M. A. E. Dummett, *Frege: Philosophy of language*, 1973)

Introduction

Something of the range of philosophizing about language has already been introduced in the first three chapters. Philosophical issues have also emerged in relation to the discussion of innateness (Chapter Four), of grammar (Chapter Five), and of both sociolinguistics and psycholinguistics (Chapters Six and Seven). As the above quotations from Wittgenstein and Dummett suggest, moreover, the development of language theory and philosophy in the twentieth century have been closely intertwined, and it has become increasingly apparent that there is really no language theory that is *not* philosophical in nature or which is independent from some of the fundamental problems debated by philosophers over the centuries. What professional philosophers have concentrated on most, however, in distinction from linguists, biologists, psychologists or sociologists is the particular relationship between language, truth, and meaning. Philosophical positions can be most conveniently viewed in terms of the claims they embody about this relationship although, as we shall see in this chapter, the very grounds for relating the three to each other are in dispute. In the first part of the chapter, we will look more closely at the claim that the relationship between language and truth resides in formal logic. In the second part, we will turn to the more recent idea that meaning in context is the most fundamental relation and, in the third part, to the emergence of a phenomenological tradition of thinking about the nature of language in which it is argued that language, thought, and Being are in quite essential ways identical. These three parts, it will be recognized, retrace the spectrum from "object" to "subject" introduced in the first part of the book. The final chapter in this section, on semiotics, should be read as a direct continuation of this discussion.

Language, Truth, and Logic

How do we conclude that what someone else says is "true" and how, indeed, do others know when we are speaking the truth? Is it possible to "speak the truth" without what we are saying actually describing reality (even though we may *intend* that it does)? Clearly, there must be some important links between truth, on the one hand, and both logical propriety and what speakers count as meaningful, on the other but, as the review of Tarski's proposals about the relations between truth and logic demonstrate (see Chapter Two, above) the relations between truth and meaning may actually be very difficult to describe in a precise way. One of the things that makes these questions so intransigent is that satisfactory answers to them so clearly depend upon an understanding of the underlying nature of knowledge itself. This is so, since what counts as "knowledge" in any individual must to a great deal depend upon what she considers to be "true" and "meaningful." Not surprisingly, philosophers continue to wrestle with these central questions of meaning, truth, language and knowledge.

Four Traditional Interpretations of the Language-Truth Relationship

Some of the major ideas specifically developed by philosophers about the relationship between language and truth are conveniently discussed under the headings of *correspondence* theories, *coherence* theories, *pragmatic* theory, and *semantic* theory (Haack, 1978).

Correspondence

In the early period of his work, Wittgenstein, along with Russell, Whitehead and others argued that truth was guaranteed only by the correspondence of propositions to facts. Even complex propositions, then, rested according to these philosophers on the *logical atoms* out of which they were composed: They argued that truth rested on one-to-one correspondence between propositions and real-world "facts." But while this idea sounds simple and clear enough, it has led to a huge amount of controversy, since it is not always exactly evident what a "fact" is and there is no easy way to distinguish between what actually *is* and what I truly and genuinely *believe* to be the case (even though others may not see things the same way, and even if I may change my beliefs over time). Another fundamental problem in establishing "atoms" of truth upon which all other propositions rest is our inability to establish that what may look like universal truths really *are* so, since we are almost always incapable of taking into account the set of all instances upon which the correspondence rests. Even an apparently uncontroversial proposition such as *All mature elephants have a thick hide* may run into trouble if its "truth" rests on correspondence to the facts, and when it is entirely possible that there may be at least one thin-skinned elephant somewhere in the jungle.

Is it possible to modify correspondence theories so that the criterion of correspondence can be saved without being so strictly tied to these absolute logical atoms? It is in response to this question that the work of Austin is important, since his notion of correspondence rests not upon this idea of logical atoms but upon the idea that correspondence between propositions and facts was essentially a matter of *convention* (this is what makes him a "subjectivist" rather than an "objectivist"). Austin (1950) argued that correspondence should be broken down into two types of convention, *descriptive* and *demonstrative*. To illustrate descriptive conventions, if I am heard to utter (or if I write) "Major's going to fall," then you understand this as a true statement by me at a particular point in time and in terms of a particular set of circumstances we are both in touch with (either there is a British political circumstance detrimental to Major, or we can both see him on non-metaphorical thin ice, for example). There are many communicative circumstances, however, where neither of us can actually corroborate in any clear way what is or what is not the case and yet on which you may reasonably conclude that I am speaking the truth. These cases involve demonstrative convention. If I say, for instance, "Yeltsin's going to fall" even though, unlike the case of Major, you may have no direct evidence, you regard my utterance as truthful by *analogy* to other statements made by me and others (such as that about Major).

To Austin, then, correspondence needed to be understood in a quite different way from how the early Wittgenstein and Russell had described it. He argued that correspondences *are always conventional*; words and the world outside can be mapped on to each other in many ways and do not always stand in a one-to-one relationship. As we have already seen, this represents a different (and much more feasible) view of the role of language since, unlike logical atomism, the idea of language convention is not inconsistent with the idea that language is typically used to describe facts or events that are displaced from the here and now in time, space, or fictional imagination.

Coherence

Correspondence theorists held that truth lay in the relation between propositions and real-world facts and that complex propositions should be analyzed into their logical atoms. The propositions which were considered to be "atoms" were, of course, those which were considered to be the most reliable and the least controvertible, namely, those propositions which were immediately verifiable in perceptual experience. Coherence theorists such as the philosopher, Carnap, emphasized that the guarantee of truth lay not so much in the reducibility of propositions to these atoms as it did in the *logical relations* between these perceptual propositions and other statements. And since even these atomistic propositions are difficult to test in any absolute sense and are difficult to divide from firm beliefs (however well justified), the coherence theorists argued that the central test of truth must lie in the coherence or otherwise of the statements (propositions, beliefs) themselves. On this view, then, a statement like *Major's going to fall* is true or false depending upon a framework of systematically-related beliefs about the world in general, about the nature of politics, and so on, and because it fits into this framework as part of a coherent set of beliefs. This view of truth is more *epistemological* in nature than correspondence theory since it invokes the idea of knowledge (which arises only out of the perception of system and coherence in natural events) in order to explain the *experience* of truth. Central in the coherence theory of truth is the claim that knowledge changes and that it involves constant searching for "truth" and the rearrangement of beliefs and ideas, rather than being any absolute or rigid property of nature: Reality is defined as the perception of a coherent whole, although it seems clear that individuals can never see the totality of events and that they must therefore work with the "partial" truths that the scope of their experiences allows them to construct.

Just like correspondence theory, however, coherence theory is faced with a fundamental problem. With correspondence theory, the problem was to establish exactly what it is that is supposed to correspond between propositions and facts. With coherence theory, the problem resides in the impossibility of prescribing exactly what are those propositions that will count as "coherent" with others and which will not. A story can be entirely *coherent*, but can this be said to establish the "truth" of what is written? It could be argued that it is only those propositions which are *plausible* which should be included within the set of coherent propositions within some domain of truthful description, but this wouldn't get us much further since we would now need to come up with a satisfactory and watertight criterion of plausibility. In the end, then, coherence, while being an important contributor to knowledge can at best only form *part* of the nature of truth. It is not in itself a sufficiently rich notion on the basis of which to explain the necessary *and* sufficient conditions for truth.

Pragmatism

The central idea of the pragmatist philosophers, James, Peirce, and Dewey was that truth and reality were related to *actions* and *consequences*. If I believe something to be true, then in order for this belief to mean anything at all there must be some *test* that I can perform to establish that my belief is justified. According to Peirce, it is only the scientific method by which such tests can be made rigorous and which can guarantee the necessary objectivity for establishing the truth. On this view, true belief can only arise out of systematic testing of belief against reality, and it is only through repeated testing of beliefs that they become stable and no longer require skepticism or doubt. Testing of one's beliefs, of course, as James pointed out, takes place over time, and the constant verification of beliefs brings with it an element of coherence to truth. Dewey preferred to use the term "warranted assertibility" rather than "truth" in order to capture the idea that individual knowledge is built up on the basis of what individuals can with empirical justification rightly *claim* to be true (Haack, 1978, pp. 97-99).

As can be seen from a brief review of these central ideas, the pragmatists' description of the relation between meaning and truth straddles both objective and subjective orientations towards language. On the one hand, truth is held to depend upon the rigorous and objective submission of beliefs to tests of reality, but on the other, the pragmatists argue that truth *is* a matter of the subjective interpretation through the scientific method, where truth becomes a matter of *conventional* acceptance rather than any formal-logical relation. One difficulty which is avoided by the pragmatist approach to truth and knowledge is that raised by the evident *changes* in what is accepted to be true in everyday life and, even more dramatically, in the realm of science itself. Within the pragmatist framework, the fact that the Copernican, Newtonian, and Einsteinian views of the truth about the universe, for example, presents no intransigent inconsistency: Each of these revolutionary views presented the "truth" about the universe *in their time and within the conventions of empiricism*. Knowledge at these various points in history consisted in justified true belief on the basis of available tests of reality and, according to the pragmatist philosophers, the results of such available tests provide the ultimate criteria of truth, and therefore of meaning. On this view, both the criteria of correspondence and coherence, then, are *dependent*, on and can only follow *from* the constant testing of the consequences of our beliefs.

Semantics

The prime example of a theory which provides a "semantic" solution to the relation between meaning, truth, and reality, is that of Tarski, already reviewed in Chapter Two. It will be recalled that Tarski's analysis of paradoxes such as the Liar's Paradox (*This sentence is false...*) was that they were paradoxical due to certain semantic properties of the language in which they were expressed, namely, that the language contained the words "true" and "false" and that it therefore permitted reference to its own expressions. The way out of the paradox, according to Tarski, was to claim that truth or falsity cannot be reliably ascertained in any *object* language (such as everyday English in this case), but must be established by a higher-level *metalanguage* that permits the conditions of truth for the object language to be stated independently. Paradoxes can be easily resolved, on this basis, by showing that the statements that give rise to them only do so when they are semantically *bound* within a single language.

Some serious questions have been raised about Tarski's proposals, however, on the basis that they are *just* semantic in nature and that while they provide an apparent *logical* way out of the problem of having a sentence such as *This sentence is false* be false when it is true and true when it is false, the whole matter involves more than logic per se. From a purely logical perspective, the metalinguistic solution that claims that *This sentence is false* is to be interpreted as "This sentence is false in its English object language" (thus making it simply false and not paradoxical) appears to work. But is this really how truth and falsity "work" in an everyday sense? Are problems of truth and knowledge really resolved by resorting to "metalanguage?" To some philosophers, Tarski's ideas have appeared to amount more to semantic and logical trickery than to any real philosophical solution to the problem of truth, a solution which leads to greater understanding of how true belief is established.

Davidson (1967, 1974) has attempted to develop the semantic theory of truth in a way which does more to explain how normal expression and understanding take place. Davidson (1974) proposed that *interpretation* lies at the core of truth and meaning; speakers of a language hold something to be true in relation to their perception of what beliefs are held constant by others around them. This approach incorporates both truth-functional and intentional aspects of meaning since by accepting a statement to be true, a given language-user will be judging, first, that the statement reflects true belief in the community around him and, consequently, that the statement does actually represent a true correspondence to reality. Language, then, is *for expressing the truth* and things in general can only be interpreted with this in mind.

While Tarski had been ultimately skeptical about formulating a truth-functional account of any natural language in the face of so many forms which seem neither true nor false, Davidson has forged ahead in an attempt to extend Tarskian principles. Instead of attempting to define truth as a property of *sentences*, Davidson argues that it is a property of *utterances in context*, although he continues to believe that the logical form of such utterances underlies their truth and that the specification of such logical form must be part of an explanation of meaning. In this way, the truth of the utterance "There is a bear in the campground" is established precisely by it being the case that there exists something that is a bear in something that is a campground at the time that utterance is spoken. (The utterance both corresponds to the facts *and* is coherent in terms of its context). What about utterances such as "Anita blurted out that there is a bear in the campground," however? Here, the truth of the utterance no longer depends upon correspondence to reality in the cases of either the bear or the campground; their existence is irrelevant to the truth or otherwise of the reported speech. Logical reduction, moreover, might involve the claim that where *bear* = *an omnivorous mammal* then what Anita actually blurted out was that there was "an omnivorous mammal in the campground," leading to further explanatory problems.

Davidson's proposed solution to problems such as these is to break things down in another way as follows: The utterance about Anita comprises two parts--Anita said *that* (i.e. she made the claim that) and the claim *There is a bear in the campground*. In the case that there *is* a bear in the campground, then, according to Davidson Anita and I (or you, or anyone who is there at the time) stand in relation to each other as "samesayers." This same relation would hold, moreover, if Anita was a monolingual Italian speaker and made the equivalent statement in her own language while we expressed things in English. In this way, Anita's utterance is true *if* she meant exactly the same thing as someone else meant by uttering that there was a bear in the campground. If she didn't mean the same thing (or, of course, if that's not what she uttered or she didn't utter anything at all), then the entire statement is false. Unlike other logical analyses (cf. Frege, Carnap, and others), Davidson's analysis demonstrates that a claim or belief (such as Anita's about the bear) does not actually entail the presence of the bear, and that the truth or falsity of the entire utterance "Anita blurted out that there is a bear in the campground" does not depend entirely upon the truth of all of its components. While Davidson's developments of a theory of meaning and truth on Tarskian lines clearly succeed in showing how utterances in local contexts of interpretation are still logical in nature, it appears that he may not have sufficiently dealt with the critical question of what are the primitive logical forms underlying truth itself and on which his theory rests (Haack, pp. 125-127).

The presence of these competing views about truth demonstrates the considerable challenge philosophers continue to face in describing its nature. While many philosophers have chosen to concentrate upon relatively abstract logical aspects of the problems connected with truth, as the review of four major approaches shows, the whole question of truth is really inseparable from questions about the nature of knowledge and meaning. One crucial distinction in the arguments about truth, a distinction drawn, for example, between the views of Austin, on the one hand, and those of Russell and the early Wittgenstein on the other, centers on the importance of *contingency* or, to use a more familiar and less technical term, of *context*. Whereas the logical positivists (Russell, Wittgenstein, Carnap, and others) searched for a *direct* link between logic and truth--one which works for all occasions and for all types of reference--Austin and many others have argued that the fundamental logic underlying and linking truth and meaning is a logic that relates utterances to their contexts. The principal frameworks in which have debated and developed these ideas are those of *modal* and *possible-world* logics.

Modal Logic and Possible Worlds

So far, the thoughts about logic that have been described relate logic to only one "world," the "real" world of the here-and-now. But do the utterances we speak and hear or the expressions we read and write always unequivocally relate to this world of the here-and-now? It is clear that they do not and, indeed, it may even be the case that *more* expressions in natural language describe states of affairs that are "possible" or "hypothetical" rather than actual. Even everyday utterances like "Tomorrow the Dow's going to jump fifty points, I know it..." or "I bet it's just heavenly in Aruba right now" show that language is not always used to describe things as they absolutely certainly are, and that language users typically embody in their utterances certain kinds of estimates of the *probability* of things occurring. One way of doing this is by identifying their levels of *beliefs* about how things are in the world. Some clear evidence of the indirectness of truth and meaning comes from use of the *modal* verbs of the language. The propositions *Schwarzenegger **may** turn to politics, Holmes **could** regain the championship*, or *Nancy Reagan **should** be ashamed* all involve modal verbs that invoke some sort of *hypothetical* rather than "definite" reality.

Possible-world logic

Modal logicians have attempted to match these facts of everyday usage by developing logics which include operators that permit extension of logical systems to cover such types of expressions. Another way of viewing this is to say that someone uttering a modal expression like those above is stating that something is true in *some possible world*--that is to say, using the examples, that there is at least one such possible world in which Schwarzenegger will turn to politics, at least one possible world in which Homes will regain the championship, and at least one in which Nancy Reagan is ashamed. These are all *logically possible* occurrences. A *necessary* truth (for example *Two plus seven is nine*) is, then, one that is true in *all* possible worlds, while a *contingent* truth is one, like those above, which is dependent upon the prevailing conditions of *one* of many possible worlds.

Modal logic contains operators to reflect the distinction between necessary and contingent truth in terms of possible-world identification. In simple propositional or predicate logic, the utterance "Schwarzenegger will turn to politics," then, would be subject to verification in the first instance by way of assessing the quality of the speaker's "true belief," and, ultimately, by the quality of the actual outcome *necessary* to the truth. In modal logic, the utterance will be understood to be of the form "*It is possible* that Schwarzenegger will turn to politics," and the truth will be *contingent* upon the existence of the possible world in which this becomes realized. Even if this does come about, then, it is not *necessary* for it to come about for the statement to be both true and meaningful. It is necessary only that the events are *possible*. It should be recognized, indeed, that there are *many* possible worlds in which Schwarzenegger could turn to politics and, equally surely, a lesser subset of worlds in which he could become president. Reagan made it, after all, and Schwarzenegger has much better family connections. In this way, *Arnold Schwarzenegger, body-builder, and star of "The Terminator" was born on Earth* is true in *all* possible worlds (i.e. is *necessarily* true), while *Schwarzenegger will be president* is true in a number of possible worlds, while *Schwarzenegger will become Prime Minister* is much less probable (i.e. true in a much smaller set of possible worlds) and *Schwarzenegger will become Miss America* is necessarily false (i.e. not true in any possible world).

It should be noted that the domain of possible worlds extends to *fictional* worlds, too, and that once these are included into the calculation of truth, "no holds are barred." There is no doubt an imaginary world somewhere in time and space in which such an occurrence as the crowning of Arnold as Miss America might take place--one, perhaps, where body-building, steroids, and gender, become socially integrated in some ingenious way. One very important aspect of the development of modal logic and possible-world theorizing is that they do permit the rational analysis of fictional and historical worlds (see Pavel, 1986; Bruner, 1986).

Various types of modal truth are possible, and various logics have been devised to reflect this. *Deontic* logic has been formulated to reflect the semantics of permission and obligation, a formulation particularly well-suited for describing all statements having to do with law or morality, the particular forms of which are not universal across cultures and which typically apply within particular possible worlds or sets of possible worlds. The statement *Drivers must keep to the left of the highway median*, then, expresses an obligation in some possible worlds (England, Japan, Hong Kong, The Bahamas) that would lead to permission to proceed on highways in certain ways. In other jurisdictions (possible worlds), such as the United States and Canada, statements of obligation and permission relating to driving will be stated quite differently. *Epistemic* modal logic is specialized to deal with expressions of *belief*. *Boulomaic* logic contains special operators for the expression of *desire*, while *tense* logic relates alternative possible worlds to particular points in time (Allwood, Andersson & Dahl, 1977).

Conditional reasoning

One particular area where possible-world analysis has been pursued is in the analysis of *counterfactual* sentences. Counterfactual sentences, fairly typical in everyday language use, are those which express things in terms of how they might be, or might have been, *if* circumstances were different. Typically, expressions of this kind utilize the *conditional connectives, if....then*, and are of a form similar to that in *If McEnroe had attended Sunday School, he wouldn't have been fined for swearing.* Utterances such as these seem to work on an underlying all-things-being-equal assumption that the *only* change that need be wrought is that in the if-clause itself: The speaker of the utterance in this case is inviting agreement that, *had the real world stayed the same* and little McEnroe had attended some bible classes, he would not have been fined for swearing. The relevant *possible* world here, then, is only one small step from the actual or real world. Several logicians and, in particular, Lewis (1973) have moved on from this point to develop systems of modal logic in which the relations between possible worlds and the actual world can be specified precisely in terms of their degrees of similarity to each other. According to this analysis, then, we may interpret the statement about McEnroe as true in a possible world *since* this world is similar to the world in which the *if* and the *then* clause are normally related (in this case, in which respect for others and the language is a normal consequence of respect for the Bible).

One noticeable aspect of the work of logicians and philosophers working in the area of modal logic and possible worlds is just how *psychological* in nature much of the arguments appear to be. In much of the literature, possible worlds, indeed, often appear to be "projections of the mind" rather than purely *logical* entities--or, at the least, it appears that logic proceeds *after* the imaginative projection of some possible world of reference. Philosophers have themselves disputed the justifiability of blending logic and psychology in this way and, in particular, they have debated the question of whether possible worlds should be construed as purely logical in nature or as part of *constructed* reality--that is, as part of how individuals psychologically construct reality on the basis of their own individual sensations and perceptions. Most seem to have opted for some version of the constructivist alternative, although Lewis (1986), has developed his earlier position into an even more controversial stance by arguing for "modal realism," a version of modal logic in which possible worlds are treated as having the same reality status as the "actual" world of the here-and-now. The most concentrated attempt to develop a semantic theory on the basis of modal and possible-world logic is to be found in the work of Montague (1970), who incorporated these principles into what is now often called *Montague grammar* (for a concise review, see Dowty et al., 1981).

Pragmatics: Meaning in Context

The idea that truth is *contingent* on frames of reference that is central to possible-world analysis is less incompatible than is a purely truth-functional logical analysis of meaning with the idea that meaning and truth continually involve human psychological processing. The field of *pragmatics* (not to be confused with the work of the pragmatic philosophers mentioned above) can be viewed as an extension of this view of meaning, which places human perceptions and decisions in communicative contexts at the core of meaning. It will be recognized from this that many of the ideas already reviewed, such as those developed by Austin, Grice, and Searle concerning the contextualization of communication in social context fall within the domain of pragmatics (see Chapters Three and Seven).

The fundamental insight of these theorists and of the many sociolinguists and discourse-analysts now working in the area of pragmatics is that language and communication must be understood in relation to social and interpersonal interaction rather than to any formal logical system (modal or otherwise) developed in abstraction from the dynamics of intentionality and inference. Utterances are understood to be not "statements" or "sentences" but, rather, to be *acts*; acts of greeting, thanking, persuading, ordering, apologizing, and so on, having a quite different kind of logical make-up from that contained in the various calculi upon which other philosophers have relied. In *speech-act semantics*, as it is sometimes called, it is recognized that simple propositions such as, say, *The television is on*, having the same properties in relation to truth-functionality in the real or a possible world as noted in traditional logical semantics also have the *further* quality of always being embedded in the framework of some form of *intent* and *purpose*. In Chapter Seven, the idea was introduced that utterances can be varied for register, style, and so on, in such a way that they reflect types of social relationships and identities. Another more formal way in which philosophers have thought about this is to say that utterances have varying levels of *force* (following Austin, 1962). The set of possible utterances "Karen, would you please switch the television off," "Karen, would you please switch that damn thing off," "Karen, switch it off," and "Do you think you could switch the television off?" suggest that a message can be uttered in many forms which differ in terms of this *illocutionary force*. Speech act theorists claim, then, that utterances contain two types of content; *propositional content* (p), together with a level of illocutionary force (F), and all utterances have a "total act structure" of the form F(p) (Searle, Kiefer & Bierwisch, 1980). It is also clear that utterances can be broken down into *direct* acts ("Karen, switch it off.") and *indirect* acts ("Do you think you could switch the television off?").

Pragmatics: Scope and Justification

The term *pragmatics* is now used to cover types of language analysis that are founded on recognition of the kind of conversational reasoning described in speech act semantics and, indeed, on any kind of reasoning that is socially or contextually based. Searle et al. (1980), however, argue that pragmatics is a somewhat ambiguous term that has been used in various ways, and they identify three such distinct ways in which it has been used.

The first way, following Montague, Lewis, and others, has been to view pragmatics simply as a matter of relating propositions to their contexts. On this view, a proposition is what it *denotes* in any particular context. Hence, *Americans are patriotic*, stated without circumstantial or other constraint denotes all those occasions on which Americans are patriotic. Stated by a European while watching celebrations of the Gulf War victory, however, the utterance might have quite another kind of force indeed, including denotation relating to European skepticism about American geopolitical behavior. In this first tradition, pragmatics is viewed as concerning the explanation of the relations between propositions and the particular contexts in which they are uttered.

In the second tradition of thinking about pragmatics, the *sense* rather than the reference of things is considered to be most important aspect of meaning. In this second tradition, exemplified by Katz (1977), *semantics* involves the determination of all aspects of the *literal* meaning of utterances (including the definitions of words and their relations with other words through *synonymy*, *antonymy*, and logical entailment), while pragmatics should be concerned with how speakers and hearers determine the ways in which utterances are being *used*. Taking the sentences *Fiona collected her certificate* vs. *Fiona collected his certificate*, we can see that there are certain underlying rules of gender and pronoun agreement in English that bias our reading of the first towards the interpretation that Fiona collected her own certificate (although it *could* have been Jane's) and our reading of the second towards the interpretation that she collected someone else's. According to the second tradition, the analysis of why and how this comes about lies within the domain of semantics, while questions about who "he" is, or about what events could have led to such an action, are matters for pragmatics. Semantics, according to this view, would also explain the *literal* meaning of my wife's saying "Butter's pure saturated fat" (butter contains fat that doesn't melt at room temperature etc...), while my pragmatic understanding of her forceful speech act might be something like "Drop the butter knife if you want to reach retirement age intact."

In the third tradition, of Austin, Grice, Searle, and the late Wittgenstein, there simply are no "context-free" aspects of meaning, and so there can be no clear distinction between semantics and pragmatics on this basis. On this view, it is impossible to split utterances into several "kinds" of meaning, such as their "indexical," "referential," or "denotative" meaning: All utterances are fundamentally determined by their communicative purposes, what they refer to is viewed as incidental, and illocutionary force is seen to be just as significant as anything the utterance might directly or indirectly refer to.

Pragmatic Functioning

The above three approaches to defining pragmatics illustrate what a great deal of the debate in semantics has been about since Austin's innovations. The fact that the speech-act philosophers did not themselves use the term "pragmatics" to describe their theories has made it more difficult to draw the boundaries of the area precisely. It is the third tradition (that of the speech-act philosophers), however, which seems to capture most clearly the characteristics of the field now known as pragmatics. If there is one unifying theme in the field of pragmatics it is that meaning is *always* underwritten by context, purpose, and intent and, accordingly, that pure "semantic" analysis of language--whether this be in terms of logical calculi, structural relations such as synonymy and antonymy, or syntax, is doomed to failure. But if the kinds of dynamics argued to underlie communication are to be accepted as the foundations of meaning, one crucial question remains, and it is this: What is the nature of all the *background* knowledge needed for speakers and hearers to interpret each other and precisely *how* is this background information related to utterances?

Bringing lexical and contextual information together

A particularly clear analysis of how meaning emerges from the relationship between speech acts and background meaning is provided by Searle et al. (1980), who look in some detail at the various types of usage in English of the verb *cut*. Searle's basic position is that the meaning of any sentence is unitary and unambiguous when placed against an "unrepresentable" background of assumptions and practices (p. 221). Sentences such as *Bill cut the grass*, *The barber cut Tom's hair*, or *Sally cut the cake* are all, according to Searle, interpreted "literally," and there is nothing contained in them that is metaphorical or figurative. This is not the case, however, in sentences such as *Sam cut two classes last week*, or *The President cut the salaries of the employees*, where *cut* is used in a way which figuratively extends the meaning found in the first group: The distinction can be demonstrated by way of the sentence frame *The new cutting machine can cut...*, which can be completed by *the grass*, *Tom's hair*, etc., but not by *the salaries* etc.. In the sentences *Bob can't cut the mustard*, *Cut the noise*, and *Cut it out!*, *cut* is clearly used *idiomatically*, in a way which only experienced native speakers will understand and in a way which does not readily translate into other languages.

We have, then, three different kinds of usage for *cut*; literal, figurative, and idiomatic. These multiple uses, according to Searle, present a severe problem to traditional semantics such as that pursued by the logicians, or to the idea that there is any "basic" or "literal" meaning to a sentence that can be conceived of as being separate from its context, or to the idea that meaning is dependent upon its truth-conditions. Searle argues that the occurrences of *cut* in the first (literal) set of sentences undermine the idea that meaning depends upon truth-conditions, since, even in repeated uses of this literal meaning, these truth-conditions appear to be different--what satisfies any cutting having taken place seems to be different for each sentence. It might be argued that *cut*, like *bank*, or *check*, is simply ambiguous as demonstrated by looking up the multiple meanings listed in dictionaries. This will not suffice in this case, however, since the various occurrences of *cut* in the first set of sentences all conform to the *same* meaning (corresponding, roughly, to "slice with an instrument"). Another counter-argument might be that *cut* takes different "arguments" in the sentences of the first set: Thus the literal meaning of *cut* "combines with" the literal meaning of *grass, hair, cake,* and so on, to yield multiple particular meanings. Searle rejects this argument also on the grounds that *cut* can actually mean the *same* thing on two supposedly contrasting occasions: In a gardening supply store, the utterance "Cut the grass for the customer" *could* include *cut* meaning very much the same as it does in the bakery utterance "Cut the cake for the customer," where "cut the grass," in context, means *slice* off a piece of turf. Here, the interpretation of meaning involves no change in the underlying literal meaning of *cut*, nor can it be tied to the co-occurrence of *cut* with other lexical items. This seems to prove, then, that truth-conditions are primarily the function of context.

A third counter-argument might be that *cut* is simply a vaguer term for more precise ones such as *mow, stab, slice,* or *trim*. If this were the case, *Bill cut the grass* would be interpreted as "Bill separated the grass using a sharp instrument" and the precise meaning as "Bill mowed the lawn." While this seems plausible, Searle argues that it entails the idea that meaning is a matter of extrapolation from general to specific and that this, in turn, means that some fairly bizarre interpretations will be possible: What is to debar the interpretation, for example, of "Cut the grass" by someone somewhere to mean "Stab at the grass with a butcher's knife"? In the end, all of this seems to suggest that there *is* a common meaning that we learn to attach to words such as *cut* which is then modified in context. In this way, we learn the common meaning of *cut* from experiencing the range of its literal meanings in the contexts of cutting grass, hair, cakes, and so on. We then have a "basic" meaning for *cut* which is *not* context-dependent (the kind of meaning stored, perhaps, in the internal lexicon discussed in Chapter Six). On this basis, we *infer* from the context that *cut* in "Cut the flowers," for example, means "chop off the stems of the flowers using scissors" (after Searle et al., 1980, pp. 225-226). It will be recognized that these ideas bear much in common with Saussure's original distinction between *sense* and *value* (see Chapter Two, above).

The involvement of cultural background knowledge

In the end, Searle believes that semantic interpretation occurs in the way described above due to *cultural* commonality, due to the use of culturally shared information and assumptions during communication. This cultural background knowledge includes information about both institutions and nature in general, and Searle claims that we know what "Cut the grass" means when we hear it simply because we know a great deal about grass, home lawn care, and mowers, just as we also know about cakes, cake knives, and slicing cakes into portions. It is this type of knowledge together with particular contexts, then, which yields meaning, and not any particular properties of words themselves and "the literal meaning of a sentence only determines a set of truth conditions given a set of background practices and assumptions" (ibid., p. 227).

If this is so, however, should we not be able to *describe* this background knowledge in relation to interpretation and meaning, to *include* it within semantic (or pragmatic) theory? Searle believes that this cannot be accomplished. First, the background is infinite in scope, and no theorist would ever know how to delimit or complete the task. Second, we would have to describe background assumptions using words and sentences, and then would have to describe the assumptions underlying these expressions, leading to infinite regress. The fact that we cannot readily describe them, however, does not mean that cultural knowledge and assumptions are not omnipresent. (Schema-theorists such as Bartlett have made the same point in the framework of the psychology of reading and memory; see Chapter Six). Even sentences such as *Two and two make four*, supposedly "true in all possible worlds," or "analytically true" are, according to Searle, understood against a background of shared cultural knowledge (and it is certainly the case, as Wittgenstein pointed out, that a different civilization might understand and do addition in quite different ways from our own). According to Searle, the literal meaning of sentences establishes the truth-conditions for their interpretation only against culturally-shared background knowledge. This compendium of background knowledge, moreover, is in a state of flux, and it is possible, for example, that a hundred years from now people will no longer use mowers, having some other machine or having found some bio-technical solution to cutting lawns (if they still have them). Hence, the interpretations cited above would no longer be viable since the relativity by which they become meaningful would be absent. Meaning is always wrought out of and is relative to some specific *interaction* between words, contexts, and background knowledge, and even assumptions about supposed universals, such as the effects of gravity, or the color of snow are ultimately subject to change (pp. 230-231).

Intentionality and Presupposition

The cement that binds all these problems of relating literal meaning to background knowledge and context is *intentionality*, the fact that all utterances, and therefore all interpretations of utterances, rest on the intentions the speaker has in making an utterance (see, also, Chapter Three). Intentionality, in turn, involves *belief* that such and such is the case (that the grass can be cut, that the mower will work, that Bill knows how to use a mower, and that he understands that he is to use it in cutting the grass, and so on). In the end, Searle believes, the argument for a pragmatic view of meaning, one which rejects any attempt to describe meaning out of context, is inseparable from the nature of perception itself: Perception, in other words, necessarily involves both intentionality and belief, and what an individual sees or hears is largely dependent upon what she *expects* to see and hear (cf. schema theory). All notions of "reference" and "reality" are themselves also dependent on the contextual interpretation, intention, and belief, and this is perhaps the most persuasive reason of all for rejecting truth-functional accounts of meaning and for embracing the pragmatic approach. In this way, Searle incorporates the analysis of meaning into the analysis of perception, treating it as inseparable from the interpretation of phenomena in general (ibid. p. 232).

The view of language taken in pragmatics is one in which intentions and assumptions of various kinds play a central role. Communication is viewed in this framework as "a complex kind of intention that is achieved or satisfied just by being recognized" (Levinson, 1983, p. 16). Communication takes place only when *mutual knowledge* is held between speakers and hearers, and this can only come about as the result of an intentional goal (ibid.). All of this involves not only intentions and beliefs, but also *presuppositions* that things are as they really are in the world (or the possible world) and that the intent to communicate successfully is present on both sides (this is the central import of Gricean felicity conditions, see Chapter Three).

But how might presuppositions be analyzed, and how might a presuppositional semantics be developed? In semantic analysis, the term *presupposition* has a somewhat stricter meaning than it does in common everyday usage, where it occurs in statements like *Following the first successful launch, the Israelis presupposed a SCUD attack* or *The history of music presupposes a succession of composers*. In these latter utterances, the verb *presuppose* is used rather loosely to mean something like "this *entails* what follows" or "on the basis of this information, what follows is reasonable" but in the more technical sense used in pragmatics, it refers to the information *necessary* for communication. Levinson (1983) likens the relationship between inferences and background presuppositions to that between *figure* and *ground* described by the Gestalt psychologists, who observed that the figure in a picture only stands out in relation to what surrounds it. Some ambiguous figures exist, such as the familiar "old woman-young girl" drawing in which figure and ground can be easily reversed due to an absence of visual cues to differentiate either figure from any one ground.

Types of presuppositions

Semantic analyses have revealed several kinds of presupposition that may be contained in the background to communication. In particular, a set of *presupposition-triggers* have been identified, some of which can be illustrated by the following examples. In *Norman took (or didn't take) the sandwich with ham and pickles* there is a presupposition arising from the definiteness of the description that "there is a sandwich with ham and pickles." In *Norman knew (didn't know) that other sandwiches had mustard* there is a presupposition centered on the *factive* verb *know* that the other sandwiches did indeed have mustard in them (a factive verb is defined as one which presupposes the belief in the speaker of the truth of something stated. In *Norman succeeded (or didn't succeed) in getting the sandwich,* there is a presupposition based on the verb *succeed* that Norman did in fact make an attempt to get the sandwich; this is what Grice referred to as an *implicature*, something which can be deduced from the utterance. In *Norman continued to eat the sandwich* it is implied that he had already started eating it.

Another instance of presupposition arises with the distinction between *restrictive* and *non-restrictive* relative clauses (see also Chapter Five). Consider the two sentences *The politicians who wore brown boots trampled on the daisies* and *The politicians, who wore brown boots, trampled on the daisies*. The difference in punctuation (reflected by slight pauses and intonational changes in spoken form) signals that in the first sentence it is presupposed that *only* those politicians that happened to be wearing brown boots who did the trampling, while in the second sentence, it is *all* of the politicians who are referred to: In the first sentence the additional information is "restricted" to the politicians, while in the second, the information about brown boots is *incidental* and is not necessarily restricted to the politicians (it is not a defining quality of them in this case and there may well have been others with brown boots around at the same time). Another instance is to be found in the *counterfactual* conditional sentence *If Saddam had not invaded Kuwait, there would have been peace*, where it is presupposed that he did (factually) invade Kuwait. Other types of presupposition include those implicit in felicity conditions and conversational implicatures (see Chapters Three and

Seven, above).

Analytical problems

Although the above examples *seem* to establish presupposition of various kinds further analysis shows just how complex the analytical problem really is. In some of the sentences above, for instance, it is clear that the relevant presupposition is triggered in *either* its affirmative *or* the negative form; whether Norman got the sandwich or not, for example, the sentence mentioning "success" implies that he tried in either case. In the case of the *factive* verbs (including, *know*, *agree*, *realize*, and so on), however, the situation is a little different and *I don't know that it is raining in Aruba* does *not* trigger the same presupposition as its affirmative version (i.e. it cannot be concluded from the negative form, unlike its affirmative transformation that it *is* raining in Aruba--indeed, it cannot even be concluded that it is *not* raining in Aruba). This means that there is an interaction between certain types of verbs and negation such that the criterion that presupposition is constant over affirmative and negative versions of the same expression is not satisfied. Another tricky problem arises with the contrast between *Holmes shaved before regaining the championship* and *Holmes expired before regaining the championship*. Normally, information given in a sentence prior to the appearance of *before* is presupposed to be true (as in *She knelt before praying* or *Jack took off his shoes before entering the shrine*) but the verb *expire* clearly debars this presupposition since it is logically opposed to the continuation of time, even though the statement *is* interpretable. In cases where it can be shown that a presupposition can be nullified in a certain linguistic or referential context, they are known as *defeasible* (Levinson, 1983, pp. 112-113; 186-187).

Another set of problems, known as *projection problems*, arise where propositions are compounded with each other but yet where the connected presuppositions do not "survive" the transition or "add up." The sentence *The two dancers were arrested once again yesterday* triggers the presuppositions that the dancers were arrested yesterday and that they had been previously arrested. What happens when we put the sentence into a *conditional* framework, however, as in *If the two dancers were arrested once again yesterday, then the club will close*? In this case, there can be no presupposition that the dancers were actually arrested yesterday, but the presupposition that they had been arrested in the past (sometime before yesterday) survives. The same thing happens when the sentence is placed in a *disjunctive* frame, as in *Either the two dancers were arrested yesterday once again, or the club will be fined*. In a sense, these may seem like relatively trivial problems in relation to the viability of the pragmatic approach and the idea of presuppositions taken as a whole. For the philosopher, however, they represent key reasons for rejecting any purely "semantic" (i.e. formal-logical) approach to pragmatics (ibid., p. 199). One alternative route to understanding how presupposition works in communication is by way of the criterion of "mutual knowledge," the idea that reasonable presupposition takes place only if a given proposition is *mutually and conventionally known* by the participants. This has the merit of giving some psychological reality to presupposition while lacking the rigor of formal semantics in pursuit of some rigorous description of the "structure" of presuppositions.

These ideas about presupposition have been introduced since the issues lie at the heart of the field of pragmatics. It has been concluded, however, that no fully satisfactory model of presuppositional language behavior yet exists (Levinson, 1983, p. 225; see also, Kempson, 1975, 1977). Much is now understood, however, about *what needs to be explained* and the challenge to pragmatic theorists is to develop a theory which demonstrates how presupposition takes place on the basis of *both* internal aspects of the language (such as the properties of certain verbs and syntactic arrangements) *and* the psychological and contextual factors attached to communicative events.

Language from the Phenomenological Perspective

The phenomenological tradition in philosophy has brought radical new insights into the subject-object dichotomy introduced at the beginning of this book and, indeed, has initiated some searching questions about the very nature of the relationship between what we have traditionally viewed as "object" and "subject." Unlike many of the philosophers so far mentioned who, for the most part, would consider themselves "language philosophers," phenomenologists have not apparently set out to develop any specific theory of language. Nevertheless, as we shall see in the last section of this chapter, the phenomenological perspective, which is growing in influence, especially in the areas of social science and education, sheds new light on language in its relationship to consciousness in general. Phenomenology and its close relations, existentialism and hermeneutics, are not easy to introduce in brief form. The effort to identify some key concepts here is worthwhile, however, and no account of current philosophy of language could be complete without reference to this stream of thought.

Background to Phenomenology

Substances, accidents, matters, and essences

In the tradition reaching back to Aristotle, it was believed that everything in existence can be broken down into two fundamental categories: *substances* and *accidents*. Substances were the individual things in the world, such as trees, clouds, books, chairs, and so on, while accidents were the properties of those things, such as their greenness, billowiness, readability, and strength. Substances were said to exist independently and in their own right, while accidents were said to be completely dependent upon the prior existence of substances.

Although there has been considerable debate over the centuries about the precise definitions, substances (or "material substances" or "individual things") were generally said to be composed of *matter* and *essence*, where matter was the unformed "stuff" making up substances and where essence was the characteristic that organized the stuff into the particular substance-- what makes a tree a tree or a cloud a cloud. Unlike an accidental property of a substance, an essence was considered to be *part* of the substance and not a mere appendage added on to it.

Descartes' revision

One of the most important ramifications of this division of things between substances and accidental properties had to do with how the nature of human beings was understood. Until a crucial revision by Descartes in the seventeenth century, the *soul* was thought of as the essence and the body, the substance of humans and, in addition, it was believed that the soul-essence could exist apart from the body, a belief replete with obvious implications for theological dogma. Descartes argued on the contrary, however, that the mind (or soul) is not an essence but, rather, a substance in its own right. Humans, according to Descartes, were made up of two separate and interacting substances and not were not made up by a relationship between a substance and an essence. Each of these substances, it followed, must have its own essence (Grossman, 1984).

According to Descartes, the essential property of bodies that distinguishes them from minds is that they have *extension*; that is, they have shape and are located in space. Minds have no such extension, only *thought*, which has no "shape" and which is not located in space; they are the source of the entire range of mental acts including emotional response. One thing which body and mind *do* have in common, however, is that they both exist in *time;* both bodily and mental actions can exist in temporal relations to each other.

Why were Descartes' views considered to be so radical, and how have they become central to the entire development of modern philosophy--not to mention psychology and the work of transformational grammarians? The answer lies partly not in anything that Descartes "discovered" but in the new *questions* he forced philosophers to ponder. First, Descartes' proposals forced a reconsideration of the relationship between mind and body. If he was right, and there exists some kind of interaction between the two substances of the mind and the body, then what could be the precise nature of this interaction? A simple "causal" model, by which two physical substances touch each other in some way could not work, since this would require extension (physicality) on both sides, not just on the side of the body. Modern scientists, following proposals by the British philosopher, Hume, have generally adopted the view that mind and body must relate to each other by way of *laws* of conjunction: In this way, the relationship, say, between brain damage and speech is now typically viewed as a *lawful correspondence*, not as the direct result of physical exchange between body and mind (the rejection of the "locationist" view of mental events is a good indication of the general move in science towards interest in discovering lawful regularities and away from belief in direct correspondence between mind and brain; see Chapter Four). Second, according to the pre-Cartesian view of how knowledge comes about, it was believed that when humans perceive or think about things, the essences of those things exist both in the objects *and* in the mind. When I look at a VCR, then, the essence of the VCR would be said to reside both in the object itself and in my own mind in such a way that I and the VCR actually *share* the essence. This scheme of things could not work in Descartes' model, however, since the mind, being substantive and being, moreover, of a different substance from the body, could not simply incorporate essences in this way: There could be no way in which body and mind could share the essences of things. Descartes argued therefore that we perceive and think about things in terms of *ideas* which, of course, bear an indirect relationship to the things that give rise to them. Descartes' view of things is much more like the view we have become used to in modern cognitive psychology, the view that objects cause sensory stimulation leading to some kinds of mechanical changes in the brain leading (in a way not yet fully understood) to the formation of images which in some way *represent* the things we perceive but yet which are not "part of" them or in any sense really like them at all.

Descartes also argued that the mind changed to reflect sensations, but that sensations were to be treated as a separate category from ideas. The "primary qualities" of material objects were said to be their roundness, height, weight, quality of movement, and so on, while their "secondary qualities" were their color, taste, sound, odor. Primary qualities were held in the mind in terms of ideas, while secondary qualities were merely sensations.

Rationalists vs. Empiricists

As suggested, Descartes' rejection of the tenets of the Scholastic tradition that preceded him established the rockbed of central questions taken up by later philosophers. Following Descartes, both the British Empiricists, and the Rationalists entered into debate about the integrity of the notion of "substance," and about the whole distinction between substances, essences, and accidental properties still maintained in Descartes' discourse.

Under further scrutiny, the Cartesian idea that things are known not in terms of senses but in terms of ideas and the "understanding" that comes from them apparently fell down in the face of routine examples. If Descartes were exactly right on this point, then it should be the case that if, to contradict one of his own examples, I ask you to look at a ball of wax at one point in time, then ask you to leave the room while I melt the wax and then invite you back in again, you should be able to recognize that this fluid in the bowl is "the same wax" as previously shown to you. This is so, since in Descartes' view you do not know about this wax on the basis of your sensations but on the basis only of inner ideas which exist independently of sensory experience. Of course, I might have switched the wax or done any number of things to trick you, and the point is that you simply would have no basis for your judgement *other* than in terms of what you could sense. Simple logic seems to suggest, moreover, that we perceive and conceive of things in terms of the many properties we ascribe to them, and that there is no real distinction, say, between the roundness, redness, tastiness, or other properties of an apple in terms of our ascriptions; we "know" the apple by way of these ascriptions, ascriptions that can only be based on our sensations at given points in time. There simply would be no way of knowing whether a rotten insect-ridden apple were the same bright Red Delicious that was in the bowl a few days ago, the apple has no individual properties that allow us to make this judgement apart from the properties we sense. Of course, we can make reasoned judgements about the apple--that it still has the supermarket sticker on it in the same place, that it is still partly red, and that it is unlikely that someone will have deliberately replaced it, and so on, but the long and the short of it is that all these judgements and thoughts about the identification of the apple, and of all objects whatsoever, must ultimately come from our sensations of objects and from the mental "tests" we continually make to ensure that our perceptions and judgements are correct. In contrast to Descartes, later philosophers have largely treated individuals' knowledge of objects to be in terms of the sets or "bundles" of attributes that are given to them in sensation and in terms of the reasonable judgments they make on this basis. The traditional distinction between substances, essences, and accidental properties has been largely eroded.

Post-Cartesian Questions

Descartes, as previously mentioned, was the philosopher who opened the Pandora's Box of questions about the nature of the mind and mental phenomena. The Empiricist philosophers following Descartes did much to establish the logical bases upon which the traditional notion of "essences" must be rejected and to establish the idea that minds are composed of "mental acts" which work to organize the perceived properties of material things. The mere presence of mental acts, however, does not really explain the *experience* of knowledge or how the various properties of things included in mental acts relate to each other in the processes of thought and consciousness, nor does it explain the relationship between physical and psychological phenomena. In particular, what remained to be explained was just how it is that a human mind comes to the experience of "objective" knowledge, how it arrives at the state in which external objects are seen to have permanence and *identity*. We constantly make assumptions that objects have such permanence--that the apple in the basket is the same one we saw last week, that the building we work in is the same as it was yesterday, and so on--but exactly *how* or *why* this is the case does not normally concern us. From a philosophical point of view, however, a great deal needs to be explained here, and it is no trivial matter that the mind does seem to act in this way. Following the rejection of Descartes' analysis, the crucial question to be taken up by philosophers was just how this experience of "objective reality" comes to be, and the answer required something more than the claim that ideation involves the mental processing of bundles of perceived features of things.

Arguments about Identity

How, more precisely, did Empiricist philosophers believe that apprehension of the permanence or identity of objects comes about? Following the work of Locke and Berkeley, Hume argued in his *Treatise of Human Nature (1739)* that "our bodies are nothing but collections formed by the mind of the ideas of the several distinct sensible qualities, of which objects are composed, and which we find to have a constant union with each other." By "sensible qualities," Hume meant the sensations that are felt in the mind during perception, sensations that he and the other Empiricists believed to be actual elements of the mind. On these grounds, although there is no common "essence" held in both the mind and a given object, Hume believed that there were properties or elements that were common to the two; sensations themselves, then, are to be conceived of as "objects" entering the mind through the senses and becoming part of the actual *contents* of consciousness. Hume argued that our experience of the continuity of things around us arose out of the *resemblances* among sense data: When we blink our eyes several times while looking at an object, although what actually results is several quite *separate* and unique states, we have the impression that things exist continuously and without interruption. Although the sense data are in fact *not* identical, we have the *sense* that they are very similar to each other. Hence, the mind takes what is only *very similar* to be *identical,* and this, according to Hume, is how the perception of the identity of things comes about. This general process of comparing resemblance, since it occurs through time, requires memory, of course, and Hume argued that the process of maintaining the sequence of items in mind through the imagination resulted in the *illusion* that things have constant identities. This illusion, moreover, was dependent upon a constancy of attention in the subject; any change in the imagination resulting in a change of focus in consciousness such as the subject's thinking about the progress of time as he senses an object would destroy the continuity of the illusion. To use more modern terms, the experience (or illusion) of continuity and of the identity of things, according to Hume, had to be an "automatic" or "subconscious" matter.

Flaws in Hume's arguments

There is, however, a fundamental and fatal flaw in all of this, and it concerns the claims Hume makes about the nature of imagination. An object is initially represented in the mind in the form of a bundle of features or properties that enter through the senses. In order to form the illusion of identity, though, the imagination, according to Hume, must suppress the idea that there is in fact a plurality of items to be dealt with since its main task is to form the illusion that there is simply one identity. Here lies the unacceptable contradiction: The imagination cannot *both* at one and the same time set about creating an image of unity or identity in an object *and* set about destroying or suppressing the sensory elements that are its own stimulus. Hume was in effect arguing that the purpose of the imagination was its own destruction.

In Hume's theory, sense data and ideas get only "one shot" in the mind. Once they are passed over by the imagination, they disappear for ever, and memory presumably resides entirely within the aforementioned experience of resemblances between things as perception and consciousness move forward. As everyday observation makes clear, however, consciousness is not really like this, and we *are* able both to hold things as being permanent identities in our minds (chairs, tables, all objects whatsoever) while also being able to think *about* them, to reflect upon them or imagine things about them. The fact that we can see a person one day and plan to see them a week or even several years from how, that we can reflect on how things were and how they might have been, or might be, demonstrates that we are not totally dependent for our experiences of continuity and identity, as Hume suggested we are, on the unidirectional succession of temporal events. Hume viewed consciousness as proceeding in much the same way as a movie, as a series of quick frames moving in strict linear order. What is missing, however, is the aspect of the *audience* who views the pictures and whose mind in some sense constantly *interacts* with the pictures, and both analyzes and reflects upon them taking their meaning out of and beyond the strictly linear sequence of images. We are able to think about films, and even about our own thinking about films while we are in the process of watching them but *without* sacrificing the notion that the things we are watching (both *in* the film and the film itself) have "identity." If Hume were correct, and the perception of the identity of objects were dependent upon the presence of continuous sense data, then the experience we pervasively have of objects being "the same" and having the "same identity" over days or years without sensing them simply could not occur. On Hume's view of consciousness, indeed, there could not really be any "objects" at all (Gurwitsch, 1940).

Phenomenological Processing

The central problems raised in the work of Descartes and the British Empiricist philosophers who followed him had to do with reconciling the transience of mental events, on the one hand, with the experience of the stability and permanence of objects in the world, on the other. Even William James, with his well-known idea of the "stream of consciousness" did not manage to solve the logical riddle of just how it is that permanence can be experienced over substantial *breaks* or interruptions in this unidirectional stream. What was needed, in particular, was a clear distinction between objects themselves and their relationship to what goes on in the mind when (and when they are not) perceived. It was this necessary distinction that Husserl established (see, e.g., Husserl, 1964, 1970).

Direct perception: Noesis

Let us return to the chair-object mentioned earlier. There is a chair opposite me at the moment that has the qualities of being wooden, brownish-yellow, standing on its two front legs while leaning forward to the edge of a table, and standing approximately half in shade and half in direct sunlight. The perspective of the chair is such that its left back leg is the one nearest to me. The chair has also been around for some time, since I can see scratches all over it (better in the part in direct sunlight) and someone has carved a heart with an arrow through it on the back rest. The above characteristics are the ones of which I am immediately, or very nearly immediately, aware. This direct perceptual experience, the kind that we encounter all the time we are awake and conscious, is what Husserl termed *noema* (pl. *noemata*). The noema is quite independent from the actual chair object which, of course, can appear in many different ways depending on light, perspective, and so on.

But there is another level at which I am also perceiving the chair-object above and beyond this relatively automatic and sensual one, namely, at the level of its *significance* to me: In addition to the mere perception of shape, color, age, and so on, when I look at the chair other things flood into my mind--that the cleaner was responsible for tilting the chair, that I would prefer a newer one in my office, that people should not ruin furniture by carving on it, that professor Quince sat on it last week because there wasn't another one, and so on. The central point here is that, in addition to the level of *basic* sensory perception, there is always another level of consciousness in human experience which reflects our *intentions* towards objects, a level that establishes our *awareness* of the particular significance of objects at particular points of space-time interaction in our lives. This latter aspect of perception, Husserl named *noesis*. He argued that perception always involves this dual analysis in which the noemata constitute the fundamental stable "contents" in the mind. Noemata are *not* just "images," however. When I look at a chair some changes take place on my retina but it is not merely this "picture," this amalgam of legs, seat, and backrest that I see: I see a *chair*, nothing more and nothing less; it comes to my consciousness *already defined* as a *whole* chair in the form of a *gestalt*. Even if I blink my eyes while I look at the chair, then, this leads to perceptual experiences that are actually different (just like the almost imperceptible changes between the sequential frames in a film). The chair remains the "same" chair, however, due to the noemata underlying all perception, even though the acts of perception (noesis) are separate. By proposing these *two* levels of perception, with the level of noesis essentially *interpreting* the level of noemata, Husserl opened up a way to solving some of the problems proposed in one-level models such as that of Hume.

Identity: the irreducibility of perceptual elements

The key difference between this and earlier models of consciousness is that, with Husserl, perception is no longer tied to what goes on at any particular point in time: Mental events are dependent on more than what is actually present or even on what can simply be recalled from previous experience. Husserl saw noemata as the fundamental and constant elements of consciousness, as elements that stood in a one-to-one or *identical* relationship to objects and which were *irreducible* to more fundamental elements (such as bundles of features or properties) in any way. Identity is a fundamental "given" in consciousness, and we hold things to be the same in the world *without* necessarily being conscious about this all the time. At any given time, however, and for a multiplicity of reasons, the fact of an identity *may* become an object of consciousness and we may become *aware* of the identity of objects in some context of significance. In the above-mentioned case of the chair in my office, for instance, there was already a great deal going on besides my holding in mind the noema of the chair: As soon as I describe the chair even to myself and certainly to an audience, I do so with purpose and intent, and I have become fully conscious of the significance of the chair in some way. The noema, however, was the necessary trigger for this conscious interpretation--indeed it, rather than the chair, was the actual *object* of the interpretation.

A central point in all this is that my reaching this position of conscious awareness about the chair also means that I must also in some sense be aware of the *temporality of consciousness itself*. This observation is a central tenet of phenomenology and it amounts to an insistence that a central characteristic of human consciousness is its ability to recognize perceptions as individual acts in time. If we return for a moment to the analogy between Hume's more primitive model and the sequence of frames in a film, then, at some risk of oversimplification, it might be said that the phenomenological account of perception holds that we are not the mere screens upon which images are projected but are, rather, capable of looking at the projections, of making selective decisions about what they mean in terms of all our other experiences and in terms of the entire film. Crucially, according to phenomenologists we are as human-beings *aware of the nature that the impressions are having upon us in time.* At some level of consciousness, we are aware of the passage of time and our conception of the identities of things is inseparable from our conception of their "lasting" in time through the separate noemata as these are received and lost from memory.

More precisely, how are the experiences of identity and of time related to each other? The answer to this question is crucial in understanding the phenomenological theory of knowledge. If we did not have the fundamental experience of the identity of things, of their continuity, then awareness of time itself would be impossible. This is so, since we would be in the position of seeing things as they move around or as they present different aspects of themselves to us as thoroughly disconnected. When we look at things, then, we *must* be in some sense actively "discounting" the changes that are taking place through time. In order to "discount" time we must be thoroughly aware of it--not in the sense that we "time" events or look at our watches all the time, of course, but in the sense that we are aware of the *passing* of time in general, of *temporality*. Paradoxically, this awareness of what might be called "the permanence of temporality" and awareness that sense impressions are constantly and typically changing is the very *guarantee* to us that things are identical. It is in this way that identity and time are locked together in the phenomena of consciousness.

Consciousness as inner dialogue

Consciousness, then, is seen to be a kind of inner *dialogue* (or "parallelism," or "correspondence") between noemata and a level of perceptual analysis (noesis) rather than a monologic response to sensory input: In particular, while noemata are constant, in that they are *indexes* of sensory experience, there is no one-to-one relationship between them and acts of interpretation (noesis). One might say, indeed, that there is a *generative* or *recursive* relationship between these two levels in consciousness. Since these two levels are mutually interdependent, any traditional distinction between "subject" and "object" is effectively neutralized--or at least, is radically altered.

Husserl argued, further, that since the fundamental irreducible elements of consciousness are the noemata of experience, and since noemata are only singular correlates of perceived objects, any one of which can release infinite different noemata through time and changing conditions, even they involve the *subjective* involvement of the conscious mind, or "intention." If there are any "objects" in Husserl's scheme of things, then these are the noemata themselves and *not* the things as they stand in the real world. On this view, consciousness becomes a two-step process, involving a sort of oscillation between subjectivity and objectivity: The object leads to a "subjective" noema, which in turn becomes the "object" and, at the same time, the basic element or building-block of consciousness. In the stream of consciousness, of course, it is not merely *things* which give rise to noemata, but also all sorts of other encounters, including conversations and memories. Noemata create further noemata and combine into systems on the basis of which complex conscious experiences are founded, and so the experience of "reality" or of "objectivity" is inseparable from the subjectivity of individual acts of interpretation. Husserl further argued that individuals and, indeed, groups of individuals with overlapping cultural experiences (i.e. members of the same cultural groups) develop a perceptual *system* constituted by what they normally interpret to be "reality." He termed this social world of pure experience the "life-world" (*Lebenswelt*). These life-worlds do not just come about automatically like projections on to a passive screen but, rather, they involve at every moment our subjective *intentions* towards mental phenomena.

Phenomenology, Language, and Meaning

We are now in a position to see how the phenomenological perspective brings with it some radical thoughts about language and meaning in their relationship both to communication and, more fundamentally, in relation to perception and consciousness. Husserl's main proposals about language can be conveniently divided into two parts: his proposals about the relationship between elements of language vis à vis noemata, and his proposals about "pure logical grammar."

Language, thinking, and noemata

Simply stated, thinking and use of language are one thing in Husserl's phenomenology. In this unification, they constitute the most important but not the only part of consciousness. As we have seen, the fundamental phenomena of consciousness, the noemata, are held to be mental objects upon which actions of various kinds are performed (noesis). Hence, acts of perception, imagining, hypothesizing, reminiscing, and so on, are all possible during the realization of consciousness. Husserl saw language, together with its correlate, thinking, as a specialized type of action on noemata, one which gives the possibility of abstraction away from the given objects (noemata) and which gives an ability to question the *meaning* of perceptions.

But this relationship between perception and language is an extremely close one, since they are *mutually dependent*. Even the most basic type of perception is dependent upon a simple proposition--that is, upon a linguistically formed thought. In this way, the perception of a red apple, for example, depends on some kind of inner representation like "There is an apple" (together with its predicate "is red"). In addition, even the most basic thought demands comparison and verification against the fundamental "given" resident in noemata. This means that the mechanisms of language and perception are fundamentally inseparable, and language serves to give perception "sense." It is a fundamental purpose of language, moreover, to generate further objects of thoughts (ideas, descriptions, responses, etc.), that can be stored in linguistic form. Husserl thought of these mental objects created through language as ideal objects. It takes just a little introspection to realize just how much of our everyday thinking might be dependent upon our prior establishing of these "ideal" objects, to realize how much is composed of "thinking about our own prior thinking."

A central idea in Husserl's understanding of language is that it works in terms of these ideal objects. The words and other elements in any natural language, just like elements in music or visual art, can be and are, used an infinite number of times and in an infinite number of different circumstances. Like all events, linguistic events are always unique, and given expressions never mean *exactly* the same thing on different occasions. Nevertheless, there *is* a commonality to them that allows us to constantly realize their sense (just as, in music, the same notes are never played in exactly the same way even though a piece of music is recognized as the particular work of a composer). This commonality arises since words have *ideal senses* that they bring with them and, moreover, which underlie our conception of the permanence of things in general (reminding us, once again, of de Saussure's distinction between *sense* and *value*). It is through this ideality of language, indeed, and the opportunity it affords for *repeating* ideas and thinking about things in different and new ways, that our sense of culture and history and the passing of time are developed.

There is, then, a further level at which language and the foundations of perceptual experience are intertwined. The business of everyday conversation is conducted on the basis of these shared senses or ideals that have a permanent quality about them, and which become fully meaningful only when they are realized in particular communicative situations. It is important to realize that there is both some similarity and some crucial difference here with the Cartesian theory of knowledge. The similarity lies in the idea that language contains "essences" which comes with Husserl's conception of language as composed of "ideal objects." The difference, however, is that in Husserl these essences are viewed as properties of *mental phenomena* and not, as they were in Descartes, as physical objects extending directly into the mind (for further commentary, see Edie, 1987, pp 32-35).

A priori logic, grammar, and language

It will be recalled that the logical positivists (Russell, Carnap, the early Wittgenstein) believed that they could establish the fundamental logical laws to which language supposedly conforms. This search, however, took place on the basis that perception and experience existed in one realm, while logic took its place in another--what they seemed to be looking for was some kind of correspondence between these two quite distinct types of phenomena. The radical difference between this conception and that developed in phenomenology is that in the latter these two types of phenomena--the logical and experiential--are considered to be inseparable aspects of the *same* phenomenon. This is so partly, as we have seen, because perception and logic (embodied in language) are themselves inseparable; *nothing can be perceived that does not have some basic kind of logical form.* Husserl believed, further, that a universal "a priori" form of logic lay at the foundation of all language and, indeed, that the study of *grammar* was, precisely, a process of reflection on this fundamental logic.

As can be gathered from the foregoing discourse, a central part of phenomenological analysis involves deliberative awareness that how things are in the world must be determined by looking not at the world *itself* but at the mental objects that result from perceiving the world (neomata). In this way, understanding and meaning involve recognition of our subjective participation in acts of interpretation as much as upon the objects that give rise to them. Husserl argued that understanding involved what he called the *bracketing off* of the mere experience of "facts" and a deliberate turning towards mental phenomena.

Another word used to describe this turning away from the factual world and towards the deeper meaning of things was *reduction*. When we consider language in detail, then, we are, according to Husserl, performing precisely such a reduction--a turning away from "facts" themselves and towards how facts are represented in the mind, in thought and perception. In phenomenology, reduction becomes the principle *method*, moreover, by which individuals can get in touch with the "pure intuitions" that lie at the basis of meaning. The fundamental purpose of the various specific types of reduction that Husserl proposed is to rid the mind of all prejudice, of all *assumptions* about the way things are, and to get at the meaning of things by way of seeing how we have come to know them in the first place. In this way, the method or practice of reduction involves placing ourselves in a sphere of thinking which is *transcendental*--that is, which transcends the plane of the mere outward appearance of things and which searches for inner meanings. It is only through such reductions that we come into contact with the fundamental *essences* of things (see Kockelmans, 1967). Reduction, then, is a kind of inner analysis which involves both the bracketing out of things irrelevant to the essence of a given experience and some occasional implicit comparisons between the things to be understood and other things related to it. In particular, Husserl believed that traditional assumptions about science and about how the world can only be understood "empirically" themselves need to be bracketed in order for us to achieve greater insight into all those phenomena we have learned over the past few hundred years to think of as "scientific." He saw that our every perception, unless so analyzed, is culturally laden and full of assumption and prejudice. We need to pare these assumptions away in order to separate out all the conceptual encumbrances of our everyday "life-world" if we are to get at the true meaning of things. The true meaning of things lies not just in the description of "objects" or the development of sophisticated logical schemes to describe their "objective" interrelations, but also in careful and systematic analysis of their subjective aspects. In short, the reductions capture the idea that we cannot know anything whatsoever very deeply unless we pay attention to our own understanding of it. In this way, "object" and "subject" are interactive and inseparable at every turn.

When we look at even elementary grammatical facts such as the separation of subject and predicate, then, we are not looking merely at some linguistic rule abstracted for analytical purposes but at no less than one of the fundamental logical laws through which consciousness is established. This follows from the aforementioned fusion of perception and language. By "a priori logic," however, Husserl did not mean the same thing as logicians. He did not intend to refer to some kind of "calculus" set against a background of truth-tables but, rather, to an even more fundamental set of laws, reflected in language and perception, by which contradictions and errors in perception and understanding were universally avoided, and upon which other logical schemes were dependent. Husserl's radical insight was that all human thought, including all those forms which we call "science" and including the investigations conducted of language within the framework of "linguistics" themselves rested upon the even more fundamental and powerful laws underlying perception and knowledge. It is the search for *these* laws, the fundamental *grammar of thought*, that constitutes one of the primary and the most profound goals of phenomenology. Taking language and its grammatical rules as the object of analysis, however, is the cardinal starting point for this quest into a priori grammar and, as such, it constitutes in itself a key turning-away from mere facts passively experienced, a key phenomenological reduction.

Phenomenological interpretation of syntax

If grammar is seen to be inseparable from the description of the laws of thought, then how does the phenomenologist view what we are used to calling "syntax," the rules of how linguistic elements are combined? In keeping with the idea that the laws of thought are universal and underlie all languages, Husserl claimed that particular rules of syntax are all founded on fundamental laws of relationship between meanings. Husserl thought of expressions as "Gestalts," as meaning-wholes and it was their quality of unification that depended upon the more fundamental laws governing the combination of linguistic elements. Linguistic expressions, then, could only be well-formed if they conformed to these fundamental laws of relationship. Husserl's understanding of a sentence was that it comprises a whole built up of parts in a hierarchical way (and, in many ways, his view of the structure of language turns out to be remarkably similar to Chomsky's; see Edie, 1987, pp. 49-50). The most fundamental part of a sentential expression is the "object" described (e.g. *the elephant*) which brings with it a necessary predicate of some kind (e.g. *is bathing*) and possibly reference to some other object or objects (e.g. *in the river*) and which bears all kinds of possible modifications (e.g. *the turquoise elephant*). In this way, sentences are "driven" by objects (in the noematic sense already described) and then the combinations and orders of things follow naturally and lawfully from this primacy of the noun. Grammatical "operations," then, relate what must be *subordinate* in a priori grammar (adjectives and other modifying phrases) to what is *superordinate* (nouns and then verbs) working towards the building-up of more complex noun-phrases and higher-level structures, including conditional and modal structures (e.g. *If the turquoise elephant is bathing in the filthy river, then...*). The key point in all of this is that Husserl believed that the particular grammatical rules of all languages followed the same kind of fundamental a priori laws of reasoning upon which *all* perception and meaning are also dependent. It is these a priori laws, reflecting the processes connected to the interpretation of noemata, that guarantee meaning and which provide the fundamental blueprint for the grammars of all languages, no matter how they instantiate the necessary underlying relationships of dependency between parts of speech. In this way, the grammars of languages and the laws of thought are said to be synonymous.

Hermeneutics

What might appear to be an apparently disproportionate amount of space has been devoted to the ideas of Husserl since they represent a true turning point in intellectual history upon which a great deal, including the development of hermeneutics, depends. This is not to say that Husserl left an unfalsifiable theory of knowledge and, indeed, many of his successors, including his student, Heidegger, saw the need for alteration and refinement of his ideas. Phenomenology is still very much under development as a philosophical school, but the ideas reviewed above do represent a true turning-point.

Background to hermeneutics

Hermeneutics can be broadly defined as "the art of interpretation." The movement has a long history and borrows its name from Hermes, the Greek messenger of the gods, who was renowned for the effects of his interpretations of the messages he was given to transmit between the gods and mortals. In the Middle Ages and the Renaissance, hermeneutics found its focus in the interpretation of biblical and other religious texts and the key objective was the *exegesis*, or thorough explanation of the inner meanings of such texts. In the nineteenth and twentieth centuries, hermeneutics has gradually broadened out to include as an objective the explanation of spoken as well as written discourse, and this expansion of scope has brought with it important new insights into the more general nature of communication. Its closest point of relationship with phenomenology, the philosophy with which it has become most closely associated, lies in the shared belief that true knowledge and understanding arise only out of close attention both to the "messages" and the medium by which things arrive in consciousness and not merely to the things themselves. As the word *message* suggests, however, hermeneuticians are not so interested in the ideal, essential, or universal foundations of thought as they are in the ways in which language *conditions* knowledge. They are interested, moreover, in the *changing* perceptions of reality that are wrought in language through diachronic processes and, conversely, how language affects historical change.

The fundamental enterprise of paring away assumptions of various kinds in order to see the raw truth, however, is shared by both phenomenology and hermeneutics. In hermeneutical thinking, this paring away, or attempt to gain transcendence over how things are actually presented to us through language, has developed into nothing less than a critique of the nature and contents of knowledge as they have been handed down to us through history. Specifically, it is a critique of the view of knowledge founded on the duality of "object" and "subject" with its accompanying doctrine of empiricism. Within the vibrant hermeneutical tradition, these forms of thinking, which have been largely accepted without question since the time of Descartes, continue to be subjected to relentless critical re-interpretation, an activity which centrally involves forms of analysis of language which bring with them a particular and important perspective on the nature of language in all forms of communication.

Foundational ideas from von Humboldt

There are several aspects of von Humboldt's work which, in addition to those already introduced (see Chapter One, above), make him an important figure in the modern era of hermeneutics. One idea of Humboldt's from which hermeneutics has taken inspiration, an idea shared by other "Romantic" thinkers such as the philosopher, Schleiermacher, is that linguistic competence involves *both* speakers and hearers--the idea that one can only understand what one has the potential for expressing and *vice versa*.

Humboldt insisted that communication was a *co-product* of speakers and hearers and that it could not simply be the product of one of them (cf. the speaker-hearer relationship in psycholinguistic processing, Chapter Six, above). Hence meaning, for Humboldt, arose out of the underlying principles of language shared by all language-users and he, too, viewed the rules of grammar and of the mind to be inseparable.

As observed earlier, Humboldt also believed in the discreteness of cultural boundaries. He was, indeed, one of the early proponents of the idea of linguistic relativity, by which individual languages were argued to lead to different world-views in their speakers (an idea finding its clearest expression in the Sapir-Whorf Hypothesis; see Chapter Three). What follows from this discreteness of languages from each other, and what is of interest for hermeneutics, is that understanding of others from other cultures and language groups will always involve *interpretation*, interpretation, moreover, that demands some suspension from (or transcendence of) the conditioning given to individuals by their cultures and language. Humboldt held that there were two fundamental aspects to language--a universal foundation associated with the way things are structured in the mind and shared by all speakers, together with a culture-specific aspect of which speakers and listeners would have to be aware when communicating across cultures. Foreshadowing the work of modern sociolinguists and ethnographers (see Chapter Seven), it was his view that communication in general involved the constant *negotiation* of meaning in language: He saw language as a cultural and social product and that meaning only arose out of social negotiations in which speakers and hearers tested each other out. This places interpretation at the very heart of communication rather than at its periphery, as it is in many formal semantic theories. In the hermeneutical view of things expressed in the writings of von Humboldt, interpretation is central, involving language users' constant and active modification of their own impressions and assumptions as given by cultural background and experience.

A second major contribution to the evolution of hermeneutics that Humboldt made is to be found in his understanding of history. The traditional view of history (one still widely held) is that everything must be explained in terms of "causes" and "effects," on the basis that these can be "discovered." In his famous essay *On the Task of the Historian* (1822), however, Humboldt argued that historians can never really discover any "objective" underlying patterns--all they can do is bring into account as many facts as they can and then superimpose their *own* ideas about how these facts cohere or relate to each other. Historians, then, *give meaning to* history as much as history gives meaning to them: Historical interpretation involves constant oscillation between the perception of the "whole" (the large "explained" episodes) and the parts (the individual events constituting the historical data). In this way, historical interpretation is viewed as a *circular* process.

In both the processing of language and history, Humboldt's fundamental insight was that there is always a *dual* attention required, an attention to both the "subject" and the "objects" involved in any interpretation: In order to understand a speaker, a listener involves himself (subject) in what is heard (object), while in order to understand historical events, the historian must be as aware of the nature of her own subjective intuitions as much as the objective data upon which she draws. Once again, we encounter here one of the central shared themes of phenomenology and hermeneutical interpretation, namely, neutralization of the traditional dichotomy between "subject" and "object." In this way, meaning is always tied to--always arises out of a *relation* between the subject and the object and the subject is always in a sense "predisposed" towards the object both through the sharing of language and of cultural history. Meaning always arises out of active interaction, interaction involving constant awareness of the conditions in which meaning is to be derived, and is never the confrontation of "unknown object" by "unknowing subject." The conditions of this fusion of subject and object in interpretation are already there, pre-existent in cultural experience.

Heidegger: Being and Time

One of the most important twentieth century documents for hermeneutics is Heidegger's *Being and Time* (1962), in which many of the foregoing ideas are developed. In this work, Heidegger's key objective was to bring some clarity to the notion of "Being." One mystery to be explored is that humans do, indeed, have an experience of "Being," an experience by which they identify themselves in respect to the world around them. This experience, however, seems to be a "given" without having received any fully satisfactory explanation. Explanation of being-in-the-world (*Dasein*), then, since all else in perception and meaning follows from it, might be viewed as the most fundamen+tal task of phenomenology. In pursuit of this explanatory goal, Heidegger extends hermeneutic method into a wider territory than that comprised of the explanation of texts or even of communication.

Language and time:

A central feature of the universal experience of Being, Heidegger claims, has to do with the experience of the dimensionality of time. In a sense, Heidegger viewed the progress of life from the past and into the future as a kind of unraveling of Being: We come to understand what Being is only through the activities and experiences we pursue in life. In this way, this fundamental feeling about our existence provides a kind of drive to self-discovery through experience. The central hermeneutical theme picked up here from Humboldt and others, and continued later in Gadamer, is that interpretation is always grounded in what is *already present* and at least partly understood (i.e. *Dasein*) and this brings us back to the idea that interpretation and meaning must be always *circular* in nature. In later hermeneutics, this idea has become central and familiar, often referred to either as the "hermeneutic" or "critical" circle. The traditional view was that knowledge and understanding arise out of the confrontation between an *innocent* mind and unfamiliar data whose structural relations waited to be uncovered. The hermeneutical view, following Heidegger, is that the mind is never "innocent" and is always dynamically involved in the interpretation of things about the nature of which it already has some premonitions through the human experience of Being in the world.

Heidegger's interpretation of language is central to his entire thesis about the nature of Being. To Heidegger language, like time, is a fundamental *part* or *reflection* of Being, and so trying to "objectify" language in any way leads to an obfuscation of its true essential nature. This makes "defining" or even "talking about" language very difficult and, for this reason, in his writings about language, Heidegger tries to provide an *encounter* with language which reveals this nature, which "explicates" rather than "describes" it. Some of his more extended engagements with the relationship between language and Being appear in a series of lectures he gave published under the title *On the Way to Language* (1971), and they provide a rich basis for contemplation of the hermeneutical interpretation of language.

Heidegger's starting point in these lectures is to reject all contemporary "scientific" or "philosophical" investigations of language that give rise to a *metalanguage* about language as ways of getting to the *experience* of what language really is (cf. Kripke, Chapter Two). Metalinguistic investigations do have their place in the "technologized" world but, according to Heidegger, they actually take us away from the essence of language. What remains for him to attempt, therefore, is to arrange an "experience" with language (1971, p. 59). This he sees as the only valid approach to language since, in the course of everyday communication, the phenomenon of language does not normally arise as part of conscious experience, and so any discourse which mentions it or brings it into conscious attention in any way is, ironically, destined to lose its essential nature in the process. To Heidegger, the essential nature of language is, precisely, to *bring into being*; it is almost as if language is the "breath" of thought (and, therefore, of the *experience* of Being and Time). In his exploration of this idea, Heidegger focuses on the meaning of the last stanza of a poem by Stefan George:

> So I renounced and sadly see:
> Where word breaks off no thing may be.

About the last line, he comments:

> 'Where word breaks off no thing may be,' points to the relation of word and thing in this manner, that the word itself is the

> relation, by holding everything forth into being, and there upholding it. If the word did not have this bearing, the whole of things, the 'world,' would sink into obscurity, including the 'I' of the poem, him who brings to his country's strand, to the source of names, all the wonders and dreams he encounters. (1971, p. 73)

Perhaps the most significant word here is "relation." Following the tradition of Cartesian dualism, we are conditioned to think about words in various ways--that they "bear meaning," that they "stand for things," and so on--but what Heidegger seems to be suggesting is that language does *not* depend upon the subject-object correspondences or mappings embodied in these traditional ways of talking about language. On the contrary, language itself *is* the relation between subjectivities (minds) and objects. Once again, as did Husserl, Heidegger intends to neutralize the subject-object distinction, and he suggests that it is language which constantly performs this neutralization, that stands between subject and object and, most significantly of all, that this standing-for relation *is* thought, *is* Being (or it is the realization of Being to consciousness, which amounts to the same thing). In this way "Language is the house of Being" (1971, pp. 63, 135).

The poetic mode:

> A central theme in these lectures is the centrality of the *poetic* mode in language, a mode that Heidegger sees as in no manner incompatible with *thinking*. When we read poetry, we are perhaps used to thinking of the experience as in some way special or different from our thinking in general: Poems seem to "consume" us, and language perhaps seems to "reside" in our consciousness in more intimate ways than in other forms of discourse. In short, poetry (good poetry, anyway) seems in a sense to "take over our being," and it is this experience that Heidegger believes more than any other reveals to us the essence of language. But "thinking," he argues, which we typically associate with greater levels of "objectivity" than poetry, should not be understood to be of an essentially different nature. The following passage

carries this point further.

> 'Where word breaks off no thing may be.' As soon as we consider that what is named here is the relation between thing and word, and with it the relation of language to an entity as such, we have called poetry over into the neighborliness of thinking. Thinking, however, sees nothing strange in that. In fact, the relation between thing and word is among the earliest matters to which Western thinking gives voice and word, and does so in the form of the relation between being and saying. This relation assaults thinking in such an overpowering manner that it announces itself in a single word. The word is *logos*. It speaks simultaneously as the name for Being and for Saying. (1971, p.80)

As an interpretation of the poem itself reveals, the poetic experience--the "taking-over" of consciousness and Being as described above--must often give way to another perspective. In this case, this perspective lies in what the poet is "naming" in his final stanza, namely, the relationship between language and objects. This change of consciousness is a move from the "poetic" to "thinking," but, according to Heidegger, the two types are natural partners to each other: They live in the same "neighborhood" as each other, and they adhere to the fundamental principle that language is essentially *relation*, and that relation is Being. But although Heidegger appears to believe in the priority of the poetic and thinking modes through language, he contends that even these do not actually bring us to a pure understanding of what language actually *is*. In a revealing passage, he articulates what he sees as the central dilemma in defining language:

> Neither poetic experience with the word nor the thinking experience with Saying gives voice to language in its essential being. Such is the situation, and this despite the fact that since the early days of Western thinking...thinking has thought deep thoughts about language, and poetry has made stirring things into language. But we can only conjecture why it is that, nonetheless, the being of language nowhere brings itself to word as the language of being. There is some evidence that

> the essential nature of language flatly refuses to express itself in words--in the language, that is, in which we make statements about language. If language everywhere withholds its nature in this sense, then such withholding is in the very nature of language. Thus language not only holds back when we speak it in the accustomed ways, but this its holding back is determined by the fact that language holds back its own origin and so denies its being to our usual notions. But then we may no longer say that the being of language is the language of being, unless the word 'language' in the second phrase says something different, in fact something in which the withholding of the being of language--speaks. Accordingly, the being of language puts itself into language nonetheless, in its own most appropriate manner. (1971, p. 81)

According to Heidegger, then, exploration of the two aspects of language--poetry and thinking--will not in itself reveal the fundamental nature of language: They are not the "way to language." If poetry and thinking are to provide the way, we must not lose sight of *either* of them since they live in dynamic relationship to each other. The problem is that we can only come to further understanding through the realization that we *live in* the environment of these two modes, we are "already abiding in it" and we "move within it." (ibid., p. 82).

All of this means if Heidegger is right, that we can only "capture" language in the experience of the present, and we can only capture the present through the experience of language, making language fundamentally *paradoxical*. Language is fleeting and words serve as the "place-holders" of relations, which disappear with the words themselves. If we are to understand the nature of language, then, it follows, since we cannot achieve this end by "looking at" it (because this causes the fundamental relation by which we might understand it to slip away) that language must reveal *itself*. This point is well-expressed in the following, in which Heidegger's phenomenological *essentialism* concerning language is clearly revealed.

> We speak of language, but constantly seem to be speaking merely *about* language, while in fact we are already letting

language, *from within* language, speak to us, in language, of itself, saying its nature. (ibid., p. 85)

In order to reveal itself, language must have an essence, an essence which we share and of which we become part in its presence. The way to language, then, is through the *experience* of the state of being in which this essence is present and not through any form of objective exegesis. The essence of language is perhaps most clearly captured on the page, in overt language form, by Heidegger's expression "The being of language: The language of being," which, he claims "holds the primal tidings of linguistic nature (1971, p. 94). The two sides of the expression are bound together in the sense that we will only comprehend the one when we comprehend the other. Heidegger suggests that we are to think of language truly as the breath of thought and of life itself. Life itself, moreover, is founded on the experience of temporality, an experience founded in turn on the relations that live, die, reproduce, and extend each other in language. To objectify language, or to see it as a code by which objective experience is translated and understood by the knowing subject is to miss the point--to miss the essence--of language entirely.

Heidegger's investigations of language represent in themselves excellent examples of the hermeneutical enterprise since they show so clearly how constantly he "grapples" with the phenomenon before him, constantly approaching it, backing away from it, reconsidering it from different perspectives and, most important of all, *considering the impact of his own involvement and his own language* on his analysis. Heidegger's investigations of language also demonstrate the critical circle in action and this is evident, for example, in his parallel discussion of two oscillating themes--the question of analyzing language by way of its "parts," including the "poetic" and "thinking" *parts*, and the need to grasp the essence of language as a *whole*.

The part of Heidegger's philosophy of language, however, that has been developed elsewhere in the field of hermeneutics, and which makes him a strong contributor to this field, is in his establishing the inseparability of language, Being, and interpretation: The fundamental interconnectedness of language and Being brings with it, of course, the idea that all understanding must be linguistic in nature, a point made more clearly, perhaps, in "Being and Time" than in the works specifically directed towards language. Heidegger's student, Gadamer, took up this idea about language in its relation to the development of the history of human culture and knowledge more generally. Gadamer argued that all understanding necessarily involves prejudices of various kinds, prejudices that are picked up through individual and cultural history, and which are developed and passed on through the medium of language (e.g. Gadamer, 1975). The hermeneutical endeavor must always involve awareness of this state of things and, in particular, how entire cultures are enwrapped in their languages. The central understanding of language in the modern hermeneutic tradition, though, is captured in Heidegger's observations about language as the essence of cultural being. All hermeneutic interpretation thus involves the attempt to understand how things came to be as they are through language, how they are *constituted* by language.

Summary

In this chapter, we have explored some of the central issues and positions across a spectrum of contemporary philosophy of language. Four characteristic positions were outlined concerning the relationship between language, truth, and logic: the correspondence, coherence, pragmatic, and semantic positions. Following this, the nature of modal logic was outlined in relation to possible-world theories in which language use is viewed as being contingent on referential and modal contexts.

The area of language analysis now known as pragmatics concentrates on the description of all the aspects of communication that are influenced by speakers' knowledge of the communicative contexts in which they interact. This includes recognition of such matters as the illocutionary force of utterances, recognition of the distinction between the dictionary senses of words and their meanings in different contexts, and speakers' reliance on many forms of cultural background knowledge. The pragmatic approach to language also emphasizes the pervasive presence of intentionality and presupposition in communication.

In the latter part of the chapter, a view of language from the quite different philosophical tradition of phenomenology was presented. It was shown how phenomenologists take as their central objective the explanation of how things are experienced and "known," rather than how "subjective" minds interpret "objective" data. To the phenomenologist, language lies at the fusion of the object and the subject, a process that Husserl attempted to capture in his description of noesis.

Finally, we looked briefly at the emerging interest in the hermeneutical interpretation of language, in which the inseparability of all knowledge from subjective interpretation is emphasized. From this perspective, the mind is viewed as never being "innocent," and is always involved in the interpretation of phenomena. One of the profoundest expressions of phenomenological and hermeneutic thought is to be found in Heidegger's *Being and Time*, in which he struggles to find the essence of language. It is to be found, he claims, only in the "breathing" of individual thought, and not in the dualistic disengagement of language from what it signifies. Heidegger suggests in the end that language is always just the relation between subjects and objects.

CHAPTER NINE

Semiotics: The Investigation of Signs

A general semiotics studies the whole of the human signifying activity--languages--and languages are what constitutnes human beings as such, that is, as semiotic animals. It studies and describes languages through languages. By studying the human signifying activity it influences its course. A general semiotics transforms, for the very fact of its theoretical claim, its own object....[T]he categories posited by a general semiotics can prove their power insofar as they provide a satisfactory working hypothesis to specific semiotics. However, they can also allow one to look at the whole of human activity form a coherent point of view. To see human beings as signifying animals--even outside the practiice of verbal language--and to see that their ability to produce and to interpret signs, as well as their ability to draw inferences, is rooted in the same cognitive structures, represent a way to give form to our experience. (U. Eco, *Semiotics and the Philosophy of Language*, 1984)

Introduction

A brief overview of some of the main ideas developed in the field of semiotics was presented in Chapter Three, where it was also established that modern semiotics has emerged from several centuries of thinking about signs. Semiotics now covers a burgeoning number of activities all of which are predicated on an understanding that all experience, including that involving language, is essentially made up of signs of various types and is built upon the processes of sign-formation and interpretation.

Although semiotics is growing by leaps and bounds and is now influential in a number of fields, fields as diverse as literary criticism and musicology, it is still, in a sense, defining itself as it goes along. It is clear, however, that semiotics grew out of and continues to gather inspiration from a number of foundational sources, including the works of Peirce and his intellectual predecessors, the work of Saussure, phenomenology, and structuralism. Following the review of phenomenological thinking about language in the preceding chapter, it is now possible to return to semiotics and to define it more precisely as a growing intellectual tradition. It is also possible to explore more fully the contribution made by semiotic philosophy and analysis to our understanding of language. In order to accomplish this, we will delve further into each of these foundational influences in semiotics, looking at the relationship between semiotics and phenomenology, at the place of Peirce's theory of signs in the context of his other philosophical speculations, at the relationship between semiotics and structuralism, and at how semiotics has been inspired by Saussure. Finally, we will look the tradition of Russian semiotics and at some current trends in the field.

Foundations of Semiotics

Semiotics and Phenomenology

Husserl: signs and meanings

In his working-out of a phenomenology founded on the grounds of the interplay between noemata and noemesis, Husserl had a great deal to say about signs. In describing some distinctions essential to phenomenological theory, for instance, Husserl (1913) dwelt at some length on the differences between signs and "expressions." He wrote that "Every sign is a sign for something, but not every sign has a 'meaning,' a 'sense' that the sign 'expresses,' observing also that "[i]n many cases, it is not even true that a sign 'stands for' that of which we may say it is a sign' and that '...even where this can be said, one has to observe that 'standing for' will not count as the 'meaning' which characterizes the expression" (1985, p. 166). Signs that are "indications," such as notes or marks, do not express anything, he argued, unless in addition to being merely indicative, they are part of a significant function. Husserl suggests here that the mere 'indication' of things does not guarantee that signs are *meaningful* and, indeed, he goes on to argue that signs do not gain their meaning simply from what they indicate. This must be so since meaning is quite possible without any indicative function whatsoever, as in the case of thinking of things "in isolated mental life," where no indications of things are either present or necessary (ibid.).

Indicative signs

In the same essay, Husserl proceeds to analyze the distinction within signs between "expressions" and "indications" more fully. His conclusion is that a sign is equivalent to indication when it leads to an *indicative relation*, as in the cases, for example, of national flags, or canals on Mars indicating the existence of Martian life, or fossils indicating prehistoric animals, or when we leave marks of various kinds to help us remember things. It is only in cases such as these, Husserl argues, that we actually *recognize* that signs are present and doing the particular job of indicating things. It is only in such case that signs ostensibly "stand for" things. The key characteristic of the indicative function of these kinds of signs is that we believe something to be the case because we believe in the reality of the sign: In this way, we *experience* the reality of things indicated through the reality of the sign. Another way of putting this is to say that signs *motivate* belief in what they indicate by way of the indicative relation and, Husserl believes, this property of motivation leads to a *descriptive unity* in the subjective mind (1985, p. 167). In qualifying this property of "motivation" further, Husserl argues that it is fundamentally a *logical* function--it takes the form of the *logical connective* in the thought. To provide a simple example of this process, an observer seeing "an American airplane" will have arrived at this perception from, say, the combination of seeing the shape of the airplane and a U.S. flag motif on its tail wing: The two signs then *motivate* the connection "*Since* there is an

American flag, it must be a plane from the United States." He argued that propositional connectives such as *some* or *if-then* lie at the core of the indicative relation, a relation which is not *intuitive* in nature but which involves the conscious connection between signs and what they signify.

Meaningful signs

In contrast to indicative signs are truly *meaningful* signs, or *expressions*, a term Husserl uses in a quite restricted sense. Included in the class of signs called expressions are all speech forms, including inner speech forms, but not gestures, facial expressions, or inner actions "in which a man's (sic) mental states achieve understandable 'expression' for his environment, without the added help of speech," since none of these involve communicative intention towards another (1985, p. 171). Husserl holds that it is usual to assume that expressions have two aspects--their physical manifestation in the form of speech or written language, and a sequence of mental states that are closely linked to them making up their senses or meanings. He argues that this description is inadequate, however, and that in order to understand how meaning really comes about, there is a need to distinguish between what a sign "shows forth" in terms of mental states, on the one hand, and what it "means," on the other. We also need to distinguish between the *content* of a sign (i.e. what it names) and the actual thing that is named. The origin of expressions lies in communicative need and the desire to *share* ideas with others who understand the speaker's intention (cf. Grice's co-operative principle, see Chapter Three). What speakers do is to *intimate* their inner experiences and, through language, they *indicate* what these inner experiences and thoughts are like. The intimating function, however, has two sides--a narrower side in which it involves the *imparting* of the sense of things (including, perhaps, aspects of the *medium* of delivery) and a broader side which involves the meaning of the message *as* message (1985, p. 172). It is the presence of this duality of functioning in communicative signs that allows them to be more than mere "indications," and to be always *expressions*, since they are always imbued with the intentionality of communication which gives them sense and meaning. Husserl's conclusion, therefore, is that the indicative function is *both* different from and a *part of* the expressive function of signs.

Phenomenology of signs

In the end, what is probably of most interest in Husserl's analysis of signs is his argument about how expressions and indications are supposed to differ in terms of the phenomenological dynamics. To Husserl, meaning arises only when awareness of actual signs themselves disappears and when there is a kind of *fusion* between intuition, intention, and expression. In cases where signs are ostensible--where we remain aware of the links between the sign and what it signifies--it follows there is no meaning in Husserl's sense of the term, since no essential phenomenological transformation has taken place removing the sign from the experience (1985, p. 176).

In another section of *Logical Investigations* (1913), Husserl remarks on the phenomenological aspects of signs in more detail. In keeping with his theory of perception, he believed that signs should not be treated as "objects," but rather, as *constituting* meaning, understanding, and thought (1985, p. 181). He rejects the idea that signs are objects in the sense that in thinking we think "about" signs: We think according to Husserl more *through* signs than about them and even when we deliberately turn our attention to them we are still thinking *through* them. Where there are signs there is intention, and where there is intention there are signs; we can never disinter signs from consciousness (ibid.). Husserl also argues that symbolic systems such as mathematics conform to this interpretation of signs, an idea that he explains by way of the familiar analogy to chess. Chess pieces, he asserted, "are not part of the chess-game as bits of ivory and wood having such and such shapes and colors," but receive their meaning *only from their place and function in the game*. In the same way, mathematical signs when they are being used in the solution of problems gain meaning only in relation to the "game" of calculation. This is not the same as thinking about them *as symbols* of addition, subtraction, and so on, which involves another kind of intention towards them. The signs that are actually used to do calculations, and which become part of the expressions of their solutions, are actually intuitively fused into the mathematical acts themselves, and it is in this that their meaning resides (1985, p. 182).

At the end of the same article, Husserl indicates what he thinks might be the order of events, the "process" of response to signs. On first encounter, expressive signs rest on the same kinds of interpretations of basic sense-contents as perception. The first apprehension of a word is of it as a physical object, a "mere sign" that has not yet been fused with intuitive meaning. A second conception is built on this, however, which "goes entirely beyond the experienced sense-material, which it no longer uses as analogical building-material, to the quite new object of its present meaning" (1985, p. 186). This second "conception" Husserl thinks of as an "act" which effectively transports the content of the sign over from its original sensual essence to its *meaning* essence, which during this transformation relinquishes its sensual character. Meaning, then, according to Husserl, involves and arises out of the *presupposition* that signs will reveal through these acts their intuitive foundations. Husserl saw the further exploration of these matters to be of central interest for phenomenology (ibid.).

C.S Peirce: the pure logic of signs

Following Husserl's description of "acts," "presuppositions," and of the general "process" by which signs are transformed into meaning, not to mention the patent presence of psychological reasoning in the notion of his "reductions," it is not perhaps surprising that Peirce accused him of being "hopelessly involved in psychology" (*Collected Papers*, Vol. 4). Peirce refused to be lured into these "psychological" aspects of phenomenology and insisted throughout his life on pursuing a *monistic* philosophy directed towards demonstrating how reality reduces to fundamental laws of logic. We have already noted (see Chapter Three) how Peirce viewed semiotic functioning as a triadic relationship between signs (representamens), what they stand for (their objects) and the respect in which they stand for things (their grounds). Peirce went further than anyone before him in classifying signs on the basis of the three types, icon, index, and symbol, and he saw language as expressing the essential *symbolism* by which signs became related to their objects. What we have not yet explored in detail, however, and what can now be explored with greater insight following the brief review of Husserl's treatment of language, is how Peirce related his typology of signs to his own more monistic epistemology. It is Peirce's understanding of the processes of knowing through semiosis (rather than his detailed categorization of signs) which composes the most exciting and potentially influential aspect of his contribution.

Foundational categories of knowing:

In some ways, Peirce's analysis and understanding of the structures of signs is similar to Husserl's. They both believed in the fundamental inseparability of signs, language, and thought in general. Peirce claimed, indeed, that "there is no element whatsoever of man's (sic) consciousness that has not something corresponding to it in the word" and that "the word or sign that man uses is the man himself." "Thus," he continued, " my language is the sum total of myself; for the man is the thought" (Vol. 5, pp. 313-314). Peirce's view of how this fusion was wrought, however, was radically different from Husserl's, and this becomes particularly clear when we look at the categories of *Firstness*, *Secondness*, and *Thirdness*, that lie at the heart of his epistemology.

Peirce's view of phenomenology was that its central task was to discover the fundamental or irreducible categories of things, categories that are universal across human experience. He wrote that he never doubted that these categories were present to all minds and that there could be no question of (and therefore no real interest in the question of) the "psychological" reality of these elements (quoted in Feibleman, 1946, p. 145). The real task of the philosopher, then, is to identify these foundational elements, and Peirce concluded that there were just three of these categories, categories that "are supposed to be the three kinds of elements that attentive perception can make out in the phenomenon" (ibid.). All of these elements, he argued, would be present in some relationship in every phenomenon.

The first category Peirce identifies is that of the *qualities* of phenomena, qualities such as *redness, passion, height, violence*, etc.. Where there are phenomena, there are always such qualities, he argued and they typically "merge into each other" even though they exist on their own "without help from the others." His second category is that of *actual facts*. While the qualities are only general and abstract, facts involve the presence of material substances and, in particular, of individuals in situations in which qualities become "known." Qualities exist independently of and beyond facts, but it is only in facts--in the coming-together of individuals and situations that qualities actually receive their significance. His third category is that of *laws* and *thoughts* which are "neither qualities nor facts" since they are "general" and can refer to "all possible things, and not merely to those which happen to exist" (quoted in Feibleman, 1946, p. 150).

The three categories, elsewhere referred to in Peirce's writing as the *monad*, *dyad*, and *triad*, are closely tied to Firstness, Secondness, and Thirdness and, concomitantly, to the tripartite categorization of signs. Peirce gave the name Firstness to the "idea of that which is such as it is regardless of anything else" (ibid., p. 156). Firstness might be experienced, for instance, in a state of semi-consciousness in which one might have a sense of something-- of heat, of humidity, of an intruder--without yet bringing it to subjective attention. This, he wrote, would be "as nearly as possible, a purely monadic state of feeling." Significantly, there is no *relation* present in this experience, and it is timeless in the sense of all independent qualities. Secondness refers to some "reaction" to Firstness; it is the concept of "being relative to" something else, it is a "force," or "the object of experience as a reality." Secondness is, of course, logically dependent on Firstness, while the reverse does not hold: Qualities, in other words, can and do exist without the intervention of minds, while the latter impose upon, constrain, and are utterly dependent upon the existence of the former. Peirce held that true Secondness involves a dyadic relation between qualities and subjects in opposition to each other and in which one (the subject) is in "a mode of being over and above" qualities (ibid., p. 159). Thirdness is a medium between Firstness and Secondness, being the *representation* of the relation between the two. It is in this sense a *part* of the relation, not only representing it but also bringing about its connection in the first place. Peirce saw Thirdness as being akin to "composition" or "combination" in that it is "what it is owing to the parts which it brings into mutual relationship" (ibid., p. 164). Thirdness was logically dependent on the presence of both of the other two forms. Peirce believed that no further categories were needed than these and that all others were derived as recombinations and extensions of the basic triad (ibid., p. 168).

It is easy to see now how the categories set forth in Peirce's wider ontological and metaphysical speculations relate to the semiotic categories of *icon*, *index*, and *symbol* (see Chapter Three). Peirce wrote that an icon was a representamen having the quality of Firstness, whereas an index was a representamen with the characteristic of being a Second, and a symbol involved Thirdness, being a "rule" which determined how the entire triad was to be interpreted.

Peirce's understanding of meaning and knowledge:

> Peirce's proposals concerning Thirdness in relation to symbols bring us to consideration of what might be called the "semiotic theory of knowledge" or "semiotic epistemology." According to Deely (1982), for example, knowledge is "equivalent to a process of communication by signs, or semiosis," and it involves the principle to which Peirce gave the name Thirdness (p. 95). As Deely argues, Peirce's invocation of "thirdness" constitutes a radically different solution to the problem of knowledge than that to be found in his predecessors, such as Descartes, Hume, and Locke, even though it was Locke who had first written of the possibility of "a science of signs." These earlier philosophers had all argued that sense impressions be understood in terms of objective data cast in the form of mental images which go to make up the objects of awareness. In contrast, Deely summarizes Peirce's central notion about meaning and knowledge as follows:

>> ...the 'data' or 'impressions' of external sense, semiotically, should be regarded neither as intrinsic properties of physical things nor as mere modifications of the subjective faculties ('effects' wholly within the cognitive organism), but precisely as features or properties exhibiting how things are *in their action*

here and now on an organism possessed of this determinate range of sensitivities. (1982, pp. 96-97)

Thirdness is a key concept in this view of meaning and knowledge since it embodies the idea that no phenomenon whatsoever can be known by an organism without involving the bringing-together, the fusion, of two sign-phenomena. According to Peirce, then, an individual can never know "redness" as a pure (First) quality without it being attached to something else--a traffic signal to stop, the color of a book, anger, a Ferrari, and so on: We could never know "redness" or "the sound of B flat played on a tuba" without their being attached to some other quality or condition. The fundamental claim here is that we can never know anything whatsoever without the fusional process of semiosis and, moreover, that our knowledge is constituted by such semiosis.

Husserl and Peirce compared

In contrasting the ideas of Peirce with those of Husserl, several similarities and several differences become apparent. What they share is a profound belief in discovering the elements that are fundamental to all perception and knowledge, together with the idea that these are logical in nature. There seems to be a great deal of similarity also in the particulars of Husserl's ideas about *noemata*, on the one hand, and Peirce's ideas about Firstness, on the other. These notions represent the attempts of each philosopher to describe the basic forms out of which perception, understanding, meaning, and knowledge are created by conscious minds. There is also some apparent correspondence between Peirce's conception of Secondness and Husserl's process of noesis, in that both are essentially *relational* and dyadic in character, imbuing sense data with structure and significance to the individual mind. The two also share the belief that all experience, no matter how complex, is wrought out of these foundational logical elements. Where the two differ significantly, however, is in their additional understanding about the nature of phenomena in general and in their methods for arriving at the truth.

In Husserl's ideas, as we have seen, there is a continual reference to the *essences* of things and the presence of essences brings with it a series of *psychological* entailments, including the idea that our perception of things can be modified through conscious reductions, acts of bracketing, and so on. Peirce remained far more rigorously "logical" and "mathematical" in his orientation to phenomenology and, although he often referred to "essences" he did not involve himself in the details of psychological processes whatsoever believing, instead, in rigorous attention to the delineation of the logical categories. In Peirce's writing, "essences" are wrought out of logic, while in Husserl they seem to retain a life of their own that lies beyond the boundaries of empirical investigation. While Husserl pursued "reduction" as a method, a method having much in common with Gestalt psychology, Peirce pursued his own version of "Pragmatism," which concerned, precisely, this unadulterated search for truth, and the fundamental laws of cause and effect. Peirce wrote that the phenomenologist has a difficult task in which he or she must "look well at the phenomenon and say what are the characteristics that are never wanting in it," an ability that required "the faculty of seeing what stares one in the face," the faculty of "resolute discrimination which fastens itself like a bulldog upon the particular feature that we are studying," and the faculty which consists in "the generalizing power of the mathematician" (Peirce, quoted in Feibleman, pp. 145-146).

Despite the differences, however, what is of importance for the further development of semiotics is that some of its strongest roots lie in systematic phenomenology of one sort or another. In this, there is a significant shift of understanding about the nature of language, a shift even more apparent in the work of later theorists such as Heidegger, and it is, namely, the shift away from thinking of languages as codes which "represent" or "translate" perceptions and experiences already held in the mind and towards the view that there are simply no representations or experiences *without* linguistic sign-forms. Within the semiotic view of things, signs *are* our experiences and they are formed through the operation of universal logical laws that exist quite independently of the particular psychological qualities of individuals. The potential ramifications of semiotic philosophy are enormous since, if the tenets of semiotics such as those laid down by Peirce be accepted, it means that examination of all linguistic phenomena, including the traditional categories of "syntax," "morphology," "lexical semantics," and so on, should be re-ordered in relation to the priority of signs. In the context of recent linguistic terminology, it means that all distinctions between "deep" and "surface" structure will need to be redefined in terms of the fundamental relationship between what is given (Firstness, icons), the fundamental pairing of the given to a knowing mind (Secondness, indices). The primary function of language in the semiotic view is *constantly to forge relationships between these two elements* giving them meaning and significance. Clearly, higher orders of signs can be built on the basis of the initial object-subject pairings and, indeed, these pairings themselves then become available as phenomenological objects for further sign-formation. In this way, semiotics is both a "science" and *a way of looking at* things in general.

Semiotics and Structuralism

It would be impossible to characterize modern semiotics without tracing the influence on semiotics of structuralism in addition to that of phenomenology. This takes us back to the thoughts of de Saussure who, it will be remembered, asserted that language theory should be centrally involved in the analysis of signs, and who also laid the groundwork for the structural analysis of language. Some of the main characteristics of structuralism as inspired by Saussure were briefly outlined in Chapter Two, where it was identified within an "objective" orientation. At the core of the structuralist analysis of language lies the concept of elements deriving their meaning, value, or significance, from their systemic interrelationships. On this basis, the search for structural *oppositions* between phonemes was conducted, as was the later search for sets of *distinctive features* underlying various sub-systems in languages. This search for abstract features underlying the sound system reached an apotheosis in the work of Chomsky and Halle (1968) and also spread into the realm of semantic analysis (see e.g. Bierwisch, 1967).

In relating semiotics to structuralism, there seems to be something of an anomaly, however, since at first glance this "objective" mode of analysis would seem to have little in common with the phenomenological approaches outlined above. This anomaly can be resolved, though, if we recognize an important distinction between what linguists or others calling themselves "structuralists" actually *do* in their work, on the one hand, and the central *philosophy* of structuralism, on the other. All too easily, structuralist analysis can revert to the type of analysis which it was intended to replace, namely, the kind of structural linguistic analysis espoused by behaviorists such as Bloomfield (1933), in which structural analysis was reduced to provision of formal inventories of linguistic elements.

The search for universals

It can be argued that approaches such as Bloomfield's do not represent the true spirit of structuralism. Its true spirit is reflected in a concern with the identification of the *universal patterns that underlie* things. This is evident in the essential *abstraction* that structuralist analysis involves: Neither phonemes nor distinctive features have any *physical* status--they are viewed as "properties" which accompany physical instantiations of things, properties that are established through cultural processes and which constitute a fundamental part of speaker-knowledge ("langue" or "competence"). Much of the early work in structuralism focused on language, but the method has also been applied to the analysis of culture and society more generally (see e.g. Lévi-Strauss, 1967). Structuralists initiated an all-important move from mere "description" of phenomena to an attempt to provide deeper "explanation" of things in terms of their underlying relationships. In this way, much more general statements could be made about matters such as the ways in which all phonological systems seem to operate, and so on. The quest of the Prague School linguists, for example, was to describe the fundamental and *universal logic* by which all phonological systems work in languages, and the work of Chomsky and Halle was directed to finding the "ideal" forms which underlie the English sound system.

In this search for "ideal" and "universal" forms, of course, structuralism clearly shares much with phenomenology. However, there appears to be a central ambiguity in structuralism having to do with the attitude it brings to the subject-object distinction. In one way, structuralism appears to lead to a form of objective abstraction which divorces the study of language from its subjects and thus from communication, while in another way, since it is directed towards discovering universal ideal forms it is directed, just like Husserl's phenomenological method, towards describing the forms of subjective knowledge. In some ways it is the tension between these two interpretations of structuralism which leads to much of the controversy over the psychological reality of generative grammars (see Chapter Seven). In the end, it appears that whether structuralism is viewed as being pre-eminently an "objective" or a "subjective" mode of analysis depends upon which of its aspects are seen to predominate. From a semiotic perspective, structuralist analysis of "objective" forms is part of the larger endeavor of relating objective and subjective structures to each other.

Another feature of structuralist thinking is that it concerns explanation of things as they are in the here-and-now (in what Saussure referred to as the *synchronic* dimension), rather of how they came to be or where they are going to in the future (Saussure's *diachronic* dimension). And here we find some further connection between structuralism and phenomenology in that the latter also stresses the *immediacy*, the *presentness* of experience necessary to the understanding of things. In several works, Husserl himself had actually expressed an interest in semiotics, and he clearly recognized the importance of studying signs as a part of studying "general" or "universal" logic. Husserl was also influenced by the earlier work of the Prague philosopher, Bolzano, who distinguished between two aspects of signs: signs as "objects" and as "connections" (see Jakobson, 1987, pp. 339-340). What structuralism, semiotics, and phenomenology share is a belief in the search for fundamental structures in all experience, in the "ideal" and "universal" structures that underlie everything and which give them objective shape. Like phenomenology, moreover, structuralism and semiotics have developed in response to the challenge of explaining the underlying *logic* of experience, a logic even more fundamental than "psycho-logic," which underlies perception universally, which is quite abstract in form, and which transcends the vicissitudes of *individual* behavior or function. Husserl's starting point was the question of how we can know ideal forms such as numbers or geometric states, and he developed methods--in particular the method of reduction--as part of his solution to how, in general, we must bracket away thinking irrelevant to the essence of matters. In a similar way, the starting point of the structuralist and the semiotician is to search for underlying abstract systems in which things are given meaning. Rather than bracketing, their method involves comparison and contrast of elements within systems, although in terms of the everyday perception of things, structuralists, along with both phenomenologists (and Gestalt psychologists) believe that perception (e.g. of phonemes) proceeds in terms of *holistic* given structures and *not* in terms of any components formal analysis might yield.

Saussurean Semiotics

It is interesting to notice the strong correspondences between the chess analogy given by Husserl (above) and that of Saussure, who placed his greatest emphasis on the notion of the *values* assumed by linguistic units. Saussure wrote that a game of chess "is like an artificial realization of what language offers in a natural form....[t]he respective value of the pieces depends on their position on the chessboard just as each linguistic term derives its value from its opposition to all the other terms" (p. 88). The system depends on convention, and each piece in the game can easily be replaced by an equivalent piece if we declare this replacement to hold the same value as its predecessor. "We see then," he wrote, "that in semiological systems like language, where elements hold each other in equilibrium in accordance with fixed rules, the notion of identity blends with that of value and vice versa" (Saussure 1974, pp. 88, 110). In comparing the two chess analogies (cf. Husserl, above) it can be seen that both Saussure and Husserl recognized the close relationship between meaning and structural positioning. In Saussure's *Course*, however, the analogy is tied to his insistence on the importance of the arbitrariness of signs and on the mutual dependency of this idea with that of structural opposition. In this way, Saussure made it clear that the particular form of signs is of no importance since they gain meaning only in relation to other signs co-existing within the same system (see Chapter Two, above).

In a recent analysis of Saussurean language theory, Tobin (1990) has attempted to interpret Saussure in greater detail and to show how semiotic analysis should be developed in line with the principles that he laid down. According to Tobin, it was Saussure's original intention to retire all the traditional categories of linguistic analysis in favor of analyzing language signs in their own terms (1990, p. xii). He argues that there has been a failure in North American linguistics to recognize the importance Saussure's call to semiotic analysis, and structural linguists (as opposed to those working in the true light of structuralism) have typically chosen to take "sentences," "utterances," or "speech acts," rather than signs, as their fundamental analytical categories (ibid, p. 14). One thing that makes these traditional categories so ubiquitous in linguistic analysis (together with all the traditional categories of parts of speech and so on) is that they are "convenient" and "easy." As Saussure had suggested, however, the convenience of language categories does not necessarily make them *valid*; they bring with them preconceptions about how language fits together which do not actually arise out of *language*, and which therefore serve to obscure the *signs* out of which language is truly wrought. Linguists, Saussure claimed, work "continuously with concepts forged by grammarians without knowing whether or not the concepts actually correspond to the constituents of the system of language" (Saussure, 1974, pp. 109-110; quoted in Tobin, p. 29).

One key aspect of Saussurean semiotics follows from his distrust of linguistic categories and analytical levels as they have been developed by linguists: If signs be accepted as the only unit of analysis then all of these "linguistic" categories become redundant. This is so since all linguistic elements, at the phonological, morphological, and syntactic levels, will be understood in terms of their oppositional relationships. In this way, the sentence *The linguist convinced the semiotician* is in opposition to *The semiotician convinced the linguist* in just the same way that /b/ opposes /p/ within the English phonemic system. According to Saussure's radical (and as yet unfulfilled) view of how language analysis should ideally proceed, meaning *at any level whatsoever* in language can be most readily analyzed in terms of the *contrasts* between elements within systems of signs. As Tobin points out, this brings an essential *unification* of method across all the traditionally compartmentalized levels of language analysis (p. 30). In contrast to the traditionally-accepted notion of the task of linguistics, Saussure's view was that the generation of more and more elaborate schemes on the bases of pre-established categories was worthless. The true objective should be, rather, to *discover* what are the true categories of language. This search for fundamental categories appears to share much in common with that of Husserl and Peirce. Like Husserl and Peirce, too, Saussure's ideas about sounds bring with them the necessary conclusion that sign-elements, especially more complex ones such as words and utterances, involve recognition of *wholes* rather than atomistic parts. This holistic aspect of sign recognition is captured in the term *synergesis*, which may be defined as the "cooperative action of discrete agencies such that the total effect is greater than the sum of the discrete effects taken independently" (Tobin, 1990, p.48). Synergesis is the process by which the *invariant* "definitions" of signs (i.e. their "dictionary" meanings) are always combined by intentional communicators with *variant* aspects of context to yield their real communicative meanings. The process does not yield meaning via *decomposition* of signs but by way of fusing signs together. It is in this way that word sign-forms can be used endlessly through new acts of synergesis. The general process is especially clear in the case of homophones, such as *bank* or *plant*, where definition depends entirely upon the selected use of a sign from a set of possibilities, but it is also at work in the formation and interpretation of *all* sign forms in language (ibid.).

Semiotics and grammar

In this analysis, it is also possible to see "grammar" as a system of signs which combines synergetically with lexical items (morphemes and words) in semiosis. This is a highly significant point for language analysis, since it suggests, counter to most of the work conducted in the mainstream of linguistics, that lexical signs must be considered *prior* to syntax; syntax, in other words, would seem to proceed from lexis rather than the other way around (cf. Chomskyan standard theory, Chapter Five). The purpose of grammar is on this view to "refine the relational aspects of what is being talked about" (Tobin, 1990, p. 64).

The era of transformational-grammatical theorizing has biased many linguists towards thinking about lexical items almost as if they "slot into" pre-established sentence frames. This is precisely the mode of analysis in standard transformational grammar, even though it has also been recognized just how rich the lexicon is in terms of the syntactic information that it contains *without* any assistance from an independent theory of syntactic ordering. This tradition of thinking about language has also conditioned us to think of grammar in terms of words and morphemes rather than signs. The counter-position following a re-analysis of Saussure's ideas about signs, however, is that *both* lexical *and* grammatical forms should be considered as signs. From the point of view of Saussurean semiotics, the sentence *The semiotician impressed the linguist* should be thought of as involving the synergetic combinations of several kinds leading to a "whole" which is the sign making up the entire sentence. First, there are the invariant meanings of *semiotician, linguist*, (which are in opposition to each other in this context), *impress*, (in opposition to *amused, bored*) and so on. Second, there are choices of signs from the English grammatical system. Informally, we might say that for this utterance there is a choice between the frame *subject--active transitive verb--object* or *object--passive transitive verb by--subject*, where each of these choices is a sign in just the same way as are *semiotician* and *linguist*, and where active and passive voices are in opposition to each other. Third, there is the synergesis between these signs and the signs intended by me as the writer and you as the reader in the context(s) in which *we* communicate. In this regard, it is clear that I have deliberately set up an opposition between semioticians and linguists as part of my own text: I fully *intend* you, the reader, to recognize this opposition in my textual references semioticians and linguists.

From this small example, we can see just how inseparable, how synergetically related, are signs from intentions and contexts. Perhaps the most important point of all, however, is that all of this synergesis of signs is accomplished *holistically*, and, indeed, description of any underlying categories in language in the framework of Saussurean semiotics must proceed on the basis that wholes cannot be explained merely on the basis of the addition of their parts. In their oppositional relationships, moreover, it is clear that signs gain value as much *from what they are not* as from the parts out of which they are supposedly composed. Analysis of language, then, proceeds precisely on the basis of showing how meaning comes about through the place of arbitrary language signs in particular contexts of space, time, and modality. The simple sign *linguist*, to take just one example, can enter any number of oppositional *relations* with other language items within other contexts. In the sentence *Linguists like garage-sales*, the sign *linguist* yields a somewhat different sense from that when it was placed in opposition to *semiotician* (in the previous example, above). In the case of *Linguists like garage-sales*, the reader will no doubt have to do a little more (synergetic) work to make adequate sense of the sentence but the point is that, in order to make any sense whatsoever, the interpreter must find *some kind of* opposition for *linguist*. The particular contrast made will be a matter of individual difference, but might oppose *linguist* to *biologist*, *philosopher*, or (perhaps more realistically) *normal people*. Once an opposition has been found, then the utterance takes on a semblance of meaning. In these latter examples, the context for the interpretation of *linguist* has already been partly set by the previous examples, and its sense is woven into the text of this chapter. At the heart of all this semiotic processing is the idea that *linguist* has *value* in the systems in which it resides which, together with the *sense* given by the textual and extra-textual context, yields a "whole" and particular meaning on each separate occasion of its use. According to Saussure, what is true of individual words is also true of all other signs ranging from phonemes to entire utterances.

Current Semiotics: Themes and Trends

The genesis of recent semiotics can be traced to the work of Peirce and Saussure on the nature of language signs. Rather than consolidating their work within a unitary paradigm, though, semioticians have begun to explore the relations between language signs and signs within other cultural systems such as art, film, music, and also with the signs used by other animal species. This breadth of interest seems likely to continue and semiotics, by its very nature, is unlikely to become constrained by a unitary paradigm since semioticians are in general more interested in exposing the nature of paradigms than they are in following them.

Any categorization of semioticians into different groups is hazardous because, in addition to being varied, the field is rich in its cross-fertilization of ideas. Major individual contributions have been made, however, in the context of Russian semiotics as well as that of European-American semiotics. In the reaming sections, it will be the objective to identify and review some of the major contributions made within each of these cultural groupings.

Russian Semiotics

The mainstream of Russian semiotics comes by way of the linguists, Jakobson and Trubetskoy, and the Moscow Linguistic Circle (Lucid, 1977). In the school of Russian Formalism which flourished in the 1920s, there was an attempt to analyze literature and other artistic phenomena from a strictly structuralist perspective, and formalists such as Propp undertook intense studies of folktales to find their structural commonalities and their reflections of social organization. The revival of semiotics in the 1950s and 1960s was partly inspired by this kind of structural analysis, extending some of the Formalists' interests in the structure of language, literature, visual art, sociology, and mythology, and also by research on machine translation and mathematical linguistics. One particular focus in Russian semiotics has been the investigation of sign systems as "models of the world," a type of investigation predicated on the notion that a modeling system is "a structure of elements and of rules for combining them that is a state of fixed analogy to the entire sphere of an object of knowledge, insight or regulation" (ibid., p. 7). Language is viewed as the "primary modeling system, " while other sign systems are viewed as "secondary." Like language, all other semiotic modeling systems are viewed as having "grammatical" rules which govern what can and what cannot occur and co-occur, and this gives the basis for considering the violation of norms not only in language, but also in mythology, games, jurisprudence, or whatever semiotic system is in question.

A good illustration of this interest in the detailed description of rules and structural relations is to be found in the study by Revzin (1977) entitled *Language as a Sign System and the Game of Chess*, which can usefully be compared with the chess analogies of Husserl and Saussure (see above). Using Saussure's comparison as his starting point, Revzin extends the analogy by considering the kinds of parallels between chess and language in much greater detail.

Revzin's elaboration of the chess-language analogy includes the following central points. First, in terms of their fundamental elements, the parallel of the squares on the chess board is the "non-sign background" in language. Against this background, the chess pieces have the equivalent in language of the morphemes. Second, there is a finite number of possible moves in chess which mean something different in each instance in which they are moved. Corresponding to this in language, there is a finite number of morphemes that are realized as new meanings within a finite set of words. In chess there is a finite number of ways in which the pieces can be configured, and each piece has its own particular "trait" of being a pawn, a rook, and so on, while in language each word has its own parallel trait, or semantic value. Third, while chess moves are finite in number, there is an infinite set of positions in which pieces can be arranged at given moments. These positions are either correct or incorrect and correct positions can only be arrived at by way of correct plays (i.e. by following the rules correctly). Correct and incorrect positioning in chess corresponds to correct (grammatical) and incorrect (ungrammatical) forms. Fourth, the match in chess corresponds to the text, to the fabric of utterances in language, where the outcome in the former is winning, drawing, or losing, and in the latter is understanding, partial understanding, or lack of understanding (Revzin, p. 89).

In terms of the parallel *relations* in chess and language, Revzin finds that the interaction of pieces in chess involves certain "valences" or tensions between them given by their structural relationships in the game. In language, such valencies exist between words. Chess involves recollection of previous moves, while language involves recollection of the connections between words and sentences not given by the text. Recollections guarantee that certain *plays* can be used, such as the flanking movements or the deliberate removal of pieces undertaken to make the game of chess clearer, or the use of pronouns and other devices in language to the same end. In terms of their parallel *operations*, chess and language are similar in that they share "tactics" and "strategies"; they both involve deliberative analysis of what is going on and how to gain advantage (ibid.). The thrust of Revzin's argument, then, is that both chess and language are intricate cultural systems. He suggests that what they, and perhaps all similar cultural systems, share is an underlying purpose which governs the interaction and use of the systemic elements. They also share the elements of a game in that both chess and language are underscored by the question of individuals to gain greater understanding of (and therefore greater control over) the symbolically-encoded information at hand. In both language and chess, greater symbolic control, greater mastery over valences and relationships, leads to the gaining of some kind of socio-cultural advantage.

Bakhtin: semiotics and ideology

Bakhtin's *Marxism and the Philosophy of Language* was published in Russian in 1929, but in its English translation only in 1973. The authorship of the book has been hotly contested as can be inferred from the fact that the book is actually published under the name of Vološinov, a contemporary of Bakhtin's who was strongly influenced by him. Since this and other works were written within a climate of potential danger from Soviet authorities who might not agree with any particular interpretation of Marxist ideas not in keeping with their political aims, it is possible that Bakhtin and other theorists deliberately wished to obscure their authorship. In any case, sufficient arguments have been developed in favor of Bakhtin's authorship of *Marxism and the Philosophy of Language* (for details of related arguments here, see Morson, 1986).

Bakhtin's book is a tour de force of semiotic and linguistic theory, reaching deeply and critically into the nature of language, philosophy, and psychology, and concluding that language is an inextricable part of *social* life. The book is divided into three parts, the first being an analysis of the potential relationship between Marxist ideology and the philosophy of language, the second being a more direct attempt to outline a Marxist semiotic theory of language, and the third being an analysis of indirect speech in line with the arguments developed in the preceding parts. The first two parts of the book are of special interest since, in addition to the particular contribution they make to semiotic theory, they return us full-circle to a reconsideration of the subject-object dichotomy in language analysis, and since Bakhtin's arguments contain an articulate critique of Saussure, whose *Course*, as we have seen, seems to stand at the intersection of so many theories of language.

The starting point for Bakhtin's analysis is the realization that everything that is meaningful is also ideological. The communist state ideologies prevalent in Bakhtin's time governing Soviet workers, for instance, had particular meanings which were encoded in their related sign-systems. Bakhtin argues that ideology and signs in general are interdependent (*Marxism and the Philosophy of Language*, p. 9). Accordingly, tools (such as the hammer and sickle) readily lead to signs and, as such, they become "material things" which go beyond their own significance and which "reflect and refract another reality" (ibid., p. 10). So close is the relationship between ideology and signs, indeed, that "Wherever a sign is present, ideology is present, too. Everything ideological possesses semiotic value" (p. 11). Bakhtin proceeds from this recognition of the inseparability of ideology and signs to an attack on the notion that signs are "contained" in consciousness, where (as in the psychological tradition generally) consciousness is understood to be some kind of entity that is *separate* from the signs it "contains." In the psychological tradition, ideological signs are treated as mere outward effects of inner thoughts that are not intrinsically linked with them. For Bakhtin, they are one and the same thing since understanding can only arise through signs. Hence, consciousness itself is comprised of--is co-terminous with--sign forms:

> The understanding of a sign is, after all, an act of reference between the sign apprehended and other, already known signs;

in other words, understanding is a response to a sign with signs. (1986, p. 11)

Signs, however, (and therefore individual consciousness) are only possible through processes of interaction between individuals *in society*, and cannot be explained without reference to the societies and the ideological circumstances in which they are created. It follows from this that consciousness is a *social* phenomenon and that:

> Consciousness takes shape and being in the material of signs created by an organized group in the process of its social intercourse. The individual consciousness is nurtured on signs; it derives its growth from them; it reflects their logic and laws. The logic of consciousness is the logic of ideological communication, of the semiotic interaction of a social group. If we deprive consciousness of its semiotic, ideological content, it would have absolutely nothing left. (*Marxism and the Philosophy of Language*, p. 13)

If ideology, rather than individual psychology, provides the essential substance of signs, then *words* are the primary ideological tools. Bakhtin views words as the "purest" of signs which have, in addition, the property of being *neutral* (p. 14). They are neutral in the sense that they can participate in *any* kind of ideological functioning, be it political, religious, or scientific, or whatever. Words also serve as the "material of inner life--of consciousness," in other words as the substance of *inner speech*, a phenomenon which Bakhtin identifies as one of the most "vital" in the philosophy of language (ibid.). He suggests here that one of the key objectives in semiotics must be the analysis of words *as social signs*; this is the gateway to understanding individual consciousness. Another significant claim he makes about inner speech as constituted in word-signs is that *all* sign systems, including those of the visual arts, music, and so on, are rooted in inner language; they are "bathed by, suspended in, and cannot be entirely segregated or divorced from the element of speech" (p. 15). Accordingly, then, *all* consciousness must be verbally constituted.

How are ideologies, together with their supporting language forms, established? Bakhtin's answer is that they are created out of hierarchical social and communicative interaction. Signs are conditioned through the social organization of communicators and by their immediate conditions. In this way, ideologies are tied to signs, signs are tied to social intercourse, and communication is always tied to the material conditions in which it takes place. Bakhtin thinks of signs, society, and ideology as constituting an organic whole in which individual choice "can have no meaning at all" (p. 21). Individuals live by the themes carried by the signs that they themselves give birth to within particular social communities. This view of consciousness as being socially, and not individually, constituted brings with it a vibrant rejection of traditional scientific approaches to consciousness as "object," and to Cartesian dualism as a whole. Bakhtin argues that inner experience is solely constituted by signs and that it is continuous with outer experience. On this view, there is no psyche without signs; they are made up of the same material, and

> ...there are physiological processes, processes in the nervous system, but no subjective psyche as a special existential quality fundamentally distinct from both the physiological processes occurring within the organism and the reality encompassing the organism from outside, to which the psyche reacts and which one way or another it reflects. (*Marxism and the Philosophy of Language*, p. 26)

Bakhtin sees the subjective psyche, moreover, as existing at the border, or interface, of the individual psyche and the outside world, and this is precisely where they intersect in signs. Clearly, though, the actual form of signs in the subjective psyche must be different from those of outer speech, and it is here that Bakhtin returns to bring greater clarity to his conception of inner speech.

Although inner speech must be closely interactive with other basic forms such as motor reactions which have their own semiotic value, he believes that the word forms of inner speech are primary in human functioning. Unlike the functional psychologists who, in keeping with the empirical-scientific tradition, treat psychic phenomena as inner processes of data interpretation of various kinds, Bakhtin argues in sympathy with Husserl that the form and *content* of psychic experience cannot be prised apart. The study of subjective consciousness, then, involves understanding the contents of signs as well as the ways in which they are "processed," and it turns out that both their forms and their contents are given through the interactions between ideological construction and social identification (pp. 32-33).

According to Bakhtin, the difference between inner and outer signs lies mainly in the directions in which signs are turned. Inner language meaning is turned toward the individual and is constituted by individual experience, although even this inner experience, since it is in turn constituted by social signs, will have an ideological character in the context of which thoughts will find a structured place. Outer signs are "purely ideological," and individual subjective understanding comes from the relating of outer to inner signs. Bakhtin claims that outer speech can be directed either towards the subjective psyche, in cases where speech invites understanding of individual experience, or outwards, in which case it will take its place in some ideological context. Inner speech he believes to be composed of signs that are not classifiable in terms of regular grammatical or phonetic categories. They work in the form of inner *dialogue*. He believes this dialogue of inner speech to be not "grammatical" or "logical" in nature, but emotional-evaluative, and dependent upon the current of social experience. Individuals and their socio-ideological contexts are inseparable. They are in a continual dialectic with each other since, *as long as outer signs remain vibrant and meaningful*, "the psyche effaces itself, or is obliterated, in the process of becoming ideology, and ideology effaces itself in the process of becoming the psyche" (p. 39). The process breaks down, however, where there is no resonance between subjective inner and objective outer signs. It follows from all of the above that it should be a primary task of the philosophy of language to identify these ideological sign forms. (Here, it is tempting to speculate just how closely related the current disintegration of Soviet Communism is, in keeping with Bakhtin's observations, to the erosion of the ideological sign-forms by which it was once constituted).

Bakhtin's analysis of "subject" vs. "object":

In the second part of his treatise, Bakhtin reviews the two major trends he sees to have emerged in the history of the search for a definition of language. These are, namely, those around which some of the present work has been organized, the "individualistic subjectivist" and the "abstract objectivist" trends. The four characteristics of the first trend are the perception that language is an individual *creative activity*, that the laws of linguistic creativity are the laws of individual psychology, that creativity is meaningful in a way that is analogous to creative art, and that language conceived as a stable system (*ergon* Humboldt's terms; *langue* in Saussure's; *competence* in Chomsky's) is the "hardened inner crust" of linguistic creativity (p. 48). The first trend is, in keeping with the analysis pursued in earlier chapters here, *anti-positivist*, and it is consistent with a *poetic* or *aesthetic* understanding of language, a view captured in the words of the Russian philologist, Vossler: "Linguistic thought is essentially poetic thought; linguistic truth is artistic truth, is meaningful beauty" (quoted in Bakhtin, p. 51).

The second "objective" trend focuses on language *system* and as an essentially *static* phenomenon not governed by creativity and change. Objective treatment of language depends upon the *normative identity* of linguistic elements such as phonemes or words, and it is only through this normative identity that communication is held to be possible. Certainly, such an analytical approach to language fails to recognize the social and ideological forces which, in Bakhtin's view, provide both the matrix and the substance for all language activity. As Bakhtin sees it, the characteristics of this second trend are, in summary, that language is viewed as *stable* and *immutable*, and that language laws (grammatical rules) are viewed in terms of specific connections between linguistic signs within closed linguistic systems. Further, these connections are not themselves related to external *values* and, finally, individual speech acts are viewed as "distortions" of normative or ideal language forms and they are disconnected from any historical properties of the language (p. 57).

Bakhtin's critique of Saussure:

Bakhtin's unsympathetic appraisal of abstract objectivism in language finds both motivation and focus in his critique of Saussurean linguistics which, he writes, was at that time having great and, in his view, unwarranted influence in Russia. Bakhtin first attacked Saussure's assumption that the study of language cannot focus on *speech* forms (*parole*) but must focus on the inner system of language (*langue*) since this is the only stable or normative form of language. Second, he attacked Saussure's rejection of the *diachronic* dimension of language study in favor of the *synchronic* dimension in which logical and psychological relations between linguistic elements are essentially formed. Given the views expressed by Bakhtin about the inseparability of sign forms, on the one hand, and both creative speech and ideological history, on the other, it is not surprising that he found these two central ideas of Saussure's inimical. What Bakhtin objected to most strongly both in Saussure and in other areas of emergent structuralism is *the separation of language from the question of consciousness*. Saussure, he claimed, is the main spokesman for the "spirit of rationalism" (initiated by Descartes) which regards "history as an irrational force distorting the logical purity of the language system" (p. 61).

Is Bakhtin correct in his appraisal of Saussure, and is he fair in branding him in this way as an abstractivist-objectivist? We have already seen how Saussure's ideas are in many ways difficult to characterize. In some ways, he appears to think of language in the way Bakhtin suggests, as disembodied from social creativity and consciousness, but in another way his structuralism can be viewed as a form of idealism that is highly compatible with some of the central tenets of semiotics (see above). As has already been pointed out, what *is* true is that Saussure has been *interpreted* as having laid the foundations of the kind of abstractivist structuralism Bakhtin inveighs against, but it is also true that, as we have seen, there are strong lines of compatibility between his structuralism and the idealist structuralism of Husserl and Peirce. Moreover, linguists such as Tobin (see Tobin, 1990, above) have begun to realize that the abstractivist tendencies in Saussure were *not* what he would have wished to inspire. His ideal program was, rather, to lead to a *semiotic* understanding of language, and he appeared to view "structural-linguistic" analysis as a relatively insignificant part of the enterprise. In this way, Saussure's *Course* should perhaps best be read as a series of heuristic distinctions *on the way* to a more fully-developed semiotic theory and *not* as a reflection of any deep disinterest he supposedly had in creative or historical aspects of language.

If we look more closely, indeed, at one of the quotations from Saussure's course that Bakhtin apparently believes stands in condemnation of itself, there is some reason for skepticism about his critique. In the context of his formal distinction between the synchronic and diachronic dimensions, Saussure wrote that:

> Diachronic linguistics...must study relations binding successive terms together, which relations are not perceived by the collective mind and replace one another without forming a system. (Quoted in *Marxism and the Philosophy of Language*, p. 61)

But it is clear from reading the *entire* passage in the *Course* from which this extract was abstracted by Bakhtin that Saussure was essentially reacting to the period of what he saw as very sterile language analysis that had lasted throughout much of the previous century. This was the period of *philology* in which there had been an overwhelming preoccupation with the question of the origins of language and, concomitantly, with the minute changes in meanings and grammars that take place over time. Why Saussure saw this kind of analysis as unproductive was precisely because it led the study of language *away from* communication and from the dynamics of communicative interaction. The point he makes most forcefully of all in support of this turn away from historical linguistics is that *since individual speakers are not conscious of the history of the language when they use it* this should not play a central role in any explanation of how language and communication relate to each other. Communication, in other words, always takes place in present time and therefore must be explained by way of what *is* in consciousness, and individuals are simply not aware, for instance, of the history of how the verb *to be* gained its present grammatical forms over the course of the history of the language. This realization led Saussure to the very reasonable conclusion that what linguistics need to concentrate on is the description of the dynamics of the relations between semiotic elements as they underlie linguistic performance in present time. It was this, in turn, which led to development of the notion of dynamic structural oppositions, a notion not incompatible with a phenomenological interpretation of consciousness.

While it can be argued that Saussure's remarks and his true intent are distorted at the hands of Bakhtin, he is clearly right in his perception that Saussure's distinction does stress systematic norms rather than variations. Saussure was correct in his assertion that speakers are not normally conscious of diachronic aspects of linguistic elements, but the key difference between him and Bakhtin is that the latter simply views consciousness in a different way, as being *constituted by* language. Since consciousness is actually formed by language in Bakhtin's semiotics, it makes little sense to make the claim that speakers "are not conscious" of their language; they are simply conscious *through* language signs, and these bring with them all the history of the ideologies and social interactions they bear. But, of course, there could be no more justification for Bakhtin's saying that speakers are conscious of *these* (ideological) aspects of signs (unless they are specifically brought to attention by way of another, ideologically conditioned, sign-system) than for Saussure's claiming that people are aware of the diachronic aspects of their language. In the end, what we have in the contrast between Saussure's and Bakhtin's views is itself a genuine philosophical opposition. This opposition is rooted however, not so much in what Bakhtin *identifies* as its foundation, but rather, in their own quite different perceptions of the nature of consciousness. There seems, moreover, little reason to believe that Saussure's structuralism, as interpreted in terms of *semiotic oppositions* in shared linguistic consciousness (*langue*) are fundamentally or logically incompatible with Bakhtin's theory of the ideological sign.

As pointed out above, Saussure's insistence on the centrality of the synchronic dimension in linguistics was wrought out of his rejection of what he saw as being the vapidity of philology. It is all the more ironic that

Bakhtin continued his own attack on abstractive objectivism and on structural linguistics in general with a parallel rejection of philology, the central characteristics of which he apparently felt were merely continued in the work of Saussure. Linguists, according to Bakhtin, typically divorce language forms from their ideological or social metier and they are concerned with *signals* rather than signs. The metalinguistic character of linguistics means that linguists cannot be describing the same phenomenon that is in the mouths and minds of everyday language-users, for whom "there is no direct access to the system of language envisioned by abstract objectivism" (p. 71). Linguistics is unable to escape the philological orientation since, like the philological tradition in which, according to Bakhtin, it still exists, it is driven by recognition and analysis of *alien* language forms; that is, by forms that are not taken from the everyday flow of ideologically and socially embedded speech. Hence, "dead, written, alien language is the true description of the language with which linguistic thought has been concerned" (p. 73). He continues:

> The isolated, finished, monologic utterance, divorced from its verbal and actual context and standing open not to any possible sort of active response but to passive understanding on the part of a philologist--that is the ultimate 'donnée' and the starting point of linguistic thought. (*Marxism and the Philosophy of Language*, p. 73)

The philological orientation is partly due, moreover, to the description of foreign languages for teaching purposes. For this reason, linguistics has been in a sense trapped by the foreign or "alien" word with which it has been primarily concerned and which has led it away from involvement with the truly *philosophical* investigation of language. In sum, according to Bakhtin, linguistics fails entirely by concentrating on immutable forms, on abstractness as opposed to concrete living language forms, on synchronic phenomena as opposed to "historical actuality" (by which he means, of course, ideological circumstance, not the evolution of grammars), on the singularity of word meaning as opposed to its multiplicity, on the notion of language as a "ready-made artifact handed down from one generation to another" (ibid.). All of this involves, further, an "inability to conceptualize the inner generative process of a language" (a criticism which Bakhtin might have withdrawn or at the very least modified, had he lived to see the inception of transformational-generative linguistics) (ibid.). A final apparent inconsistency in Bakhtin's critique of Saussure should be recognized in that it was Saussure, the "abstractive-objectivist" par excellence, of course, who quite contrary to Bakhtin's point about the "singularity" of linguistic forms, stressed the *arbitrary* nature of signs (Saussure, 1974).

Although most of Bakhtin's intriguing analysis of semiotics, linguistics, and the philosophy of language, is devoted to this attack on abstractive-objectivism in linguistics, he also rejects the other extreme of individualistic-subjectivism, since, as we have already seen in his placing of language within an ideological matrix, there can be no such thing as an "individual subjectivism" that is in any sense separate from or non-contiguous with this matrix (Bakhtin, p. 82). Just like objectivism, extreme subjectivism becomes "monologic" in its concentration solely on the inner stream of consciousness, a concentration most strongly espoused in Romanticism. In the social semiotics of Bakhtin, the word is neither purely objective nor purely subjective but is, rather, a "two-sided act" determined equally by the speaker and by the person or people for whom it is intended; as he puts it "A word is a bridge thrown between myself and another. If one end of the bridge depends on me, then the other depends on my addressee. A word is territory shared by both addresser and addressee" (ibid., p. 86). Physiologically, a speaker "owns" his words, but as a sign, it is the joint possession of the community in which he is a communicative member, and meaning is jointly determined within social situations which, with their ideological underpinnings, serve to shape the outward manifestation in speech of inner language. A hearer typically becomes involved with two types of experience; either speech is referred to inner consciousness and thereby loses its ideological meaning or it is referred within the "we-experience" to the ideological framework in which the communication takes place. In keeping with his entire argument, Bakhtin believes that the growth of consciousness and the development of inner experience are tied to and are greatly enhanced by this referral of speech to its social and ideological contexts. All of this means that speech must be understood not in terms of any abstractive linguistic system, nor in terms of psychological processes, but in terms, solely of *social events*: Utterances are moments that only receive meaning in the context of the continual historical process of sign and language use. This process is, finally, a *generative* one which leads to the continual production of new forms (and therefore new ideological circumstances). Since all speech must be social in origin and in form, moreover, the idea that there could ever be such a thing as an "individual speech act" is, in Bakhtin's view, a contradiction in terms (ibid., p. 98).

Vygotsky: language as mediation

Although Vygotsky (whose views on thought and language were introduced in Chapter three) would never have regarded himself as a "semiotician," he was a thinker who left as part of his legacy many potent thoughts about signs, especially in relation to thinking and learning. For this reason, his work has become of such great interest in the relations between child development and language education (see e.g. Wertsch, 1985a, 1985b). Vygotsky's contribution to semiotics is founded in his own very broad intellectual interests, ranging from literature to psychiatry, and in his rejection of the scientific decomposition of mental phenomena in favour of *holistic* anlaysis: Signs, he believed, were more than the sum of their parts.

One of Vygotsky's concepts relating to his view of the place of signs is that of the *psychological tool* (cf. Bakhtin's "ideological" tool, above). Vygotsky thought of psychological tools as being akin to external or mechanical tools, and as serving as *mediators* in mental activity in much the same way as mechanical tools serve to mediate material objects. What they share in common is that they are used to gain *control* over activities. Psychological tools serve to transform basic mental schemes, such as sensation and motor activities into higher mental functions. Sign systems, then, become part of the fundamental fabric of mental activity since they are viewed, precisely, as tools with which to form new cognitive relationships between things. It is a crucial part of Vygotsky's ideas about human intellectual development that these sign-tools become progressively *internalized* with age, along with growing realization in individuals of the need for constraints on social behavior. On this point about development, it is well-known that Vygotsky disagreed with Piaget, who believed that language and thought were first internal and then social (see, e.g. Kozulin's introduction to the revised edition of *Thought and Language*, 1986). When sign-tools are internalized, Vygotsky claimed, they constitute forms of *inner speech*, which serve to regulate behavior and, indeed, which regulate conceptualization itself. Vygotsky saw inner speech not merely as some kind of internalized "talking to oneself" but, rather, as a *function* which served to relate inner thought with external, socialized, communicative speech: he saw it as the interface between "culturally sanctioned symbolic systems" and "private 'language' and imagery" (Kozulin, 1986, p. xxxviii).

In an insightful study, Lee (1985) makes it clear that Vygotsky's understanding of the processes of semiosis drew in part from the influence of Marxism, although it is equally clear that Vygotsky was neither politically a "Marxist" nor believed in the direct adoption of the Marxist method to science. One commonality between Marx and Vygotsky, however, is that both viewed consciousness as arising out of individuals interacting with the objective world, and their accompanying creation of subject-object relations. The concept of "subject" and "object," then, are themselves *constructed* through practical activity and interaction with the world. But while Marx traced social consciousness to the forces of the workplace, yielding a *social-political* theory, Vygotsky interpreted the idea of the subject-object-activity relation in *psychological* terms.

A second commonality lies in their *functionalism*. Both Marx and Vygotsky insisted that things should be analyzed in terms of their connected and interrelating functional roles within systems, an idea very close to that of structural oppositions (see above). While Marx related such matters as production and consumption to each other, Vygotsky saw that consciousness involves relations between psychological states. Memory, for instance, involves functional relationships between attention, perception, and comprehension (Lee, 1985, p. 70). Vygotsky was interested, however, not in the atomization of functions, in the examination of *separate* functions but, rather, in the entire orchestration of all functions in consciousness *as a whole*. He firmly believed that the kind of functionalist psychology which concentrated on treating functions as separate entities, abstracted from organic consciousness as a whole, led investigators *away* from the truth about consciousness.

Vygotsky and Marx both also viewed the development of consciousness in *dialectical* terms. In society, according to Marx, there is a dialectic between forces of production and consumption which lead to changing relationships over time and, according to Vygotsky, psychological processes also develop "genetically" in this way.

A fourth similarity lies in their belief in the interaction between the natural, or genetically given aspects of human life, and *social* life. Marx argued that what made humans different from animals was that they organized production and labour in social terms and not merely in terms of consumption, a fact which lent itself to his theory of dialectical materialism. Vygotsky drew distinction between the *natural* and *social* lines of development of humans, and argued that social development is closely attached to communicative development (and therefore to the development of language and semiosis) (Lee, 1985, pp. 66-74).

The reason why humans have been able to transcend animal forms of tool-use is, according to Vygotsky, because they are capable of language, the system of signs (or sign-tools) which permits them to gain control over their environment and through which consciousness develops and changes over time. The following extracts from the revised edition of *Thought and Language* (1986) illustrate Vygotsky's more precise ideas about signs in relation to language, concepts, and the development of thinking:

> Our experimental study proved that it is a functional use of the word, or any other sign, as means of focusing one's attention, selecting distinctive features and analyzing and synthesizing them, that plays a central role in concept formation. (p. 106)

> Words and other signs are those means that direct our mental operations, control their course, and channel them toward the solution of the problem confronting us. (pp. 106-107)

> Real concepts are impossible without words, and thinking in concepts does not exist beyond verbal thinking. That is why the central moment in concept formation, and its generative cause, is a specific use of words as functional 'tools.' (p. 107)
>
> Learning to direct one's own mental processes with the aid of words or signs is an integral part of concept formation. The ability to regulate one's actions by using auxiliary means reaches its full development only in adolescence. (p. 108)
>
> Speech itself is based on the relation between a sign and a structure of higher intellectual operations, rather than on purely associative connections. (p. 109)

The following passage further reveals the connections between Vygotsky's psychological theorizing with the historical tradition of semiotic philosophy, in its implicit reduction of the subject-object dichotomy and in its insistence on the inseparability of signs (language) from thought and consciousness:

> The relation of thought to word is not a thing but a process, a continual movement back and forth from thought to word and from word to thought. In that process, the relation of thought to word undergoes changes that themselves may be regarded as development in the functional sense. Thought is not merely expressed in words; it comes into existence through them. Every thought tends to connect something with something else, to establish a relation between things. Every thought moves, grows and develops, fulfills a function, solves a problem. This flow of thought occurs as an inner movement through a series of planes. An analysis of the interaction of thought and word must begin with an investigation of the different phases and planes a thought traverses before it is embodied in words. (p. 218)

By "planes," Vygotsky means the outer (phonetic) aspects of speech and the inner (semantic) aspects, aspects which he claims move in "opposite directions"; outer speech moving from part to whole and inner from whole to part. The process of semiosis guarantees the unification of these planes in thinking and language-use--unification not in the sense of "neutralization" but in that of their systematic interaction.

Vygotsky's view of grammar:

If words and thoughts exist in a complex relation of interaction with each other through signs, then what might be the function of grammar in these processes? Vygotsky thought that the study of grammar in school was actually "of paramount importance for the mental development of the child" (1986, p.184). Although children come to school with a natural command of grammar, their knowledge is largely unconscious; in other words, they are able to *follow* rules without having conscious knowledge of the form of these rules or the ability to state them. The reason why the study of grammar is valuable, then, is because it raises these rules to consciousness and, in this way, they become part of the inventory of semiotic tools at the core of intellectual growth and control. Through grammar and other forms of consciousness, the planes of inner and outer speech become progressively differentiated, and this differentiation between the two, of course, is a necessary prerequisite for their unification through dialectical interaction.

In another way, the signs of the grammatical system of a language are also *psychological* categories since "behind words, there is the independent grammar of thought, the syntax of word meanings" (1986, p. 222). Like Saussure and many other semioticians, Vygotsky emphasizes the arbitrariness of signs, but what he also reveals is that arbitrariness is only achieved as a process of interaction between the two planes of language. The development of grammatical understanding in Vygotsky is inseparable from development towards success at arbitrary signification. At first, the child is unable to distinguish between the senses of words and the phonetic (outer) forms and so words, to the child, are really "parts" of the objects they refer to. Children have "primitive linguistic consciousness" in which "the name is the thing," so to speak, and they are unwilling to call objects by different names because the names they have are equated to the properties of the objects they denote. According to Vygotsky, language (i.e. semiotic) development involves the progressive differentiation of the two planes, together with the child's growing abilities to tell the difference between the meanings in consciousness and those contained in the outer form of language to which they relate but with which they are not synonymous. Concomitant with this idea is the realization that language signs have both a "nominative" (i.e. referential) and a "significative" function. Conceptual growth is intimately connected with the ability to recognize the difference. The heart of Vygotsky's semiotic analysis lies in this realization that semiosis, the human ability which develops from this distinction between outer and inner language and which is rooted in the ability to use language signs as tools, lies at the core of *all* learning and conscious experience. Vygotsky's specific observations about human development through the manipulation of signs represents an influential theme in Russian semiotics.

The scope of semiotics

Contemporary semioticians working within the Euro-American tradition believe that a science of signs can form the basis for explaining a wide range of phenomena. Semioticians such as Eco and Deely, furthermore, clearly believe that semiotic analysis will even lead to a revolutionary new understanding about the history of thought itself, since they believe that all intellectual positions or philosophies are inseparable from the cultural (and therefore semiotic) phenomena that underlie them. According to Deely (1982, 1990), all the traditional kinds of theoretical reduction of language represent a major fallacy. Since these approaches are all part of a general attempt to tie language to static calculi of various kinds, they fail to recognize the *changeability* of natural language that is central to its dynamic and creative character. On this view, any symbolic system that philosophers engender, despite their theoretical claims to the contrary, must be considered as a subset of natural language, a subset which cannot be taken to characterize language as a whole. From the semiotic perspective, which views language as an unbroken and dynamic stream of semiosis, this kind of abstraction away from ordinary language violates two principles of natural language. First, it fails to recognize the complex contemporary and historical network in which and through which each individual speaker mediates *subjective* experience. Any artificial language designated by philosophers to conform to the rules of particular calculi by definition reduces natural language to a restricted and unchanging corpus. As Deely puts it:

> Artificial languages...reduce ...linguistic and cultural tradition down to the state or 'size' of a purely current understanding, suppressing or making 'invisible' the questions of how this understanding was achieved and what it fails to bring into account...if they are deployed without critical attention to their proper ground. (1982, p. 90)

Second, from the perspective of semiotics the view of most recent language philosophers fails to take into account the linkage of natural languages to other *non*-linguistic and *non*-conceptual channels of meaning. As previously stated, semiotics takes *all* sign systems as its subject matter, and it is also clear to the semiotician that animals, just as much as humans, depend upon systems of signs for their existence and identity. As Sebeok (1985) points out, animals have their own "life-worlds" which are established and maintained through signs. An essential point about human languages, moreover, is that they are *dependent* upon such wider systems, although they function to secure greater control over these "pre- and non-linguistic communicative channels" (Deely, 1982, p. 91). Yet another count against the traditional modes of language analysis pursued in linguistics is that, from the semiotic point of view, they fail to recognize this dependency of natural language on other systems, in the same way that those who theorize on the basis of "artificial" languages ignore the dependency of these upon natural languages. Deely claims that linguists typically "overstipulate" language. Even stipulations such as the "English speaking world" are insensitive to the embedding of language in the total universe of signs. For the semiotician, indeed, *any* abstraction of language away from its constituting role in human experience and in the human definition of "reality," obscures its true nature (ibid.).

While semiotics continues to expand into the analysis of all types of cultural phenomenon, several European and American theorists continue to work towards an understanding of language as the primary semiotic system in human experience. It is impossible in the confines of a single chapter to capture the complete range of this theorizing in sufficient detail, but some reference to the ideas of Eco, Lacan, and Kristeva may give some flavor of current directions in semiotics.

Eco: the infinity of signs

Eco's output on semiotics (not to mention his novels) is already legendary. He has been responsible for writing a fascinating history of signs in relation to the philosophy of language (Eco, 1984a), a profound analysis of texts in relation to readers from a semiotic perspective (Eco, 1984b), and for a fully-fledged theory of semiotics (Eco, 1979). In this latter work, Eco has essentially attempted to rework Peirce's categories of *icon*, *index*, and *symbol*, which he prefers to see in terms of "semiotic categories" by which it will be easier to form theoretical descriptions of actual *strategies* of signification (for a concise review, see Eco, 1985, pp. 177-178). Calling Peirce's attempt to create a complete typology of signs an "impossible dream," Eco argues that any complete classification of signs should be impossible *in principle* (ibid., p. 178). In particular, Eco rejects Peirce's notion of the *icon* as the absolute reduction of a language-sign to its content, preferring to emphasize the semiotic centrality of the principle of *aliquid stat pro aliquo*-the "standing of something *for* something *else*" (ibid.; italics added). Concerning language:

> Nobody has said that this correlation (i.e. *aliquid stat pro aliquo*) necessarily and exclusively constitutes what is commonly called a sign. Nobody has ever said that a sign is necessarily something homologous to a word. In fact, verbal language is perhaps the only semiotic system in which one gets the impression that to a single expression unit corresponds a single content unit. So it seems but, as with all other semiotic systems, an expression (a word) corresponds to a changing network of semantic components, content units. Any single

expression unit refers back to a more complex portion of verbal discourse. (1985, p. 178)

According to Eco, any sign, whether in the form of a map or of language, involves the continual "play" of a "semiotic game," and there is simply no way of tying signs to what they may signify; a map, for instance, may signify anything from a direction indicator to a reminder of a holiday, or signification may oscillate between these and infinite other significations. For this reason, Eco believes, semiotic theory must concentrate on the modes sign *production* and not on classes of signs treated as having "contents." Here, he appears to move away from the essentialism apparent in Peircean phenomenology.

In place of Peirce's essential categories, Eco proposes classes of sign production, classified partly in terms of the types of "labor" needed to produce expressions and of the complexity of the semiotic system in which expressions are produced. Signs, moreover, are built into *texts* through which they convey both their functions and their connotations. In language, he argues, words are always worked into a fabric of signification which includes accompanying gestures, intonation patterns, and other indicators of communicative intention. Language is always *clustered*, moreover, and clichés such as "It goes without saying" are used as ready-made "stylizations" that are worked into the total text. Eco's central point here is that semiotic production in language can never be the result of any *one* semiotic system and that it always involves a confluence of systems of signifying, referring, connotating and expressing. In all his work on semiotics, Eco asserts that language cannot be understood independently from its interplay with other cultural codes, including those which carry social and historical understanding.

Lacan and Kristeva: Language, signs, and the subconscious

It is a Freudian axiom that it is only by way of their language that psychoanalysts can come into contact with the "subjects" they examine (Kristeva, 1989). Freud treated language forms as *symptoms* of inner states and also considered dreams to take shape in linguistic form. By listening to subjects, the psychoanalyst can begin to detect their entire subjective reality, together with the underlying motivations for disordered thinking. Freud saw the conscious mind as being both contained within and dependent upon the larger context of the unconscious mind. The relationship between subject and psychoanalyst, then, can be viewed as a kind of prototype of communication in language since it reveals so clearly how every discourse is "destined for another" (Kristeva, 1989, p. 267).

Lacan has observed the very close relationship between the language used by subjects in psychoanalysis and their discovery that their subjective selves are, in fact, constructed entirely through semiotic forms. Through their attempts to describe what is going on "inside" them, subjects end up "by recognizing that this being has never been anything more than [their] construct in the imaginary and that this construct disappoints all [their] certainties" (1977, pp. 41-42, quoted in Kristeva, 1989, p. 267). In revealing themselves to the analyst, patients thus, in a sense, both sacrifice and discover their subjectivities and, in constructing their description for another (the analyst) they discover how their own subjectivities have been put together by *others* and may therefore be appropriated by the analyst. In more Freudian terms, psychoanalysis involves the constant discovery through language of the structure of the ego. This means, in Lacan's terms, that "the unconscious of the subject is the discourse of the other" (ibid.).

According to Kristeva, psychoanalysis has pioneered the notion that language is *dual* structure shared by speaking subjects and their interlocutors. The language recognized in psychoanalysis is to be distinguished entirely from the object studied by formal linguists. It is, rather, to be viewed as a *secondary* system of signs which "superimposes" itself on this object (langue), and this secondary system is much more compact than langue, working in larger units of discourse. Freud found this secondary system at work in dream symbols, which may have multiple and ambiguous meanings. In particular, these kinds of symbols are *holistic* and cannot be decomposed into their parts, of which they are more than the sum (cf. Vygotsky, above). Freud also observed that dreams bring disparate thoughts together in time in the formation of *logical* relations between things (not, of course *formal-*

logical relations, but the intuitive logic by which subjects "know" what is signified by them). Freud observed, further, that the syntactic symbolization in dreams also appeared in folklore, myth, and legend.

To Kristeva, the significance of these Freudian observations is that they open up a reconsideration of the relations between, to use Saussure's terms, *signifier* and *signified*; between signs and what they mean. The tendency of objectivist formal linguistics is to relate what is signified to a relatively stable underlying system (langue), but the aforementioned characteristics of dreams and inner symbolization which come to light in psychoanalysis suggest, to the contrary, that the power of the connections between the two has been wrongly conceived and greatly overestimated. Psychoanalytical and dream phenomena suggest that sign forms may become *detached* from langue, that they may *have a life of their own* and are not necessarily exclusively connected to the normative system of langue; there must be symbol systems created out of langue but which are of a separate order from it. Semiotics and grammar, then, are neither synonymous nor coterminous. On this view, linguistics and a psychoanalytically-inspired semiotics represent two quite separate trends of analysis (Kristeva, 1989, p. 274). The former permits and encourages the separation of subject and discourse, while the latter insists that language simply does not exist outside the bounds of subjectivity: Accordingly, language simply does not "exist" in the sense in which it is modeled in Cartesian-inspired Chomskyan linguistics but, rather, is always *being made*. The conclusion for the future of language studies must be that the objective and subjective orientations to language captured, respectively, within the diverging trends of structural linguistics and semiotics must begin to modify each other. Only in this way can the vision of Saussure of a linguistics which makes examination of signs its central task be realized (ibid., p. 277).

Summary

The field of semiotics is devoted to the analysis of language in terms of sign-systems. Several traditions of thought have come together in semiotics, including the work of phenomenologists such as Husserl, the work of Peirce, and the work of structuralists. These three aspects of semiotics are examined in this chapter.

Unlike Peirce, Husserl did not deliberately set out to construct a typology of signs. Husserl nevertheless realized that signs have many aspects, all of which are brought together in subjective experience. To Husserl, indeed, perception and meaning only arise when there is a fusion through signs of the processes of intuition, intention, and expression. When signs are still ostensible in experience, when they are still a matter of attention then, according to Husserl, no meaning is present. Signs, then, are to be treated as *constituting* meaning, not as objects: Individuals think *through* signs, and in this way signs *are* conscious experience.

In some ways, Peirce's views on signs were similar to Husserl's, and both emphasized the inseparability of signs from language and thought. Peirce, however, saw the central task of the philosopher as being the search for fundamental irreducible logical categories underlying signs rather than the description of psychological processes. His analysis of signs into the categories of Firstness, Secondness, and Thirdness leads to a rich theory of sign-formation in which many types of signs are at play in experience. All knowledge, according to Peirce, involves the *bringing together* of signs; there can be no thought whatsoever that is not somehow connected to other experience through signs.

Structuralists such as Saussure have made it clear that signs are partly defined by their structural positioning in relation to other items in signifying systems. Every sign, then, has some function in a system, a function which it gains from the oppositions it enters into with other signs. Structural oppositions exist at every level of language analysis including the sentence level where, for example, passive and active sentences oppose each other. This leads to the idea that even grammatical structure might be interpreted in terms of semiotic structuring. Both communication and language analysis depend upon perceiving just what are the intended oppositions, what is the intended significance, of language on given occasions. The central idea contributed to semiotics from structuralism is that signs have *values* in the contexts of the systems in which they play their parts.

There has also been a rich tradition of thinking about signs in Russia. In particular, Russian semioticians such as Bakhtin and Vygotsky have revealed the inseparability between signs, individual, and ideologically-governed consciousness. According to Bakhtin, inner language meaning is turned toward the individual and is constituted by individual experience, while outer signs are ideological in nature. Human experience is intimately involved with the relating of these two realms of sign-formation, realms that are themselves dynamically inter-related. The breakdown of the resonance between inner and outer sign-systems, according to Bakhtin, leads to a breakdown in the psyche itself. Bakhtin found fault with Saussurean structuralism in that it apparently failed to acknowledge the close connections between signs and social consciousness.

Vygotsky emphasized the use of language signs as tools, as implements that are used in mediating the relationship between individuals and their outer contexts. Both the learning and use of language, according to Vygotsky, depend upon conscious recognition of an inner and an outer plane of language; an inner, semantic, plane working from whole ideas to parts (phonetic or grammatical units) and an outer, phonetic, plane working from parts to wholes. Children must learn to differentiate between these two planes.

Current work in semiotics continues along the various lines established by earlier theorists, although the scope of semiotic analysis has been greatly expanded to include the examination of literary and cultural systems. As Eco has observed, language cannot be approached without recognizing its role in the formation of cultural codes of various kinds and, therefore, without reference to the cultural and historical influences in the formation of all signs. Both Kristeva and Lacan have emphasized that signs are not always merely connections between elements in stable systems but that in many respects they have lives of their own. This becomes clear in the analysis of dream phenomena, where quite new connections between signs are continuously created.

The major overall conclusion from semiotic theory lies in the need to take both subjective and objective qualities into account in the analysis of signs. Signs, indeed, appear to lie at the intersection of the objective and subjective spheres, and they appear to be partly governed by each. Semioticians suggest that experience is inseparable from the constant and creative reassignment of sign-forms in relation to their meanings through cultural interaction, historical change, and ideological circumstance. In this way, semiotics brings together many of the themes pursued in earlier chapters.

CHAPTER TEN

Theory and Practice: The Epistemic Spectrum of Language

[I]f you follow the pragmatic method, you cannot look on any [one] word as closing your quest. You must bring out of each word its practical cash-value, set it at work within the stream of your experience. It appears less as a solution, then, than as a program for more work, and more particularly as an indication of the ways in which existing realities may be *changed*. *Theories thus become instruments, not answers to enigmas, in which we can rest.* We don't lie back upon them, we move forward, and, on occasion, make nature over again by their aid. Pragmatism unstiffens all our theories, limbers them up and sets each one at work. (W. James. *What Pragmatism Means*, 1907)

Introduction

One of the initial claims in this book was that no *single* approach to the description of language can suffice as a basis for decisions in contexts of educational practice. The overview of contemporary theories was initiated by identifying eight foundational ideas about language divided into "objective' and "subjective" orientations. In subsequent chapters, we have seen how these and other related ideas have been examined and elaborated in various ways within the disciplines of biology, linguistics, psychology, sociology, and philosophy. The main purpose of this final chapter is to examine the question of how a framework can be established for educational practice which acknowledges the potential value of the range of thinking about language while not violating the principle of internal consistency.

What is needed in order to achieve such a broad framework for practice is some further principle of *integration*. In Chapter One, several kinds of questions faced by language educators were also raised, and it was suggested that a fully integrated approach to challenges in language education is one which takes into account the full range of subjectively- and objectively-oriented observations and which minimizes the risk of denying the significance of any aspect of language processing that may be relevant on a given practical occasion. Some primary areas of educational decision-making were identified, and some questions were raised in relation to these specified domains. Concerning the close connection between linguistic and cognitive development, for instance, questions were raised about how academic work should best be sequenced, about measurement and assessment of language impairments, about language enrichment in special education, and about the possible constraints on second language learning that are attributable to the prior establishment of first-cultural cognitive-linguistic schemata. Regarding the equally close relationships between language and social development, questions were raised about the relations between social development, language, and academic achievement, about the effects of teachers' own social identities in classrooms, about the linguistic characteristics of sub-cultures in schools, and about children who face language switches of various kinds between home and school. Finally, questions were raised about abnormal language processing, about the relations between language and physiological structures, and about the very nature of "normal" language processing.

While it is not the purpose here to give specific and detailed answers to all of the above questions, an attempt will be made to show how they can be best approached only from an integrated, pragmatically-inspired, and multi-modal framework. Within the compass of contemporary thinking, there are several closely related streams of thought not so far considered which promise to provide a solid basis for defining the necessary principles of integration in this framework. The first is the stream of critical thinking about the entire process of theory-building and about the cultural and ideological conditions in which language theorizing takes place. The second concerns the involvement of *metaphorical* thought in theories of language and in language more generally. The third concerns the place of *gestalt* phenomena in both everyday and theoretical discourse. These three streams of thought naturally combine with a *pragmatic* orientation to the interpretation of language theories for educational practice.

The Nature of Language Theorizing

The nature of theories is to explain phenomena, and the nature of most theorists is to compete with others to come up with the most impressive explanation in the fastest time. As the various groups of language theorists, such as the Logical Positivists or Transformational Grammarians or Speech Act Theorists, have demonstrated, the typical way in which ideas move forward is through the establishment of tight-knit and mutually-supportive circles in which arguments are further justified and elaborated. This naturally means that many ideas become "theory-driven" in the sense that they are predicated on a need to defend theoretical territory rather than a need to seek consonance with ideas in rival theories or to find bridges between different theories. These sociological aspects of academic life have no doubt been responsible for much of the compartmentalization evident in language theories, the most fundamental aspect of which is the division between seeing language as either object or subject.

Language and the Mirror of Nature

Even more significant than this tendency towards discrete theoretical paradigms in language theorizing has been that towards adopting many of the analytical schemata that have developed over the past few centuries in the more general contexts of *epistemology* and *science*. There has been a growing realization that many of these traditionally-accepted schemata, however, sometimes predominate over contemporary ideas in ways which tend to obscure rather than clarify the explanation of phenomena. This may have been an especially severe problem in the development of language theories since the schemata in question are powerful enough to obscure the nature of their own creation, a creation itself embodied in linguistic creativity and expression. A number of philosophers have begun to grapple with this problem of the constraints imposed on thinking by aspects of our intellectual inheritance in the context of what can be described as a hermeneutical and deconstructive enterprise. One proponent of this revision has been Rorty (e.g. Rorty, 1979, 1982), who has argued that the entire division between subjects and objects is itself a result of the powerful assumptions lying at the heart of the Western intellectual tradition.

Rorty's "ocular" metaphor

According to Rorty (1979), ever since the work of Descartes and Kant the entire enterprise of explanation has been predicated on the notion that the mind is a "great mirror" and that clarity derives from "polishing" it. He writes that:

> Without the notion of the mind as mirror, the notion of knowledge as accuracy of representation would not have suggested itself. Without this latter notion, the strategy common to Descartes and Kant--getting more accurate representations by inspecting, repairing, and polishing the mirror, so to speak--would not have made sense. Without this strategy in mind, recent claims that philosophy could consist of 'conceptual analysis' or 'phenomenological analysis' or 'explication of meanings' or examination of 'the logic of our language' or of 'the structure of the constituting activity of consciousness' would not have made sense. (p. 12)

What seems to have been at work during the period of development of modern thought is an "ocular" metaphor which forces us into a particular way of thinking about explanation. Quoting Dewey, Rorty argues that our idea of what it means to "know" something is largely modeled after this ocular metaphor and that the closely-related extended metaphor of "the mind's eye" reinforces the idea further by portraying knowledge as a matter of "inspection" of unchanging "representations." This "spectator theory" of knowledge, as Dewey called it, forges a distance, an "aloofness," from any phenomena being investigated (Rorty, 1979, p. 39).

What is the alternative to thinking of knowledge in this way, as the result of scrutinizing images? Rorty argues that a more accurate and sensitive portrayal of human knowledge may have been captured in the pre-Cartesian intellectual tradition where, as Shakespeare expressed it, the center of knowledge was a "Glassy Essence." This Glassy Essence image of the seat of the human intellect, while it shares something of the mirror metaphor, differs from it in significant ways. In the mind of the pre-Cartesian thinker, the Glassy Essence was not the source of mere reflection but was, as Bacon put it, rather, an "enchanted" glass, "full of superstition and imposture" (quoted in Rorty, p. 42). The Glassy Essence, then, unlike the image of the clear, bright, accurate, mirror, is partly clear, partly opaque. It is an image replete with the idea that the human mind is never able to *fully* grasp reality, and is always partly subject to deceptions of various kinds. As the term "essence" suggests, too, the metaphor centered on the notion that the intellect was partly *shared* with those of others. Rorty traces the two contrasting ideas about knowledge captured, respectively, in the metaphors of the mirror and the Glassy Essence back to debates of the Classical philosophers and, in particular, and argues that they represent truly different epistemological attitudes. In keeping with the Glassy Essence metaphor, Aristotle's conception of the mind was not as a *duality* of "mirror" being inspected by "inner eye," but rather "both mirror and eye in one" (Rorty, 1979, p. 45). In contrast, according to the dualistic Cartesian mirror metaphor which has so strongly influenced modern epistemology, the mind contains "representations" which "[t]he Inner Eye surveys...hoping to find some mark which will testify to their fidelity" (ibid.), an idea underwritten by Descartes' even more fundamental separation between "mind" and "body." One further ramification of the various levels of Cartesian dualism has been a further commonplace idea in the modern intellectual tradition that clear distinction can be made between what is "conscious" and what is not. All of these apparently clear dichotomies, however, are supported by dualistic metaphors that have been assumed in modern intellectual life, which dominate the ways in which research is conducted and theories are constructed, but which are less resilient to detailed scrutiny than is widely believed.

The first crucial point of realization about the development of modern language theories, then, is how strongly they have been inspired by Cartesian mirror-imagery. This is clearly more true of "objective" theories such as those of the Logical Positivists or Chomskyan grammarians, but even the construction of categories of subjectively-driven language functions followed by the elaboration of "systems" of functions (see, e.g. Systemic Grammar, Chapter Five) appears to fall in with the concept of theory as "polished glass." Language theories as we have seen them are full of the positivism implicit in the assertion that clarity of explanation can be achieved *if all forms of ambiguity are eliminated*. But attention to the mirror and other related metaphors inspired by Cartesian dualism forces us to ask how theories enhance our understanding of language if its nature *cannot* be clarified in this way. Deconstruction of the mirror metaphor raises the question of whether forcing any absolute distinctions between representations and analysis, between object and subject will lead us in the right direction.

Moving beyond traditional epistemology

If modern language theories, like other theories, are hopelessly tainted with the metaphors of dualism, and make assumptions about the nature of knowledge that wither under scrutiny, what is a more optimistic way forward? According to Rorty and others (e.g. Bernstein, 1983), it lies through the rejection of traditional epistemology which takes representation as the central characteristic of language and in the direction of a bi-modal approach which recognizes the dangers of such a monolithic and culturally-conditioned perspective. Another crucial feature of epistemology which Rorty identifies is its insistence on maximal *commensurability*. The construction of a theory of knowledge, in other words, has typically been based on the search for the "maximum amount of common ground with others." But why do we assume such common ground exists in the first place? And why does knowledge have to be explained in terms of such supposed commonality? As Rorty suggests, philosophers and others have sought for the supposed common ground in all sorts of locations, including "within ourselves" and "within language." This search for common ground is, of course, intimately related to admiration for the "objective," the "true" as the basis for knowledge. A total flight from commensurability, however, does not appear to work any better: Any theory of knowledge based on the priority of individual over collective understanding of the "truth" leaves itself open to the attack of spurious *relativism*, the charge that knowledge is thus reduced to the subjective whims of individuals. Total rejection of the epistemological program, then, may lead to the unacceptable position where such alternatives "seem to license everyone to construct his (sic) own little whole--his own little paradigm, his own little practice, his own little language-game--and then crawl into it" (p. 317). A third possibility, however, is that of the *hermeneutics*, which "sees the relations between various discourses as those of strands in a possible conversation, a conversation which presupposes no disciplinary matrix which unites the speakers, but where the hope of agreement is never lost so long as the conversation lasts" (p. 318). Rorty is careful to point out that hermeneutics does not totally *deny* epistemology, though. Neither does he view them as being mutually exclusive. He argues that they should be permitted to live in a complex and ambiguous relationship in which epistemology proceeds only where we have reached a point of sufficient understanding of what we are doing and need to codify our thoughts, and where a hermeneutical stance is taken "where we do not understand what is happening but are honest enough to admit it" (p. 321). If the relationship between the hermeneutical and epistemological enterprises are viewed in the manner of being complementary discourses concerning what we are certain about (as in so-called "normal" science paradigms) and what we are not certain about (the "abnormal" discourse of doubt and foundational exploration), then yet another unhelpful dichotomy can be avoided (p. 346).

The overall thrust of Rorty's arguments is to indicate the dangers inherent in *any* approach to knowledge and, on this foundation, in all theory-building which adheres dogmatically to a particular vision of what is to count as being "true." According to Rorty's deconstruction of the metaphors and ideas that surround our contemporary understanding of knowledge and science, there is a need to recognize the value of multiple ways of looking at things within an over-all context of realizing that certitude, such as that implicit in epistemology, should always be understood as being contextualized within given theoretical enterprises. Epistemological certainty, then, is context-dependent, and what has been missing in much of modern scientific exploration, including that into language, has been recognition of the need to complement the drive to codify knowledge with the need to question the nature of codification itself and to examine the nature of the changes that such knowledge brings about. It is this latter task which the hermeneutical attitude pursues. In the end, Rorty, suggests that progress in theoretical understanding will continue only if these two modes of thinking, these two intellectual attitudes, live in a relationship of dynamic alternation.

The pragmatic alternative

The direction taken by Rorty is in many ways an extension of the ideas of the *pragmatist* philosophers and, in particular, Dewey. One essential property of pragmatism, as Rorty sees it, is its rejection of the idea that the cornerstone of knowledge is the pursuit of the "ultimate truth" about things (1982, p. xiv). Since the time of Plato, there have been two fundamental ideas about the nature of truth. The first idea, propounded by Plato, is that truth goes beyond the confines of the spatio-temporal world while the second, implicit in the development of modern science and technology, is that truth resides only in the spatio-temporal world, a world whose laws can be fully described in one form or another. These ideas appear today in the form of a division between "empiricists" and "transcendentalists," who accuse one another of barking up the wrong tree. Pragmatists, however, attempt to "cut across this transcendental-empirical distinction by questioning the common presupposition that there is an invidious distinction to be drawn between kinds of truths" (1982, p. xvi). The pragmatist is highly skeptical of any version of truth that is "absolute" either in terms of its empirical correspondence to the facts or to moral principles. The pragmatist, indeed, "drops the notion of truth as correspondence with reality altogether, and says that modern science does not enable us to cope because it corresponds, it just plain enables us to cope" (Rorty, 1982, p. xvii; see also the discussion of the pragmatic theory of truth in Chapter Eight).

This non-traditional perspective on truth clearly lays the groundwork for an eclectic theory of language which admits many kinds of statements about what is "true" without treating any of them as ultimate or inviolable: From the pragmatic perspective, the history of debate about all kinds of phenomena, including the truth itself, clearly illustrates the need for openness. It views knowledge as arising out of this continuing and open-ended dialogue and is not to be located in any one theory, however grandiose. This attitude brings with it a view of language which has more in common with Heidegger or Vygotsky than Chomsky, and which views language as a "tool," rather than a "system." The tool, however, is inseparable from the user and "there is no way to think about either the world or our purposes except by using our language" (1982, p. xix). From the perspective of pragmatism, this means that we should never *compare* ourselves or our thoughts or our actions with some external "absolute," since, however hard we try, it is mere conceit to consider that we can ever escape the confines of our own language. Rorty makes the essential point here as follows:

> The ubiquity of language is a matter of language moving into the vacancies left by the failure of all the various candidates for the position of 'natural starting-points' of thought, starting-points which are prior to and independent of the way some culture speaks or spoke. (Candidates for such starting-points include clear and distinct ideas, sense-data, categories of the pure understanding, structures of prelinguistic consciousness, and the like.) (1982, p. xx)

This view of language brings with it one further consequence, namely, the need to accept that knowledge arises in the context of a possibly infinite regress, a regress that epistemologists and empiricists apparently believe is to be avoided at all costs. To the pragmatists, there is simply no way out of the regress by which things can only be "explained" in relation to the manner in which they are codified; there simply is no code that can be used to explain anything that is independent of the knower. The belief that there are such codes, instantiated in physics, psychology, transformational-generative grammar, and so on, is just one more manifestation of the mirror of nature metaphor.

Rorty's arguments constitute a well-known reference point in what is now a large framework of ideas about possible complete demise of traditional epistemology. This "post-modern" direction in thinking incorporates ideas originating in pragmatic philosophy, semiotics, hermeneutics, and many other perspectives, but is united in a disaffection with all the traditional positivist ways of thinking which search for ultimate "scientific" truth in the form of supposedly value-neutral forms of description. Before moving on to consider the relevance of this massive contemporary reorientation of ideas about human knowledge to language in education, some of the more critical aspects of the debate need to be pointed out. In keeping with the direction of current thinking, it would, after all, be paradoxical if even the definition of the "pragmatic attitude" were treated as sacrosanct. The pragmatic attitude towards theories and knowledge is one which itself requires a great deal of active and open-ended interpretation. As Rochberg-Halton (1986) has shown, for instance, there has been a tendency to *mis*interpret the work of the great American pragmatic philosophers, Peirce, James, Dewey, and Mead in ways which fail to make distinct the nature of their rejection of positivism.

Pragmatism misunderstood

A prime example of how pragmatism may have been misappropriated, according to Rochberg-Halton, is the interpretation of Peircean semiotics by later theorists. In much recent work in semiotics, there has been a tendency towards treating sign-systems in the same way as other structural or taxonomic systems, towards treating signs as "commodities" (1986, pp. 2-5). The pragmaticism which underlay Peirce's ideas about signs, however, had little to do with the elaboration of a complete or "objective" scientific system but, rather, with the elaboration of a "method of reflexion having for its purpose to render ideas clear" (quoted in Rochberg-Halton, p. 4). Peirce's fascination with signs was truly more phenomenological in orientation than many recent semioticians have interpreted it to be. The connection between Peirce's theory of signs and his pragmatism lies in the elucidation which recognition of sign-formation brings as a "method of reflexion which is guided by constantly holding in view its purpose and the purpose of the ideas it analyzes" (ibid.; and see the discussion of Peirce and phenomenology in Chapter Nine). Rochberg-Halton criticizes many later exponents of semiotics, and especially those following in the footsteps of the American semiotician, Charles Morris, and including Eco, for being guilty of a "fetishism" of signs, an obsession with the structural identity of signs rather than with a further elaboration of signs in the pragmatic attitude expressed by Peirce (1986, pp. 95-105). The crucial lapse in much modern thinking about signs is to ignore the question of what they are *for*. This question, essential within the pragmatic attitude, has often been replaced by a neo-positivist drive towards some "complete elaboration" of meaning through the construction of sign-systems, the construction of "brilliant apparatus[es] ...in which all the cogwheels mesh so perfectly that not the slightest hole remains open for the meaning of the whole" (see Rochberg-Halton, 1986, p. 97). To Rochberg-Halton, even Rorty's attempts to revamp philosophy as a pragmatically-inspired "conversation" are too deeply founded in "conceptual reason" to the exclusion of more reflective modes of thought (1986, p. xii).

Despite the continuing controversy over precise interpretation, it is clear that the pragmatic attitude provides a significant alternative to many of the more constraining metaphors that are now realized to pervade the modern mind. It is time, too, to reconsider language theorizing in this new post-modern context. Within this context, it becomes possible to neutralize the apparent dichotomy between subjective and objective aspects of language, and to see them both as part of an integrated dialectic on language.

Language Users and Language Theorists

But if the above comments go some way towards clarifying certain aspects of how language *theories* have taken their places on the polarized canvas of post-Cartesian thought, what do they have to say about the position of language-users? The answer to this question is crucial to the formation of a pragmatically-oriented framework for practice and it is, of course, that language-users and language-theorists in many ways exhibit identical traits. First, as the pragmatic interpretation of theorists suggests, all theorists are pre-eminently language-users; their theories are couched in language which reflects their most fundamental attitudes and beliefs. The language of all theorization, then, must be seen to be just some limited set of terms that are functionally directed towards some explanatory end. This theoretical language, though, is a subset of language in general and, as such, exhibits the same functional qualities of the language of all discourses in being directed towards some end, an end inscribed within the subjective intentions of theorists.

As has been pointed out by many post-modern thinkers, the idea that a language theory is in some way "independent" from language use in general is a misconception, an illusion. In addition, close observation of language-use outside the limited confines of theory-building reveals that language-users themselves continually switch or oscillate between many different language modes, modes which are founded on just the same kinds of epistemic categories that are identified across the range of so-called objective and subjective theorizing. The crucial difference between the mode of theorizing and the mode of wider discourse, then, may be simply that while the latter involves continual and imperceptible *shifts* between these epistemic modes, which are not normally a matter of consequence, the former, in the modernist spirit, unnaturally elevates particular epistemic modes to positions of explanatory significance. In this way, the grammarian counts knowledge of grammatical rules as primary linguistic knowledge, while the psychologist elevates "linguistic representations" to a similar level of primacy, and the sociolinguistic elevates functions or speech acts in a similar way. On the hermeneutical side of things, the literary theorist, too, follows the same trend when he elevates the "direct symbolic experience" of poetry to a level of experiential primacy. According to a pragmatic consideration of the range of linguistic activities in which individual speakers typically engage, though, this tendency towards elevating one epistemically-rooted model of language over any other makes little sense. Such elevation satisfies the need of language theorists for a *hierarchical* explanation of language behavior in which language use is embedded, according to given theories, in "grammar," "society," or "the semiotic flow," or even "communication," but it does not apparently reflect the truly mercurial nature of language-use: Individuals, unlike the "subjects" (i.e. objects) who are reported in experiments or transcripts do, after all, have real lives extending well beyond the range of any theoretical domain. In striving for further metaphors, that of the chameleon may be very appropriate, however, since the epistemic colors exhibit through language-use change with their surroundings, making them all the more difficult to perceive and comprehend.

Shifting epistemic modes in discourse

Although the epistemic qualities of language use may not be a matter of conscious concern, this does not imply that they cannot be identified. It is perhaps worth creating some informal examples of just how typical are these shifts between the modalities of language that have become the compartmentalized focus of independent language theories. In a recent communicative sequence, three individuals conversed as they walked to a lecture theatre. One was the professor about to give the lecture (Ted Thomson), the second was a prize-winning senior undergraduate (Gillian), and the third was a foreign student from Mexico who is still in the process of learning English as a Second Language (Carlo). The interchanges unfolded as follows. The bracketed numbers (#) will be used for later reference.

Gillian: (1) "Hi, Professor Thomson! Marked our papers yet?"
Ted: "Hi, how're you doing? Nope, can't says I have. Unfortunately for you guys, my wife's folks came for the weekend and so what with that and the..."
Gillian: "So, you've basically been partying all weekend!"
Ted: "Well, I wouldn't say 'partying' exactly, but you know how it is...gotta pay attention to your elders and betters. (2) Anyway, how are you

nowadays, Carlo? Are you managing to keep up with all this European stuff--not to mention the archaic English?"

Carlo: "Oh yes, thank you. I've been studying very hard and lucky for me Gillian was helping me with some new definition."

Ted: "Good for you. Do you find it as interesting as Mexican literature... (3) I guess I shouldn't ask you that should I!"

Gillian: (4) Professor Thomson, what do you think about the raised tuition fees for next year? What a bummer..."

Ted: "Well, I haven't thought about it all that much--although I was at a few meetings where it was discussed. Seems inevitable. How much are they going up? I didn't see the newspaper yet."

Gillian: "Thirty per cent, if you can believe it. My parents are going to be broke. Just the thought of it! Really depressing.

Ted: (5) "What do you mean--don't you value the education we're giving you, Gillian? The fact of the matter is that recession plus increased taxes equals no more books for the library, bigger classes, and a general decline in standards--not to mention a reduction in the fatted calf for my in-laws! So *somebody's* got to come up with some more cash or we're all up a gummybaum.

Gillian: "*Gummybaum?*"

Ted: "German for 'gum tree'--you must have heard the expression 'up a gum tree?' Basically means you're stuck--just like being up a certain kind of creek without a paddle. (6) The point about the fees is that it just wouldn't be logical to do anything else. If we don't bring in some more money, then salaries will be frozen. If salaries are frozen, then good faculty members are going to leave. If they leave, then in the end it becomes more difficult to attract students. If we can't attract students, we can't pay anybody. It's a great big vicious cycle.

Gillian: (7) "Okay. But surely the government could pitch in the difference...I mean education's supposed to be the gate to the future and all that?"

Ted: (8) "You deal in fantasy my friend. What does the word *politics* mean to you? Remember, politics is 'of the people'--that means, basically, the people have to pay up!"

Carlo (laughing): "Yes, it is the same in Mexico City--whenever the politicians need bigger houses, the price of gas goes up!"

Gillian: "Well, I suppose you're right. After all, quality is what it's all about--and quality definitely means keeping the classes as small as possible. And I *know* they're right when they talk about 'decline.' I was in the library just the other day and found out that a journal I used to look at regularly last semester has just been cancelled. (9) So I guess the university motto about 'excellence in all things' means something after all."

Ted: "Yes, you're right--although I'm not sure the decision to raise fees was made on such an ideal basis. More a matter of balancing out the various whines of the students, the public and the university and deciding which one they could get away with ignoring. We're all basically after our own interests. (10) You students don't want to pay back huge loans to your parents or to the banks, which is understandable--by the way Gillian what *are* the payments on that nifty little Geo I saw you driving the other day?--and the university administrators don't want the embarrassment of going into the red--although they express their concerns in terms of things like the idealistic motto you mentioned--and we professors...well, I think we're just in the middle 'perishing' even though some of us are publishing too! See you later. Enjoy the lecture--it's on the meaning of 'materialism,' suitably enough."

Gillian: (11) "Gee, Professor Thomson, I thought that *was* the lecture! See you at the pawn shop, anyway!"

(Gillian and Carlo take two seats half way down the lecture-hall as the professor takes his place at the podium.)

Carlo: (12) "Gillian, please, what did he say about 'fatted car'? I didn't understand him."

Gillian: (13) "Fatted *calf.* Oh, he was just saying that if his salary didn't keep going up, he wouldn't be able to feed his in-laws--you know, his wife's parents--well enough. A calf--you know the word calf I think, 'c-a-l-f' means a young cow or bull--actually it also means this part of your leg (pointing). 'Fatted calf' means a calf that has been fed up so that it's real good to eat. It's just an image. Comes originally from the bible I think, when fathers would kill a fatted calf for a special dinner to welcome their wandering sons back--probably not daughters..."

Carlo: **(14)** "'Fed up'? I thought that meant 'disgusting.'"

Gillian: "Idiot boy--don't joke with me!" Anyway, that reminds me, I meant to give you another grammar lesson. Do you remember what you said to Professor T. just now..when you were talking about me helping you with your English?"

Carlo: "No."

Gillian: **(15)** "You said 'Gillian *was helping me* with some new definitions.' What's wrong with that?"

Carlo: "It should be 'Gillian was help me'...no...'Gillian helps me'...no, I know...'Anna was helping...'"

Gillian: "Pea-brain! No, it should be 'Gillian *has been* helping me.' You remember what I told you about 'present relevance' the other day? Well, I'm still helping you, aren't I?"

Carlo: "Oh, yes, you're right! But I think professor Thomson understood. **(16)** I think he understands me even when I make a mistake because he has such a logical mind. He is the professor, after all."

Ted: "Good morning. Can I have you're attention, please. The weekend is now officially over--at least for some of us! Welcome to week three of *Language and Culture*. **(17)** I want to start today by asking you just to jot down on a piece of paper exactly what you understand by the term 'materialism.' Don't just give me a dictionary definition, though. Put down something about how the word makes you *feel*. What does it really *mean* to you--what associations, if any, does it conjure up?"

(The students attend to the task.)

"So let's hear some of these responses. Who'd like to offer something?"

Peter (a front row participant): **(18)** "The first thing I wrote down was 'Material *Girl*.' If you've seen the video, she's just flaunting the idea that being rich and having lots of things is important. I think the real meaning there is that she's saying that's what love is like nowadays--a matter of having property--and she expresses the idea that this is okay. So materialism means thinking of everything in material terms."

Ted: "Good. Yes, I think I did once catch a glimpse of Madonna doing that song, although the image that really sticks in my mind is the one of her being a virgin on a gondola in Venice. That image also fits in very well with your description of materialism, though. Anyone else?"

Susan: **(19)** "Well, all those images of Madonna were of course created by *men* I hope everybody realizes! I must admit, I thought of Madonna too, but I rejected it. I don't think Madonna has anything to do with the *meaning* of materialism...which is what we were asked to provide. I think Orwell's novel *1984* is much more to the point. I get images of a world reduced to material things--a harsh world with not much love or feeling of any kind--just like a shopping mall. Seriously, though, I would define materialism as something like 'the pursuit of material possessions--in economic terms, it means a society which is based on the free flow of goods in a context of supply and demand. That's what professor Freeman said the other day, according to my notes."

Ted: "Good. Nice to see my colleague Freeman saying something of note to the Culture class! One more? Gillian, yes."

Gillian: **(20)** "Well, I think the last speaker was right (Gillian doesn't know Susan, it being a very large class) but if I understood professor Freeman's lecture the other day, he was saying this was only one possible definition--the Marxist view of things. I don't think this is the *only* way of thinking about materialism. Marx was trying to say something about the bad things materialism does to the human spirit, but there are some *good* things about materialism. I really like my new Geo, for instance, and in a capitalist society I don't see anything wrong with enjoying possession of things. So I think it depends on your perspective what materialism means...whether it's a good or a bad thing...."

Ted: "Good answers. **(21)** So we have three versions of 'materialism.' The first was a rather colorful one based on Madonna. The second ended up, I agree with Gillian, by being rather Marxist in orientation. And then we heard the view that 'materialism' actually means different things in different contexts. All these views are right in their own way, although it's really interesting to note the different approaches to definition that each of you took. The important thing to realize here, of course, is that they are all to some extent *culturally conditioned*. The Madonna imagery is culturally conditioned in the sense that it has entered the head of Peter and has obviously to some extent influenced his feelings about the relationship between gender and possession. Susan's apparent Marxist sympathies, following my colleague's lecture, are obviously culturally conditioned--in this case by the university. Gillian, though, seems to recognize this cultural conditioning more overtly by suggesting that there may be more than one definition of materialism--although she also experiences the term somewhat subjectively, as is apparent from her fondness for the new Geo." (At this point, Ted launches into the main body of the lecture, following the changes in sense and value of the term materialism from the beginnings of the Industrial Revolution to the present day. Carlo follows with difficulty, and with occasional scribbles from Gillian).

The purpose of the above interaction is not to provide a basis for detailed transcription. Its purpose is simply to establish the range and variety of epistemic shifts that might be found in such typical interaction. Various kinds of discoursal shifts have already been referred to, including those involved in changes of *topic*, *turn*, *style*, or *register* (see Chapter Seven). But the point to be emphasized here is that these kinds of shifts are only part of larger network of transitions in language-users' attitudes towards the "truth" and towards the nature of language in relation to the truth. In typical discourse, participants do not seem to adhere to any *single* epistemic mode, and they seem capable of changing their modes of knowing and believing even as they negotiate between social and more formal modes of discourse. An informal analysis of this kind of interaction in the above dialogue is as follows:

(1) At the beginning of the engagement, both Gillian and Ted are clearly in a *social* mode of discourse. This social functioning is evident

in the informality of the language used and the personal-subjective topics identified.

(2) The point of transition at which Ted turns his attention to Carlo (who, thinking in his social mode, probably thinks Carlo should be included at this point) is also an epistemic transition. In turning his attention to Carlo, a second language speaker, Ted exhibits awareness of both of the linguistic and cultural gap that Carlo experiences. In this, he gives evidence of the more general inseparability of language and culture.

(3) When Ted realizes he "shouldn't ask" Carlo whether he likes his class, he is partly joking, but at a deeper level demonstrates awareness of the presence of reciprocal politeness constraints in English. He realizes he can't put Carlo on the cross-cultural spot like this.

(4) Gillian changes the topic to "tuition fees" in a much more formal mode than her opening gambit. Her greater formality reflects her knowledge of the pairing of topic and language, as it does a switch of register (demonstrating that register-switches can occur even during interactions with the *same* individual if there is a change of topic or situation).

(5) Ted's initial response is fairly light-hearted, including two deliberate uses of *figurative* language--*fatted calf* and *Gummybaum*. He knows his response is a little harsh and not likely to make Gillian feel any better. The use of the figurative language reflects his knowledge of how to soften his discourse when necessary. Once again, this reflects an epistemic shift--his realization of the need to be less confident of his own particular understanding of the "truth" of the situation.

(6) At this point, however, Ted becomes carried along by the tide of his own logical impetus. He switches gear into a more formal mode of discourse in which the language is driven by a series of conditional (if...then) connectives, rendering the whole sequence in much the same way as a formulation in simple propositional calculus. In this way, language is being used as a *logical* tool. Ted follows the formula exactly, committing none of the notorious fallacies, and by so doing

demonstrates his knowledge that in some contexts of expression language is *formulaic* and that the formula must be treated "objectively." The *truth* (and therefore the argumentative power) of Ted's response is guaranteed within the formulaic-logical discourse. He knows that he and everyone involved in tuition fee hikes is bound by it. He hopes his display of these logical dictates impresses the point on Gillian and Carlo.

(7) It doesn't. Either that or, more likely, Gillian doesn't want to lose face and so deliberately keeps the whole conversation going by bringing it back onto a more social footing.

(8) Ted's corresponding play on the word *politics* once again reflects his ability to deal with the language as "object," although the result in this case is *irony* rather than symbolic logic.

(9) It is possible here that Gillian is herself caught up in the objectivizing drift of the conversation, since she chooses to promote the historically-inscribed school motto as a possible guideline for action. Her attempts to deal with the matter on a subjective, social, and emotional basis have been finally eclipsed, and she knows it.

(10) Having beaten everyone over the head with his formality, Ted, being a well-adjusted sort of guy, knows that he can revert to finishing the matter off in a far more informal way, one which reveals his own "subjective" involvement in the situation and which correspondingly makes use of less formal language.

(11) Ted is successful in his discoursal switch. Gillian knows there has been an invitation to be less formal and that it is her turn to be less serious about the topic.

(12) At this point, a sequence is initiated in which Carlo demonstrates something of the special kinds of knowledge often exhibited by second language learners, and Gillian demonstrates how a native-speaker taking on the role of *teacher* (even an untrained one) is capable of raising language to a level of conscious analysis. Carlo initially shows his strategic competence implicit in his knowledge that his status as a second language learner gives him permission to ask such questions of his teacher friend.

(13) In her response about the fatted calf, Gillian is acting as a "lexicon" for Carlo, although she fully realizes in this figurative case she needs to provide some historical context to complement the purely synchronic meaning.

(14) Carlo has a lively sense of humor and knows he can get away with it in the social and topical context.

(15) When Carlo comments on Ted Thomson's abilities to understand him, he illustrates two significant points. First, he has a personal tendency to equate linguistic and *logical* abilities. Second, he appears to have a good deal of respect for professors simply because they *are* professors. Individuals from different cultures have quite different expectations about teacher-student relationships which fact, in itself, reflects culturally-driven epistemic contrasts.

(16) Here, Gillian takes on a fully formal-grammatical role. She has never taken a course in Chomskyan grammar, only Ted's second year course in grammar for English majors, but she both shows natural native-speaker ability to recognize an ungrammatical sentence when she sees or hears one and sufficient objective grammatical knowledge to articulate the reason for the mistake. She also apparently realizes the advantage of casting her explanation in terms of the actual meaning of Carlo's statement, not satisfied to leave it as a purely objective matter.

(17) The beginning of the formal lecture marks a return to the terms and expressions of formal discourse. In his request of the students to analyze *materialism*, however, Ted is clear to emphasize his recognition of the fact that words have both sense and value, and that meaning cannot be located in dictionaries alone.

(18) Peter demonstrates Ted's point by offering up some vibrant *imagery* as part of the definition of the word. He gives a definition grounded in subjective imagery, finally linking it to the more objective *sense* of "property."

(19) Susan's response is subjective in a quite different sense from Peter's. It is subjective in the sense that she emphasizes the presence of an ideological web in which meanings such as those underlying

materialism are created--she "permits" the ideology to give the word its meaning. As a feminist, she has a particular (subjective) view of material society, but in the later parts of her response, she also demonstrates the need to strive for further objectivity, to disengage her first reactions in some way from the more commonly-understood, or conventional, definition.

(20) Gillian goes even further in straddling the subjective and objective modes of definition by showing that even Susan's more objective definition remains ideologically constrained and by suggesting, further, that there may be parallel definitions of materialism depending *both* upon the ideological contexts *and* the subjective experiences of possession. She, more than the other respondents, recognizes the value of looking at definition from multiple perspectives. She demonstrates the ability to make conscious epistemic shifts between subjective and objective interpretation.

(21) Ted summarizes, having capitalized on the speech acts of his students, by arguing that definition and, by extension, language is, indeed, multi-faceted; a matter of response to cultural-conditioning, the history of words, individual feelings, and the oppositional relations between words in the current language system.

In this one short analysis of a sequence of interaction in English, then, it is possible to detect a very wide range of epistemic and linguistic shifts. Although they do not *formalize* their knowledge in the same way as theorists tend to formalize theirs, these speakers variously demonstrate that they make decisions based upon their socio-cultural knowledge, their grammatical and lexical knowledge, their formal-logical knowledge their historical knowledge, and on the relations between these various factors in meaning. In some places in the discourse, knowledge of language *is* consciously expressed--in the case of Gillian's teaching Carlo and of Ted's final support for a multi-faceted view of meaning. Such conscious discourse *about* language represents the beginnings of *theoretical* discourse, although at this level, there is no establishment of a formal theoretical system of explanation.

The salient points in all this are as follows. First, while the speakers are not working in the disconnected mode of language theorists, they yet demonstrate types of knowledge instantiated in theories across the objective-subjective range: At given moments, they actively think of language as an objective phenomenon having, in a sense it's own life to which they are subject (as in the case of the relation between language, truth, and predicate calculus, or in that of culturally-instantiated principles such as those in mottos). Second, and more significantly for our understanding of language competence, unlike theorists, language-users in contexts of everyday language use, are typically able to *shift* very nimbly between these various modes of thinking about language. These shifts are apparent in the various transitions within the discourse, the various strategic and epistemic tacks the speakers take in the course of their utterances. The total fabric of the interaction is made up of *oscillations* between various kinds of objective and subjective notions of language. This kind of oscillation supports both the social and the intellectual substance of the exchanges at one and the same time. Third, language-users sometimes appear to be *consciously aware* of these linguistic and epistemic shifts, and sometimes not. Alternatively, like Carlo, they can be made consciously aware of aspects of their performance at a later time. On occasions, it appears that typical language-users actually monitor epistemic transitions deciding, for instance, to approach a topic from another "more or less objective" point of view, while on others their attention may be geared to a range of other matters such as "meaning of a word" or "face-saving" or various functional objectives.

All of the above suggests that the relationship between conscious monitoring and language-use is an extremely complex one, one which is extremely variable and individual in nature. Consideration of discourse at large, however, suggests that epistemic switching of the kind mentioned above is characteristic of language-use, whether or not speakers are "consciously aware" of it. There is an apparent need, then, to *separate* the level of knowledge generally involved in making transitions from that level of conscious monitoring which *may* become involved on given occasions. Certainly, transitions do not seem to be *dependent* on conscious monitoring, and it is possible to view such monitoring itself in terms of a shift of attention rather than as a hierarchically superordinate or "executive" level of "control" over the epistemic transitions.

This leads to a fourth point, namely, that theorists, rather than reflecting this continual switching in discourse, have tended to emphasize only *one* mode of language-use, generally attempting to make this singular mode the focus of a consistent and coherent explanation. In this way, theories apparently deny the very changeability of modal processing inherent in most discourse, together with the complexity of interaction between monitored and unmonitored knowledge. One of the characteristics of theories, indeed, is that they depend upon a steady, monotonic, descriptive focus, reflecting and elaborating the particular conscious intentions of the theorist (in his role as theorist, not as language-user in general).

What transpires from closer examination of the transitions in discourse, though, is that language may not be such a steady-state phenomenon as theorists tend to treat it. One of the myths that we need to dispose of is that language is any *one* thing across the range of its usage. Language is, rather, a *collection*, an orchestrated conglomerate of expressive and epistemic tools. The point that theorists apparently often miss is that *all* language-users are "theorists" in the sense that they realize in one way or another some of the many possible types of interaction between truth, subjectivity, objectivity, and language--they have to in order to use language in the multifarious ways necessary for social survival and direction. Individuals, of course, vary in the exact range of modalities in which they can communicate. In this way, Ted has mastered a slightly wider range of modalities than Gillian, and so on. But what unites them as language-users is their ability to negotiate transitions, to view things from different directions, an ability which depends upon being able to shift quickly from the idea that meaning arises both *through* their own personal language and their knowledge *about* language. Sometimes they are locked into one perception, sometimes another. Both the total communicative episode though, and the meanings of individual propositions, depend upon this context of varied epistemic modality. This leads to a revitalized interpretation of notions such as "communicative competence" and the "ideal speaker-hearer," then, in which the ability to make transitions itself becomes a focal point. Language is conceived of not as "a tool" but as a *set* of tools which work always in counterpoint and harmony with one another in the construction and interpretation of meaning.

Before returning to take up these comments further, there are several further questions which need to be addressed before approaching the task of describing a framework for practice. First, while the foregoing has drawn a distinction between theoretical as opposed to everyday comprehensions of language, the reasons for this discrepancy are not yet sufficiently clear. *Why* is it that theoretical abstractions tend to lead away from recognition of the multi-faceted nature of language? Second, it has been claimed that epistemic *transitions* lie at the heart of normal language processing, but *how* and *why* do these transitions take place? How is it that language-users are apparently so able to use language as a social tool one minute, to use it as a logical tool the next, and as a vehicle for exploring subjective experience the next, and to combine any or all of these modalities the next? Each of these questions could obviously be the subject matter of an entire book. Two areas of investigation, however, appear to be very promising in the search for answers. The first of these is the recent work on *metaphorical* expressions as they are involved in both the theorist's and the language-user's views and uses of language. The second concerns the status of *gestalt* phenomena in language processing.

Metaphorical Interpretations of Language and Knowledge

We have already encountered Rorty's attempt to deconstruct what he claims to be a predominant metaphor in the science of our time, what he calls the "ocular" metaphor, the image of knowledge as the "mirror of nature." The metaphor embodies a dualistic notion that knowledge consists of representations that are "studied" and "interpreted" by the knower. Rorty deeply questions this idea as a possible foundation for knowledge, essentially arguing that it must replaced by a less static and more pragmatic view of reality as inscribed within cultural influence and change.

Just how powerful a matter a metaphor can be, though, can be gauged from some subsequent criticisms of Rorty's analysis which attempt to re-establish the mirror of nature as a worthy image if only it be dealt with in different terms. Such a re-analysis of the metaphor is to be found in the context of a vitriolic critique of Rorty by Munz (1984), who sees Rorty's arguments as nothing less than an attempt to establish the "true foundations" of knowledge. Munz counters that the mirror metaphor

> ...is not as silly as Rorty thinks. Of all the human senses, the sense of vision has a very special significance. Unlike other animals, we depend more on vision than on smell, fee, or touch or hearing. There are well known neurological reasons for this and it has something to do with our bipedal, upright posture. Hence also our common speech habits. When we want to say that we understand we say 'I see!' but not 'I hear' or 'I smell.' (p. 355)

Turning the tables on Rorty, Munz claims that he commits a major fallacy by treating the metaphor as a "literal truth," an interpretation not representative of the philosophers such as Kant against whom he inveighs (p. 359). According to Munz, abandoning the metaphor merely leads to a position of epistemic circularity in which knowledge "ceases to be a relation between knower and known...and becomes, instead, something like a state of mind" in which "one gets a euphoria of consensus" with one's philosophical "friends" (p. 363).

This critique suggests that while metaphors may be troublesome, they may be necessary in our grappling with complex issues such as consciousness and knowledge. But we can also see from this that metaphors, just like language in general, can be treated subjectively (in their being thought *through* as an image) or objectively (as a piece of evidence about thinking that may be disputed). Recent insights into the nature of metaphor suggest that they enter our thinking about both knowledge and language in profound ways. It is unlikely that any theory of language or of language practice can (or should) avoid them.

Non-literal Images of Language

One matter upon which all contributors to the ground-breaking compendium of metaphorical analysis, *Metaphor and Thought* (A. Ortony, Ed., 1979), appear to agree is that the use and comprehension of metaphor involves *non-literal* meaning. In this way, even a familiar metaphor like "the sunset of life" involves the perception of a relationship between the qualities of two phenomena in which one (literal) is illuminated (suitably enough in this case) by the other (non-literal; for especially clear analyses of literal vs. non-literal meaning see e.g. the chapters in Ortony by Black, Sadock, and Searle). As Searle points out, there have been two traditions of thinking about the nature of the relationship established between the two references in metaphors. The first, following Aristotle, views metaphors as *comparisons* between two objects, while the second, following Beardsley (1962) and Black (1962), views the relationship as a verbal interaction (Searle, 1979, p. 99). After wrestling with the idea that metaphors might be explained in terms of truth conditions, Searle himself concludes that metaphors actually convey *more* than mere truth conditions. He argues that a metaphor "conveys its truth conditions by way of another semantic content, whose truth conditions are not part of the truth conditions of the utterance." He concludes that:

> The expressive power that we feel is part of good metaphors is largely a matter of two features. The hearer has to figure out what the speaker means--he has to contribute more to the communication than just passive uptake--and he has to do that by going through another and related semantic content from the one which is communicated." (p. 123)

In the end, metaphorical expressions seem to demand all of comparison, interaction, and creativity. To take a now rather dated but familiar metaphor as an example--Mrs. Thatcher as the "Iron Lady"--we can see how the metaphor may take effect in several ways. First, there is an obvious comparison between Thatcher's personality and modus operandi with the qualities of iron, which is rigid, unbending, and long-lasting. Second, there is a certain more direct interaction between *iron* and *Thatcher* dependent upon the simple juxtaposition of *iron* and *Thatcher* in momentary structural opposition to each other. Third, and most importantly, the receiver of the metaphor may create further relationships between the two objects depending on individual experience and associations: *Iron*, after all, is not only rigid, unbending, and durable, but also *rusty*, an appropriate addition in the years following Thatcher's demise, and the "Iron Lady" is also reminiscent of the "Iron Maiden"--a formidable medieval instrument of torture. The interpretive possibilities are almost endless, which makes the point that metaphorical interpretation is at least partly a matter of individual creativity: The values that may be given to the references in metaphors are constrained only by the imaginations and motivations of individual minds operating within the general convention that the purpose of metaphors is, in general, to illuminate the nature of some object or idea by indicating a potential relationship between it and something else with which it is perceived to share certain qualities. The individual and creative aspects of metaphorical expression may be one central reason why they can be misunderstood and why, especially when they are used in the course of philosophical or scientific argument (as in the case of the "mirror of nature"), they require especial care in their interpretation.

The Conduit Metaphor

Reddy (1979) argues that our entire conceptualization of language and communication is governed by a frame of reference that is grounded in the metaphorical structures of the language itself, and which is essentially biased. This bias is apparent in the ways in which we talk about communication when it goes wrong. Some examples Reddy gives of typical reactions to such instances are as follows:

> "Try to *get* your *thoughts across* better."
> "None of Mary's *feelings came through to me* with any clarity."
> "You still haven't *given me* any *idea* of what you mean." (1979, p. 286)

Statements such as these give evidence of an underlying "conduit" metaphor, a frame of reference in terms of which we think about language as the *transmission* or *transfer* of *messages* through conduits, or passageways, erected between communicators. If a speaker is to *transfer* his thoughts effectively, moreover, she must know how to manipulate the language-objects that are to be sent down the conduit. Hence, we have expressions like:

"You have to *put* each *concept into words* very carefully."
"Try to *pack* more *thoughts into* fewer *words*." (p. 287)

According to Reddy, all of this leads to a notion of language in which words have "insides" and "outsides," and also that words have "content" comprised of ideas and meanings. All of this is connected to the idea that linguistic items are "inserted" by speakers (see, for instance, the notion of "lexical insertion" in TGG, Chapter Five). The central characteristics of language as perceived in this metaphorical frame are that language items are considered as "materials" and that communication consists in the transfer of these materials in a stable environment.

An alternative frame, or metaphor, for language that Reddy explores is one which he calls the "toolmakers paradigm" (not to be confused with the metaphor of "language as a tool") (pp. 292-297). This second idea about language is established by way of an illustrative narrative in which communicators are placed in different segments of a circle, each having essentially different material circumstances, and different languages, in which situation they are able to communicate to others only by depositing messages in a central hub. Individuals in this "radical-subjectivist" world wish to communicate to each other about various tools they have discovered in their own environments. To cut a long story short (sic), these individuals do, indeed, manage to convey and discuss these ideas, but only after a struggle to grasp each others' meaning (sic), and after considerable trial and error. The point of comparison is that, in terms of the conduit metaphor, information is either conveyed whole, directly, and as a "replica," or it fails. The toolmakers paradigm, on the other hand, demonstrates the opposite point, namely, that "[h]uman communication will almost always go astray unless real energy is expended" (p. 295). According to this view, the conduit metaphor continually requires us to explain "what went wrong" in communication, and to reject any communication which is only partially successful or which yields divergent interpretations. The toolmakers paradigm, on the contrary, views partial miscommunication and divergent interpretation as being inherent in the language system: Meanings require constant productive energy (pp. 295-296).

Reddy makes it clear that none of us can easily free ourselves from the grips of the conduit metaphor, since it is deeply embedded in the language we use. His "conservative estimate," indeed, is "that, of the entire metalingual apparatus of the English language, at least seventy percent is directly, visibly, and graphically based on the conduit metaphor" (p. 298). Clearly, the conduit metaphor has had great impact on language theorizing. In particular, this is true with any information-processing approach invoking the notion of "source," "message," "channel," and "receiver," but even talk of communicative "conventions," or "conditions" or "discourse-signals" may not entirely escape the clutches of the conduit frame of thinking.

In addition to its effect on theorists, Reddy finally suggests two ways in which the conduit metaphor affects everyday language-users. One is that as everyday speakers of the language, we are lured into talking and thinking about thoughts "as if they had the same kind of external, intersubjective reality as lamps and tables" (p. 308). This form of reification in language is essentially "dehumanizing" in the sense that when communication in this vein brakes down, we begin to think of ourselves as being in charge of some kind of computer for which we have been given the "wrong instruction manual." Furthermore, we pass this delusion on to our children (ibid.). A second is that the conduit metaphor has, by various extensions, convinced us that ideas exist *in books*, *in libraries*, and *on pages*, and so on. In this way, these "objects" are ultimately understood to *be* our culture. The toolmakers metaphor, however, makes it clear that there can be no "culture" without the *reconstruction* of knowledge by language-users who interpret cultural artifacts in terms of their own environments and experiences (pp. 309-310). In summary, Reddy believes that the conduit metaphor, together with its tendency to reify all aspects of language, is pervasive both in theory and in everyday usage. It continually lures us away from a true understanding of language as a creative, social, and approximative phenomenon. In this, he revitalizes many of the subjectivist themes identified by previous theorists, together with the central Saussurean idea that language involves sense, value, and the arbitrary pairings of symbols and meanings. In discussing Reddy's conduit metaphor, Lakoff and Johnson (1980) argue that if a concept, such as language, is structured by a certain metaphor, this means that it is "partially structured and that it can be extended in some ways but not others" (p. 13). In this way, a metaphor such as the conduit metaphor can be viewed as embodying a set of constraints on, or rules for, further interpretation of a phenomenon. Lakoff and Johnson go on further to consider how metaphors ground the entire conceptual system and how the presence of metaphors means that "most concepts are understood in terms of other concepts" (p. 56). The way in which metaphors work to "structure" experience, according to Lakoff and Johnson, is through *experiential gestalts*. Hence, when we are having a conversation which becomes polemic, for example, the metaphor "argument is war" becomes a gestalt, "war," through which the experience becomes a structured whole. The metaphor, then, triggers a gestalt, which is a coherent frame for understanding the experience, a frame which leads to other feelings and ideas--for instance, those of *being under attack*, *defense*, *retreat*, *counterattack*, *surrender*, *victory*, and so on (pp. 80-81). It is in the form of these multidimensional gestalts, they argue, that all "definition" of the world takes place. In this way, they endorse the idea proposed by Beardsley (1982) and Black (1962) (see above) that metaphors involve *interactions* between concepts as they are presented in language and as they enter into the experience of individuals (pp. 119-120).

The structured gestalts that are often triggered by metaphors become the ground in which the objective and subjective are negotiated. Lakoff and Johnson propose an *experientialist* interpretation of metaphor in which issues of truth and falsity are dealt with in the following way:

> In most cases, what is at issue is not the truth or falsity of a metaphor but the perceptions and inferences that follow from it and the actions that are sanctioned by it. In all aspects of

life, not just in politics or in love, we define our reality in terms of metaphors and then proceed to act on the basis of the metaphors. We draw inferences, set goals, make commitments, and execute plans, all on the basis of how we in part structure our experience, consciously and unconsciously, by means of metaphor. (p. 158)

This leads, in turn, to an epistemology founded on the notion that:

We understand a statement as being true in a given situation when our understanding of the statement fits our understanding of the situation closely enough for our purposes. (P. 179)

As they admit, there is nothing radically new in this position, and it contains elements of the pragmatically-inspired rejection of epistemological foundationalism also apparent in Rorty. The combination of metaphorical and gestalt processing within this "experientialism," however, brings some new insight into how both ordinary language-users and theorists may be conditioned in their thinking and expression by the ideas about language that are instantiated in the language itself.

The mythology of objectivism and subjectivism

Lakoff and Johnson conclude their analysis of metaphor with the view that both objectivism and subjectivism are myths--myths that are only understood if we understand just how deeply rooted our thinking is in metaphor. In the myth of objectivism, there is a failure to recognize that all understanding is relative to cultural systems and that it can never be "neutral." In the myth of subjectivism, there is a failure to recognize that all our thinking, however, metaphorical, is grounded in our functioning within our cultural and physical environments: "It also misses the fact that metaphorical understanding involves metaphorical entailment, which is an imaginative form of rationality" (p. 194). They cite Chomskyan linguistics as a prime example of the objectivist fallacy, with its treatment of linguistic expressions as "objects" and with its notion that grammar is "independent" from meaning. While Lakoff and Johnson, like most other contemporary critics, see more evil arising from objectivist than subjectivist metaphors, they point also to some of the standard dangers identifiable with the subjectivist position: the assumption that meaning can be *private*; the assumption that experience is purely *holistic*; the assumption that meanings have no natural *structure*; the assumption that *context is unstructured*; and the assumption that meaning cannot be adequately *represented* (p. 224). As previously stated, their alternative to the traditional dichotomy is to view all experience as structured by metaphors, and by the gestalts they give rise to, where such metaphors and gestalts arise out of the continual experiential negotiation of "objects" and "subjects" within individual consciousness.

Metaphor, imagination, and the human body

Continuing this analysis of metaphor, Johnson (1987) argues that metaphorical thinking is inseparable from human *imagination*. Pursuing the idea that both metaphor and imagination are grounded in physical experience, Johnson further argues that they are both ultimately grounded in our experiences of our *bodies* in their interactions with the environment. Even metaphors based on something so fundamental as verticality are constrained by our upright bodily functioning (pp. ix-xv). Metaphors, according to Johnson, have a certain "force" of meaning which is above and beyond the propositions they contain; they exist at an irreducible level of schemata and imagery (pp. 20-26). This force is the central property of gestalt structures which, he argues, are operating all the time in language use; they structure expression within different *modalities*--the actual, the possible, the necessary--and they structure speech acts.

Although Johnson's idea of force in speech acts shares much with Austin's "illocutionary force," it goes beyond it in certain important respects. The more traditional notion is that all speech acts combine some *proposition* with some illocutionary force giving them direction and purpose. Hence a statement such as "The river is drying up" might on one occasion carry the force of an *assertion*, while on another the force of *causing* someone not to put a boat in the river. Johnson extends this idea by claiming that speech acts are themselves always the *result* of some force given by circumstances. What he has in mind as being the origins of such forces is just the kinds of metaphors about language already mentioned. As in his earlier work with Lakoff, Johnson sees a central correspondence between the presence of metaphors and gestalt-structures and, in this interpretation, the conduit metaphor becomes "one elaboration of [a] force gestalt" (p. 59). Johnson views the conduit metaphor of language as being part of a more general *compulsion* metaphor which exerts a force on the creation of forms of expression in speakers, on how a listener will interpret a given message, and which exerts force as it is embodied within the strength of the utterance itself. Finally, the metaphor gives force to what Austin called the "perlocutionary" aspects of the utterance, the action responses it may cause (pp. 59-60).

Elaborating his thesis that much of our most fundamental metaphorically-supported imagery of the world around us is rooted in our bodily experience, Johnson shows how our conceptions of space, weight, color, and time are fundamentally conditioned in this way. The metaphors are experienced in the form of gestalts which carry us forward in the stream of interpretation. The result is what he calls *embodied understanding*, a form of understanding which transcends the traditional object-subject dichotomy (p. 205). Metaphor, truth, and imagination, on this view, are all inseparable from the processing of gestalt-structures within human psychology. Johnson's ideas on how these various strands come together to yield meaning can be summarized as follows:

> We are dealing...with psychological patterns or schemata that make it possible for us to have structured, coherent experiences that we can make sense of. We are dealing with levels of organization that are on the borderline between bodily processes and conscious or reflective acts that we can focus our attention on, if we choose. We are dealing with preconceptual levels at which structure emerges in our experience via metaphorical extensions of image schemata. (p. 85)

Taken as a whole, much of the recent work on metaphors, including their close relation to the formation of gestalts in psychological processing, can be interpreted as an extension of *schema theory* in general. This is a dangerous analogy, however, since earlier work in schema-theory, especially that conducted in the domain of reading theory (see Chapter Six), has been conducted within the context of a positivistic information-processing approach, and so reflects many of the conduit-driven characteristics of this approach. The real significance for establishing new foundations in educational practice of this recent work, however, lies in its promise of a way *out* of these old modes of thinking. Understanding how thought is permeated by fundamental metaphorical forces is the first essential step in understanding how our language constrains us in our thinking about the relations between language theories and practice. Since metaphors, imagination, and meaning appear to be inseparable, this further justifies a *pragmatic* approach to language and to language education, an approach which transcends the rigid opposition between object and subject, and which views the opposition as itself being metaphorical in nature. In this way, the dichotomy, experienced through gestalts, becomes part of the larger attempt made by all individuals in their search for meaning, and both theoretical "truth" and the everyday "truth" of utterances can be seen to arise from the interaction between the forces of language and of experience. All of this supports the idea that individuals, as suggested in the analysis of the dialogue above, typically operate in a *range* of epistemic modalities through their language. It is possible that these modalities themselves shift with the metaphors and gestalts which underlie them and which constitute their essential epistemic frames of reference

Gestalts

The ideas that our everyday experiences live in an interactive relationship with metaphorical forms, and that the psychological forces which hold this relationship together find their focus in gestalt images, requires at least some brief exploration of the relationship of all this to what is commonly referred to as "consciousness." As Rorty (1979) has noted, there are many dangers inherent in the very notion that there is a divide between "conscious" and "unconscious" processing, a divide which he traces back to Cartesian dualism and the idea that an "inner mind" looks at a mirror (pp. 34-38; 51-56). Under this interpretation, the idea of "consciousness" is a misleading one, obfuscated by its own metaphorical connotations. There have, nevertheless, been many quite *different* attempts to give meaning to the notion of consciousness, and it is important at least to identify the tradition in which gestalt psychology fits in the course of a more general investigation into its relation to metaphor.

Traditions of Thought about Consciousness

One way in which we think of consciousness now is certainly due to Descartes' realization (*Cogito ergo sum*) that thinking, the guarantee of existent being, was inseparable from conscious *awareness*. One test of conscious awareness is the ability of a (human) organism to be *deceived*, although he or she can never be deceived to the point of denying their own existences. Since Descartes also believed that the substance of consciousness in the mind was different in kind from that of the body, this idea lays the foundation for mind-body dualism, together with many of the conceptual problems previously reviewed.

The psychologist, Wundt, later developed a notion of consciousness as being in constant flux. In his method of *introspection*, however, he claimed that there was a level of *inner perception*, the mode of consciousness of most untrained individuals, and a separate level of *introspection* which, through training, made awareness of these internal events possible.

In America, in keeping with the spirit of pragmatism, William James and others took a *functionalist* approach to consciousness which, in contrast to the structuralist approach of his European predecessors, turned away from any attempt to isolate "atoms" of consciousness in favor of a view of consciousness as *process*. This idea is crystallized in James' now famous metaphor of *the stream of consciousness*. In *The Principles of Psychology*, James described consciousness as having the attributes of being personal, as being in a state of flux (although not a state of flux amenable to atomistic reduction), as being continuous, intentional, and selectional. The criteria of intention and selection suggest that consciousness is always comprised of attention "on something" and that thinking always involves choosing from among the array of possible attributes some particular qualities upon which attention is to be focussed. This stream of attention and selection is unending. It can never be abandoned, and it can never be reversed.

In many respects, the later approach of Gestalt psychologists, such as Katz, Wertheimer, and Kohler, is compatible with that of James. Their thinking, however, can be traced back to a quite different source, that of phenomenological psychology and the doctrine of *intentionality* pursued by Brentano and his pupil, Husserl (see also Chapter Eight). Husserl's division between intentional acts of consciousness (*noesis*) and the objects of consciousness (*noema*), and his phenomenological method of bracketing, were developed partly in order to guarantee that the study of consciousness could be rigorous and scientific. Following these ideas, the Gestalt psychologists referred to direct experiences as *phenomena*. Their central tenet, however (in keeping with the thinking of James), was that individual experience was based on "wholes" rather than "parts," and, indeed, that the psychological whole was always more than the sum of its parts. Individuals see movement, or recognize objects or faces, or hear music, or become conscious of (i.e. attend to) anything whatsoever as a "whole" and without being aware of any of the elements that are irrelevant to the phenomenon in attention. It makes no sense, as a result, to speak of consciousness other than in terms of these holistic phenomena of experience.

It is in this latter tradition that the foregoing analysis of the relationship between gestalts and metaphor is most clearly grounded. We can now give more precision to the idea that metaphors have force through gestalts in conscious experience: Metaphors have this force precisely because they are *wholes*--irreducible phenomena, not decomposable into any component parts. To say that metaphors may be experienced as gestalt images, then, is to say that they are irreducible phenomena in consciousness. It follows that any attempt to analyze a metaphor through some form of decomposition faces a *loss* of its meaning. The metaphorical web that Reddy, Lakoff, Johnson, and many others have recognized and investigated, then, is foundational in consciousness. Individuals are conscious *through* not *of the structure of* metaphors during their normal language processing.

Towards an Integrated Framework for Language Practice

It has been suggested that everyday language use, unlike the use of language within the special domain of theory-construction, involves a wide range of epistemic modalities. These separate modalities, distributed across a spectrum between subjectivity and objectivity, are reflected in separate theories--theories of grammar or speech acts and so on--but here they are treated as being discrete rather than dynamically interactive. In this way, language theories, driven by the need to decompose particular gestalts, together with any educational theorizing which may depend upon them, may have typically failed to capture one of the central features of human language processing, namely, that it *involves successful transition between many epistemic modes.*

Although perhaps not predictable in any precise way, it is clear that successful language-use typically involves oscillation between such modes. Sometimes the transitions are a matter of immediate conscious attention, and sometimes they appear to be more automatic in nature and below the threshold of awareness. What normal discourse often seems to involve however, is a continual switching from a subjective mode in which meanings are driven by individual interpretation, involving imagery, association, and the belief in these as providing an integral part of the "truth" of whatever is being discussed, to an objective mode in which meaning is derived more from the senses of words as they are presented in their outer conventional form. In this latter mode, the logical frames in which language is cast may also have their own force.

While it may be characteristic of *special* types of discourse, then, such as scientific arguments, sermons, or theoretical descriptions, adherence to any one epistemic modality does not seem to be characteristic of everyday discourse, in which participants are typically far more eclectic in their behavior. The overall motivation for such transitions is no doubt largely social in nature. In this, everyday discourse shares much with the formal construction of arguments, sermons, or theories. In the dialogue presented above, there were several examples where an epistemic switch was triggered as much by the need not to appear "too serious" or "formal" as it was by the need for an alternative epistemic vantage point. More generally, however, it is likely the case that such epistemic transitions serve the even more fundamental purpose of *pragmatic* interpretation: Individuals appear to realize in general that the "truth" about anything generally depends upon looking at things from multiple perspectives, and not on the elaboration of any particular linguistic formulae. Although everyday language-users may not be able to elaborate precisely how the use of language interacts with these various perspectives, it is clear that they are typically able to consciously analyze the different ways in which a word may be interpreted on a given occasion, and even to compare the subjective meanings of words as they find them "stored" in their memories with some new and more objective meaning which may be presented to them. (The classroom interaction concerning the interpretation of *materialism* showed how individuals may do this to different degrees).

A Pragmatic Orientation to Practice

The observation of this kind of continual shifting of epistemic grounds in normal discourse is highly compatible with a *pragmatic* philosophy of language, one which rejects both the dogma of any particular view of the relationship between language, meaning, and truth, and the idea that there can be any one interpretation of the truth in general. From the pragmatic perspective, truth and meaning are matters of continual negotiation. This has been pointed out at the level of theoretical discourse and within the context of the centuries-old dispute about the nature of knowledge, but it seems an equally appropriate perspective on language-use in general: The epistemic transitions reflect, precisely, this idea of the construction and abstraction of truth and meaning through multiple perspectives.

Another aspect of these transitions in discourse that makes them fundamentally pragmatic is that successful communicators are always aware of the *consequences* of what they are saying. The adoption of a "logical" mode of discourse, for instance, as illustrated in the dialogue, may have the social consequence of making the speaker appear "biased," "unsympathetic," or simply "boring." Speakers, then, may be aware that taking a particular perspective on something being negotiated in discussion may itself have consequences for how the deeper meanings of messages and intentions are interpreted. This strong relationship between meaning and analysis of the consequences of what is described in language is a central theme of pragmatic philosophy, sharply distinguishing it from any notion of truth and meaning founded on *correspondence* or *cohesion*. A pragmatic orientation is a necessary part of any framework for educational practice which recognizes that there is an array of epistemic modes in which language-users typically operate.

Interpretation of Metaphor

The investigation of metaphor strongly suggests several further characteristics that a pragmatically-based framework for practice should have. First, there is a need to recognize how metaphors typically become over-extended. A good example is that of the conduit metaphor, together with all its supportive expressions, which reinforces the idea of language as a system of signal-objects. At the other extreme, there is a need to be equally careful about metaphors which stress language as purely subjective creation. A metaphor such as Heidegger's "house of being," for instance, if not adequately interpreted, may lead us to a solipsistic view of language in which any idea of *conventional* symbolization is lost. On the other hand, metaphors are a central mode of expression through language, and constitute a central part of a pragmatic analysis of meaning. They provide an invaluable avenue to rethinking old ideas about language in new ways. We need, then, to be alert in distinguishing between dead metaphors, such as those which polarize the subject and object in restrictive ways, and productive metaphors, such as the notion of language as a set of creative tools, which are still dynamic and open-ended, still leading to new insight.

Current metaphors in socio-cultural context:

There is, though, a danger inherent in dealing with metaphors for language within a pragmatic framework for language education. It is that of an *over*-reaction to certain metaphors which, although we may wish to dispose of them on ideological grounds, yet still have currency and which remain in wide circulation (see, for example, Munz's comments on Rorty's possibly premature retirement of the mirror metaphor, above). As an example, the conduit metaphor, together with all the extended and related imagery of humans as "computers," as "word- or information-processors," as "programmers," or of language as "input/output," as "sequences of symbols," as "internal lexicon," to mention but a few of myriad possible examples, still has a very wide currency but yet tends to emphasize only a techno-objective view of language. But how are we to deal with this fact within a pragmatic framework for language education? Following Rorty and other recent philosophers, we would no doubt work to eradicate these kinds of expressions and to replace them with others which develop and support a less modern and technological view of things. The view taken here, however, is rather different. It is that while we may be at a point in cultural history where we have identified the suspicion with which such metaphors need to be treated in terms of their power to determine ways of thinking in a *global* sense, it would be unrepresentative of the current state of both Western culture and language to reject them altogether. After all, the metaphors attached to technology, to computers and all sorts of other machines in relation to the humans around them, are not likely to disappear overnight, however powerful new post-modern ideologies may prove to be. They are here to stay for the foreseeable future and, what is of particular importance for educators to realize, they form an essential component part of the typical sociolinguistic conditioning of students actually in current education systems.

The interpretation of pragmatic principle adopted here, then, is that a viable framework for practice in language education must *include* the language and imagery of objectivizing technology, but only as *one epistemic modality among many*. The key point to realize, however, is that in a fully pragmatic approach, one ultimate aim in language education will be to attain points of recognition of just what each of these separate modalities "means," just what *consequences* result from thinking about language in any particular way. There may be many domains in which language-as-object may be found to be an entirely appropriate mode of discourse. It will take some time before the full impact of post-modernist deconstruction reaches the schools. Certain danger arises, however, just as we have found to be the case in the elaboration of theories in general, when one epistemic mode is overgeneralized into the domain of another. In this way, the machine-based metaphors of human language processing may work productively in domains ranging from the technological to models of management and administration, but will not survive extension into the interpretation of poetry or drama. Conversely, the subject-mode discourse of literary interpretation will fail to suffice in these objective domains. The present framework is predicated on a perceived need for language-users to be capable of working *across the spectrum of these modalities* and, more important, to come to recognize during the course of language development the characteristic strengths and limitations of each.

The place of gestalts

The background of Gestalt psychology provides the final essential principle to a pragmatic framework. If, as is claimed here, it is a central part of language processing (and of thought in general) to shift across different epistemic modalities, then the presence of gestalts is a crucial part of the explanation of how this takes place, if only for the simple reason that the mental processing of individual atoms of information that would have to take place without them would constitute an unmanageable "cognitive overload." Although humans are clearly capable of both conceiving things in terms of wholes and their parts or, correspondingly, from a top-down or a bottom-up perspective, it is perception of wholes which allows all kinds of thought, comprehension, and expression to take place at the speed that it does. As psychologists have long pointed out, we are unable to attend to *all* the stimuli that our senses may apprehend: Selective attention lies at the heart of the construction and interpretation of meaning.

The abilities apparent in successful language-users to negotiate the transitions between various possible worlds, between different social levels of discourse and between the epistemic modalities that accompany these, are only explicable through the presence of various kinds of gestalt organization. Piper (1985b) conducted research that demonstrated that as children develop from what Piaget termed the stage of *concrete operations* to that of *formal operations* they become more adept at dealing with a multiplicity of discourse worlds. It was argued, indeed, that this ability at discoursal transition itself constitutes a better measure of cognitive-linguistic development than do alternative measures concentrating upon the particular "logical operations" children "acquire" and add to their cognitive repertoires. It was noted in this research just how logical and overpowering a ten-year old can be when processing within the context of some video-game, no matter how sophisticated or complex. Sometimes ten-year olds, indeed, appear to believe that life in general is underwritten by the logic of causes and effects typically found in such games. What distinguishes the level of formal operations in older students is the ability to recognize that different discoursal domains require distinct kinds of interpretation, and that what appears quite logical or "obvious" in one framework may not be so in another. The more mature thinker and language-user, then, becomes more capable of these transitions, more adept at traveling between various discourse-worlds and more adept at adjusting interpretations to suit distinct frames of reference. At the root of all these kinds of advanced language processes lie transitions between objective and subjective orientations, transitions that are supported by holistic mental organizations (gestalts) and which are associated, in turn, with distinct ideas of how language is being used, for what purpose, and how it works towards the establishment of truth and meaning.

Outline of Principles

We will now conclude this discussion of the foundations of a framework for educational practice by presenting a brief and more concise outline of the central principles and their implications for interpreting language development.

An Integrated Multi-modal Framework for Educational Practice

A: Central concepts:

1. Central to the framework is its accordance with pragmatic philosophy in both recognizing and accepting the entire range of epistemic modes by which truth and meaning are accessed.
2. In particular, there is a recognition that competent adult language-users regularly switch between these epistemic modes in the general pursuit of meaning and truth. In this way, objectivizing and subjectivizing aspects of language are viewed as being *interactive* and *complementary* rather than *inconsistent* with each other.
3. A reassessment of the notion "communicative competence" in terms of the framework leads to the inclusion of a criterion of ability to negotiate these epistemic transitions. Fluent transitions between epistemic modalities, together with closely associated transitions between the various discourse worlds referenced during communication, requires the concomitant ability to recognize the distinct ways in which truth is justified in discrete domains or, alternatively, whether or not truth and justification are relevant to meaning in any particular domain. While theorists have tended to concentrate on elevating the characteristics of *one* epistemic mode such as "truth as correspondence," "truth as coherence," or "truth as individual construction or reconstruction," this pragmatic framework recognizes the heterogeneity of epistemic modalities even within ordinary non-technical discourse. The pragmatic framework places the requirement for diverse epistemic processing at the core of communicative competence.
4. The ability for fluent transitions between modes is supported by a recognition of the *arbitrary* and *productive* nature of metaphors as they affect ways of knowing. Communicatively competent individuals are aware that metaphorical expressions, such as those which reflect a

strongly objectivizing tendency towards experience and tending, for instance, to reify communication into the machinery of the "conduit," are merely specialized ways of looking at things for particular purposes. Metaphorical expressions are viewed, then, as one facet of the arbitrary nature of language. In disagreement with some of the positions taken by various post-modern philosophers concerned with the deconstruction of metaphors viewed to be constraining, it is argued as part of the present framework that both objective and subjective metaphors still need to be recognized as viable and current ways of seeing the world. Certainly, recognition of the typical range of language actually used within contemporary schooling leads to the conclusion that language education should reflect the entire spectrum of objectively- and subjectively-oriented language and metaphorical expression.

5. The reappraisal of the "ideal speaker-hearer" in these terms suggests that she is not only capable of epistemic transitions, but also able to negotiate them *quickly*. The criterion of speed is necessary in order to explain the *combination* of epistemic modes within the scope of even very brief communicative encounters (such as the illustrative dialogue, above). Central to this necessary speed in processing is the formation of gestalt images of various kinds, and especially the formation of such gestalts through the metaphors which capture the characteristics of epistemic modes themselves.

B: Interpretation for practice within the framework:

6. The idea that language-processing is essentially multi-modal in the manner described leads to a new general metaphor for language processing, namely, that of *epistemic orchestration*. The ultimate aim of language education that proceeds from this metaphor is that of developing students' abilities to orchestrate, to coordinate a range of objective and subjective ways of knowing through language within their own integrated frameworks of language-use. In very general terms, this process goes beyond any traditional division of language

studies into "language" vs. "literature" or the traditional modes of rhetoric to the idea that even these categories cross epistemic boundaries: In this way, the study of grammar, just as much as the study of a Shakespeare play, will involve both subjective and objective aspects of knowing and will not be constrained (as they have been, and often continue to be) by monolithic perspectives.

7. The metaphor of epistemic orchestration is one which can be further *extended* in fruitful ways for language education. Orchestration demands that ways of knowing (cf. ways of "playing a theme," "coloring sounds by use of different musical tools having different instrumental and tonal qualities") are *both kept separate and together at one and the same time.* In current psychological terms, orchestration is a metaphor which includes the possibility of *parallel processing*: Just as an orchestral performance requires the separation of instrumental sections together with the potential for combination and interaction with other sections, so, too, does language use require these organizational qualities. More than this, one orchestral section typically takes up a musical theme (cf. discoursal theme) dealing with it in its own tonal mode (cf. epistemic mode) only to pass it through a point of transition to another section where processing continues in an alternative mode. Finally, an orchestral performance, just like language performance, emerges not only out of the concatenation of separate thematic interpretations but out of the *relations between* these discrete parts: Just like a symphonic composition, then, knowledge through language appears to be built up out of the interrelating of modalities. In this way, linguistic meaning, just like musical experience, is both composed out of its parts and yet is more than them at the same time.

8. The particular nature of communicative competence suggested by the framework leads naturally to the idea that one key approach in language education is to *exercise* language-users' developing abilities to negotiate transitions. There are many ways in which curriculum materials can be developed to this end, but in general terms they will include questions and answers which depend upon epistemic

transitions. Many English teachers have pursued this direction in, say, the teaching of Shakespeare by helping their students build up their understanding of characters by a combination of the objective study of theme, background, and language together with a more subjective and phenomenological approach to inner meaning. (It might be noted in passing, moreover, that much of the power of Shakespearean characters such as Hamlet, Macbeth, Lear, or the various English kings derives from our seeing *them* wrestle with epistemic transitions between the subjective and objective worlds.)

9. Within the framework, a central aspect of language development will be the gradual increase in abilities to deal with multiple modalities. As previously stated, the ultimate objective will be achievement of the ability to *orchestrate* modes of knowing through language, an ability which itself depends upon the assumption of several epistemic *roles*, including those of *composer*, *player*, and *conductor*. This process, however, is a gradual one, starting with the child's capability for understanding and expression within the frame of different and discrete modalities and leading, during the period of formal operations, to increasing abilities to negotiate transitions across epistemic boundaries. It is further supposed that this kind of language growth continues throughout adulthood. It is proposed that the central criterion of language growth is not the acquisition of many of the traditional categories (such as "vocabulary," "grammar," or even "social" competence) but that these are themselves dependent upon the ability to deal in multiple epistemic domains. A key point of development is that identified in another manner by Piaget (e.g. Piaget, 1960), that between concrete- and formal-operations. In the current analysis, the crux of this developmental transition lies in the later ability to recognize and negotiate the subjective and objective "faces" of truth and meaning.

10. Overall, the framework suggests that schooling across the curriculum should have both the particular aim of establishing language fluency within *and across* separate domains of knowledge. While the traditional approach has certainly pursued the former objective, the

latter has been lacking perhaps due in part to methodological dogmas which emphasize one part of the epistemic spectrum to the exclusion of others. This framework suggests that language education should fully accept the presence of a complete range of separate, discrete, modalities, but that, further, full communicative competence depends upon establishing individual recognition and, ultimately, orchestration of these separate modes of knowing and expressing.

11. Questions such as those posed in Chapter One concerning the relations between language and cognition are to be interpreted within the framework as being most fundamentally questions about facility with the range of epistemic-linguistic interactions across the subject-object spectrum. The relationship is no longer viewed as being uniquely tied to objective processing or to the idea that knowledge through language is culturally and subjectively conditioned. Language and cognition are related through the *range* of modal shifts enacted by each communicatively-competent individual, and cognitive-linguistic growth, therefore, is viewed as being crucially dependent upon the increasing ability to recognize, to manage, and relate these discrete domains.

12. The framework suggests that the relationship between language and social identity, too, is underwritten by epistemic fundamentals. Discoursal shifts which may be perceived at one level to serve communicative and social functions of various kinds are ultimately inseparable from movements between subjective and objective assessments of things. Even the ability to negotiate *dialectical* transitions of various kinds--between Black English and more formal dialects of English, for instance--would seem to involve epistemic shifts between discoursal worlds in which justifications and meanings are established in contrasting ways. The framework suggests that the best way to approach social modalities is on the basis of shifting epistemic modalities that can be ultimately orchestrated and *managed* in social contexts.

13. The framework suggests that a fruitful way of approaching communicative disabilities will be to view then as the result of various

kinds of constraints on the ability to perform linguistic transitions. It is known that one of the key characteristics of poor readers and writers is that they are restricted by certain kinds of unitary belief about language processing--that reading is primarily "phonological" in nature or that writing has to be well-formed "immediately" and without revision, for example. In addition, Broca's aphasics are limited to one mode of language, while Wernicke's are limited to yet another (see Chapter Six). Within the multi-modal framework, once again, abilities to supplement one mode of thinking with others will be a key objective in remediation.

Concluding Comments

Several key questions may help to further clarify the multi-modal framework for thinking about language education. First, how is this framework different from what at this time is fast becoming the dominant paradigm in language education, namely, *Whole Language*? Second, while the presentation in this book has been largely conceptual, founded on a consideration of the range of language theorizing together with further theorizing about the nature of the relationship between language and knowing, what kinds of *research* does the framework lead to? Third, what are some further conceptual directions suggested by the framework?

The multi-modal framework and Whole Language

One authoritative definition of the whole-language approach is that of Froese (1990), who defines whole-language as "a child-centered, literature-based approach to language teaching that immerses students in real communication situations whenever possible" (p. 2). As points of consensus about the whole-language concept, Froese goes on to list the idea that "language is a naturally developing human activity," that it is a "social phenomenon used for communication purposes," that it must be "personalized in order to respect the uniqueness and interest of the learner," and that it is a "part of making sense of the world." Finally, language is learned "holistically in context rather than in bits and pieces in isolation" (ibid.).

Froese further states that the motivation behind the whole-language approach comes from several sources; linguistics, psychology, and pedagogy. Within the scope of linguistic influence, Froese includes the idea that language is equivalent to a *social semiotic* (following Halliday, 1978), that children develop *metalinguistic awareness*, and that linguists "have provided us with the basic organizational concepts of our language," as inscribed in the levels of phonological, syntactic, and semantic analysis. Psycholinguists, he continues, "have taught us about how our memory is organized, what motivates our use of language, and how we use language for different purposes," and about the "internalization of information or 'rules' about language" (p. 6). Pedagogy has contributed some respect for "collaborative learning" and "peer tutoring" and, crucially, by the retreat from the traditional view of learning as *receptive* to the idea that it is *constructive*.

While the approach is supposedly partly founded on linguistic and psychological grounds, however, it is clear from the wider literature on whole-language that it is primarily a pedagogical movement which rests upon a *child-centered* philosophy of teaching and learning. This is made clear in the idea that "Teaching should be personalized, based on students' individual needs," and that "Each student is a unique individual, different from others, and that is to be expected--it is the norm" (Froese, 1990, pp. 8-9). Should there be any doubt that whole-language theorists believe they have a secure epistemological basis for their theory, Froese identifies as a fundamental idea in the approach that "Language is learned and used holistically first; it is differentiated and refined later" (p. 9). This is compatible with the educationally far-reaching principle that "Language is part of our environment and need not be separated into 'subjects' to be taught" (p. 8).

Key differences:

Stated briefly, the differences between the whole-language child-centered approach and the multi-modal framework are as follows: First, the whole-language approach appears to provide no principle for the *integration* of knowledge, either at the theoretical level (for instance, the integration of "linguistic" and "psychological" principles in teaching and learning) or at the level of individual discourse. A multi-modal framework, on the other hand, articulates a fundamental principle for integrated language-use, namely, that of epistemic transition across the subject-object spectrum represented in both language and language theorizing. Second, on the same point, although lip-service is paid to linguistic analysis (i.e. the treatment of language as object within the various levels of linguistic analysis) there is no mention, at least in the statement of principles, of how this approach might play any significant part in children's learning. From the multi-modal framework flows the idea that able language-users are able to deal with the entire range of epistemic modalities in language, utilizing the gestalt of language as object and as subject in free alternation. Third, the ideologically-driven ideal of child-centered language and learning at the core of the approach in any case overpowers any tendency towards or passing recognition of epistemic objectivity in language: The approach is unabashedly subjectivist in its promotion of language and meaning as subjective *construction*. The multi-modal approach, on the other hand, treats both subjective-constructive and objective-receptive aspects of language *equally*--it gives them equal status within a framework of interactive processing. Fourth, while the whole-language approach is biased towards a top-down notion of language processing, an idea inherent in the idea that language "first holistic" and then "differentiated and refined," the multi-modal approach views language processing as involving highly *complex* interactions between "wholes" and "parts," viewing these as complementary facets of thinking in general, and as part of the general oscillation between subject and object conducted in language-use.

Finally, while whole-language theorists, at least as they are represented by Froese, apparently believe in the holistic *fusion* of subject matter, the multi-modal framework works against this tendency to homogenize language and towards the view that communicative competence truly depends upon the ability to orchestrate *discrete* linguistic-epistemic frames of reference. It is an implication of the multi-modal framework that education that fails to deal with epistemic domains *both separately and together* (through the processes of orchestration), while it may produce learners fluent in the articulation of their own perceptions of meaning, will not equip them to deal with situations where language *is* working in harmony with an objective domain of description which must be interpreted in isolation from subjective (although not from conventional) meaning. The claim inherent in the multi-modal approach is that children need to be able to *switch* and to *relate* the objective worlds of machinery, algorithms, and rules, with the subjective worlds of constructive meaning. In contrast to whole-language theorizing, the multi-modal framework suggests that some language *is* "receptive" in the sense that language-users must learn to decode symbols that are instantiated within systems of which they are *not* yet part. In its constructivist bias, whole-language appears to undervalue this kind of relationship between language-users and their language, and the relationship between these two types of knowing more generally.

Future research

In the experimental study mentioned earlier, Piper (1985) explored the shifts in logical processing which occur when identical logical sequences are placed in differing narrative frames. The study supported the idea that children as they move from concrete- to formal-operations are able to process the transitions between discoursal frames with increasing ease and that this ability, indeed, may constitute an important measure of cognitive and linguistic development. The idea that language processing naturally involves even more fundamental epistemic shifts than those originally explored is in some senses an extension of this earlier work.

Several key new research questions emerge from the development of a multi-modal framework. Some of them are as follows. First, what are the more precise characteristics of the epistemic modalities which underlie cognitive-linguistic processing, and what are the structures of the gestalts which support these modalities? Second, how do individuals develop the ability to orchestrate these transitions and to take on the variety of roles in relation to their language and knowing that are apparent in advanced language-users? How aware are individuals of these transitions as they are negotiated, and what part does such awareness play in both language-use and language learning? Answers to such questions await the development of appropriate experimental procedures which, in the spirit of the framework itself, will likely involve both objective and subjective protocols.

Further conceptual development

Another way of asking the question of how the framework can be conceptually extended is to ask how the epistemic-orchestral metaphor can be linked to other productive metaphors. Just like theories, the present heuristic framework for language education is partly dependent upon metaphorical expression. The central metaphor here is one of the "ideal" communicatively-competent language-user being in charge of the *orchestration* of different cognitive-linguistic modalities. This is a metaphor which shares something in common with that in systemic grammar (see Chapter Five), even though the primary categories are of a different nature. As has been suggested, though, the epistemic-orchestral metaphor is intended to be extended in specific ways that earlier similar metaphors are not. For instance, the language-user is viewed in the course of development, first, as an orchestral *player*, moving on later to the varied roles of *player*, *composer*, and *conductor*. The richness of the metaphor lies in its ability to reflect different levels of conscious processing both of linguistic expression and of epistemic transition. The metaphor is more in keeping with an eighteenth-century interpretation of orchestral performance (nor often reproduced in performances with original instruments) in which the conductor takes on the other roles--sometimes in parallel--of player, arranger, and improvisor, frequently switching these during the musical presentation.

Another current and productive metaphor which may bear close relation to this idea is that of the "society of mind" (Minsky, 1985), which portrays the mind in a similar way as a *collective* of discrete and closely interactive parts. A further idea which is also not yet explicit in the present framework is that of language as *energy* rather than as *atom*. The orchestral metaphor is one which represents language as being in a state of constant flow, even though it also embraces the idea that the component parts of language may on occasion become objects of attention both at the theoretical and communicative levels. Recent work in physics and the philosophy of science following Bohm (1980) suggests that the oscillation between the idea of matter as "atoms" and as pure "energy" developed through quantum theory may also have some bearing on our understanding of language. It is likely that the pragmatic multi-modal framework of language, together with the orchestral metaphor which supports it, can be further developed in terms of these and other current metaphors from sociology and science.

Objects, subjects, wholes, and parts

A concept central to the multi-modal framework is that of the necessity of including in any set of proposals for language education a recognition of the involvement in language processing of both objective and subjective modalities. As we have seen, this idea bears a close correspondence to holistic vs. atomistic processing: There is a close relationship between subjective experience of the world and the formation of holistic gestalt structures, on the one hand, and between analysis of wholes into their parts and the objective modality of thought, on the other. According to the framework, advanced communicative competence depends upon the abilities of language-users to oscillate between these polarities and the intermediate positions between them on the epistemic spectrum and, ultimately, the ability to recognize the domains in which objective-atomistic language-use or subjective-holistic language-use are most appropriate for the expression of meaning or, alternatively, when there is a need to think in both modalities in parallel.

A good point on which to end this preliminary discussion of the multi-modal framework is to emphasize how these ideas are extensions of a fundamentally *pragmatic* philosophical outlook. In a different article to the one quoted at the beginning of this chapter, William James (1879) wrote about the "sentiment of rationality" within the pragmatic orientation. In this essay he wrote of the fundamental human need for *simplification* in the explanation of things around us, of the "pleasure at finding that a chaos of facts is the expression of a single underlying fact" (p. 4). Putting a musical metaphor to his own particular use, he added that the feeling of achieving simplicity in explanation was "like the relief of the musician at resolving a confused mass of sound into melodic or harmonic order" (ibid.). It is clear that by "simplification" James was thinking in terms of the subjectivizing modality of metaphor and gestalt, since he further illustrates his point by asking: "Who does not feel the charm of thinking that the moon and the apple are, as far as their relation to the earth goes, identical; of knowing respiration and combustion to be one; of understanding that the balloon rises by the same law whereby the stone sinks...?" (p. 5). But James then adds that

> ...alongside of this passion for simplification there exists a sister passion, which in some minds...is its rival. This is the passion for distinguishing; it is the impulse to be acquainted with the parts rather than to comprehend the whole. It loves to recognize particulars in their full completeness....Clearness and simplicity thus set up rival claims, and make a real dilemma for the thinker. *A man's (sic) philosophic attitude is determined by the balance in him of these two cravings.* (James, *The Sentiment of Rationality*, 1879, p. 5, italics added)

It is exactly within this pragmatic spirit that the multi-modal framework for the interpretation of language theories for educational practice finds its roots and the inspiration for its development.

APPENDIX A

Left-side View of the Brain

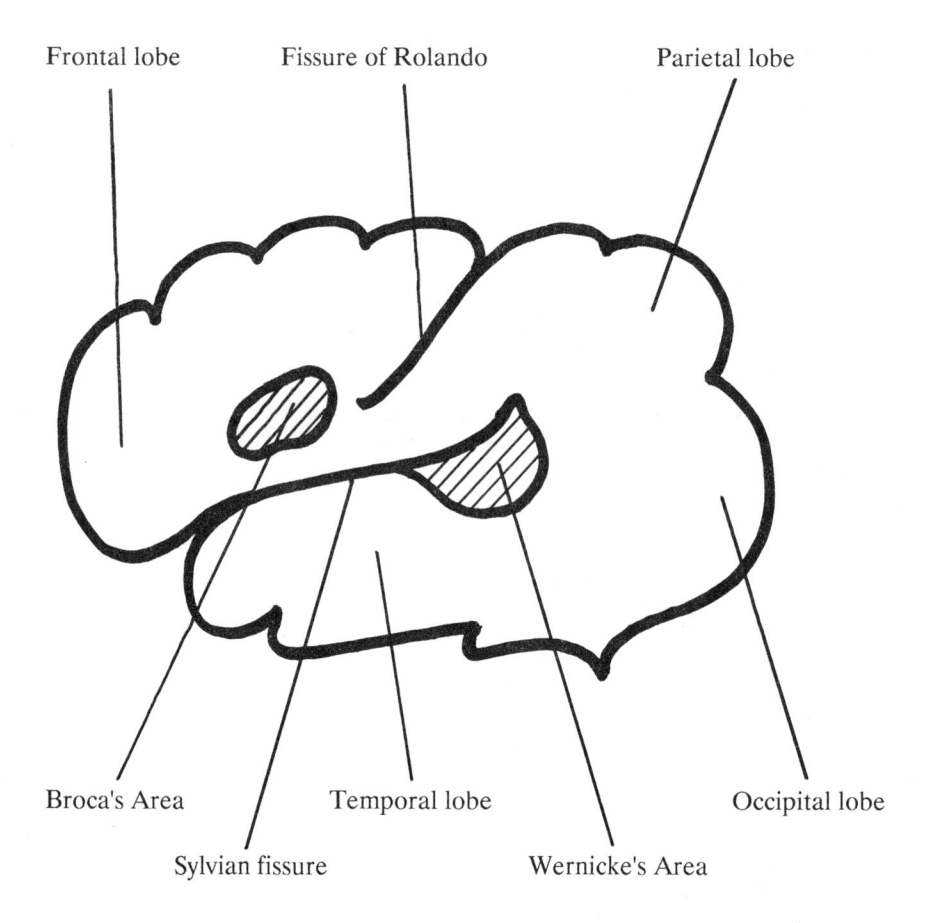

Frontal lobe • Fissure of Rolando • Parietal lobe

Broca's Area • Temporal lobe • Occipital lobe

Sylvian fissure • Wernicke's Area

APPENDIX B

Gender in Chinese Characters (see Text p. 260)

The modern Chinese character for woman, 女 , derives from the earlier character woman-glyph , which is a representation of a kneeling woman in servile position. The male character 男 derives from 田 , a picture of a field and a plow, implying 'tiller of the soil.'

Other forms containing the servile woman figure include:

> 婪 = *greedy* ('forest' over 'woman': 'a woman desires a forest--a multiplicity--of things)
>
> 奸 = *vicious* ('woman' and 'work': 'if a woman works outside the home, she becomes vicious')
>
> 妇 = *wife* ('woman' and 'broom': 'a woman's place is working in the home')
>
> 妾 = *concubine* ('figure standing on top of a woman')

Also, *hostess* 空姐   *waitress* 女招待
       daughter 女儿   *mother* 妈妈
       sister 姐姐

Terms of abuse include 婊子 , for *bitch*; 婊子养的 , for *son-of-a-bitch* .

REFERENCES

Aarsleff, H. (1982). *From Locke to Saussure: Essays on the study of language and intellectual history*. Minneapolis, MN: University of Minnesota.

Akmajian, A., Demers, R. A., Farmer, A. K., & Harnish, R. M. (1990). *Linguistics: An introduction to language and communication (3rd ed.)*. Cambridge, MA: Massachusetts Institute of Technology Press.

Allan, K. (1986). *Linguistic meaning (Vol. 1)*. New York: Routledge & Kegan Paul.

Allan, K. (1986). *Linguistic meaning (Vol. 2)*. New York: Routledge & Kegan Paul.

Allport, A., MacKay, D., Prinz, W., & Scheerer, E. (Eds.). (1987). *Language perception and production: Relationships between listening, speaking, reading and writing*. London: Academic Press.

Allwood, J., Andersson, L. G., & Dahl, O. (1977). *Logic in linguistics*. Cambridge: Cambridge University Press.

Andersen, R. (Ed.). (1983). *Pidginization and creolization as language acquisition*. Rowley, MA: Newbury House.

Anshen, F. (1969). *Speech variation among Negroes in a small southern community*. Ph. D dissertation, New York University.

Arthur, B., Weiner, R., Culver, M., Ja Lee, Y., & Thomas, D. (1980). The register of impersonal discourse to foreigners: Verbal adjustments to foreign accent. In D. Larsen-Freeman (Ed.), *Discourse analysis in second language research*. Rowley, MA: Newbury House.

Atchison, J. (1981). *Language change: Progress or decay?* Bungay, Suffolk: Chaucer Press.

Atkinson, P. (1985). *Language, structure and reproduction: An introduction to the sociology of Basil Bernstein*. London: Methuen.

Austin, J. L. (1950). *Truth*, Proceedings of the Aristotelian Society, 24.

Austin, J. L. (1962). *How to do things with words*. Oxford: Clarendon Press.

Baddeley, A. D. (1976). *The psychology of memory*. New York: Basic Books.

Bartlett, F. C. (1932). *Remembering: A study in experimental social psychology*. Cambridge: Cambridge University Press.

Bates, E. & MacWhinney, B. (1987). Competition, variation, and language learning. In B. MacWhinney, (Ed.), *Mechanisms of language acquisition*. Hillsdale, NJ: Erlbaum.

Bates, E. (1976). *Language and context: The acquisition of pragmatics*. New York: Academic Press.

Beardsley, M. C. (1962). The metaphorical twist. *Philosophy and Phenomenological Research*, 22, 293-307.

Berko-Gleason, J. (1989). *The development of language (2nd ed.)*. Columbus, Ohio: Merrill Publishing.

Bernstein, B. (1958). Some sociological determinants of perception. *British Journal of Sociology*, 9, 159-174.

Bernstein, B. (1962). Linguistic codes, hesitation phenomena, and intelligence. *Language and Speech*, 5, 31-46.

Bernstein, B. (1970). A sociolinguistic approach to socialization: With some reference to educability. In F. Williams (Ed.), *Language and poverty*. Chicago: Markham Publishing.

Bernstein, B. (1972). A critique of the concept of compensatory education. In C. Cazden, D. Hymes, & V. John (Eds.), *Functions of language in the classroom*. New York: Teacher's College Press.
Bernstein, R. (1983). *Beyond objectivism and relativism*. Philadelphia: University of Pennsylvania Press.
Bever, T. G. (1970). The cognitive basis for linguistic structures. In J.R. Hayes, (Ed.), *Cognition and the development of language*. New York: John Wiley.
Bever, T. G., Fodor, J. A., Garrett, M. F., & Mehler, J. (1966). *Transformational operations and stimulus complexity*. Cited in Fodor, Bever, Garrett (1974).
Bickerton, D. (1975). *Dynamics of a creole system*. Cambridge: Cambridge University Press.
Bickerton, D. (1977). Language acquistion and language universals. In A. Balman (Ed.), *Pidgin and creole linguistics*. Bloomington, IN: Indiana University Press.
Bierwisch, M. (1967). Some semantic universals of German adjectivals. *Foundations of Language, 3*, 1-36.
Black, M. (1962). *Models and metaphors*. Ithaca, NY: Cornell University Press.
Black, M. (1979). More about Metaphor. In A. Ortony (Ed.), *Metaphor and thought* (pp, 19-43). Cambridge: Cambridge University Press.
Block, N. (Ed.). (1981). *Readings in philosophy of psychology* (Vol. 1). Cambridge, MA: Harvard University Press.
Block, N. (Ed.). (1981). *Readings in philosophy of psychology* (Vol. 2). Cambridge, MA: Harvard University Press.
Blonsky, M. (Ed.). (1985). *On signs*. Baltimore, MD: Johns Hopkins University Press.
Bloomfield, L. (1933). *Language*. New York: Holt, Rinehart & Winston.
Blumenthal, A. L. (1970). *Language and psychology: Historical aspects of psycholinguistics*. New York: John Wiley & Sons.
Blumstein, S. E. (1988). Neurolinguistics: An overview of language-brain relations in aphasia. In F. J. Newmeyer, (Ed.), *Linguistics: The Cambridge survey III: Language: Psychological and biological aspects*. (pp. 210-236), Cambridge: Cambridge University Press.
Bodine, A. (1975). Sex differences in language. In B. Thorne & N. Henley (Eds.), *Language and sex: Difference and dominance*, Rowley, MA: Newbury House Publishers.
Bohm, D. (1980). *Wholeness and the implicate order*. London: Routledge & Kegan Paul.
Bousfield, W. A. (1953). The occurrence of clustering in the recall of randomly arranged associates. *Journal of General Psychology, 49*, 229-240.
Bradley, R., & Swartz, N. (1979). *Possible worlds: An introduction to logic and its philosophy*. Indianapolis, IN: Hackett Publishing.
Bransford, J. D., & Franks, J. J. (1971). The abstraction of linguistic ideas. *Cognitive Psychology, 2*, 331-350.
Bregman, A. S., & Strasberg, R. (1968). Memory for the syntactic form of sentences. *Journal of Verbal Learning and Verbal Behavior, 7*, 396-403.
Bresnan, J. (1978). A realistic transformational grammar. In M. Halle, J. Bresnan, & G. A. Miller (Eds.), *Linguistic theory and psychological reality* (pp. 1-59). Cambridge, MA: Massachusetts Institute Technology Press,
Bresnan, J. (Ed.).(1982). *The mental representation of grammatical relations*. Cambridge MA: Massachusetts Institute of Technology Press.
Broca, P. (1865). Sur le siège de la facultè du langage articulè. *Bulletin d'Anthropologie, 6*, 377-393.
Brown, R. (1958). *Words and things: An introduction to language*. New York: The Free Press.
Brown, G., & Yule, G. (1983). *Discourse analysis*. Cambridge: Cambridge University Press.
Brown, R. (1973). *A first language: The early stages*. Cambridge, MA: Harvard University Press.

Brumfit, C. J., & Johnson, K. (Eds.). (1979). *The communicative approach to language teaching.* Oxford: Oxford University Press.
Bruner, J. (1986). *Actual minds, possible worlds.* Cambridge, MA: Harvard University Press.
Caplan, D., Baker, C., & Dehaut, F. (1985). Syntactic determinants of sentence comprehension in aphasia. *Cognition, 21*, 117-175.
Caplan, D. (1987). *Neurolinguistics and linguistic aphasiology: An introduction.* Cambridge: Cambridge University Press.
Carnap, R. (1947). *Meaning and necessity.* Chicago: Chicago University Press.
Carrell, P. L. (1983). Some issues in studying the role of schemata, or background knowledge, in second language comprehension. *Reading in a Foreign Language, 1*, 82-92.
Carroll, D. W. (1986). *Psychology of language.* Monterey, CA: Brooks/Cole.
Chomsky, N. (1957). *Syntactic Structures.* Gravenhage: Mouton.
Chomsky, N. (1959). Review of Skinner, B. F: Verbal Behavior. *Language, 35*, 26-58.
Chomsky, N. (1965). *Aspects of the theory of syntax.* Cambridge, MA: MIT Press.
Chomsky, N. (1967). Recent contributions to the theory of innate ideas. *Synthesis, 17*, 2-11.
Chomsky, N. (1968). *Language and mind.* New York: Harcourt Brace Jovanovich.
Chomsky, N. (1970). Remarks on nominalization. In R. Jacobs & P Rosenbaum (Eds.). *Readings in English transformational grammar.* 184-221.
Chomsky, N. (1975). *Reflections on language.* New York: Random House.
Chomsky, N. (1981). *Lectures on Government and Binding.* Dordrecht: Foris.
Chomsky, N. (1982). *Some concepts and consequences of the theory of Government and Binding.* Cambridge, MA: MIT Press.
Chomsky, N. (1988). *Language and problems of knowledge: The Managua lectures.* Cambridge, MA: MIT Press.
Chomsky, N., & Halle, M. (1968). *The sound pattern of English.* New York: Harper & Row.
Clark, H. H., & Clark, E. E. (1977). *Psychology and language: An introduction to psycholinguistics.* New York: Harcourt Brace Jovanovich.
Clark, H. H. (1985). Language use and language users. In G. Lindzey & E. Aronson (Eds.), *Handbook of social psychology* (3rd ed.) (Vol. 2). New York: Random House.
Cole, P. & Morgan J. L. (Eds). (1975). *Syntax and semantics 3: Speech acts.* New York: Academic Press.
Cole, P. (Ed). (1978). *Syntax and semantics 9: Pragmatics.* New York: Academic Press.
Collins, A. M., & Quillian, M. R. (1972). Experiments on semantic memory and language comprehension. In L. W. Gregg (Ed.), *Cognition in learning and memory* (pp. 117-148). New York: Wiley.
Conrad, C. (1972). Cognitive economy in semantic memory. *Journal of Experimental Psychology, 92*, 149-154.
Cook-Gumperz, J. (Ed.). (1986). *The social construction of literacy.* Cambridge: Cambridge University Press.
Cooper, D. (1973). *Philosophy and the nature of language.* London: Longman Group.
Cooper, D. E. (1975). *Knowledge of language.* London: Prism Press.
Coulthard, M. (1977). *An introduction to discourse analysis.* London: Longman Group.
Crosstalk (1986). London: BBC Documentary.
Crowhurst, M. (1980). Syntactic complexity in narration and argument of three grade levels. *Canadian Journal of Education, 5,* 6-13.
Cruse, D. A. (1986). *Lexical semantics.* Cambridge: Cambridge University Press.
Crystal, D. (1971). *Linguistics.* Middlesex: Penguin.
Crystal, D. (1985). *A dictionary of linguistics and phonetics (2nd ed.).* Oxford: Basil Blackwell.
Crystal, D. (1987). *The Cambridge encyclopedia of language.* Cambridge: Cambridge University Press.
Crystal, D., & Davy, D. (1969). *Investigating English style.* London: Longman Group.

Das, J. P., Kirby, J. R., & Jarman, R. F. (1979). *Simultaneous and successive processing*. New York: Academic Press.
Davidson, D. (1967). Truth and meaning. *Synthese, 17*.
Davidson, D. (1974). Belief and the basis of meaning. *Synthese, 27*.
Davies, A. (Ed.). (1975). *Problems of language learning*. London: Heinemann.
Davis, P. W. (1973). *Modern theories of language*. Englewood Cliffs, NJ: Prentice-Hall.
de Castell, S., Luke, A., & Egan, K. (Eds.). (1986). *Literacy, society, and schooling: A reader*. Cambridge: Cambridge University Press.
Deely, J. (1982). *Introducing semiotic: Its history and doctrine*. Bloomington, IN: Indiana State University.
Deely, J., Williams, B., & Kruse, F. E. (Eds.). (1986). *Frontiers in semiotics*. Bloomington, IN: Indiana University Press.
Deely, J. (1990). *Basics of semiotics*. Bloomington, IN: Indiana University Press.
Deese, J. (1962). On the structure of associative meaning. *Psychology Review, 69*, 161-175.
Department of Education and Science. (1975). *A Language for Life: Report of the Committee of Inquiry appointed by the Secretary of State for Education and Science under the Chairmanship of Sir Alan Bullock*. London: Her Majesty's Stationery Office.
Devitt, M., & Sterelny, K. (1987). *Language & reality: An introduction to the Philosophy of language*. Oxford: Basil Blackwell.
Dewey, J. (1938). *Logic, the theory of inquiry*. New York: Henry Holt & Company.
Dingwall, W. O. (1988). The evolution of human communicative behavior. In F. J. Newmeyer (Ed.), *Linguistics: The Cambridge Survey III. Language psychological and biological aspects*. (pp. 274-313). Cambridge: Cambridge University Press.
Downes, W. (1984). *Language and society*. London: Hartnolls.
Dowty, D. R., Wall, R. E., & Peters, S. (1981). *Introduction to Montague Semantics*. Dordrecht, Holland: D. Reidel.
Dreyfus, H. L. (Ed.). (1982). *Husserl, intentionality, and cognitive science*. Cambridge, MA: Massachusetts Institute of Technology Press.
Ducrot, O., & Todorov, T. (1972). *Encyclopedic Dictionary of the sciences of language* (C. Porter, Trans.). Baltimore, MD: John Hopkins University Press.
Dummett, M. A. E. (1973). *Frege: philosophy of language*. London: Duckworth.
Eco, U. (1979). *A theory of semiotics*. Bloomington, IN: Indiana University Press.
Eco, U. (1984a). *Semiotics and the philosophy of language*. Bloomington, IN: Indiana University Press.
Eco, U. (1984b). *The role of the reader: Explorations in the semiotics of texts*. Bloomington, IN: Indiana University Press.
Eco, U. (1985). Producing signs. In M. Blonsky (Ed.), *On signs* (pp. 176-183). Baltimore, MD: John Hopkins University Press
Edie, J. M. (1987). *Edmund Husserl's Phenomenology: A critical commentary*. Bloomington, IN: Indiana University Press.
Feibleman, J. K. (1946). *An introduction to the philosophy of Charles S. Peirce*. Cambridge, MA: Massachusetts Institute of Technology.
Ferguson, C. A. (1971). Absence of copula and the notion of simplicity: A study of normal speech, baby talk, foreigner talk, and pidgins. In D. Hymes (Ed.), *Pidginization and creolization of languages*. New York: Cambridge University Press.
Ferguson, C. A. (1972). Toward a characterization of English foreigner talk. *Anthropological Linguistics, 17*, 1-14.
Fillmore, C. (1966). A proposal concerning English prepositions. *Monograph Series on Languages and Linguistics, 19*, 19-34.
Fillmore, C. (1968). The case for case. In E. Bach & R. Harms, (Eds.). *Universals in linguistic theory*. New York: Holt, Rinehart and Winston.

Fillmore, C. (1971). Some problems for case grammar. *Monograph Series on Languages and Linguistics, 24,* 35-56.
Fink, B. R., & Kirschner, F. (1959). Observations on the acoustical and mechanical properties of the vocal folds. *Folia Phoniatrica, 11,* 167-172.
Firth, J. R. (1957). *Papers in Linguistics 1934-1951.* London: Oxford University Press.
Fischer, J. L. (1958). Social influences on the choice of a linguistic variant. *Word, 14,* 47-56.
Flower, L., & Hayes, J. R. (1981). A cognitive process theory of writing. *College Composition and Communication, 32,* 365-387.
Fodor, J. A. (1983). *The modularity of mind.* Cambridge, MA: Massachusetts of Institute of Technology Press.
Fodor, J. A., Garrett, M. F. (1967). Some syntactic determinants of sentential complexity. *Perception and Psychophysics, 2,* 289-296.
Fodor, J. A., Bever, T. G., & Garrett, M. F. (1974). *The psychology of language: An introduction to psycholinguistics and generative grammar.* New York: McGraw-Hill.
French, P. A., Uehling, T. E., Jr., & Wettstein, H. K. (Eds.). (1980). *Midwest studies in philosophy: Studies in epistemology* (Vol. 5). Minneapolis, MN: University of Minnesota Press.
Froese, V. (1990). *Whole-language practice and theory.* Scarborough, ON: Prentice-Hall Canada Inc.
Fromkin, V. (1971). The non-anomalous nature of anomalous utterances. *Language, 47,* 27-52.
Fromkin, V., & Rodman, R. (1978). *An introduction to language* (3rd ed.). New York: Holt, Rinehart and Winston.
Furnham, A., & Bochner, S. (1986). *Culture shock: Psychological reactions to unfamiliar environments.* London: Methuen.
Gadamer, H. G. (1976). *Philosophical hermeneutics* (D.E. Linge, Trans.). Berkeley: University of California Press.
Gadamer (1975). *Truth and method.* New York: Seabury Press.
Galton, F. (1880). Psychometric experiments. *Brain, 2,* 149-162.
Gardner, R. C., & Lambert, W. E. (1959). Motivational variables in second language acquisition. *Canadian Journal of Psychology, 13,* 266-272.
Gardner, R. C. (1979). Social psychological aspects of second language acquisition. In H. Giles & R. St. Clair (Eds.), *Language and social psychology* (pp. 193-220). Oxford: Basil Blackwell.
Garrett, M. F. (1975). The analysis of sentence production. In G.H. Bower (Ed.), *The psychology of learning and memory* (Vol. 9, pp. 133-177). New York: Academic Press.
Gazdar, G. (1982). Phrase structure grammar. In P. Jacobson & G. Pullum (Eds.). *The nature of syntactic representation.* 131-186.
Gazzaniga, M. S. (1983). Right hemisphere language following brain bisection: A twenty year perspective. *American Psychologist, 38*(5), 525-537.
Gibson, E. J., & Levin, H. (1975). *The psychology of reading.* Cambridge, MA: Massachusetts Institute of Technology Press.
Giglioli, P. P. (Ed.). (1972). *Language and social context.* London: Penguin Books.
Gleason, H. A. (1961). *An Introduction to Descriptive Linguistics.* New York: Holt, Rinehart and Winston.
Glucksburg, S., & Danks, J. H. (1975). *Experimental psycholinguistics: An introduction.* Hillsdale, NJ: Lawrence Erlbaum Associates.
Goffman, E. (1976). Replies and responses. *Language in Society, 5*(3), 257-313.
Goodglass, H. (1968). Studies in the grammar of aphasics. In S. Rosenberg & J. Koplin (Eds.), *Developments in applied psycholinguistics.* New York: Macmillan.

Goodglass, H., & Baker, E. (1976). Semantic field, naming, and auditory comprehension in aphasia. *Brain and Language, 3,* 359-374.
Goodman, K. S. (1967). Reading: A psycholinguistic guessing game. *Journal of the Reading Specialist, 6,* 126-135.
Gough, P. B. (1966). The verification of sentences. The effects of delay of evidence and sentence length. *Journal of Verbal Learning and Verbal Behavior, 5,* 492-496.
Greene, J. (1972). *Psycholinguistics: Chomsky and psychology.* Middlesex: Penguin Education.
Grice, H. P. (1957). Meaning. *Philosophical Review, 67,* 377-88.
Grice, H. P. (1975). Logic and conversation. In P. Cole & J. L. Morgan (Eds.), *Studies in syntax (Vol. 3): Speech acts* (pp. 41-58). New York: Academic Press.
Grice, H. P. (1978). Further notes on logic and conversation. In P. Cole (Ed.), *Syntax and semantics 9: Pragmatics* (pp.113-128).
Grossmann, R. (1984). *Phenomenology & existentialism: An introduction.* London: Routledge & Kegan Paul.
Gumperz, J. J. (1982). *Discourse strategies.* Cambridge: Cambridge University Press.
Gumperz, J. J. & Cook-Gumperz, J. (1982). Introduction: Language and the communication of social identity. In J. J. Gumperz (Ed.), *Language and social identity.* Cambridge: Cambridge University Press.
Gurwitsch, A. (1940). On the intentionality of consciousness. In M. Farber (Ed.), *Philosophical essays in memory of Edmund Husserl.* Cambridge, MA: Harvard University Press.
Haack, S. (1978). *Philosophy of Logics.* Cambridge: Cambridge University Press.
Hacking, I. (1975). *What does Language Matter to Philosophy?*. Cambridge: Cambridge University Press.
Hallahan, D. P., & Kauffman, J. M. (1988). *Exceptional Children: Introduction to Special Education* (4th. ed.). Englewood Cliffs, NJ: Prentice-Hall.
Halliday, M. A. K. (1961). Categories of the theory of grammar. *Word, 17,* 24 1-292.
Halliday, M. A. K. (1973). *Explorations in the functions of language.* London: Edward Arnold Publishers.
Halliday, M. A. K. (1975). *Learning how to mean: explorations in the development of language.* London: Edward Arnold.
Halliday, M. A. K. (1978). *Language as social semiotic: The social interpretation of language and meaning.* London: Edward Arnold.
Halliday, M. A. K., & Hasan, R. (1976). *Cohesion in English.* London: Longman Group.
Harland, R. (1987). *The philosophy of structuralism and post-structuralism.* London: Routledge.
Harris, R., & Taylor, T. J. (1989). *Landmarks in linguistic thought: The western tradition from Socrates to Saussure.* London: Routledge.
Harris, R. (1980). *The language makers.* Ithica, NY: Cornell University Press.
Harris, Z. (1951). *Methods in structural linguistics.* Chicago, IL: University of Chicago Press.
Hartnack, J. (1965). *Wittgenstein and Modern Philosophy.* London: Methuen.
Hatch, E. M. (1983). *Psycholinguistics: A second language perspective.* Rowley, MA: Newbury House.
Hatch, E., & Long, M. (1980). Discourse analysis, what's that? In D. Larsen-Freeman (Ed.), *Discourse analysis in second language research.* Rowley, MA: Newbury House Publishers.
Hattiangadi, J. N. (1987). *How is language possible? Philosophical reflections on the evolution of language and knowledge.* La Salle, IL: Open Court.
Hawkes, T. (1977). *Structuralism and semiotics.* Berkeley: University of California Press.
Hawkins, E. (1984). *Awareness of language: An introduction.* Cambridge: Cambridge University Press.
Head, H. (1926). *Aphasia and kindred disorders of speech.* Cambridge: Cambridge University Press.

Heidegger, M. (1927). *Being and Time.* (J. Macquarrie & E. Robinson, Trans.) New York: Harper & Row.
Heidegger, M. (1971). *On the way to language.* (P. D. Hertz, Trans.). New York: Harper & Row. (Original work published 1959)
Heidegger, M. (1977). *Basic writings.* New York: Harper & Row.
Held, D. (1980). *Introduction to critical theory: Horkheimer to Habermas.* Berkeley: University of California Press.
Hilgard, E. R., Atkinson, R. L., & Atkinson, R. C. (1979). *Introduction to psychology* (7th ed.). New York: Harcourt Brace Jovanovich.
Hodge, R., & Kress, G. (1988). *Social Semiotics.* Ithica, NY: Cornell University Press.
Hörmann, H. (1971). *Psycholinguistics.* New York: Springer-Verlag.
Horrocks, G. (1987). *Generative Grammar.* London: Longman.
Howatt, A. P. R. (1984). *A history of English language teaching.* Oxford: Oxford University Press.
Huddleston, R. (1984). *Introduction to the grammar of English.* Cambridge: Cambridge University Press.
Humboldt, W. von (1836). *Uber die Verachiedenheit des Menschlichen Sprachhaus.* Berlin-Bonn: Dummler.
Humboldt, W. von (1822). On the task of the historian. In K. Mueller-Vollmer (Ed.).(1986), *The hermeneuics reader* (pp. 105-118). Oxford: Basil Blackwell.
Hume, D. (1967). *Treatise of human nature,* L. A. Selby-Bigge (Ed.). Oxford: Clarendon Press. (first published in 1739)
Hunnings, G. (1988). *The world and language in Wittgenstein's philosophy.* New York: State University of New York Press.
Hurford, J. R., & Heasley, B. (1983). *Semantics: A coursebook.* Cambridge: Cambridge University Press.
Husserl, E. (1913). The phenomenological theory of meaning and of meaning-apprehension. In Mueller-Vollmer (Ed.). (1986), *The hermeneutics reader.* Oxford: Basil Blackwell.
Husserl, E. (1970). *The idea of phenomenology.* (W. P. Alston & G. Nakhnikian, Trans.). The Hague: Marinus Nijhoff. (Original work published 1964)
Hymes, D. (1971). Competence and performance in linguistic theory. In R. Huxley & E. Ingram (Eds), *Language Acquisition: Models and Methods.* London: Academic Press.
Hymes, D. (1972). On communicative competence. In Pride, J. B., & Holmes, J. (Eds.), *Sociolinguistics: Selected readings* (pp. 269-293). Harmondsworth: Penguin Books.
Innis, R. E. (Ed.).(1985). *Semiotics: An introductory anthology.* Bloomington, IN: Indiana University Press.
Jackendoff, R. (1969). An interpretive theory of negation. *Foundations of Language, 5,* 218-241.
Jackendoff, R. (1983). *Semantics and cognition.* Cambridge, MA: Massachusetts Institute of Technology Press.
Jakobson, R. (1968). *Child language, aphasia, and phonological universals.* (translated from the German original published in 1941). The Hague: Mouton.
Jakobson, R., & Pomorska, K. (1988). *Dialogues.* Cambridge, MA: Massachusetts Institute of Technology Press.
Jakobson, R. (1980). *The framework of language.* University of Michigan: Michigan Studies in the Humanities.
Jakobson, R. (1987). *Language in literature.* Cambridge, MA: Harvard University Press.
James, W. (1879). The sentiment of rationality. Reprinted in James, W. (1948). *Essays in pragmatism.* New York: Hafner Publishing Company.
James, W. (1907). What pragmatism means. Reprinted in James, W. (1948). *Essays in pragmatism.* New York: Hafner Publishing Company.

James, W. (1907). *Pragmatism*. London: Longman Group.
James, W. (1948). *Essays in pragmatism*. New York: Hafner Publishing Company.
Johnson, M. (1987). *The body in the mind*. Chicago, IL: The University of Chicago Press.
Johnson, N. A. (Ed.). (1976). *Current topics in language: Introductory readings*. Cambridge, MA: Winthrop Publishers.
Joos, M. (1967). *The five clocks*. New York: Harcourt Brace Jovanovich.
Kaplan, R. (1966). Cultural thought patterns in inter-cultural education. *Language Learning, 16*, 1-20.
Kaplan, R. & Bresnan, J. (1982). Lexical-functional grammar: A formal system for grammatical representation. In J. Bresnan (Ed.). *The mental representation of grammatical relations*, 173-281. Cambridge, MA: MIT Press.
Katz, J. J. (1977). The real status of semantic representations. *Linguistic Inquiry, 8*, 559-84.
Katz, J. J., & Fodor, J. A. (1963). The structure of a semantic theory. *Language, 39*, 170-210.
Katz, J. J., & Postal, P. (1964). *An integrated theory of linguistic descriptions*. Cambridge, MA: MIT Press.
Kempson, R. M. (1975). *Presupposition and the delimitation of semantics*. Cambridge: Cambridge University Press.
Kempson, R. M. (1977). *Semantic Theory*. Cambridge: Cambridge University Press.
Kennedy, A. (1984). *The psychology of reading*. London: Methuen.
Kieras, D. E. (1981). Component processes in the comprehension of simple prose. *Journal of Verbal Learning and Verbal Behavior, 20*, 1-23.
Kimura, D. (1983). Sex differences in cerebral organization for speech and praxic functions. *Canadian Journal of Psychology, 37*, 19-35.
King, R. (1991). *Talking gender*. Toronto: Copp Clark Pitman.
Kintsch, W. (1974). *The representation of meaning in memory*. Hillsdale, NJ: Lawrence Erlbaum Associates.
Kintsch, W., & Keenan, J. M. (1973). Reading rate and retention as a function of the number of propositions in the base structure of sentences. *Cognitive Psychology, 5*, 257-274.
Kintsch, W., Kozminsky, E., Streby, W. J., McKoon, G., & Keenan, J. M. (1975). Comprehension and recall of text as a function of content variables. *Journal of Verbal Learning and Verbal Behavior, 14*, 196-214.
Kockelmans, J. J. (Ed.). (1967). *Phenomenology: The philosophy of Edmund Husserl and its interpretation*. Garden City, NY: Doubleday Anchor.
Kozulin, A. (Ed.).(1986). Vygotsky in context. In L. Vygotsky *Thought and language* (pp. xi-lvi). Cambridge: Massachusetts Institute of Technology Press.
Kress, G. (Ed.). (1976). *Halliday: System and function in language*. London: Oxford University Press.
Kristeva, J. (1989). *Language the unknown; An initiation into linguistics* (A. Menke, Trans.). New York: Columbia University Press. (original work published 1981)
Labov, W. (1972). *Sociolinguistic Patterns*. Philadelphia: University of Pennsylvania Press.
Labov, W. (1969). The logic of nonstandard English. In *Report of the twentieth annual round table meeting on linguistics and language*. Washington, DC: Georgetown University Press.
Lacan, T. N. (1977). *Ecrits: A selection*. (A. Sheridan, Trans.). New York: Norton.
Lakoff, G. (1974). Interview. In H. Parret, (Ed.) , *Discussing language*. The Hague: Mouton.
Lakoff, G. & Johnson, M. (1980). *Metaphors we live by*. Chicago, IL: The University of Chicago Press.
Langendoen, D. T. (1968). *The London School of Linguistics: A study of the linguistic theories of B. Malinowski and J. R. Firth*. Cambridge, MA: MIT Press.
Lambert, W. E. (1975). Culture and language as factors in learning and education. In A. Wolfgang (Ed.), *Education of immigrant students* (pp. 55-83). Toronto: OISE press.

Landau, B., & Gleitman, L. R. (1985). *Language and experience: Evidence from the blind child.* Cambridge, MA: Harvard University Press.
Larsen-Freeman, D. (1980). *Discourse analysis in second language research.* Rowley, MA: Newbury House.
Lashley, K. S. (1951). The problem of serial order in behavior. In L. A. Jeffress (Ed.), *Cerebral mechanisms in behavior* (pp. 112-136). New York: Wiley.
Lee, B. (1985). Intellectual origins of Vygotsky's semiotic analysis. In J. M. Wertsch (Ed.), *Culture communication and cognition: Vygotskian perspectives.* Cambridge: Cambridge University Press.
Leech, G. & Svartvik, J. (1975). *A communicative grammar of English.* London: Longman.
Leiter, K. (1980). *A primer on ethnomethodology.* New York: Oxford University Press.
Lenneberg, E. H. (1967). *Biological foundations of language.* New York: John Wiley & Sons.
Levi-Strauss, C. (1967). *Structural anthropology.* Garden City, NY: Anchor.
Levinson, S. C. (1983). *Pragmatics.* Cambridge: Cambridge University Press.
Lewis, D. (1986). *On the plurality of worlds.* Oxford: Basil Black.
Lewis, D. K. (1973). *Counterfactuals.* Cambridge MA: Harvard University Press.
Lichtheim, L. (1885). On aphasia. *Brain,7,* 433-484.
Lieberman, P. (1984). *The biology and evolution of language.* Cambridge, MA: Harvard University Press.
Lieberman, P. (1968). *Journal of the Acoustical. Society of America, 44,* 1574-1584.
Lightfoot, D. (1982). *The language lottery: Toward a biology of grammars.* Cambridge, MA: MIT Press.
Lock, A., & Fisher, E. (Eds.). (1984). *Language development.* London: Croom Helm.
Locke, J. (1690). *Essay Concerning Human Understanding: Book Four.* Reprinted in J. Deely, B. Williams, & F. E. Kruse (Eds.). (1986). *Frontiers in Semiotics.* Bloomington, IN: Indiana University Press.
Luria, A. R. (1973). *The working brain.* New York: Basic Books.
Luria, A. R. (1975). *The man with a shattered world* (L. Solotaroff, Trans.). Hammondsworth, Middlesex: Penguin Books.
Lucid, D. P. (Ed.). (1977). *Soviet semiotics: An anthology* (D. P. Lucid Trans.). Baltimore, MD: Johns Hopkins University Press.
Luria, A. R. (1978). The development of writing in the child. In M. Cole (Ed.), *The selected writings of A. R. Luria* (pp. 145-194). White Plains, NY: Sharpe.
Luria, A. R., & Yudovich, F. La. (1971). *Speech and the development of mental processes in the child.* Middlesex: Penguin Books.
Lyons, J. (1968). *Introduction to theoretical linguistics.* London: Cambridge University Press.
Lyons, J. (1977). *Semantics* (Vol. 2). Cambridge: Cambridge University Press.
Lyons, J. (1981). *Language, meaning & context.* Bungay, Suffolk: Chaucer Press.
Lyons, J., & Wales, R. J. (Eds.). (1966). *Psycholinguistics papers: Proceedings of the Edinburgh Conference.* Edinburgh: Edinburgh University Press.
Macksey, R., & Donato, E. (Eds.). (1970). *The structuralist controversy: The languages of criticism and the sciences of man.* Baltimore, MD: Johns Hopkins University Press.
Macnamara, J. (1972). Cognitive basis of language learning in infants. *Psychological Review, 79,* 1-13.
Malinowski, B. (1936). The problem of meaning in primitive languages. In C.K. Ogden & T. A. Richards (Eds.), *The meaning of meaning.* London: Kegan Paul, Trench, Trubner.
Mandler, J. M., & Johnson, N. S. (1977). Remembrance of things parsed: Story structure and recall. *Cognitive Psychology, 9,* 111-151.
Marie, P. (1906). Rèvision de la question de l'aphasie: L'aphasie de 1861 a 1866: Essai de critique historique sur le genese de la doctrine de Broca. *Semaine Medicale,* (Paris) *26,* 565-571.

Martin, R. M. (1987). *The meaning of language.* Cambridge, MA: Massachusetts Institute of Technology Press.
Marckworth, M. L. & Prideaux, G. D. (1978). *Workbook for Linguistics: Modern English Grammar 2 (4th. Edition).* Edmonton: Department of Linguistics, University of Alberta.
Martinet, A. (1960). *Elements of general linguistics* (E. Palmer, Trans.). London: Faber and Faber.
McArthur, T. (1983). *A foundation course for language teachers.* Cambridge: Cambridge University Press.
Mc Cawley, J. (1968). Lexical insertion in a transformational grammar without Deep Structure. *Papers from the Fourth Regional Meeting of the Chicago Linguistic Society,* 71-80.
McCrum, R., Cran, W., & MacNeil, R. (1986). *The story of English.* New York: Viking Penguin.
McGlone, J. (1977). Sex differences in the cerebral organization of verbal functions in patients with unilateral brain lesion. *Brain, 100,* 775-793.
McGlone, J. (1980). Sex differences in human brain asymmetry: A critical survey. *Behavioural and Brain Sciences, 3,* 215-263.
McKoon, G. (1977). Organization of information in text memory. *Journal of Verbal Learning and Verbal Behavior, 16,* 247-260.
McKusick, J. C. (1986). *Coleridge's philosophy of language.* New Haven: Yale University Press.
McManis, C., Stollenwerk, D., & Zhang, Z. S. (1987). *Language Files.* Reynoldsburg, OH: Advocate Publishing Group.
McNeil, J. D. (1984). *Reading comprehension: New directions for classroom practice.* Glenview, IL: Scott Foresman and Company.
McNeill, D. (1985). Do you think gestures are nonverbal? *Psychological Review, 92,* 350-371.
McNeill, D. (1987). *Psycholinguistics: A new approach.* New York: Harper & Row.
Merleau-Ponty, M. (1964). *Signs* (R. C. McCleary, Trans.). Evanston, IL: Northwestern University Press. (Original work published 1960)
Meyer, B. J. F. (1975). *The organization of prose and its effect on memory.* Amsterdam: North-Holland.
Miller, G. A. (1962). Some psychological studies in grammar. *American Psychologist, 17,* 748-762.
Miller, J. (1983). *Many voices: Bilingualism, culture, and education.* London: Routledge & Kegan Paul.
Miller, G. A. (1956). The magical number seven plus or minus two, or, some limits on our capacity for processing information. *Psychological Review, 63,* 81-96.
Millikan, R. G. (1984). *Language, thought, and other biological categories: New foundations for realism.* Cambridge, MA: Massachusetts Institute of Technology.
Minsky, M. (1985). *The society of mind.* New York: Simon and Schuster.
Montague, R. (1970). Pragmatics and intentional logic. *Synthese 22.*
Montgomery, G. (1989). The mind in motion: *Discover, 10*(3), 58-61.
Montgomery, M. (1986). *An Introduction to language and society.* London: Methuen & Company.
Moore, T., & Carling, C. (1982). *Understanding language: Towards a post-Chomskyan linguistics.* London: Macmillan Press.
Morson, G. S. (Ed.). (1986). *Bakhtin: Essays and dialogues on his work.* Chicago: University of Chicago Press.
Morton, J., & Marshall, J. C. (Eds.). (1979). *Structures and processes.* London: Paul Elek.
Mouter, F. (1908). *L'Aphasie de Broca.* Paris: Steinheil.
Mueller-Vollmer, K. (Ed.). (1986). *The hermeneutics reader.* Oxford: Basil Blackwell.

Munz, P. (1987). Philosophy and the Mirror of Rorty. In G. Radnitzky & W. W. Bartley, III (Eds.), *Evolutionary epistemology, rationality, and the sociology of knowledge*. La Salle, IL: Open Court.

Negus, V. E. (1949). *The comparative anatomy and physiology of the larynx*. New York: Hafner.

Nelson, K. (1974). Concept, word and sentence: Interrelations in acquisition and development. *Psychological Review, 81*, 267-85.

Newmeyer, F. J. (1986). *Linguistic theory in America* (2nd ed.). San Diego, CA: Academic Press.

Ogden, C. K., & Richards, I. A. (Eds.).(1936). *The meaning of meaning: A study of the influence of language upon thought and of the science of symbolism*. London: Kegan Paul, Trench, Trubner.

Olson, D. R., Torrance, N., & Hildyard, A. (Eds.). (1985). *Literacy, language, and learning: The nature and consequences of reading and writing*. Cambridge: Cambridge University Press.

Ortony, A. (Ed.). (1979). *Metaphor and thought*. Cambridge: Cambridge University Press.

Osgood, C. E., Suci, G. J., & Tannenbaum, P.H. (1957). *The measurement of meaning*. Urbana, IL: University of Illinois Press.

Osherson, D. N., & Lasnik, H. (Eds.). (1990). *An invitation to cognitive science: Language* (Vol. 1). Cambridge, MA: Massachusetts Institute of Technology Press.

Palmer, F. R. (1965). *The English verb*. London: Longman Group.

Pavel, T. G. (1986). *Fictional worlds*. Cambridge, MA: Harvard University Press.

Pearson, P. D., & Johnson, D. D. (Eds). (1978). *Teaching reading comprehension*. New York: Holt, Rinehart and Winston.

Peirce, C. S. (1931-1958). *The collected papers of Charles Sanders Peirce*. Cambridge, MA: Harvard University Press.

Perfetti, C. A. (1985). *Reading ability*. New York: Oxford University Press.

Perlmutter, D. & Postal, P. (1977). Toward a universal characterization of passive. *Papers from the Third Annual Meeting of the Berkeley Linguistics Society*, 394-417.

Perl, S. (1980). Understanding composing. *College Communication and Composition, 31*(4), 363-369.

Piaget, J. (1960). *Psychology of intelligence*. Paterson, NJ: Littlefield Adams.

Piper, D. (1985a). Formal vs. content schemata in the reading of adult Vietnamese students. *Reading-Canada-Lecture, 3,* 187-197.

Piper, D. (1985b). Syllogistic reasoning in varied narrative contexts: Aspects of logical and linguistic development. *Journal of Psycholinguistic Research, 14*(1), 19-43.

Piper, D. (1989). Socio-political influence on cultural identity in Canada: Implications for cross-cultural communication in English. In O. Garcia & R. Otheguy (Eds.), *English across cultures; Cultures across English* (pp. 191-184). Berlin: Mouton de Gruyter.

Platt, J., Weber, H., & Ho, M. L. (1984). *The New Englishes*. London: Routledge & Kegan Paul.

Porter, R. J., Jr. (1987). What is the relation between speech production and speech perception? In D. G. MacKay, A. Allport, W. Prinz, & E. Scheerer (Eds.), *Language perception and production: Relationships between listening, speaking, reading, and writing* (pp. 85-108). London: Academic Press.

Porter, J. (1965). *The vertical mosaic*. Toronto: University of Toronto Press.

Porzig, W. (1934). Wesenhafte Bedeutungsbeziehungen. *Beitrage zur Geschichte der Deutschen Sprache und Literatur, 58,* 70-79.

Quirk, R., Greenbaum, S., Leech, G. & Svartvik, J. (1972). *A contemporary grammar of English*. London: Longman.

Quirk, R., & Greenbaum, S. (1973). *A university grammar of English*. London: Longman.

Radford, A. (1981). *Transformational syntax: A student's guide to Chomsky's extended standard theory*. Cambridge: Cambridge University Press.

Radnitzky, G. & Bartley, W. W., III (Eds.), *Evolutionary epistemology, rationality, and the sociology of knowledge*. La Salle, IL: Open Court.

Reddy, M. J. (1979). The conduit metaphor - A case of frame conflict in our language about language. In A. Ortony (Ed.), *Metaphor and thought* (pp, 284-324). Cambridge: Cambridge University Press.

Revzin, I. I. (1966). *Models of Language* (N. F. C. Owen, & A. S. C. Ross, Trans.). London: Methuen & Co. (Original work published 1962)

Revzin, I. I. (1977). Language as a sign system and the game of chess. In D. P. Lucid (Ed.), *Soviet semiotics: An anthology* (pp. 87-92). Baltimore, MD: The John Hopkins University Press.

Ricoeur, P. (1981). *Hermeneutics & the human sciences* (J. B. Thompson, Trans.). Cambridge: Cambridge University Press.

Robins, R. H. (1967). *A short history of linguistics*. London: Longmans, Green and Company.

Robins, R. H. (1984). *General Linguistics: An introductory survey*. London: Longman Group.

Robinson, I. (1975). *The new grammarians' funeral: A critique of Noam Chomsky's linguistics*. Cambridge, MA: Cambridge University Press.

Rochberg-Halton, E. (1986). *Meaning and modernity: Social theory in the pragmatic attitude*. Chicago, IL: University of Chicago Press.

Rorty, R. (1979). *Philosophy and the mirror of nature*. Princeton, NJ: Princeton University Press.

Rorty, R. (1982). *Consequences of pragmatism*. Brighton, Sussex: Harvester Press.

Rose, M. A. (1980). *The cognitive dimension of writer's block: An examination of university students*. Unpublished doctoral dissertation, University of California at Los Angeles.

Rosenblatt, L. (1978). *The reader: the text: the poem*. Carbondale: Southern Illinois University Press.

Rumelhart, D. E. (1977). Understanding and summarizing brief stories. In D. Laberge & S. J. Samuels (Eds.), *Basic processes in reading: Perception and comprehension*. Hillsdale, NJ: Erlbaum.

Sachs, J. S. (1967). Recognition memory for syntactic and semantic aspects of connected discourse. *Perception & Psychophysics, 2*, 437-442.

Sacks, H., Schegloff, E., & Jefferson, G. (1975). A simplest systematics for the organization of turn-taking for conversation. *Language, 50*, 696-735.

Sacks, H. (1971). Mimeo lecture notes. Quoted in Coulthard, M. (1977). *An introduction to discourse analysis*. London: Longman Group.

Sacks, H., Schegloff, E., & Jefferson, G. (1974). A simplest systematics for the organization of turn-taking in conversation. *Language, 50*(4), 696-735.

Sadock, J. M. (1979). Figurative speech and linguistics. In A. Ortony (Ed.), *Metaphor and thought* (pp, 46-63). Cambridge: Cambridge University Press.

Saffron, E. (1985). *STM impairment and sentence comprehension*. Paper presented at the second international cognitive neuropsychology meeting.

Sankoff, G., & Cedergren, H. (1971). Some results of a sociolinguistic study of Montreal French. In R. Darnell (Ed.), *Linguistic diversity in Canadian society*. Edmonton and Champaign.

Sapir, E. (1970). *Language: An introduction to the study of speech*. London: Rupert Hart-Davis.

Sarles, H. B. (1977). *Language and human nature*. Minneapolis, MN: University of Minnesota.

Saussure, F. de. (1974). *Course in General Linguistics* (W. Baskin, Trans.). Glasgow: Collins Sons. (Original work published 1959)

Savignon, S. J. (1983). *Communicative competence: Theory and classroom practice: Texts and contexts in second language learning*. Reading, MA: Addison-Wesley.

Saville-Troike, M (1982). *The ethnography of communication*. Oxford: Basil Blackwell.

Savin, H., & Perchonock, E. (1965). Grammatical structure and the immediate recall of English sentences. *Journal of Verbal Learning and Verbal Behavior, 4,* 348-353.
Schank, R. C., & Abelson, R. P. (1977). *Scripts, plans, goals and understanding: An inquiry into human knowledge structures.* Hillsdale, NJ: Erlbaum.
Scheffler, I. (1965). *Conditions of Knowledge.* Glenview, IL: Scott, Foresman and Company.
Schegloff, E. (1968). Sequencing in conversational openings. *American Anthropologist, 70,*(4), 1075-1095.
Scinto, L. F. M. (1986). *Written language and psychological development.* Orlando, FL: Academic Press.
Scinto, L. F. M. (1982). *The acquisition of functional composition strategies for text.* Hamburg: Helmut Buske.
Searle, J. R. (1969). *Speech Acts.* Cambridge: Cambridge University Press.
Searle, J. R. (1976). The classification of illocutionary acts. *Language in Society, 5,* 1-24.
Searle, J. R. (1979). Metaphor. In A. Ortony (Ed.), *Metaphor and thought* (pp, 90-123). Cambridge: Cambridge University Press.
Searle, J. R., Kiefer, F., & Bierwisch, M. (1980). *Speech act theory and pragmatics.* Dordrecht, Holland: D. Reidel Publishing.
Sebeok, T. A. (1985). Zoosemiotic components of human communication. In R. E. Innis (Ed.), *Semiotics: An introductory anthology* (pp. 292-324). Bloomington, IN: Indiana University Press.
Sells, P. (1985). *Lectures on contemporary syntactic theories: An introduction to government-binding theory, generalized phrase structure grammar, and lexical-functional grammar.* Stanford: Center for the Study of Language and Information.
Shafer, R. E., Staab, C., & Smith, K. (1983). *Language functions and school success.* Glenview, IL: Scott, Foresman and Company.
Shallice, T. (1988). *From neuropsychology to mental structure.* Cambridge: Cambridge University Press.
Shankweiler, D. & Liberman, I. Y. (1972). Misreading: A search for causes. In J. F. Kavanagh & I. G. Mattingly (Eds.), *Language by ear and by eye: The relationships between speech and reading.* Cambridge, MA: MIT Press.
Shapiro, G., & Sica, A. (Eds.). (1984). *Hermeneutics: Questions and prospects.* Amherst, MA: University of Massachusetts Press.
Shattuck-Hufnagel, S. (1979). Speech errors as evidence for a serial-ordering mechanism in sentence production. In W. E. Cooper & E. C. T. Walker (Eds.), *Sentence processing* (pp. 295-342). Hillsdale, NJ: Erlbaum.
Shaver, P., & Hendrick, C. l. (Eds.). (1987). *Sex and gender.* Newbury Park, CA: Sage Publications.
Silverman, K. (1983). *The subject of semiotics.* Oxford: Oxford University Press.
Skinner, B. F. (1957). *Verbal Behavior.* New York: Appleton-Century-Crofts.
Smart, W. K. (1959). *English review grammar.* New York: Appleton-Century-Crofts.
Smith, F. (1971). *Understanding reading.* New York: Holt.
Smith, F. (1982). *Writing and the writer.* New York: Holt, Rinehart and Winston.
Smith, F. (1988). *Joining the literacy club.* Portsmouth, NH: Heinemann.
Solomon, R. C. (Ed.). (1980). *Phenomenology and existentialism.* Lanham, MD: University Press of America.
Sperber, D., & Wilson, D. (1986). *Relevance: Communication and Cognition.* Cambridge, MA: Harvard University Press.
Sperry, R. W. (1966). Brain bisection and consciousness. In J. Eccles (Ed.), *Brain and conscious experience.* New York: Springer-Verlag.
Sperry, R. W. (1968). Mental unity following surgical disconnection of the cerebral hemispheres. *The Harvey Lectures Series, 62,* 293-323.

Springer, S. P., & Deutsch, G. (1981). *Left brain, right brain*. San Francisco, CA: W. H. Freeman.
Stanovich, K. E., & West, R. F. (1981). The effect of sentence context on ongoing word recognition: Tests of a two-process theory. *Journal of Experimental Psychology: Human Perception and Performance, 7,* 658-672.
Stanovich, K. E., & West, R. F. (1983). On priming with a sentence context. *Journal of Experimental Psychology: General, 112,* 1-36.
Stein, N. L., & Glenn, C. (1979). An analysis of story comprehension in elementary school children. In R. Freedle (Ed.), *New directions in discourse processing*. Norwood, NJ: Ablex.
Steinberg, D. D. (1982). *Psycholinguistics: Language, mind and world*. London: Longman House.
Stern, H. H. (1983). *Fundamental concepts of language teaching*. Oxford: Oxford University Press.
Sternberg, R. J. (1990). *Metaphors of mind: Conceptions of the nature of intelligence*. Cambridge: Cambridge University Press.
Stock, P. L. (Ed.). (1983). *Fforum: Essays on theory and practice in the teaching of writing*. Upper Montclair, NH: Boynton/Cook.
Strawson, P. F. (1971). *Logico-linguistic papers*. London: Methuen.
Strevens, P. (1972). *British and American English*. London: Collier-Macmillan Publishers.
Stubbs, M. (1983). *Discourse Analysis: The sociolinguistic analysis of natural language*. Chicago, IL: University of Chicago Press.
Stubbs, M. (Ed.). (1985). *The other languages of England: Linguistic minorities project*. London: Routledge & Kegan Paul.
Stubbs, M. (1986). *Educational Linguistics*. Oxford: Blackwell.
Studdert-Kennedy, M. (1987). The phoneme as a perceptuomotor structure. In D. G. MacKay, A. Allport, W. Prinz, & E. Scheerer (Eds.), *Language perception and production: Relationships between listening, speaking, reading, and writing* (pp. 67-84). London: Academic Press.
Swinney, D. A., & Hakes, D. T. (1976). Effects of prior context upon lexical access during sentence comprehension. *Journal of Verbal Learning and Verbal Behavior, 15,* 681-689.
Swinney, D. A. (1979). Lexical access during sentence comprehension: (Re) consideration of context effects. *Journal of Verbal Learning and Verbal Behavior 18,* 645-660.
Tamir, L. (1984). Language development: New directions. In A. Lock, & E. Fisher, (Eds.), *Language development*. London: Croom Helm.
Tannen, D. (1982). Ethnic style in male-female conversation. In J. J. Gumperz (Ed.), *Language and social identity* (pp. 217-231). Cambridge: Cambridge University Press.
Tannen, D. (1986). *That's not what I meant! How conversational style makes or breaks your relations with others*. New York: William Morrow.
Tannen, D. (1989). *Talking voices: Repetition, dialogue, and imagery in conversational discourse*. Cambridge: Cambridge University Press.
Tannen, D. (1990). *You just don't understand: Women and men in conversation*. New York: Ballantine Books.
Tarski, A. (1969). Truth and Proof. *Scientific American*, June 1969. Reprinted in O. Hanfling (Ed.), *Fundamental problems in philosophy*. Oxford: Basil Blackwell.
Taylor, C. (1985). *Human agency and language: Philosophical Papers 1*. Cambridge: Cambridge University Press.
Thorndyke, P. W. (1977). Cognitive structures in comprehension and memory of narrative discourse. *Cognitive Psychology, 9,* 77-110.
Thornton, G. (1986). *Language ignorance and education*. London: Edward Arnold.

Tierney, R. J. (1983). Writer-reader transactions: Defining the dimensions of negotiation. In P. L. Stock (Ed.), *FForum* (pp. 147-150). Montclair, NJ: Boynton/Cook.

Titone, R., & Danesi, M. (Eds.). (1985). *Applied psycholinguistics: An introduction to psychology of language learning and teaching.* Toronto: University of Toronto Press.

Tobin, Y. (1990). *Semiotics and Linguistics.* New York: Longman Group.

Traugott, E. C., & Pratt, M. L. (1980). *Linguistics for students of literature.* New York: Harcourt Brace Jovanovich.

Trier, J. (1934). Das sprachliche Feld. *Neue Jahrbücher für Wissenschaft und Jugendbildung, 10,* 428-449.

Trudgill, P. (1983). *Sociolinguistics* (2nd ed). Harmondsworth: Penguin.

Turner, E. A., & Rommetveit, R. (1968). The effects of focus of attention on storing and retrieving of active and passive voice sentences. *Journal of Verbal Learning and Verbal Behavior, 7,* 543-548.

van Dijk, T. A. (1977). *Text and context explorations in the semantics and pragmatics of discourse.* London: Longman Group.

Volosinov, V. N. (1986). *Marxism and the philosophy of language* (I. Matejka & I. R. Titunik, Trans.). Cambridge, MA: Harvard University Press. (Original work published in 1973)

Vygotsky, L. S. (1978). *Mind in Society: The development of higher psychological processes.* Cambridge, MA: Harvard University Press.

Vygotsky, L. S. (1986). *Thought and language* (rev. ed.) (A. Kozulin, Trans.). Cambridge, MA: Massachusetts Institute of Technology Press.

Wachterhauser, B. R. (1986). Introduction: History and language in understanding. In B. R. Wachterhauser (Ed.), *Hermeneutics and modern philosophy.* Albany, NY: State University of New York.

Wagner, H. R. (1983). *Phenomenology of consciousness and sociology of the life-world: An introductory study.* Edmonton, Alberta, Canada: The University of Alberta Press.

Wardhaugh, R., & Brown, D. (Eds.). (1976). *A survey of applied linguistics.* Ann Arbor, MI: University of Michigan Press.

Wells, G. (1986). *The meaning makers; Children learning language and using language to learn.* Portsmouth, NH: Heinemann.

Welton, D., & Silverman, H. J. (Eds.). (1987). *Critical and dialectical phenomenology.* New York: State University of New York Press.

Werner, H., & Kaplan, B. (1963). *Symbol Formation: An organismic-developmental approach to language and the expression of thought.* New York: Wiley.

Wertsch, J. V. (Ed.). (1985a). *Culture, communication and cognition: Vygotskian perspectives.* Cambridge: Cambridge University Press.

Wertsch, J. V. (1985b). *Vygotsky and the social formation of the mind.* Cambridge, MA: Harvard University Press.

Whorf, B. L. (1956). *Language, thought, and reality.* Cambridge, MA: Massachusetts Institute of Technology Press.

Wilson, E. O. (1978). *On human nature.* Cambridge, MA: Harvard University Press.

Winzer, M., Rogow, S., & David, C. (1987). *Exceptional Children in Canada.* Scarborough, ON: Prentice-Hall.

Wittgenstein, L. (1958). *The Blue and Brown Books.* New York: Harper & Row.

Wittgenstein, L. (1922). *Tractatus logico-philosophicus* (C.K. Ogden, Trans.). London: Routledge and Kegan Paul.

Wundt, W. (1912). *Die Sprache* (A.L. Blumenthal, Trans.). Leipzig: Englemann.

Zaidel, E. (1978). Auditory language comprehension in the right hemisphere following cerebral commissurotomy and hemispherectomy: A comparison with child language and aphasia. In A. Caramazza & E. Zurif (Eds.), *Language acquisition and language breakdown: Parallels and divergences*, (pp. 229-275). Baltimore: The Johns Hopkins University Press.

INDEX OF NAMES

Abelson, 204
Akmajian, 227, 229
Allwood, 282
Andersson, 282
Aristotle, 39, 295, 374, 396
Arthur, 240
Atkinson, 76, 234-235, 237
Austin, 47, 49-50, 273-274, 279, 284, 286, 402-403
Bacon, 374
Baddeley, 97
Baker, 96
Bakhtin, 345-356, 368
Bartlett, 195, 204, 289
Bates, 9
Beardsley, 396, 400
Berkeley, 300
Berko-Gleason, 206
Bernstein, B., 233-235, 237, 269
Bernstein, R., 375
Bever, 9, 13, 180, 182, 183
Bickerton, 256
Bierwisch, 285, 335
Black, 396, 400
Block, 104, 105
Bloomfield, L., 19, 336
Bloomfield, M., 45
Blumenthal, 171, 172, 178
Blumstein, 94, 95
Bochner, 267
Bodine, 259
Bohm, 423
Bolzano, 337
Bousfield, 187
Bransford, 194
Bregman, 195
Brentano, 406
Bresnan, 159, 183-185
Broca, 14, 78-83, 88, 95, 99
Brown, G., 251
Bruner, 282
Bullock, 2
Caplan, 79, 80, 83, 97, 99
Carnap, 38, 48, 275, 280, 308
Carramazza, 97
Carrell, 205

Carroll, J., 60, 186, 191
Carroll, D.W., 197
Cedergren, 259
Chomsky, 1, 11, 19, 20-24, 33-37, 58, 103, 104, 105, 106, 107, 108, 109, 114-118, 120, 125-126, 131, 141-142, 144, 146, 147, 149, 158, 160, 167, 170, 175-177, 179, 192, 201, 221, 238-239, 335, 340, 350, 366, 378
Clark, E., 170, 250
Clark, H. H., 249-250
Collins, 189-190
Conrad, 190
Cook-Gumperz, 12
Coulthard, 249-251
Crowhurst, 210
Crystal, 216, 258-259
Dahl, 282
Danks, 186
Darwin, 74, 107, 108, 109, 113, 115
Das, 172
Davidson, 38, 44, 278
Davis, 164
de Saussure, 24, 25, 26, 27, 28, 29, 31, 63, 66, 67, 109, 164, 238, 308, 325, 335, 338-356, 360, 366, 399
Deely, 332, 361-362
Deese, 187-188
Descartes, 35, 107, 108, 115, 271, 297-299, 302, 308, 313, 332, 351, 366, 373-374, 405
Deutsch, 100
Dewey, 38, 276, 373-374, 377, 379
Dingwall, 113, 114
Dowty, 283
Dummett, 271
Eco, 63, 324, 361, 363-364, 368, 380
Edie, 308
Fawcett, 164
Feibleman, 330, 334
Ferguson, 240
Fillmore, 144, 145, 146
Fink, 75
Firth, 55, 56, 160, 163, 164, 168
Fischer, 259
Flower, 210

Fodor, 94, 113, 141, 143, 144, 152, 180, 182-183
Franks, 194
Freud, 364-366
Froese, 418
Fromkin, 197-198
Furnham, 267
Gadamer, 316, 322
Galton, 172-173
Gardner, 267
Garrett, 113, 180, 182-183, 197-198
Gazdar, 158
Gazzinga, 100
George, 317
Geschwind, 80, 81, 82
Gibson, 202
Gleason, 61
Gleitman, 14
Glenn, 205
Glucksberg, 186
Goffman, 252-253, 261
Goodglass, 93, 96
Goodman, 203
Gough, 181
Greenbaum, 159-160, 161-162
Greenspoon, 175
Grice, 47, 49, 52, 53, 54, 224, 284, 286, 327
Grober, 96
Grossman, 296
Gumperz, 12, 268
Gurwitsch, 302
Haack, 273, 276, 279
Hacking, 46
Hakes, 191
Halle, 33, 335
Halliday, 11, 12, 55, 56,160, 164, 165, 166, 241-245, 269, 418
Harris, 118
Harris, 21
Hartnack, 48
Hatch, 253
Hawkins, 3
Hayes, 210
Head, 83, 91
Heidegger, 316-323, 378
Hilgard, 76
Hörmann, 19, 174
Horrocks, 150, 185
Humboldt (see von Humboldt)
Hume, 296, 300-301, 304, 332

Husserl, 302-312, 318, 323, 325-330, 333-334, 337, 338-340, 349, 351, 366-367, 406
Hymes, 11, 238-239
Jackendoff, 146
Jakobson, 33, 66, 91, 92, 93, 337, 343
James, 276, 302, 370, 379, 405-406, 423-424
Jefferson, 246
Jenkins, 187
Johnson, 205
Johnson, M., 399-402, 406
Joos, 222, 226
Kant, 373, 395
Kaplan, 159
Katz, 141, 142, 143, 144, 152, 285, 406
Keenan, 194
Kempson, 294
Kent, 188
Kiefer, 285
Kieras, 194
Kimura, 99
King, 259
Kintsch, 193-194
Kirschner, 75
Kockelmans, 310
Kohler, 406
Kozulin, 357
Kripke, 317
Kristeva, 363-366, 368
Labov, 226-229, 234
Lacan, 363-365, 368
Lakoff, 144, 399-401, 406
Lambert, 267
Landau, 14
Langendoen, 164
Lashley, 120, 177-178
Lawton, 235
Lee, 357-358
Leech, 159-160,
Lenneberg, 75, 111
Levi Strauss, 237
Lèvi-Strauss, 336
Levin, 202
Levinson, 291-294
Lewis, 283, 285
Liberman, 203
Lichtheim, 80, 83
Lieberman, 73, 74, 108, 109, 110, 111, 112, 113, 114
Locke, 35, 64, 300, 332
Long, 253

Lucid, 343
Luria, 83, 84, 85, 86, 87, 88, 89, 90, 91, 102, 110, 208
Lyons, 17
Macnamara, 8
MacWhinney, 9
Malinowski, 54, 253
Mandler, 205
Marbe, 173
Marckworth, 121, 129, 131
Marie, 83
Marx, 357-358
McArthur, 3
McCawley, 143
McGlone, 99
McKean, 180-181
McKoon, 194
McManis, 216, 229
McNeil, 205
McNeill, 198-200
Mead, 379
Mehler, 182
Meyer, 193-194
Miller, 180-181
Millikan, 69
Minsky, 422
Montague, 283, 285
Montgomery, G., 101, 102
Montgomery, M., 224, 235-236, 256-257
Morris, 213
Morris, 380
Moutier, 83
Munz, 394-395, 410
Negus, 73, 75, 108
Nelson, 8
Newmeyer, 141, 143, 159
Ortony, 395
Osgood, 188-189
Pavel, 282
Pavlov, 174
Peirce, 63, 64, 65, 66, 67, 276, 325, 329-330, 332-334, 340, 342, 351, 363-364, 367, 379-380
Perchonok, 181
Perfetti, 204
Perl, 210
Piaget, 59, 210, 412, 416
Piper, 205, 265-267, 412, 421
Plato, 109, 115, 377
Porter, 201, 265
Porzig, 187

Postal, 141, 142, 143, 158
Pratt, 254-255
Prideaux, 121, 129, 131
Propp, 343
Putnam, 104, 105, 106, 107
Quillian, 189-190
Quine, 38
Quirk, 159-160, 161-163, 168
Reddy, 397-401, 406
Revzin, 344-345
Robins, 5
Rochberg-Halton, 379-380
Rommetveit, 195
Rorty, 373-378, 394-395, 401, 404, 410
Rosanoff, 188
Rose, 210
Rosen, 234
Rosenblatt, 210
Rumelhart, 204
Russell, 187, 273-274, 279-280, 308
Sachs, 192, 195
Sacks, 246, 248-249, 251
Sadock, 396
Saffran, 97
Sankoff, 259
Sapir, 60, 314
Saussure (see de Saussure)
Savignon, 11, 239
Saville-Troike, 12, 239
Savin, 181
Schank, 204
Schegloff, 246-248
Schlick, 48
Scinto, 207-209
Searle, 47, 49, 51, 284-285, 287, 289, 396
Sebeok, 362
Sells, 154, 155, 185
Shakespeare, 374
Shallice, 83
Shankweiler, 203
Shattuck-Hufnagel, 197
Shaw, 216
Skinner, 19, 116, 174, 176, 177
Slobin, 180
Smart, 117
Smith, F., 205
Sperry, 100
Springer, 100
Sraffa, 48
Stanovich, 191
Stein, 205

Stollenwerk, 216
Strasberg, 195
Strawson, 17, 18
Strevens, 219
Stubbs, 3
Studdart-Kennedy, 201
Suci, 188
Svartvik, 159-160
Swinney, 191, 203
Tannen, 261-263
Tannenbaum, 188
Tarski, 38, 39, 40, 41, 42, 43, 44, 46, 47, 272, 277-278
Thorndyke, 194
Thumb, 173
Tierney, 210
Tobin, 339-341, 351
Traugott, 254-255
Trier, 187
Trubetskoy, 29, 33, 343
Trudgill, 10
Turner, 195
Verplank, 175
Vološinov, 345
von Humboldt, 5, 19, 20, 23, 24, 58, 59, 171, 208, 213, 221, 313, 315-316, 350
Vossler, 350
Vygotsky, 57-58, 88, 197-200, 207, 356-361, 368, 378
Wachterhauser, 5
Wells, 205
Werner, 208
Wernicke, 14, 79, 80, 81, 83, 88, 99
Wertheimer, 406
Wertsch, 356
West, 191
Whitehead, 273
Whorf, 59, 60, 61, 62
Whort, 314
Winzer, 14
Wittgenstein, 47-49, 245, 271-273, 280, 286, 308
Wundt, 171, 172, 405
Young, 164
Yule, 251
Zaidel, 101
Zasetsky, 84, 85, 86, 87, 88, 91
Zhang, 216

INDEX OF SUBJECTS

A priori logic, and language, 308-310
Abnormal language growth, 13-14
Aboriginal peoples, in Canada, 267
Abstract speech, and Bernstein's theory, 233-235
Abstraction; in phonology, 33; in structuralism, 335
Academic achievement, 13, 2, 371
Accents, 11; Australia, 225; Britain, 225; Canada, 225; Scottish, 240; Second language, 269; United States, 225
Accidents, 295
Accusative case, 145, 157
Acoustic transformation in speech, 75
Acquisition of language, 10
Active sentences, 126
Adaptation, 70; in evolution, 109
Addition(s), of culture, 232; in phonological errors, 95; in speech error, 197
Additive language learning, 267
Adjacency pairs, 248, 252
Adjectives, 144-145, 153, 173
Administration, 3
Adolescence, 89
Adverbs, 144; Adverbial clauses, 137, 140, 142, 173
Aesthetic functioning, 103
Affirmative(s), 21; sentences, 126
Affix shift, in TGG, 129
Affixes, 197
Agent, 145, 156, 184
Agrammaticality, 93
Agrammaticism, 83, 97-98
Agreement, subject-verb, see Subject-verb agreement.
Air stream, see exhalation
Alveolar ridge, 29, 32
Ambiguity, 139, 141, 288
American, Indian languages, 59-60; semiotics, 343; school of Thought in linguistics, 92; Sign Language (ASL), 112; speakers, 30
Amphibians, 114
Analogies, 274

Analysis by synthesis model, 203
Anaphors, 157, 158
Anatomic comparison, 73
Angular gyrus, 81
Animal(s), 72, 111, 175; communication system, 112
Animate, feature of lexical items, 150
Anomia, 96
Anthropologists, 15
Antilanguages, 257, 269
Antinomy of the liar, 42
Antonymy, 287
Apes, 112
Aphasia, 14, 78-79, 92; Aphasics, 93; Aphasic patients, 81; Aphasic processing, 94
Arbitrariness, of language symbols, 65; of signs, 26, 339, 355
Argument, in X-bar theory, 153; structures, 155
Articulatory system, 29
Artificial languages, 362
Arytenoid cartilage, 70
Aspects model, 146, (see also, Standard Theory)
Aspectual system, 255
Aspiration, 32
Assessment, 3
Assimilation, into culture, 232
Associations, 87, 171, 172; of information in the brain, 79
Associative meaning, 187, 188
Asymmetry, of hemispheric functioning, 78
Atomism in linguistic description, 4; atoms, in linguistic analysis, 340
Attention, conscious, 407
Attention, selective, 411
Auditory, cortex, 81; impairment, 13-14; processing, and aphasia, 81
Australian English speakers, 30
Autism, 175
Autopsy, 78, 79
Awareness, conscious, 392, 405
Aztecs, 61

Baby-talk, 240
Back-channel feedback, 252
Background knowledge, 287; and reading, 204; cultural, 289, 322
Base; in a TGG, 124,148, 150, 180; in GB theory, 155; Base phrase marker, 126
Bassa, 62
BBC English, 225
Behaviorism, 18-19, 66, 116, 172, 174-177, 179, 201; 208, 211
Being, in Heidegger, 316
Belgium, 264
Belief, 51, 273, 276, 280, 290
Bengali, 259
Binary relations, 31
Binding, in GB theory, 157-158
Binocular vision, 112
Bio-genetic theory, 109
Bipedalism, 72, 111
Bird calls, 112
Black English, 219-220, 228-231, 253, 256-257; Black English dialects, 257
Blends, in speech error, 197
Blood, in brain scans, 101
Bogoras, 259
Bottom-up processes, 191-192, 203-204
Boulomaic, 282
Bracketing, in Husserl, 309, 338
Bracketing convention, in TGG, 128
Brain, central core, 76; layers, 76; lesions, 14, 79, 82 (see also aphasia); stem, 76; tissue, 84; trauma, 14
Breathing, 76, 111, and eating, and speech, 74; mechanism in fish, 73
British, linguists, 159, 168; speakers, 30; tradition, of grammatical analysis, 163
Broca's aphasia, 418
Broca's Area, 78, 81, 102
Bullfrog, 111
C-commands, see constituent commands.
Calculi of thought, in Peirce, 65
Calculus, 48
Cameroons, 254
Canadian; English speakers, 30; Canadian Official Language Policy, 264; Canadian raising, 217
Cantonese, 264
Caribbean English, 256
Cartesian Dualism, 318, 348, 374-375, 404

Case; 118, 156-157; filter, in GB theory, 157; grammar, 144-146; relations, 145-146
Cause and effect, 314
Central nervous system (CNS), 76
Cerebellum, 103
Cerebral; cortex, 77; dominance, 77, 78, 99; functions, 88; hemispheres, 77; palsy, 14; processing, 101
Cerebrum, 76-77
Channels of discourse, 252
Chess, 105; chess analogies, 344
Child language acquisition, 57, 111, 241
Child-centered view, and whole language, 419
Chimpanzees, 74
Chinese writing system, 260
Choice, in systemic analysis, 164
Chômeur, in RG, 159
Chomskyan, analysis, 147; grammar (see also Transformational-generative grammar), 23; linguistics, 168, 401; model of language, 108
Class, and language, and social codes, 232-237; Britain, 233-234; Canada, 233; United States, 233; in systemic analysis, 165
Classical thought, 63
Clauses, 165
Clusters, 198
CNS, see central nervous system
Co-operative principle, 53
Code(s), 11; cultural, 364; social, 269; switching, 232; coding, 113
Cognition, 3, 85, 113
Cognitive, ability, 94; development, 8, 15, 205, 371; domains,106; psychology, 179; linguistic mapping, 8
Coherence, in discourse, 251
Coherence theory, of meaning, 38; of truth, 274-276, 322
Cohesion, truth and meaning, 409
Colonization, 254
Commensurability, 375-376
Common code, in speech and listening, 201
Communication, 4, 125, 170; and language and society, 238-253; the game of, 245-246; disorders, 2

Communicative competence, 13, 15, 238-241, 269, 393, 413, 415, 420, 422; context, 39, 52, 284, 322; delay, 13; disorder, 18; exchanges, and discourse analysis, 246-247; communicative functions, see Functions; intentions, 52; interaction, 49, 348; processes, 111, 117; processing, 45; situation, 187
Communicative disabilities, 417
Community, language, 215
Comparative sentences, 88
Competence, 20, 25 109, 148, 180, 206; vs. performance, 238-239
Competition model, 9
Complements, 155; complement structures, 156
Complex sentences, 194
Computer-based models, 189-190
Computerized axial tomography (CT), 101
Concrete, feature of nouns, 134
Concrete operations, 412, 421
Concrete speech, and Bernstein's theory, 233-236
Conditional connectives, 388
Conditionality, 293; conditional reasoning, 282; conditionals, 311
Conduit metaphor for language, 397-401, 402-403, 409-410
Conjunction(s), 197; of sentences, 41
Connectionism, 80-83
Connotative meaning, 189
Conscious processes, in reading, 202
Consciousness, 6, 45, 60, 171, 300-302, 304-305, 307, 310, 346-349, 351, 353, 355, 365
Consequences, and pragmatism, 408, 411
Consonant clusters, 255
Constituent(s) 153, analysis, 118; commands, 156; structure, approach to analysis, 125; structures, 122
Constraints, in UG, 149; in X-bar theory, 153
Constructive learning, 419
Constructive memory, 194-195
Contemporary grammar of English, 162-163, 168
Content words, 98
Context(s), of utterances, 278; of meaning, 203; of situation, 54; and meaning, 341; of situation, in Firthian linguistics, 164
Contextual analysis, 164; information, 287; variation, 146
Contingency, 280; contingent truth, 281
Continuity, theory of evolution, 113-114
Convention, 274; conventionality, 294, 338; conventionality of language symbols, 65
Conversation, 11
Conversational implicatures, 54; maxims, 53-54; slots, 253
Coordinators, 161
Core grammar, 148
Corpus, 41
Corpus callosum, 77, 100
Correspondence theory of meaning, 38; of truth, 273-274, 322, 409
Cortex, 90, 103
Cortical locations, 82
Cortical zones, in Luria, 89-90
Counselling, 3
Counterfactuals, 282; conditionals, 292
Creativity, linguistic, 350; in language, 20
Creoles, 254-255
Critical circle, 316, 321
Critical period, 111-112
Cross-cultural interactions, 264-269, 388; in studies of reading, 205
Cross-lateralization, see lateralization
Cultural background, and memory, 196; and context, 164; expectations, 250; and experience, 315; groups and sub-groups, 13; and identity, 12, 253-264; learning, 211; systems, 345
Culture(s), 174; and language, 59; and lexical categories, 61; and grammatical categories, 62; and history, 308
Curriculum, 2-3, 416
Cycles, in transformational component of TGG, 22, 133, 135
D-structures, in GB theory, 150
Darwinian model of evolution, 107
Dative case, 145, 157
Declarative sentences, 21, 37, 39, 47, 126, 165
Decoding of meaning, 92
Decomposition, of lexical information, 144; of signs, 340

Deconstruction, 373, 376
Decreolization, 256-257
Deductive theory, 116
Deep structure, 21-22, 124-125, 127-128, 132-133, 139-140, 142-143, 147, 150, 167; and psychological processes, 184
Definiendum, in Tarski's theory, 40-42
Definiens, in Tarski's theory, 40-42
Delayed auditory feedback (DAF), 199
Deletion(s), 94; of relative pronouns, 162; in speech error, 197
Denotation, 285
Denotative meaning, 188, 286
Deontic logic, 282
Derivation, of sentences in TGG, 126, 131
Derivational theory of complexity (DTC), 180-185
Derived sentence, 22
Descriptive grammar, 118; linguistics, 12; determiner, 122, 124, 132, 145
Devoicing, and pidgin English, 255
Diachronic, analysis, 28, 351; dimension of linguistic description, 171
Diachronicity, 337
Diagram-makers, see connectionism
Dialectical materialism, 358
Dialects, 11, 214-221
Dialects, 252, 269; British, 218-220; Canadian, 218; definition, 219-220; sub-standard, 228-232
Dialogue, 207
Diaphragm, 89
Dichotomies, in Saussurean theory, 24
Diphthongs, 217; and style, 226
Direction towards, and case, 145
Disciplines, 16
Discontinuity, theory of evolution, 113-114
Discourse, theoretical, 391
Discourse, analysis, 12, 245-253, 284; channels, in Goffman's theory, 252-253; competence, 11; worlds, 260-262
Discrimination, 268
Disjunctives, 294
Displacement, 93
Distinctive features, 31-32, 34, 95, 186, 189, 335
Ditransitive verbs, 137
Dominance, 100
Double-negation, 230

Drawing, 101
Dreams, and signs, 365
DTC, (see Derivational theory of complexity)
Dyad, 331
Dyslexia, 14
Eclecticism, 7
Economy of information storage, 190
Education, 205, 295; domains of discussion, 7-16; educational background, and dialects, 228; educational linguistics, 3; educational practice, 7; educators, 15
Elaborated code, 233
Electrical stimulation, to the brain, 114
Embedded sentence, 22, 132-133, 163
Embodied understanding, 403
Emission, linguistic mechanism of, 92
Emotional, associations, 101; disorder, 18; and discourse, 252
Empirical method, 172
Empiricism, 277, 313; vs. rationalism, 35
Empiricism, 377
Empiricist(s), 103; position, 70
Encounter with language, Heidegger, 317
Energeia, 19
English as a second language, 7, 371, 382, 388-389
Entailment, 291
Epiglottis, 74
Epistemic logic, 282
Epistemic orchestration, metaphor, 414
Epistemic spectrum of language, 370-424
Epistemic transitions, 382-424
Epistemology, 275, 330, 372, 375-377
Equal opportunity, and dialects, 231-232
Ergon, 19
Errors, in reading, 203
Eskimo languages, 59
ESL, see English as a second language
Esophagus, 71
Essences, 295, 299-300, 308-309
Essentialism, 320
Ethnography, and discourse analysis, 246-247
Euro-American tradition, in semiotics, 361-366
European, school of thought in linguistics, 92; semiotics, 343
Eventuating cycles, 61

Evolution of language, 202
Evolutionary development, 75, 108; of language, 70
Exceptionality,13; exceptional students, 10
Exclusion, in social groups, 221, 225
Exegesis, 312
Exhalation, 72
Existentialism, 295
Experiencer, in case grammar, 145-146
Experimental procedures, 422
Experimental psycholinguistics, 186
Explanatory status, of TGG, 138
Exponent, 57
Expressive linguistic abilities, 78
Extended standard theory, 147-148
Extension, 295
Extralinguistic aspects in communication, 164
Facial expression, 110
Factive verbs, 292-293
Factor analysis, 188
Falsity, 39-44
Falsity, 400
Families, of sentences, see Sentence families.
Felicity conditions, 50-51, 224, 292
Feminine suffixes, 258
Feminism, 257
Fetishism, of signs, 380
Fictional worlds, 281
Field, 223
Figurative meaning, 287
Figure, and ground, 291
Filler-role, in conversation, 253
Final output string, 130, 136
Finite, set of sentences, in TGG, 131; finite state language, 120; finite state machine, in Chomskyan theory, 120
Finnish, 145
Firstness, 330, 333, 335
Fissures, of the brain, 77
Flaps, in phonetics, 217
Flowcharts, 166
Focus, 165
Force, of utterances, (see Illocutionary force)
Force, in metaphor, 402
Foreigner talk, 240
Form, vs. substance, 25-26
Formal logic, 272

Formal operations, 412, 421
Founding races, in Canada, 265
Frames, syntactic, 152; of reference, and gender, 261; framing, 252
French, 60, 63, 152, 259
French, and English, in Canada, 265-267
Fricative sounds, 71, 95
Function, language, see Language, functions
Function words, 98
Functional, approach, 7; functional-semantic analysis, 57; language, 11; language behavior, 164; functionalist psychology, 348, 358
GB, see Government and Binding
Gender, 257-264, 286; differences, development of, 262; genderlects, 260-264
General intelligence, 105
Generalizations, in grammatical descriptions, 162
Generalized phrase-structuure grammar (GPSG), 158-159
Generation, of grammatical rules, 118; in TGG, 122, 148
Generative, process in language, 355-356; approach to grammatical description, 167; grammar, 21; rules, 20; semantics, 141, 146-147, 167; generativity, 178
Genetic, basis for lateralization, 100; determinism, 104; endowment, 35; inheritance, 103
Genitive case, 145, 157
Geordie, Newcastle dialect, 220
German, 60, 145, 152, 259, 264
Gerund, 117
Gestalt psychology, 291, 334, 406
Gestalts, 303, 311, 372, 394, 400, 404-407, 411, 423
Gesture, 11, 113, 239, 247; and speech, 198-200
Gist, 211
Glottis, 70
Goal(s), in case grammar, 145; of linguistic theory, 20
Government, in GB theory, 156
Government and binding, theory of (GB), 141,149-158, 168
GPSG, see Generalized phrase-structure grammar.

Grammar(s), 106, 116; and ethnography of communication, 249; and semiotics, 340-342, 366; of thought, in phenomenology, 311
Grammatical approach, 7; complexity, 93; complexity, and Black English, 230; constraints, 121; forms, 107; options, 120; relations, 88; rules, 11, 117, 214; sentences, 121, 122, 126, 137; system,11, 59; utterances, 118
Grammaticality, 118, 178, 344
Gros Ventre, 259
Ground, and object, in Peirce, 64
Habit(s),18-19; chains, 176; formation, 174; habit-strength, 173 (see also, Behaviorism)
Hand-dominance, 82
Hard palate, 32
Head(s), 155-156, in X-bar theory, 152; adjectives, 153; nouns, 153; verbs, 153
Hearing, 70, 80, 11; impairment, 13
Hemispheres, in the brain, 82
Hemispherical specialization, 82
Hermeneutics, 295, 312-322, 373, 376, 379
Heuristic function, 243-245
Hierarchical, networks in psycholinguistic processing, 190; processing, 177; structuring, 144
Hierarchical models of language, 382
Hierarchy, competition, and gender, 261-263; of languages, 43
Hispanic English, 231-232
Historical linguistics, 352
History, and hermeneutics, 314
Holistic processing, 423-424
Home-school language switching, 13
Hominoids, 112
Homonymy, 186
Homophones, 178, 216
Horses, breathing in, 73
Human, feature of nouns, 134; feature of lexical items, 150
Hypercorrection, 227
Hypothetical reality, 280
Icon, 65; in Peirce, 329, 332, 335, 363
Ideal, objects, 307; senses, 307; speaker-hearer, 109, 238; idealism, 351
Ideal speaker-hearer, 393, 414
Ideas, in Descartes, 297

Ideation, 300
Identical noun-phrases, in TGG, 134
Ideology, 345-350; ideological bases of schooling, 2; ideological conditions, 372, 390-391
Idiolects, 220
Idioms, 287
Illocutionary force, 51, 285, 322, 402
Imagery, 390
Imagination, 402
Imaginative function, 243-244
Immersion education, 267
Impairment, of language functions, 96, 371
Imperative, 165-166
Implicatures, 292
In-groups, 253; and language variety, 225
Inanimate, feature of nouns, 134
Inclusion, in social groups, 221, 225
Independence of linguistic abilities, 105-106
Index, 65; in Peirce, 329, 332, 335
Indexical meanings, 286
Indian English speakers, 30
Indicative, expressions, 165; signs, in Husserl, 326-327
Inference, 289
Infinite potential of language, 42
Infinite set, of grammatical sentences, 125
Infinity, of utterances, 120
Inflectional, morphemes, 93, 98; system, 118
Inflectional complexity, and Creole, 256
Inflections, 255
Information-processing, approaches, 208; processing models, 202
Information-processing, 403
Innate, capacities, 107, 148, 150; grammar, 34; language abilities, 105-106; language mechanisms, 18, 110; universals, 35-36
Innateness, 70; hypothesis, 75, 103-114, (see also LAD)
Inner language, 24, 57-58,197, 199-200, 347, 355, 357
Input, to language learning, 107
Instrument, in case grammar, 145
Instrumental function, 242
Integrated framework for practice, 413-424

Intelligence, 36 (see also General intelligence)
Intentionality, 278, 284, 290-294, 322, 327, 340-341, 367, 406
Intentions, 6, 46, 51, 170, 328; in Husserl, 306
Interactionist model of language acquisition, 9
Interactive, function, 242; language processing, 91; processing, 201
Interconnectedness, of language and Being, 321
Intercostal muscles, 89
Interdisciplinary approach, 3-6, 15-16
Interethnic, communication, 268-269; discourse, 260
Internal lexicon, see Mental lexicon
Internal lexicon, 410
Interpretant, 64
Interpretation, in Davidson's theory, 278; in hermeneutics, 312-314, 321
Interrogative, 165
Intonation, 11, 58, 79; and interethnic communication, 268
Intransitive verb, 122, 124, 129, 131, 185
Introspection, 171, 307, 405
Intuition, 327-328, 365, 367; native speaker, 167
Iron Lady metaphor, 396
Irony, 47, 52
Irregular, past tense, 36; verbs, 9, 137
Isoglosses, 215
Isomorphism, 93
Italian, 60, 264
Japanese, 152
Jargon aphasia, 79
Katz-Postal hypothesis, 142
Kernel sentence, 21-22, 125-126, 142, 181-183
Kinship terms, 173
Knowledge, 272, 279, 299, 365
LAD, see Language Acquisition Device
Language Acquisition Device (LAD), 35, 37
Language, acquisition, 8, 104, 107; as a tool, 378; as a logical tool, 388; as action, 45; and the brain, 78-103; breakdown, 14, 79; change, 25; cognitive development, 8-10; communities, 27; competency, 92; as use in context, 45; courses for teachers, 2; and culture, 322; culture, and society, 213-270; delay, 175; development, 1, 8, 14; diverse aspects of, 5-6; is dynamic, 18; dominance, 82; education, and culture, 267-268; errors, 177; formal analysis of, 115; functions, 12, 46, 213, 241-245, 269; habits, 87; historical properties of, 350; and identity, 12-13; impairments, 15; inner form of, 20; learning, 3, 10, 72; as object (see objectivity); outer form of, 20; phenomenology, 294-323; phenomenology, meaning, 306-312; processing, 166; productive use of, 25; reduction of, 361; rules, 17; as a rule-governed system, 19, 113; shock, 253; social development, 10; and space perception, 85; structure, 17, 91; is structured, 18; system, 99; systems and subsystems, 9; thought, 9, 46, 58, 67; as a tool, 11, 73; truth, and logic, 272-283; truth, and meaning, 272, 407-424
Language-users, and language theorists, 380-394
Langue, 24, 26-28, 109, 238, 351, 353
Larynx, 70-73, 75, 108, 113
Lateralization, 77, 82, 99
Latin, 145; terms in grammar, 117-118; categories in grammatical description, 139
Laws of thought, and grammar, in phenomenology, 312
Lax vs. tense vowels, 71
Learning disabilities, 10, 14
Lebenswelt, 306, 310
Left hemisphere, of the brain, 79, 85, 99-101
Left-handedness, 77, 82
Lesions, in the brain, see brain, lesions
Leveling, 196
Levels of analysis, in linguistic description, 118
Levels of processing, 422
Lexical, constraints, 145; differences, and gender, 259; elements, 152; entry, in GB, 156; errors, 96; information, 287; insertion, 124,

130, 143; interpretation, 141; module, 94; signs, 340; terms, 147
Lexical Functional Grammar (LFG), 159, 184
Lexical insertion, 398
Lexicon, 94, 124, 151, 153, 167, 390
Lexis, 60
LFG, see Lexical Functional Grammar
Liar's paradox, 277
Life-world(s), 362, (see also Lebenswelt)
Limbic system, 76
Linear processing, 177
Linguistic analysis, 3; linguistic aphasiology, 91-92, 99; behavior, 15; categories, 3; creativity, 214; determinism, 60; development, 15; features, 12; levels of, 94-99; protectionism, 253-257; relativism, 59; relativity, 62, 233, 314; science, 3, 25; structuralism, 66; theories, 6
Linguistic representations, 381
Linguistics, 4, 17, 354, 362; European school of thought in, 92; and psychology, 170-176
Linguists, 91
Listening, 170
Literacy, 14, 100, 205-206
Literal meaning, 287-289
Lobe(s), of the brain, 77; left-frontal, 78, 425
Localization, 100; of brain function, 77
Localized areas, in the brain, 89
Location(s), 156; of action, 144; in case grammar, 145
Locationism, 297
Locationist model, 110
Logical, atoms, 273; connectives, 326; form (LF) rules, 150; frames, 62; positivism, 48, 144; positivists, 308; relations, 275; systems, and meaning, 38-39; theory, 43
Logical positivism, 372, 375
Logicians, 18
Logos, 319
London School of Linguistics, 55, 164
Lower animals, 110
Lungs, 72, 108
Magical function, 55
Mammalian stage, 76
Mammals, 110
Mandarin, 259, 264

Mands, 174
Marbe's Law, 173
Marxism, 346
Mathematical functioning, 103
Mathematics, 21, 107
Matrix sentence, 131; in RG, 159
Matters, 295
Maximal projection, X-bar theory, 154
Maxims, see conversational maxims
Maximum bracketing, in systemic linguistics, 165
Meaning, 146, 327; as use in context, 46-47, 272; in conversation, 249; integration with function, 166; and language and truth, 37-38
Meaningful signs, in Husserl, 327
Mediation, 177, 192; of behavior, 19
Medieval thought, 63
Medulla, 114
Memory, 80, 85, 90; constructive, see Constructive memory; for gist, 192-193; for sentences, 192-195; for text, 192-195
Mental, lexicon, 184-185, 190; operations, 23; processing, 19; states, 19; storage, 96
Mental dictionary, see Mental lexicon
Mentalism, 66
Mentally challenged students, 13
Meta-level description, in Tarski's theory, 40
Metacognitive abilities, in reading, 205
Metalanguage, 42, 277, 317
Metamessages, and gender, 261
Metaphor, and interpretations of language and knowledge, 394-404; interpretation of, 409-411; in modern science, 376-377; and thought, 372
Metathesis, 95, 197
Middle ages, 118
Mind, 19, 170; in Descartes, 296
Minimal pairs, 31
Minimum-bracketing, in systemic linguistics, 165
Minority groups, 2
Mirror of nature, 372-380, 394-395
Miscommunication, 398
Miscues, 203
Misunderstandings, and gender, 261

Modal, forms, 311; logic, 280-283, 322; realism, 283; verbs, 137
Mode, 223-224
Modernism, 381
Modifies, in X-bar theory, 154
Modularity, in neuropsychology, 94; in grammatical components, 147-148, 167
Molecular biology, 109
Monad, in Peirce, 331
Monism, 329
Monitoring, conscious, 392-393
Monolingual speakers, 39
Montague grammar, 283
Mood, 117-118, 165
Morphemes, 25-26, 124, 127, 130, 193, 344; level of analysis, 180, 198; system, 118
Morphological context, in systemic analysis, 164
Morphology, 120; and dialects, 217
Morphophonemic component, 130; of a TGG, 180; rules, 134, 137, 167
Moscow Linguistic Circle, 343
Mother tongues, 8, 105
Motherese, 240
Motor control, 111
Motor cortex, 81
Move-α rule, in GB theory, 151
Movement, of lexical items, 148; in GB theory, 150; rules, in GB theory, 151
Multi-ethnic societies, 1
Multi-modal framework for practice, 370-424
Multicultural education, 63; ideology, 265
Multidisciplinary approach, see Interdisciplinary approach
Multiple perspectives on language, 6-7
Multiple sclerosis, 14
Musical functioning, 103
Mutual intelligibility, criterion in dialectology, 220
Naming, of things, 48, 96
Narrative function, 55
Nasal cavity, 70
Native speaker(s), 118, 141; intuitions, 167
Nativism, 35
Natural logic, 144, 146
Necessary truth, 281

Negation, 137
Negative(s), 88, 142; modifiers, 147; transformation, 180-181
Negotiation, of meaning, 249, 314
Neo-cortex, 114
Neo-Darwiniaan model of evolution, 108
Neo-Firthian linguistics, 56 (see also London School)
Neo-Rationalist position, 108
Neo-Vygotskyan model, 200
Neologisms, 25, 98
Neural, mechanisms, 108, 110-111; system, 110
Neurolinguistic(s), 84, 91, 99-103; processes, 83
Neurological, disorder, 90; models, 90; science, 90
Neurologists, 91
Neurology, 103
Neurons, 110
Neuropsychological modeling, 94
Neuropsychology, 84; of language, 91, 99
Neuroradiology, 101-103
New Brunswick, 264
Newborn infants, 74
Noema, 406
Noemata, 303-305, 309, 333
Noesis, 302-304, 406
Nominalization, 147
Nominative, function of signs, 361; case, 145
Non-literal images, in metaphor, 395-404
Non-natural meaning, 52
Non-restrictive relative clause(s), 160-161, 292
Normal processing, compared to aphasia, 87
Normalization, 251
North American generative approach to grammar, 166
Nouns, 103, 132, 144, 153; noun-phrases, 121, 144
Number, 118, 132; agreement, 177
Object(s), 184; case, see accusative case; in case grammar, 145-146; language, 43, 277; in RG, 159; in Peirce, 64; in sentences, 131, 151; in X-bar theory, 152
Object-subject negotiation, 400
Objective perspective on language 6, 15, 17-44, 370 (see also subjective)

Objectivism, 274; as a myth, 401
Objectivization, 389
Obligatory deletion, 162
Ocular metaphor, 373-375
Official Language Policy, see Canadian..
Ontogenetic development, 74, 108
Openings, in conversation, 247
Oppositions, 31-33, 335; structural, 338-339; in meaning, 342; structural, 353, 367 (see also structural oppositions)
Optional transformations, 138
Oral cavity, 70-72
Oral language, 207
Orchestration, metaphor in language processing, 393
Orthodox model of brain and languuage, 81-83
Outer language, 24
Overgeneralizations, 9; in children, 36
Oxbridge English, 225
Paired associates, 173, 176
Paradigm-shift, Chomskyan, 117, 160
Paradigmatic vs. syntagmatic dimensions of language analysis, 28
Paradoxes, in logic and language, 43
Paralanguage, 113; features of, 239
Parallel processing, 415; in reading, 204
Parietal lobe, 79
Parieto-occipital regions, 85
Parole, 24, 26, 109, 351
Parsimony, in grammatical description, 138
Parsing, 97
Parts of speech, 144
Passive transformation, 146, 180-181; and memory, 192
Passive trigger, in TGG, 132
Passive(s), 131, 147, 167; sentences, 127
Past participle, 98, 137
Patient(s), 156,184
Pedagogy, 419; principles, 115
Perception, 85, 90, 171, 290; in phenomenology, 304
Performance, 18, 20, 25, 109 (see also competence); vs. competence, 238-239
Performative utterances, 49, 51
Perlocutionary aspects of utterances, 403
Person, grammatical marker, 118
Personal function, 243-244

Personal identity, 12
PET scans, see Positron emission tomography
Pharyngeal region, 114
Phenologists, 78
Phenomenologists, 6
Phenomenology, 325, 329, 335-337, 380
Philology, 213, 221, 352, 354
Philosophers, 15; of language, 47
Phonemes, 30-31, 193
Phonemic contrasts, 31
Phonemic level of analysis, 180, 198
Phonemic opposition, 34
Phones, 29-30
Phonetic(s), 29; context, in systemic analysis, 164; level, 95
Phonological, errors, 94; form, in surface structure, 137; phonological Form (PF) rules, in GB theory, 151; level, 56; shape of utterances, in TGG, 130; system, in aphasia, 95; systems, 27, 32, 59
Phonology, 26, 29, 94, 186; errors, 245-246; and gender, 258-259
Phrase-structure component, 131; in TGG, 137
Phrase-structure (PS) rules, 121-122, 130, 137, 139, 151-152, 180-181
Phylogenetic, change, 72; development, 75, 108, 202
Physiological, basis of language, 14, 69; structure, 75
Pidgins, 254
Pig Latin, 242
Planes, of language, in Vygotsky, 359-361, 368
Planning, as a psycholinguistic process, 177; and speech errors, 197; in writing, 211
Plausibility, 275
Plural formation, see pluralization
Pluralization, 61, 93. 256
Plurals, 98
Poetic mode, 318
Polynesian languages, 54-55
Pongidae, 72
Positivism, 379
Positron emission tomography (PET), 101
Possessive case, 157, (see also genitive case)
Possessive(s), 93, 98; adjectives, 98; pronouns, 98

Possible world logic, 280-283
Post-colonial English, 256
Post-modernism, 380, 410-411
Practitioner-based eclecticism, 7
Pragmatic, orientation to practice, 408-412
Pragmatic function, 55, language functioning, 51, theory of truth, 276-277, 322
Pragmatic method, 370
Pragmatics, 251, 284-294, 322
Pragmatism, philosophy of, 334, 377-380
Pragmatist theory of meaning, 38
Prague School, 29-30, 33, 208, 336
Pre-empt signals, 252
Pre-linguistic stage, 57
Predicate(s), 121; in Vygotsky, 58; grammatical, 98; in inner speech, 199-200
Prejudice, 268
Prepositional phrases, 144
Prepositions, 98, 140, 144, 197
Prescriptivism, 230; in grammar, 117, 160
Present perfective, 217
Present progressive, 256
Prestige, social, and language variety, 225-226
Presuppositions, 291-293, 322, 329
Primary qualities, in Descartes, 297
Primates, 73, 110, 113-114
Pro-forms, 148
Process model, in neuropsychology, 91; of brain functioning, 83
Productive forms, 9
Productivity, 178; of languages and grammars, 132
Progressive aspect, 137
Projection, 155, 168; problems, and presupposition, 293
Projection rules, 142, 144; in GB theory, 152
Pronominal reference, 157
Pronominal system, in Black English, 230
Pronominalization, 134, 147
Pronoun agreement, and gender, 286
Pronouns, 145, 163, 173, 197
Pronunciation, and dialects, 216-217
Propositional processing, 193-194
Propositions, 193-194; logical, 273
Prosodic features, 193
Psychoanalysis, 365
Psycholinguistic explanation, 4

Psycholinguistic guessing game, 203
Psycholinguistics, 172, 176, 179, 185, 187, 202, 271
Psychological complexity, isomorphism with grammatical complexity, 181
Psychological processes, 170-212; processing, 23, 30; reality, of grammars, 337; reality of linguistic descriptions, 179-186; units, 179
Psychologically-realistic grammar, 183-185
Psychologists, 15
Pure logical grammar, in Husserl, 307
Pygmalion, 217
Quebec Separatist Movement, 265
Queen's English, 225
Question transformation, 180-181
Questions, 137, 142
R-coloring, 216
R-expressions, see referential expressions
Radioactive oxygen, in brain scans, 102
Raising, Canadian, in phonology, 159
Rap, 253; rapping, 253
Rationalism, vs. Empiricism, 35, 298-299
Rationalist position, 70, 103
Rationalizing, 196
Reading, 80-81, 102, 185, 201-206
Reading-writing relationship, 210-211
Realization statements, in systemic grammar, 165
Received Pronunciation, 225
Reception, linguistic mechanism of, 92
Receptive learning, 419, 421
Receptive linguistic abilities, 78
Reconstructive knowledge, 399
Recursion, in TGG, 130-132
Recursive processing, in reading 201
Reduction, in dialects, 229; method of, in Husserl, 309, 338
Referential, expressions, in GB theory, 157; meanings, 286
Reflective processing, 90
Reflexes, 76
Reflexive pronouns, 157
Registers, 10, 223-224, 252, 387-388
Regular verbs, 9, 137
Regulatory function, 242
Reification, in language theorizing, 399
Reinforcement, 174
Relational grammar (RG), 158, 159

Relative clauses, 88, 131,134, 137-138, 159, 160-161, 207, 255
Relativism, 376
Relativization, 148-150, 161-163, 181
Relativization transformation, 134- 135
Relexicalization, 257
Remediation, 3, 29, 72
Repairs, conversational, 247; in interethnic discourse, 268
Representamen, 64, 329
Representational function, 243-244
Resonation, 73
Respiration, 89, 111
Restricted code, 233
Restrictive relative clauses, 160-161, 292
RG, see Relational Grammar
Rhemes, 209
Right hemisphere, 99-100
Right-handedness, 77, 99
Risorious Santorini, 75
Ritual constraints, 252
Role-playing, in conversation, 247-249
Role-switching, in reading and writing, 210-211
Roles, and epistemic transitions, 416
Root form of verb, 129
Rules, of language, 8, 107
Russian, 63, 145, 264; Formalism, 343; semiotics, 325, 343-345, 361; tradition, in psychology of language, 88
S-structures, in GB theory, 150
S-symbol, in TGG, 131-132
SAE, see Standard American English
Sapir-Whorf Hypothesis, 59, 261
Saussurean principles, 28-35
Scanning, 202
Schema theory, 195-196, 251, 289, 403; and reading, 204
Scholastic tradition, 298
Science, 64
Scope, of modification, 147, 152, 155, 161
Scripts, 204
Second language learning, 10, 239, 371
Secondary qualities, in Descartes, 297
Secondness, 330, 335
Semantic(s),142; associations, 101; classes, 96; decoding, 81, 102; differential scale, 189; field, 187-188; in Generative semantics, 141; information, in grammatical description, 161; maps, 205; module, 94; roles, of lexical elements, 147; structure, 187; systems, 69; theory of truth, 277-280, 322
Semeion, 63
Semiology, 63
Semiosis, 65-67, 239
Semiotic(s), 63, 324-369; code 66; and ideology, 345-350, 379
Semioticians, 6
Sense, 327, 342; vs. reference, 285; vs. value, 308
Sensory impairment, 13-14
Sentence(s), 214, 339; families, 125; production, see Sentential processing
Sentential processing, 97
Setting, in stories, 204
Sex differences, in hemispheric dominance, 99
Sharpening, 196
Shattered world, the man with, 84-88
Shona, 61
Short-term memory, 88
Sign systems, 13, 46, 379
Sign-formation, process of, 325
Significative, function of signs, 361
Signified, vs. signifier, in Saussure, 26
Signs, 8, 64, 68, 324; and phenomenology, 328-329; secondary systems, 365
Simultaneous vs. successive processing, 172
Situation, and style, 224
Situational context, in systemic analysis, 164
Skimming, 202
Social, class and dialects, 228; development, 10, 12, 15, 205, 371; formation, in Bernstein's theory, 236; identity, 1, 11-12, 206; and language variation, 221-228; interaction, 11; learning, 211; psychology, and grammar, 168; psychology, and language variation, 221; science, 295; speech, 58; strata, and language, 222-223; systems, 237; social-psychology, and grammar, 166
Social context, and discoursal shifts, 417
Socio-cultural context, 206; and knowledge, 391

Sociolinguistic(s), 214-238, 271; competence, 11; explanation, 4; variation, 13, 146
Sociolinguistics, and schooling, 410
Sociologists, 15
Sound image, 26
Source, in case grammar, 145
Soviet communism, 349
Spatial associations, 101
Speaking, 80, 170
Specifiers, in X-bar theory, 154
Spectator theory of knowledge, 374
Speech, 70, 111, 185, 196-201; act theory, 251; acts, 11, 49, 287, 339, 372, 402; community, 19, 238; errors, and planning, 197; impairment, 13; mechanisms, 72-78; processes, combination of 198-200; sounds, physiological control of, 71-72; speech-act semantics, 284; vs. writing, 224-225
Spinal cord, 76
Split brain research, 100-101
Spoonerisms, 178
Standard, American English, 226, 231; Average European (SAE), 60; dialects, 225-228; theory, 117, 121, 147, 149-150, 152; theory of TGG, 124, 137- 138, 140, 148-149, 167
Stereotypes, and gender, 258-259
Stigma, and dialects, 231
Stimuli, and reinforcement, see Behaviorism
Stimulus-response, 174-176
Stops, 32, 71, 95
Story grammars, 204
Strategic competence, 11, 239-240, 389
Strategies, communicative, 239
Stream of consciousness, 302, 405
Strings, of lexical elements, 127
Strong verb, see also Weak verb, 117
Structural, ambiguity, 141; analysis of language, 24 (see also, Structuralism); Structural change, in TGG, 127, 128; description, 116; description in TGG, 127-128; function, in systemic analysis, 165; levels, 21; linguistics, 66, 339; oppositions, 27-28 (see also Oppostions, structural)

Structuralism, 18, 31, 213, 335, 337, 351
Structuralist analysis, 237; approach, 33-34
Student-based eclecticism, 7
Style(s), 222-223; in Black English, 230; and dialects, 236
Sub-cultures, and gender, 260; in schools, 371
Subcategorization, in GB, 156
Subconscious, 364-366
Subject, 121; and predicate, 93, 310
subject-object dichotomy, 337, 346, 350; subject-predicate relations, 62
Subject-verb agreement, 127, 129
Subjective, knowledge, 64; perspective on language, 6, 15; intentions, 381 (see also objective...)
Subjectivism, 274, 306, 389; as a myth, 401
Subjects, grammatical, 98; of sentences, 131, 151; in RG, 159
Submersion, 267
Substance(s), 295, 298; vs. form, 25-26
Substitutions, 94; in speech error, 197
Subtraction, of culture, 232
Subtractive language learning, 267
Summons-answer sequences, 247
Super-tribe, 213
Surface structure, 22, 125-126, 130, 134, 138-140, 143, 151, 167, 193; and psychological processes, 184
Swallowing, 74
Swimbladder in fish, 108
Switzerland, 264
Syllables, processing of in aphasia, 86
Sylvian fissure, 77, 425
Symbolic, behavior, 109; representations, 8; tool use, see Language
Symbols, 8; symbolism, 329; symbolization, 199; in Peirce, 65, 329, 332
Synchronic analysis, 28, 171, 351, 354
Synchronicity, 337
Synergesis, 340-342
Synonymy, 186, 287
Syntactic, ambiguity, 139; categories, 161; context, in systemic analysis, 164; errors, 96; level of analysis, 180; module, 94; ordering rules, 118; processing, 179; structure, 140; systems, 69
Syntactic-linear thinking, 198
Syntagmatic vs. paradigmatic dimensions of language analysis, 28

Syntax, 11, 94, 97, 120, 141-142, 287; and Creole, 256; and dialects, 218-219; and phenomenology, 311; and semantics, 143-144
Synthesizing process, 87
System structure theory, 56 (see also Systemic Grammar)
System-network, in systemic linguistics, 165
Systematicity, 18
Systemic grammar, 163-167, 375, 422
Tabula rasa, 35
Tacts, 175
Tagalog, 259
Teachers, 2
Technology, 410
Tegulu, 259
Temporal lobectomy, 82
Temporality, of consciousness, 304-305
Tenor, 223
Tense, 117-118, 122; tense vs. lax vowels, 71
Territoriality, and language groups, 257
Text, 208
TGG, see Transformational-generative grammar
Thai, 32
Thematic relations, in Case grammar, 144
Themes, 209; in systemic grammar, 165; music and discourse compared, 415
Theoretical linguistics, 4
Theta theory, in GB theory, 155-156
Third person singular inflection, 93, 98, 127, 129, 217
Thirdness, 330
Thought and language, 9
Time, and case, 145; categorization of and culture, 61; and language, 316
Toolmakers paradigm, 398-399
Top-down processes, 191-192, 203-204
Topics, 165, 245, 269, 387-388; negotiation of, 249-252
Total communication approach, 13
Trachea, 70, 73-74
Traditional grammar, 17
Traditional linguistic analysis, 180
Transactions, in reading, 211
Transcendentalism, 309, 377
Transcription, 29

Transformational, complexity, and psychological processing, 183
Transformational-generative grammar (TGG), 23-24, 36, 117, 121-141, 151, 159, 163, 167, 168, 180, 197, 239, 296, 341; and generative linguistics, 208, 213; generative rules, 23-24, 36, 125, 129-130, 134-141, 162, 167; generative theory, 20
Transformational grammarians, 33, 372
Transformations, 21; and meaning-preservation, 143
Transitive verb, 122, 124, 127, 129, 131, 151-153, 156
Transitivity, 165
Transmission, of messages, 113; and the conduit metaphor, 397
Trauma, to the brain, 82, 84, 91, 102
Tree-diagrams, 121, 125, 128-129, 137, 156, 186-187
Triad, 331
Truncated passives, 140
Truth, and meaning and language, 37-38
Truth, 39-44, 387, 389, 400; values, 18, 46-47; definition of, 41; functionality, 278, 291; and language, 273-280; in all possible worlds, 290; and falsity, 275; conditions, 288
Truth or falsity, of propositions, 46; of utterances, 50
Truth-functional explanation of meaning, 38-44
Turn-taking, 246, 250, 269
Turn-taking, 387
Turnover signals, 252
Turns, 11
UG, see Universal Grammar
Underlying string, 127
Ungrammatical, sentences, 127; utterances, 118
Universal constraints in communication, in Goffman's theory, 252
Universal Grammar (UG), 35, 37, 104, 107, 149, 151, 168
Universal(s), 336; features of language, 18; hypotheses, in language acquisition, 104; properties of grammar, 148-149; set of

distinctive features, 34; system of
language rules, 20; truths, 160
Unvoiced sounds, 29, 71
Utterances, 339
Valences, in chess and language, 344-345
Value(s), 34, 342; of linguistic items, 27,
338, 368
Velum, 74
Verb particles, 137
Verb-phrases, 121-122, 137, 152
Verbal behavior, 93, 116, 175
Verbs, 100, 144, 152-153
Verifiability, of truth or falsity of
utterances, 50
Vertical ethnic mosaic, in Canada, 265
Visual, acuity, 112; impairment, 13-14;
processing, and aphasia, 81
Vocabulary, 105; in aphasia, 88; and
dialects, 218
Vocal cords, 29, 70, 72, 74
Vocalization, 111
Voiced sounds, 29, 71
Voicing, phonetic feature, 31
Vowels, 71, 216
Wenicke's, area, 79, 81; aphasia, 95-96, 418
West African pidgins, 254
Western culture, 410
Wh-forms, 148
Whole language, 418-420
Whorfian hypothesis, see Sapir-Whorf
Hypothesis
Word(s), 124; classes, 97; processing of in
aphasia, 86
Working-class language varieties, 232
Writing, 80; ability 100
X-bar theory, 152-155
Zones, see Cortical zones